Ramblin' on My Mind

AFRICAN AMERICAN MUSIC IN GLOBAL PERSPECTIVE

Portia K. Maultsby and Mellonee V. Burnim, Editors

Archives of African American Music and Culture
Indiana University

*A list of books in the series appears
at the end of the book.*

Ramblin' on My Mind

New Perspectives on the Blues

EDITED BY **DAVID EVANS**

UNIVERSITY OF ILLINOIS PRESS

Urbana and Chicago

♾ This book is printed on acid-free paper.

Library of Congress Cataloging-in-Publication Data

Ramblin' on my mind : new perspectives on the blues /
edited by David Evans.
     p.   cm. — (African American music in global perspective)
Includes bibliographical references and index.
ISBN-13 978-0-252-03203-5 (cloth : alk. paper)
ISBN-10 0-252-03203-9 (cloth : alk. paper)
ISBN-13 978-0-252-07448-6 (pbk. : alk. paper)
ISBN-10 0-252-07448-3 (pbk. : alk. paper)
1. Blues (Music)—History and criticism.   I. Evans, David, 1944–
ML3521.R29   2008
781.643—dc22   2007030753

Contents

Ramblin' on My Mind

Introduction

DAVID EVANS

The years since the late 1950s have seen a dramatic growth in scholarly and popular literature about blues music. Blues was certainly mentioned in print before this time, but previous writers had almost universally viewed it as either simply a type of folk music, more or less anonymous and unchanging, or a "root" form of jazz, worthy of a chapter or two at the beginning of any study of that genre. While it was recognized that blues had been popularized and commercialized, folklorists generally viewed this process with alarm, equating commercialization with a decline in artistic quality and cultural relevance. Jazz writers were more favorable toward commercial blues, but few had heard enough of it to do more than comment on selected artists and recordings that came to their attention, especially those that contained good jazz instrumental work. What was lacking, except among musicians themselves and their immediate audiences, was a sense of blues as a distinct type of music with its own personalities, stylistic variety, and history of musical development.

The modern era of blues scholarship and the significant growth of our knowledge of this genre began with the publication of Samuel B. Charters' *The Country Blues* (1959) and Paul Oliver's *Blues Fell This Morning* (1960), followed soon by the launching of the British magazine *Blues Unlimited* and a steady stream of albums featuring both reissues of historic commercial recordings and contemporary recordings in a full variety of styles. Blues artists were interviewed and profiled in magazines. New artists were discovered, while older recording artists were "rediscovered" and had second careers. Folklorists began to explore the relationships between folk and popular blues and place more emphasis on the personalities of their informants. Historians began to write the story of this music in particular cities and regions, identifying both an array and evolution of styles. Musicians from outside the traditional blues community began to learn how to perform the music and teach others, both directly and through instructional books and articles. There are now books that analyze blues as music, literature, and culture, that profile individual artists, producers, songwriters, and record companies, and that explore the relationship of blues to religion, philosophy, history, sociology, anthropology, and ethnicity. The music is today more popular and widespread than ever, as witnessed by the growth of an international club, concert, and festival circuit, blues magazines in some ten languages, thousands of available CD recordings, university courses and archives, radio and television programs, blues as theme music for advertising, blues awards programs, museums, and even blues tourism. One now hears increasingly of a "blues industry."

Interest in blues has particularly increased since the early 1990s, coinciding with the maturing of rock music and the rock generation, rock's fragmentation into a variety of competing subgenres, the rise in interest and availability of world and ethnic music, and the challenge that rap has presented to rock and older styles of African American popular music. Blues was able to find a niche in the spectrum of popular music and has been interpreted variously as a more authentic alternative to bloated rock music, something that preserves a spirit of rebellion, anarchy, or "chaos," a true ethnic expression, or something that generates pleasant nostalgic feelings without the aggression of rap or hard rock. Many new and younger fans of blues have emerged in this recent period, and one would expect a corresponding increase in blues scholarship, with new and younger writers and new interpretations expanding, refining, revising, or challenging old information and assumptions. There has been plenty written about blues in recent years, to be sure, including a number of groundbreaking works. Most of them, however, are by writers who were already active in blues research some twenty years ago or earlier. Much of the work by newer writers, on the other hand, has been journalistic interviews and artist profiles. Many are admittedly quite good, but they largely add to the storehouse of information about blues rather than provide new interpretations. Beyond this material we observe a proliferation of photo essays and picture books, instruction guides for performers, accounts of blues history that perpetuate or even simplify old understandings, and attempts to explain the blues as a whole according to some fashionable intellectual current or by means of a theory or methodology drawn from some other field of study. Sometimes it seems as if younger and newer scholars of the blues wish to avoid tackling the wealth of material that the genre has come to offer or the wealth of information and previous interpretation about blues, its personalities, history, social context, and meaning that has been compiled over the years.

The purpose of the present collection of essays is to offer new perspectives on the blues by exploring previously neglected aspects, reinterpreting familiar material, conducting broader and more scientific surveys, and exploring specific blues performances in great depth and detail. These essays are by well-established blues writers, distinguished scholars in other fields of music, and several newly emerging writers. The authors represent the diversity of backgrounds that have contributed to blues scholarship over the years: folklorists, musicologists, anthropologists, musicians, fans, and collectors. Three of them are based outside the United States, reflecting the internationalization of blues music and blues research in recent decades. The authors' approaches to the blues include fieldwork and other direct encounters, analysis of recordings, and research in the printed literature. Each of the essays is the product of careful and wide-ranging scholarship, not a brainstorm dashed off quickly. All can serve as models for future study both of the blues and other types of music. These essays include a comparative study of the blues and African music, broad surveys full of detail about solo blues guitar styles, blues nicknames, and lyric themes of disillusion in the years following World War II, an in-depth portrait of an important but neglected early blues "advocate," detailed studies of individual performances by Son House, Robert Johnson, and Ella Fitzgerald from literary and musicological perspectives, an exploration of an early phase of blues in sheet music and vaudeville prior to commercial recording, and a reinterpretation of a particular style of blues known as *zydeco.* Four of these essays were published previously in the journal *American Music.* My experience in editing them and their favorable reception among scholars prompted me to gather this larger collection and make this scholarship more accessible not just to specialists in American music but to scholars in related disciplines and the many seriously interested lovers of blues music.

There has long been an assumption that blues is somehow historically related to African music. At a general level, of course, this should be an obvious fact if only due to the African ancestry and cultural inheritance of the creators of the blues. The problem has always been to identify which specific traits are African and determine how these traits can be isolated from other traits found in the same music, and which are clearly of Western derivation or are original American creations. How can we discuss African traits in the blues when there is almost a century of earlier non-blues music by African Americans between the time when the last Africans entered America and the time when the blues came into being? For many years, writers wrestled with these problems. At first they were stymied by the diversity of African music and the lack of a broad knowledge of its characteristics. Writers would sometimes discuss the music of one particular region or ethnic group as if it represented all of sub-Saharan African music, finding similarities between it and the blues or jazz. Others would hear vaguely "bluesy" characteristics here and there in African music and point to them as sources or "roots" of the blues. Few blues experts, however, had more than a superficial knowledge of African music, and few African music specialists knew much about the blues. A breakthrough came in 1970 with Paul Oliver's *Savannah Syncopators: African Retentions in the Blues,* in which the author identified a number of musical and contextual traits shared by the blues and the music of the savanna region of West Africa. In 1999 the eminent Africanist Gerhard Kubik published *Africa and the Blues,* undoubtedly one of the most important works of blues scholarship in the last decade. There he refined Oliver's observations and gave them a musicological basis, showing how the blues scale was created from specific African sources.

In Chapter 1, Kubik elaborates on some of the ideas presented in his book, isolating the concepts of bourdon and pentatonism as crucial in the formation of music with a true blues quality and showing that a "west-central Sudanic scalar template" is the likely basis for most blues scales. These scales normally contain "blue notes" at the third and seventh degrees. Kubik goes on, however, to discuss the more difficult problem of the blue note at the fifth degree of the scale and its likely African source in an extended version of the same scalar template. Mississippi blues artist Skip James's highly acclaimed 1931 recording of "Devil Got My Woman" serves as an example for discussing these issues. Using the same example, Kubik provides a somewhat more speculative analysis of possible relationships between scalar and textual elements in the blues. His observations stand entirely outside the framework of Western musicology and come from someone with field experience in seventeen African countries over more than forty years and numerous publications on many types of African music.

Lynn Abbott and Doug Seroff write on early blues sheet music and vaudeville performance in Chapter 2, an essay that should cause a revision in the prevailing view of blues prior to 1920, the year in which the first commercial blues recordings by black singers were made. Until recently our view of this era has been influenced by the reports of early folklorists, analysis of a small amount of sheet music, the songs and autobiographical writings of W. C. Handy, the man commonly known as the "Father of the Blues," and the later recollections of singers and musicians who had been active in this early period. Abbott and Seroff reveal a body of almost completely unexplored contemporary information about blues in the black vaudeville theater circuit drawn from black newspapers of the time, particularly the Indianapolis *Freeman*. We begin to visualize a vibrant professional music scene in which blues was a growing and controversial element, a scene not dominated by W. C. Handy but including many other interesting personalities, some of whom had already become stars and passed away before 1920. The authors show that popular blues was a cultural, social, and musical *movement* in the early years and not simply the creation of one or a few individual songwriters. They also show that blues began to enjoy widespread popularity in the South within a few years of its initial appearance as a new type of folk music, a fact that is not surprising, as the early participants in the popular blues movement were, like their audiences, little removed from a folk culture themselves.

Elliott S. Hurwitt presents in Chapter 3 a different view of W. C. Handy by focusing on Handy's friend, advisor, and collaborator Abbe Niles. Just as Handy played an important early role in giving the blues an appeal to white American and international audiences, Niles played a parallel role in interpreting and explaining this music to the same audiences. In doing so, he became a blues advocate. In reviews, articles, and an introductory essay to a book-length blues collection by Handy, Niles expressed views and understandings that were remarkably perceptive at a time when blues was still in its early stages of development. As a fan, historian, critic, and promoter, coming to the music from outside its core culture, he paved the way for many other blues "advocates" in later years.

In "The Hands of Blues Guitarists" (Chapter 4), Andrew M. Cohen offers a new treatment of an old issue. Since the 1960s one of the main approaches to the discussion of guitar-accompanied folk blues has been to categorize the material on a regional basis. Terms such as "Delta blues," "Piedmont blues," and "Texas blues" have become enshrined in the literature, indicating not only the blues of a particular place but also blues in a particular style. Most of the writing linking region and performance style has been superficial and impressionistic. Judgments made some thirty or forty years ago, when we knew much less about blues than we do now, have continued to be generally accepted by fans and scholars alike. They may, of course, prove to be essentially correct. Surprisingly, however, they have not been tested in a scientific or objective way despite the vast amount of documented musical material now available. Cohen, a guitarist with anthropological training, has taken a first step toward testing the older judgments and assumptions by constructing a sample of ninety-four blues guitarists born over a span of sixty-six years from all regions of the South. He restricts the discussion of style to a single but vital characteristic, the use of the right thumb for time-keeping and making melodic figures, demonstrating clear patterns of regional variation in the thumb's role as well as showing development of these patterns and roles over time. Cohen adds a further dimension to the discussion by correlating the players' hand postures with thumbing styles, regions, and changes over time. Ninety-four is still a relatively small segment of the total number of fingerpicking blues guitarists of whom there exist recordings or visual and biographical data. Cohen's visual and aural judgments need to be confirmed or revised by other scholars, and the sample needs to be enlarged. Whatever the final outcome, he has moved the discussion off the impressionistic level where it had stood for over thirty years, and it is likely that his approach will form the basis for future studies of this issue. One could envision the discussion of style expanded to include favorite keys and tunings, scales, other techniques besides thumbing patterns, and the vocal dimension of the music. The general approach could also be adapted to the study of other instrumental styles, particularly solo piano blues.

My own essay on the nicknames of blues singers (Chapter 5) surveys a large sample of over three thousand blues artists, more than six times as large as any previous sample. It considers all artists who recorded blues between 1920 and 1970, the genre's peak years of development as an African American art form. The essay is concerned with the types of nicknames that artists have and the normal meanings of these nicknames in African American culture rather than with explanations of their origins in particular personal characteristics or experiences of the singers. It recognizes that many nicknames combine more than one meaning or can be understood on multiple symbolic levels. There are several distinct categories of nicknames and their percentages of use vary over time, especially before and after World War II. There are also significant differences in the types of nicknames held by male and female blues singers. Taken as a whole, the nicknames and their categories give a deep insight into the world of the blues and the meaning of this music within African American culture.

"Preachin' the Blues" (Chapter 6), Luigi Monge's study of the text of Son House's 1930 recording of "Dry Spell Blues," is a penetrating look at one of the most unusual blues lyrics by one of the greatest artists in the genre's history. House alternated between being a preacher and a blues singer over his long life, and his personality embodied the conflict between sacred and secular values, between God and the devil. His blues songs were always serious and often deeply philosophical. He sang in a manner reminiscent of many later "soul" singers and often mentioned God in his verses, as well as another spiritual being that he called The Blues. His "Dry Spell Blues" was composed and recorded in the midst of a severe drought in his native Mississippi Delta. Monge relates House's text to this historical event and through a very precise and detailed analysis shows that it is a "blues prayer," a novel type of expression that matched House's conflicted personality. Monge also reveals a remarkable symmetrical structure to the text and multiple levels of meaning encoded within it. It shows that Son House was one of the great composers of the blues as well as a great performing artist.

Son House inspired Robert Johnson, who is viewed by many as one of the greatest figures in the blues in the period before World War II. This opinion has received recent support from the extraordinary sales success of a boxed set of Johnson's complete recorded works more than fifty years after his death. But what is it that makes his music in general and his individual performances great? Questions like this have been addressed for many years by musicologists in the study of Western art music, especially in respect to composers, and often in great detail. In recent decades ragtime and jazz composers and performers have begun to receive similar attention. Such detailed discussion is seldom given, however, to performers of blues and other simpler types of folk and popular music. When their individual works are cited for greatness, it is usually on account of one or more fairly obvious features, such as compositional or literary originality, improvisational ability, technical virtuosity, or emotional expression. After transcribing a partly improvised performance by Robert Johnson (thus making it appear more like a composition), musicologist James Bennighof examines these and other features of the piece in detail in Chapter 7, showing how Johnson combined them to produce a work of great complexity and creativity. While we may never know Johnson's ultimate intentions with respect to this or any other piece nor all of the forces that impelled his apparently tormented genius, Bennighof's rigorous application of musicological methodology enables us to understand a few moments of this highly creative composer/performer at work. In applying this methodology, he has adapted it to the blues tradition, avoiding jargon alien to the tradition and examining relevant aspects of Johnson's life, time and place, and overall musical output. More such studies of generally acknowledged great works in the blues would be welcome.

Blues is not the exclusive property of those who define themselves as blues singers and blues musicians. In our desire to treat blues as a distinct and separate musical genre with its own characteristics, historical development, and personalities, we often lose sight of the fact that throughout its history blues has interacted with other types of folk music as well as popular genres such as ragtime, jazz, country and western, gospel, rock and roll, and rap. This interaction has been a two-way street, with blues drawing musical influences and personal participation from these other musical communities as well as contributing stylistic influences and specific songs to them. Many blues tunes are embedded in these other genres, and often they enjoy great popularity there, while falling outside the purview of scholars and commentators who deal with blues in a narrower sense. A case in point is the song "St. Louis Blues." Composed and published by W. C. Handy in 1914, it became a national, and eventually international, hit in mainstream popular music—in fact, one of the biggest hit songs of the twentieth century. For a period of several years following the publication of "St. Louis Blues," blues was a significant part of the spectrum of mainstream music. This is a fact that we easily overlook nearly a century later when blues once again enjoys this status. "St. Louis Blues" has been sung and recorded over the years by countless jazz and pop singers. The late Ella Fitzgerald was one such singer who featured this song in her repertoire. Although she is known as a jazz singer, even as one who never gave great emphasis to blues material, it would be fair to say that her versions of this song reached far more listeners than versions by most so-called blues singers.

In Chapter 8, Katharine Cartwright analyzes in detail Fitzgerald's treatment of "St. Louis Blues" in one particular performance. The singer makes this song interesting by her use of the device of "quotation," that is, the interpolation of bits and pieces of this and other songs as performed and recorded by other singers. In using this device, Fitzgerald reveals many influences on her own style of singing. Cartwright explains these influences in a way that allows us to see Ella Fitzgerald as a truly original performer with wide ranging musical tastes, even when working with a song that many would consider to be overly familiar.

Writers and commentators have long investigated the lyrics of blues songs for the light that they can shed on African American community life and history. In the first half of the twentieth century writers tended to view these lyrics as expressions of "the Negro." Eventually they came to realize that blues represented the thought of only a segment of the African American community or even the thoughts of individuals. But whatever the case, most of the songs are shared with others and represent at least fairly widely held feelings and opinions. In "Beyond the Mushroom Cloud: A Decade of Disillusion in Black Blues and Gospel Song" (Chapter 9), Bob Groom, one of the pioneering British blues commentators of the 1960s, examines a number of blues songs composed in the decade following World War II to gauge feelings and attitudes toward contemporaneous events and conditions. Most previous research on blues lyrics has dealt with the period up to and including World War II, a fact that is surprising since the blues has experienced a longer history after the war than before it. Groom's article is innovative not only in exploring this more recent period but also in the sense that it reveals and examines a *mood* during this period, specifically a mood of disillusion. It does not merely relate a series of songs to specific historical events and trends. Writers in other fields can determine whether this mood in the blues is correlated with moods expressed in African American literature, press reports, and other vehicles of expression in the same period of time.

In Chapter 10, folklorist John Minton has combined fieldwork with a study of recordings and literature to explore the origins of a regional and ethnic derivative of blues called *zydeco,* a style prevalent among musicians of Louisiana Creole background. In the late 1940s and early 1950s blues was bursting out from its geographical and cultural confines in the black Anglophone rural South and urban ghettos, reaching white audiences through recordings on independent labels, radio, migration, and integration. One result of this process was rock and roll, which became for a time a biracial mainstream popular music. Another group that lay in the path of blues influence at this time was French-speaking and bilingual Louisiana Creoles. This population was actually most susceptible to blues influence in Texas cities, particularly Houston, where many Creoles had settled and come into contact with black Anglophone culture. Out of this contact, as Minton shows, zydeco was created. This music did not gain significant attention from outside the Creole community until some years later, by which time it had diffused back to the Creole homeland in South Louisiana. Its early development predominantly, if not exclusively, in Texas cities remained largely unknown outside those cities. Zydeco's advocates today associate its origins almost entirely with rural South Louisiana, where it frequently serves as a symbol of Creole ethnicity and tradition and as a lure to promote tourism and local pride. Minton's detailed examination of source material shows clearly that zydeco in its earliest manifestations was Louisiana music only in the sense that its creators had been born in Louisiana and were familiar with an older tradition of Louisiana Creole music. But to call it simply a Louisiana music without taking into consideration the urban Texas synthesis that it underwent would be like calling Chicago blues a Mississippi tradition because most of its chief practitioners came from that state. Minton's article serves as a corrective to facile assumptions and adds significantly to our knowledge of what zydeco is and where it came from.

Taken together, these chapters contain some of the most innovative recent scholarship on the blues, examining it as literature, music, personal expression, and cultural product. It is hoped that they can serve as models and inspirations for future scholarship.

I would like to thank all of the authors for their great patience while this collection went through the process of compilation, editing, revision, and final acceptance. I would also like to thank Judith McCulloh, Joan Catapano, Sara Luttfring, Christina Walter, Rebecca Crist, and Cope Cumpston at the University of Illinois Press as well as Carol Bifulco at BookComp for their editorial help and Scott L. Hines and William Lee Ellis at the University of Memphis for help in assembling the final version and supplementing my meager computer skills.

1

Bourdon, Blue Notes, and Pentatonism in the Blues

AN AFRICANIST PERSPECTIVE

GERHARD KUBIK

A Memorable Visit

On the afternoon of August 1, 1997, David Evans, Moya Aliya Malamusi, and I set out to visit the blues singer and guitarist Robert "Wolfman" Belfour at his home in Memphis (Fig. 1.1). Moya, who had intensively studied the music and lyrics of blues-like *bangwe* (board zither) playing minstrels in his home area in southeast Africa during the 1980s and 1990s,[1] and I had long wished to make the Wolfman's personal acquaintance. For some time I had played to students in various parts of the world his recordings released on the CD *The Spirit Lives On,*[2] including "Poor Boy Long Way from Home," "Old Black Mattie," and "Catfish Blues," among others.

Robert Belfour was born in 1940 near Holly Springs, Mississippi. His father was a blues singer and guitarist who was of considerable inspiration to the son, who tried to imitate his father's music already when he was five years old. At his father's death, Robert, aged thirteen, inherited his guitar. He began to listen to blues musicians such as John Lee Hooker, Howlin' Wolf, and others on the radio, while working on a dairy farm during the day, playing blues guitar in the evenings and weekends. By the time he was about eighteen, he played at juke houses in the area. In the 1960s he changed from acoustic to electric guitar and moved with his wife to Memphis. It was only relatively recently that he began to appear at festivals, making his first overseas tour in 1993 to Germany. Robert Belfour's music pertains to a stylistic cluster of the northern Mississippi hill country heavily relying on the concept of the "riff," similar to the style of other older Mississippi blues artists from

Fig. 1.1. Robert Belfour in front of his house in Memphis, August 1, 1997. (Photo used by permission of Moya A. Malamusi.)

nearby such as the late Junior Kimbrough (who at one time was his mentor), R. L. Burnside, Jessie Mae Hemphill, and the late Fred McDowell.[3]

Fans have given him the name "Wolfman," thereby perpetuating the concept of fear-instilling alter egos that had permeated the blues world since the days of Howlin' Wolf (1910–76) and, more recently, the She-Wolf (Jessie Mae Hemphill). Robert turned out to be a warm, friendly and circumspect person with no signs of any hidden ferocity. He escorted us to his study, a room full of paraphernalia including historical personal photographs and posters from his trips to Europe. He plugged in his pick-up to a small amplifier and first tuned the guitar to the standard tuning, which he calls "natural," the third string slightly flattened, with his fingers in an E-chord position. As he began to perform, he allowed me to videotape the entire session, several songs, and his talk with David Evans.

It was probably the first time that Belfour received visitors from southeast Africa.[4] Although rooted in a somewhat different style, Moya—a guitarist and one-string bass player—was certainly not a total stranger to the blues. In the group in which Moya has played since his childhood, there are some songs in the 12-bar (more often in a strangely reduced 10-bar) blues form.[5] For almost an hour, we were voluntarily fastened to three chairs in Robert's study, face to face with the artist. Moya listened to this music with obvious delight, his eyes concentrated on the elaborate fingering patterns on the guitar. In conversation with Evans, Belfour talked about events and significant encounters in his life, and he portrayed his father from memories, saying that his father had once tried to teach him one particular pattern that he never mastered. In the process of his narration and performances he retuned his guitar to an open chord tuning which he called "Spanish": high to low, E–C-sharp–A–E–A–E. This is somewhat similar to the tuning Moya and other musicians in southeast Africa have used when playing *hauyani* ("Hawaiian"), using a bottle as a slider;[6] in relative notation (from the highest to the lowest tone) G–E–C–G–E–C; sometimes also G–E–C–G–F–C. In southeast Africa the term "Spanish" is also found, but it refers to a different tuning that is used for *five*-string guitar played in vamping style to support a band. The A-string is removed and the remaining five strings are tuned, in relative notation (from top to bottom) E–C–A–F–(gap)–B-flat. It is said that this tuning has a penetrating power, and it is used therefore on occasions when no one-string bass is in the group.

Perhaps because the videocamera was running, Robert Belfour sang not with his usual powerful voice, but in a somewhat attenuated manner. However, his guitar performance showed all the characteristics we know from his recordings. Many songs, such as "Down the Road of Love," "Holding My Pillow Crying," and "I Have Lots of Bad Luck" refer to the composer's personal struggles during his life and his hard work to escape from rural poverty. Some others, such as "Old Black Mattie," are original adaptations of blues commonly heard in the area.

Driving home to Evans' residence, I asked Moya what his first impressions of this music were, whether he could recall anything he had recorded during his fieldwork in Malawi, Zambia, and Namibia that was comparable in style to Robert Belfour's music, or perhaps any tradition he had come to know on our joint lecture and concert tour to Senegal, Ivory Coast, Ghana, Nigeria, Cameroon, and Zaïre in 1981. He replied that Robert Belfour's music was not reminiscent of anything he had ever heard on his fieldtrips in Africa. One day later, however, he suddenly came up on his own initiative with a significant statement. He said that what had struck him most in Robert's guitar playing was that at least in one of his tunings, the open tuning called "Spanish," he would always let the fifth string vibrate unfretted, while carrying out elaborate fingerwork on the upper strings, even high up the fretboard. As a result the sound of the open fifth string functioned like a drone, like a constant reference tone permeating the entire tonal-harmonic process, in many of his pieces.

Unlike some Western musicians, Moya was not distracted by any search for "chords," "vertical harmony" and other conceptual gimmicks characteristic of a European music theory approach. In his perception he had hit with one calculated stroke at the nerve center of Belfour's tonal-harmonic world, and by implication that shared with many others in the "Delta" or "Deep South" blues style.[7] He had verbalized what indeed seems to be a central criterion distinguishing some of these artists, such as R. L. Burnside and Jessie Mae Hemphill, from other expressions of the blues, as often heard, for example, in Texas or Georgia: the tendency to organize many of their songs over a *virtual bourdon* with a powerful central tonal gravity. The use of "riffs" and short repeated melodic-rhythmic figures as a song's underlying building blocks is interrelated with this primary concept.

Scrutinizing Blues Records

I remember twenty years earlier, in 1977, during my stay with David Evans in Yorba Linda, California, how I had first heard Mississippi bluesman Skip James's February 1931 recording "Devil Got My Woman" (Paramount 13088, recorded in Grafton, Wisconsin). At that time I had become acutely aware of the vanity of analyzing this music with the concepts of Western music theory—including even some ethnomusicological concepts—in search of "chords," "blue notes," "neutral thirds," and the like. Listening to Skip James in the way I had learned to listen to west-central Sudanic and southeast African minstrels accompanying themselves with a stringed instrument, I became immersed in the inherent auditory patterns emerging from the guitar, the timbre-melodic sequences and tone oscillations of the voice, and of puzzle effects.[8] Nothing like functional harmony in the Western sense of the word would suggest itself to my mind. My attention was absorbed by Skip James's prominent use of melisma in his voice and the oscillating sound clusters on his guitar that seemed to reinforce, by some strange technique, the pervasive central reference note that functioned like a bourdon. In contrast to the auditory impression of some of my Western colleagues, the only Western element I was able to spot in this music—to be frank—was the instrument itself, a factory-manufactured acoustic guitar with its frets set according to the Pythagorean principle. But even within those limitations, Skip James seemed highly successful in manipulating the guitar according to his own designs. His non-Western approach to the guitar was obvious. It contrasted somewhat with his piano playing, such as in "22-20 Blues" (Paramount 13066) or "If You Haven't Any Hay Get On down the Road" (Paramount

13066), recordings that are no less fascinating, but in them any strategy for circumvention of the Western tempered system would have been to no avail. Clearly, in Skip James's piano playing there were progressions from tonic to subdominant and dominant degrees (though not necessarily chords).

To me this was no contradiction. I had often witnessed during fieldwork in Africa the presence in the same village, among the same people, of more than one tonal system. At Bigene village, in the southwestern corner of the Central African Republic, story-songs are sung in hexatonic three-part harmony shifting between sound clusters a semitone apart, but *kembe* lamellophones are tuned to an equipentatonic scale, with no simultaneous sounds other than unison and octaves.[9] By analogy, therefore, I expected that the hundreds of blues musicians in the history of the genre would not all proceed from unitary tonal-harmonic templates, but that there would be variety in approach and tonal ideas, sometimes even in the mind of one and the same artist.

The blues has sometimes been treated like a homogeneous expression, with the 12-bar scheme declared as paramount, along with the so-called blue notes that have been described as "a microtonal lowering of the 3rd, 7th, and (to a lesser extent) 5th scale degrees."[10] I remember one German author in the 1950s describing them as the "unification of the two tonal genders (*Tongeschlechter*) of major and minor," a stunningly sexist interpretation, probably satisfying that author's own need for symbolism. But the majority of authors have been captives of another scheme: explaining the blue notes as *deviations* from certain tones of the Western diatonic scale. This estranged me a lot. I had studied *equipentatonic* tunings in Uganda, and *equiheptatonic* ones in the Lower Zambezi valley (Moçambique, Malawi), but musicians in Africa never conceptualized their constituent pitch values as deviations from something else that they could not even have known but always as an integral framework. In some cultures, for example in southern Cameroon among Ewondo-speaking people, the tones of a xylophone are considered to be members of a family or clan, with a central authority (a chief), besides other members and their wives (= the same notes an octave higher).[11] Significantly, in the United States blues musicians do not normally talk about "blue notes" or any other intervals supposed to be special, unless they have adopted the jargon from music critics or musicologists.

I eventually arrived at the sacrilegious conclusion that the blue notes as a concept had no cognitional reality in the communities concerned but that they were a Western construct, reflecting a Western cognitive problem in the encounter with African American music. This was not meant to say that the pitch values characteristic of blue notes did not exist. They do exist, of course, but as *intrasystemic units* and not as deviations from another tonal system.

It is unclear who began to use the term "blue notes," but it seems that it was various jazz musicians and jazz critics during the 1920s, possibly even earlier. However, since then the concept has gone through a period of inflation. At first, there were only two recognized blue notes, written B-flat and E-flat (in the key of C), about whose origins musicologists began to speculate. Then, beginning in the 1940s and coinciding with the use of the "flatted fifth chord" in bebop, there were suddenly three, including a note around F-sharp. Erich Moritz von Hornbostel's concept of "neutral thirds," which he had developed to describe intonation among the Fang' of Gabon and Guinea Ecuatorial,[12] was taken up and perpetuated by others, with explicit reference to jazz by A. M. Jones in 1951. Eventually, the idea that the blue notes were neutral thirds "somewhere between E and E-flat" and "somewhere between B and B-flat," in the words of Jones,[13] gained such currency that authors became used to seeking their origins in African equi*hepta*tonic tonal systems in which thirds are characteristically about 340 cents wide (2 times 171.4), just halfway between "major" and "minor."

Clearly, neutral thirds characterize not only some instrumental tunings, for example, in xylophones of central and southern Moçambique[14] and Guinée,[15] but—as intervals *and* simultaneous sound—they also mark vocal music in several distinct cultures. They can be heard in the music of secret societies among the Cokwe, Lwena/Luvale, Lucazi and Mbwela/Nkhangala in eastern Angola[16] and the Baule on the Ivory Coast.[17] In Gabon they can be heard among the Fang' even today, although there are actually two different tonal systems in use, one hexatonic, derived from the harmonics of the musical bow called *beng*'[18] and involving a shifting tonality between two roots a whole-tone apart, the other equiheptatonic. In spite of the recent onslaught by Congo/Zaïre pop music on the Fang' ear, it is significant that one eminent Fang' guitarist, Nkogo Essono Martin, nicknamed "Jovial," who calls his guitar *mvet* (after the Cameroonian and Gabonese polyidiochord stick zither), clearly tunes it off-pitch from the Western values, allowing him to produce measurably neutral thirds. These appear both between notes on the instrument and between instrument and voice lines.[19] In a sense, the tonality of his music is comparable to that of the blues, if the term is stretched a bit, as is now common in the literature dealing with "African roots." Historical implications cannot be postulated, however, though many people from this area were deported, via Fernando Po, to the New World.

The concept of tunings and vocal intonation involving equiheptatonic neutral thirds must have been transplanted to the New World with people from the many areas in Africa where it is prominent. To what extent, however, it may have shaped vocal behavior leading to the development of blue notes is open to debate. I tend to assume that it had a minimal role in the shaping of the blue notes, if any at all, but that it was a concept lingering on in some African American cultures to *resurface* in totally unexpected realms, for example in bebop (in spite of its use of Western-tuned instruments).

The unlikelihood of an *equihepta*tonic origin of the blue notes is supported by several arguments: (1) the entrenched pentatonic framework of most blues; (2) the tendency toward disjunct intervals rather than progression in narrow step-like movement; (3) lack of recorded evidence that the higher blue note, B-flat, represents a value between B-flat and B. My impression is that there is a tendency even to *lower* the B-flat. Characteristically, the "neutral" intonation, if it occurs, always appears over a dominant chord, in which case the B-flat↑ is simply a transposition of the lower blue note E-flat↑ upward by a fifth. (4) The lower blue-note E-flat↑ fluctuates indeed very often around a neutral third, but it has a particularly wide fluctuation margin, even lower than E-flat, which is not characteristic of equiheptatonic African tunings or neutral thirds intonation in singing. This does not exclude, however, the possibility that in some rare cases an equiheptatonic approach could have survived in the blues.

In recent years the idea of the blue notes has been greatly inflated. Suddenly, there is also a "blue A," as conceptualized by Peter van der Merwe.[20] Western theorists seem to have become insatiable, never getting enough of blue notes. Almost any note that is off-pitch to the Western scale ends up being called a blue note. Blues scales are constructed with an ever increasing number of constituent notes, for example, the "octatonic" scale. Everything seems to build up toward a "star wars" of blue notes against the evil empire of the Western 12-note tempered scale.

The way out of this deadlock is simply to recognize that each vocal line in a blues performance represents an integrated, patterned whole, without any particular tones having special status. Second, the patterns formed by a blues singer's individual pitch repertoire are part of a cognitive *system* that is mostly of non-Western origins, in some individuals more, in others less. From this derives a third point useful in the research strategy, namely, that valuable data gathering can only start with the individual artist, and not with abstractions (such as "blue notes"). A fourth observation may be helpful, too, to put us on the right track: if indeed most of the Western traits during the early stages of the blues' development in the late nineteenth and early twentieth centuries came from the instrument and its tonal-harmonic conventions, namely, the guitar, then researchers who try to uncover the tonal systems behind the various forms of the blues will be more successful if they first consider the singer's vocal lines *in isolation.* Certainly, the majority of blues guitarists have also developed non-Western guitar styles and techniques. But this seems to have happened *in response to* and *imitation of* the patterns of the voice. When foreign instruments are adopted in a culture, the original heritage tends to "retreat" to the human voice as a primary instrument. For this reason, it can be expected that in the blues the non-Western traits must be particularly concentrated in the lines and timbre-melodic patterns produced by the human voice, which in turn is imitated or commented on by the guitar. A preliminary comparative scrutinizing of many blues records seems to confirm that the voice-lines of the majority of blues singers are basically pentatonic, some others hexatonic, while in the guitar accompaniment heptatonism, the three common chords, and some chromatic intermediate passages, abound. I have been able to confirm this statistically by examining Jeff Todd Titon's sample of forty-eight transcriptions of the vocal themes of "early downhome blues." According to my evaluation, seven have a tetratonic, twenty-eight a pentatonic, and thirteen a hexatonic structure.[21] Nearly three-quarters of this sample, therefore, is pentatonic or less.

Pitch Areas and Tonemes

In contrast to fixed pitch values with which Westerners mostly operate on their instruments, there is in many African traditions the concept of permissible pitch fluctuation, variously described as a *margin of tolerance,* depending on the type of tonal system that is used. Tonal systems derived from the harmonics of a musical bow tend to have a narrow margin, in contrast to those which are based on the principle of an equidistant division of the universal interval of the octave. In some xylophone and lamellophone tunings in Africa, the octaves can also be deliberately stretched or compressed by up to ± 20 cents and thereby sound almost "out of tune" to Western ears. This phenomenon was researched by A. M. Jones in 1978,[22] and it is often associated with traditions that incorporate the massive use of parallel octaves. The tunings serve to reduce the fusion effect between lines played in parallel octaves, and thereby stress their individuality. The concept of *elasticity* with regard to pitch intervals[23] is prominent particularly in those African regions where tempered, that is, equiheptatonic and equipentatonic, instrumental tunings are used, but also in some cultures whose tonal system is based on different principles. I became aware of this in the Central African Republic in 1964 among the Azande, while learning to play harp music,[24] and in Angola in 1965, when I noticed with a feeling of bewilderment how my various musician friends retuned their instruments on different occasions to what then appeared to my ear as different tunings. In Angola, I was perplexed during my work with *likembe* (lamellophone) player Kufuna Kandonga, when on one occasion he tuned the eight notes of his instrument to what seemed to be a scalar pattern incorporating (in relative notation) C, D, E↓, F-sharp↓, G, A, and on another to C, D-flat, E, F, G, A-flat, rejecting any suggestion that there was a difference.

Perhaps that rings a bell with some blues researchers. In 1982 in his book *Big Road Blues,* David Evans suggested that blues musicians proceed from an awareness of flexible pitch areas. Commenting on the apparent "neutral thirds" of the blue notes, he stated, "In fact, 'neutral' probably would best represent an *area* between major and minor where notes can be sung, rather than any specific point between them. Blues singers often waver at the third or seventh or glide from a lower to a slightly higher pitch. The lower part of the third and seventh areas tends to serve as a leading tone, respectively, to the tonic and fifth below, the upper part as a leading tone to the fifth and tonic above."[25]

From auditory mental templates that form during musical enculturation in childhood and adolescence are derived the tonemic concepts and intra-culturally accepted margins of pitch tolerance. An interval is not defined universally. What in one culture is distinguished as "major" and "minor" is certainly also *perceived* elsewhere as a difference, but not necessarily *conceptualized* as such. A distinction can be irrelevant. Its relevance is language-specific, just as color taxonomies differ from language to language. What in one language needs to be differentiated as either "green" or "blue" may encounter indifference in another, and therefore only require a common term.

The musical childhood experiences of blues artists who grew up in Mississippi and other blues-intensive areas of the Deep South during the first third of the twentieth century were comparable in kind to those in African regions. Sound impressions were absorbed and processed that came primarily from live performances in the social environment, generating memories in which sound was ordered along locally transmitted cognitional patterns. Unfortunately, very little research has been undertaken on musical enculturation in the early blues. What we rely upon comes mostly from interview accounts by artists such as Big Bill Broonzy, Muddy Waters, the writings of W. C. Handy, and some others.

| 400 | 386 | 342 | 300 | 267 |
| (major temp.) | (major natur.) | (neutral) | (minor temp.) | (below minor) |

Fig. 1.2. Variations of "the third."

It is certain that blues musicians think in terms of pitch areas. While outsiders tend towards minute tonal discrimination proceeding from the Western 12-note system as a parameter, blues artists may conceptualize adjacent frequency values as one and the same toneme. For example, the five pitch variations of "the third" given above in Figure 1.2 are acoustically defined by their cents values at 400, 386, 342, 300, and 267 cents, but the relevance of such distinctions to musicians varies with the culture.

In a blues performance the voice of a singer can fluctuate between some of these values, especially in highly ornamental styles, without any indication that they are all conceptualized as separate autonomous pitch units. It is necessary, therefore, to look at the pitch repertoire of an individual singer or instrumentalist in terms of detecting *tonemes,* that is, intraculturally conceptualized pitch values. There can be no doubt that a scaffolding of definite pitch values exists in the blues, but it exists independently of the Western-tempered scale, and there is also a margin of tolerance for fluctuations. In its internal structure such a system is autonomous. All units are integrated into the whole, with no place for any concept of "alien" or deviating tones. The pitch values can be spread across one octave, but not even necessarily so. Auditory mental templates can also cover ranges wider than an octave, especially in the blues, as we shall see later.

Scalar Patterns and Ornamentation in Blues Singers

If one considers the tonal material used by blues singers as an expression of a systemic order, one is bound to acknowledge that for a musician all the constituent tones form a framework of references and relationships. But there is in the blues also the phenomenon of microtonal wavering. Blues singers have terms to express this concept, as Muddy Waters has demonstrated in his discussion of pitch shading in Robert Palmer's book *Deep Blues.*[26] Generally, blues singers in the Deep South speak of "worrying" or "bending" the notes of the voice or on an instrument such as a guitar.

Microtonal wavering is most prominent in at least one strand of the blues, the Delta blues style. It is an inheritance in the blues from one large culture area in Africa, originally identified by Paul Oliver[27] as particularly important for the remote history of pre-blues musical forms in the southern United States: the West African savanna and sahel zone from Senegal across Mali and Burkina Faso to northern Ghana, northern Nigeria, and up to Lake Chad. This is the culture area of centuries-old contacts with the Arabic Islamic world of the Maghrib via the Saharan trading network, beginning in the seventh century A.D. Microtonal wavering in the blues can be understood as a continuation of vocal techniques that were gradually brought to the west-central geographical Sudan after the Arabic conquest of North Africa, and then exported to America. Islamization and trans-Saharan influences triggered the rise of the kingdoms of Mali in the fourteenth century, the Songhay empire, and later the Hausa states. The Arabic Islamic melismatic style was transmitted with Qur'an recitations, the call of the Muezzin for prayer and festivities of the Islamic calendar.

The Delta blues style especially is, in a sense, an extension of the west-central Sudanic Islamicized style cluster. Its earlier expressions in the region of origin are still traceable today, especially in the music of minstrels accompanying themselves with instruments such as plucked lutes[28] or the one-stringed fiddle called *gogé* or *gojé*. Like their blues singing counterparts, some of these musicians, whose music is considered to be "wicked" and "of the devil,"[29] make extensive use of vocal and instrumental melisma, expanding a basically pentatonic framework by microtonal wavering, without however losing that framework, for example, never attempting progression *between* microtones, or anything close to the 17-note classical Arabic division of the octave. A declamatory voice style and the development of melodic patterns over a bourdon-like permeating reference tone are further characteristics that link these cultures with the blues. I recorded some instructive examples in 1964 among Hausa itinerant musicians in the Adamawa mountain region in northern Cameroon/northeastern Nigeria, such as Meigogué Adamou Garoua with his one-stringed *gogé* (fiddle) and his *algeita* (reed oboe).[30]

In the African American context, the excessive use of melisma has often been misunderstood as "instability" in intonation or purposeful off-pitch phrasing, and the rough timbre qualities of the declamatory west-central Sudanic voice style misunderstood as an aesthetics of "dirty tones." However, the Arabic Islamic recitational style embraces a microtonal strategy that cannot be described as "instability." In addition, the presence of melisma in a song style does not encroach upon the simultaneous presence of a scaffolding of firm pitch values—on the contrary, ornamentation is based on the presence of fixed pitches to be circumscribed. This entitles us to search for *blues scales.*

Most helpful in this search are Jeff Todd Titon's outline transcriptions of "early downhome blues" recorded between 1926 and 1930. Titon has abstracted the vocal themes from the accompaniment, omitting guitar chords. I know that guitarists are not particularly delighted with that, but it is easier to follow one of the avenues I have suggested for cracking the tonal systems behind many blues by looking at the vocal part in isolation. Luckily, Titon adopted relative notation, that is, all the blues are transcribed in C. He must have also had a presentiment of the pitch area concept, when he spoke in his musical analysis of an "E complex," a "G complex" and a "B complex."[31]

If we take, for example, the theme of Charley Patton's "Banty Rooster Blues" (Paramount 12792, Richmond, Indiana, June 14, 1929, Yazoo L-1020, transcribed on page 65), it is obvious that E-flat↑ can be raised to some value close to E (probably E natural of 386 cents) and therefore constitute an "E area" (cf. the words "he won't" in bars 3 and 7, Ex. 1.1).

The first two lines of this twelve-bar blues show that the theme is pentatonic, but its pentatonism is spread over *more* than one octave (from top to bottom): E-flat ↑ / E → C → B-flat → G → G-flat → C. The notes G and G-flat, connected by a downward slur to end in the powerful tonic (C), are to be considered as separate tonemes, in contrast to the upper E-flat↑ / E, which constitutes one and the same pitch area. G-flat is clearly an emically distinct unit, not merely a slackening of the preceding G.

The last line in Patton's "Banty Rooster Blues" theme has a different text and, at first glance, seems to have a different tonal pattern altogether; however, this is deceptive. Closer analysis suggests that the notes going with the text fragment "with a man" (bar 10) melodically from G to B-flat↑ must be considered as a transposition of the earlier melodic motif "with a rooster" (bars 2 and 6), C to E-flat↑, a fourth down.

This brings into discussion a salient feature characterizing not only this particular title, but many other blues: that melodic motifs incorporating a blue note can in a different line appear in *transposition,* under pressure from harmonic schemes of the instrumental accompaniment. This has consequences for understanding the mechanisms involved in the blue notes and their positions in a scalar scaffolding. If E-flat↑ can appear in transposition as B-flat and vice versa, these two blue notes must have a common identity. In Titon's transcription this is corroborated by the fact that B-flat in the motif "with a man" is eventually also raised a bit, though it starts at a relatively low level. Could it be that the blue notes B-flat and E-flat↑ are quite

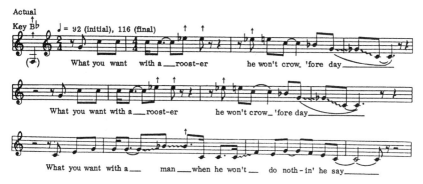

Ex. 1.1. Jeff Todd Titon's notation of the theme of Charley Patton's "Banty Rooster Blues." (Reproduced from Titon, *Early Downhome Blues,* p. 65. Reprinted by permission.)

generally transpositions of each other in the sense that each belongs to an analogous, identical scalar pattern only at a different pitch level? And that these two patterns form a merger in the auditory reference grid of many blues musicians?

Another significant indication we have obtained is that, in contrast to the conventional definition of scale as a ladder-type arrangement of tones within an octave, we can expect that in many blues the tone material will be spread across a margin larger than an octave, something that is too specific to be dismissed lightly as coincidental.

My earlier suggestion that most blues melodies have a pentatonic pitch scaffolding must therefore include these amendments. But we must also stress the diversity of pentatonism in the blues. There is no such thing as a uniform pentatonic blues scale, just as there exist also several types of pentatonism in Africa. Many African pentatonic scales alternate in whole-tone and minor third intervals within an octave framework, but in some others the layout characteristically exceeds the octave range; the lower octave can be *tetra*tonic while "new" pitches appear in the higher one, just as Charley Patton's blue third to the word "rooster" appears like a rooster's cry on the roof of the structure. Linked with it seems to be the presence of a strong central reference tone (written as C).

Scrutinizing the sample of forty-eight tune transcriptions in Titon's *Early Downhome Blues,* one discovers that all of them, except three, Blind Blake's "One Time Blues," Ma Rainey's "Lost Wandering Blues," and Furry Lewis's "Mistreatin' Mamma," end on the tonic C.[32] Blues-lines can end on a variety of tones, but the *last* line nearly always ends on that permeating reference tone. In contrast to many European folk tunes, this central reference note is generally much more powerful in the blues, as recognized by Moya in his observation of Robert Belfour.

I consider this a further signal indicating the west-central Sudanic heritage in the blues. The western Sudan was summarized by Alan Lomax in his *Cantometrics* results as the "Moslem Sudan," but it would be erroneous to consider the whole region as uniformly Islamicized.[33] The impact of the centuries-old contacts with and influences from the Maghrib is not felt everywhere with the same strength. It is prevalent in urban centers, chief's courts, among traders and minstrels, particularly among the Manding', Hausa, and Fulbe. But among many isolated mountain dwellers across the West African savanna, from the Futa Djallon to the Jos and Bauchi plateau of northern Nigeria and the Adamawa plateau of Cameroon there survive pre-Islamic singing styles based on pentatonic scalar patterns that show no Islamic traits at all. I recorded good examples in 1963 among the Chamba, Zanganyi, and Kutin in northeastern Nigeria,[34] as well as further south among the Tikar of the Cameroon grasslands. Some of these west-central Sudanic populations are the remnants of ancient millet agriculturists. Millet was planted across the western geographical Sudan already between 5000 and 1000 B.C.[35] The pentatonic scalar patterns were probably established there also for a very long duration and are most certainly derived from the formants of human speech rather than instrumental experiences of harmonics. They incorporate representations of partials up to the 8th, sometimes to the 9th, harmonic and are often constructed around a tonal scaffolding of two adjoined fourth intervals, C → G and F → C. These tonal pillars still characterize, for example, the tuning of double-bells (*tong'*) among the Kutin in the area of Kontcha, Adamawa region, northern Cameroon. They function together like the ranges of a female voice (C to G) adjoined by a lower male range (F to C), each further subdivided by just one more intermediate note that represents partial 7 to the fundamental of each "pillar," that is, B-flat↓ over a fundamental C, and E-flat↓ over a fundamental F. The juxtaposition of these two scalar patterns, each extrapolating partials 6, 7, and 8, results in an integrated bipartite pentatonic scale with a strong tonal center (C) and a secondary, ancillary center (F) (Fig. 1.3).

In acoustic structure, each section is a transposition of the other. Each can be expanded upwards by one more step in the harmonic series to include a tone representing the 9th partial (see dotted note at the beginning of Fig. 1.3).[36] Thus a variety of pentatonic scales were formed from this generalized auditory template in the history of the west-central Sudanic belt, for example:

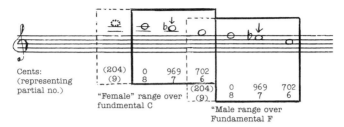

Cents:	(204)	0	969	702			
(representing	(9)	8	7	6			
partial no.)				(204)	0	969	702
				(9)	8	7	6

"Female" range over fundmental C

"Male range over Fundamental F

Fig. 1.3. Scale formed among ancient millet agriculturists of the west-central Sudan by the integration of two subscalar patterns representing symbolic female and male voice ranges, each derived from identical formants of speech.

D, C, B-flat↓, G, F or C, B-flat↓, G, F, E-flat↓ or B-flat↓, G, F, E-flat↓, C (in any notational reshuffle).

The most fascinating thing, however, is that we can retrodict what must have happened when the carriers of such a template were subjected to culture contact with Western folk and church music, as they were in the nineteenth-century South of the United States. In such a case the structure shown in Figure 1.3 would *rematerialize itself* within the framework of the Western diatonic scale in predictable ways:

1. The central reference tone (C) would be equated with the tonic of the Western system.
2. The second, ancillary center (F) would be reinterpreted in terms of a subdominant function. The carriers of this mental template will, therefore, be at ease adopting and understanding progression to the subdominant degree in the Western system.
3. The tone representing partial 6 (702 cents, written as G in Fig. 1.3) reinforces the fundamental C, but in relation to the F fundamental represents the 9th harmonic (204 cents). Both facts concur to make it difficult for carriers of this mental template to adopt and accept Western-style progressions to a dominant chord. This explains why the dominant chord is often avoided or circumvented in the blues. When it does occur, it is only in bar 9 of the standard 12-bar form (sometimes also in bar 10 and as a "turnaround" in bar 12). But since the G is also ambiguous in relation to the subscales that overlap at that point, it will have importance as a tone or degree with bilateral functions.
4. The formant-derived pitch values of 969 cents both in the upper and the lower section of the layout in Figure 1.3 represent partial 7, both

counted from their own fundamental, C and F, respectively. These pitch-values will be difficult to accommodate within the Western diatonic scale, because they are 31 cents lower than the closest equivalents in the Western tempered system. Their closest approximations in the tempered system are B-flat (at 1000 cents) and E-flat (at 300 cents). But they are also at odds with the tonic-subdominant-dominant scheme of harmonic progressions. Listeners rooted in Western music will react to their use in the diatonic system with the sensations "strange," "novel," "fascinating," etc.

The model shown in Figure 1.3 is ever-present in the blues. One may simply open to page 67 in Titon's book and find it in identical shape (up to partial 8) in the last line, bars 11 and 12, of Lillian Miller's "Dead Drunk Blues" (Gennet 6518, Richmond, Indiana, rec. ca. May 3, 1928, Origin Jazz Library OJL-6). Titon's musical sensitivity even spotted that the B-flat is somewhat lowered, suggesting the continued presence in Lillian Miller of a tonal memory that identifies the higher blue note as representing the 7th partial of the harmonic series (Ex. 1.2)

Many more examples could be cited from a variety of blues records. Historically, the presence of such tonal patterns in the blues is not surprising. The areas dominated by the Hausa city states in northern Nigeria and several Fulbe chiefdoms in the Adamawa region after the Fulbe had resettled at the end of their *jihad* beginning in 1804, were literally becoming hubs of the slave trade. Many people were still deported from those areas to New World destinations at the beginning of the nineteenth century. The "old-nigritic" millet agriculturalists especially had been defenseless victims of the slave trade throughout the eighteenth century, as is evident from the sample of languages from the interior of Nigeria identified among liberated slaves in Sierra Leone by Sigismund Koelle during the 1840s.[37] Villages in remote areas of the West African hinterland had become primary targets of slave raids. This is why, besides the Islamicized declamatory vocal style with microtonal wavering and a strong bourdon-like basis of the tonal process, the ancient savanna pentatonism of the millet agriculturists also gained a bridgehead in the United States. Some recordings that were made by Paul Oliver[38] and myself among isolated communities in the west-central Sudanic belt, can still demonstrate the connection, even though two hundred years have passed after the slave trade in that region had reached a climax. They are comparable in several traits to blues recordings; for example, the grinding song of the Tikar woman I recorded in central Cameroon in 1964.[39]

I thought I'd ___ pass ___ a - way ___

Ex. 1.2. Bars 11 and 12 in Lillian Miller's "Dead Drunk Blues" showing the presence of the west-central Sudanic speech-based tonal pattern in its original scalar layout. (Transcription extract reproduced from Titon, *Early Downhome Blues,* p. 67. Reprinted by permission.)

In vocal quality and even melodic layout it has stunning affinities with the song "Hard Working Woman" by Mississippi Matilda, recorded in New Orleans, October 15, 1936, on Bluebird B-6812, with Eugene Powell and Willie Harris accompanying her on guitars.

There is yet one more hinge to the issue of retention of a west-central Sudanic scalar template in the blues. Any tonal system that is based on a selection of harmonics—whether they are speech-derived or from instrumental experiences does not matter in this context—presupposes that its carriers are at least unconsciously aware of the fundamental (or fundamentals) on which the selection is based. Audio-psychologically, any selective use of higher partials implies that the lower partials are part of the singers' mental template. If I am correct with my model (see Fig. 1.3) in assuming that in several areas of the geographical Sudan a variety of pentatonic scales are ramifications of an auditory mental template that adjoins two identical sectors of the natural harmonic series from partial 6 to 8 at the distance of a fifth, then the carriers of such an auditory template must be unconsciously aware of the lower partials of *both sectors.* Each section will tend to be referred in the mind to its proper fundamental. The lower partials down from partial 5 to the fundamental (partial 1) will generate a vague awareness in the mind; but since there are two such columns that extend down to their fundamentals, the result will be an *interference pattern.* This can be shown best with a graphic illustration (Fig. 1.4).

What is inscribed in Figure 1.4 into the two adjoined rectangles corresponds with the tones shown in Figure 1.3. Everything that falls outside in each of the two columns constitutes partials that are activated in the mind simultaneously whenever the system formed by the two rectangles is operated. A comparison of the cents values of the two integrated columns demonstrates the emerging *interference pattern.* Some pitch values in the columns will not interfere at all; some others will supplement the opposite column with their values (see arrows); but one particular set, connected by the wavy line, will significantly interfere.

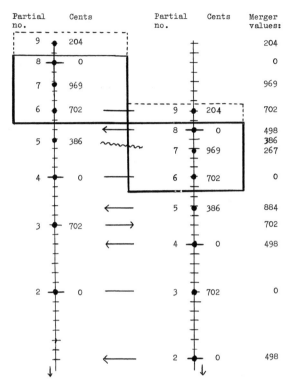

Fig. 1.4. Interference pattern between two harmonic columns based on two different fundamentals 702 cents apart, and adjoined as in Figure 1.3 to form a merger scale.

Partial 9 in the lower scale will not interfere with partial 6 of the higher one, because there is no pitch difference between them. This is the note where both scales are connected with each other, the note G in our notational layout (see Fig. 1.3). In the blues this note became the dominant (without a dominant chord). Partial 8 in the lower column will also not interfere with the opposite column, but contribute to the merger model a tone F as a secondary center. Further down, the situation is the same. Even the 386 value in the lower column will be projected easily into the empty space of the opposite column where it will constitute the note A at 884 cents (that is, 16 cents lower than the Western tempered A). This is so because the overall difference between the higher and the lower sector is 702 cents.

The two notes that seriously interfere with each other are those representing partial 5 (at 386 cents) in the higher column and partial 7 (at 969 cents) in the lower one. The ear has no choice but to declare these two tones as identical, as one and the same toneme, because first they cannot be associated with any other notes *already* forming a scaffolding of simple ratios, and secondly, they are close enough to each other—their difference being 119 cents (386 minus 267)—that they easily constitute one pitch area.

Needless to say that this is the explanation of the width of what appears in the blues as the lower blue note, "somewhere" between E and E-flat. What we have just accomplished is that we have calculated the margin of fluctuations for the lower blue note as 119 cents, a bit more than a semitone in size, and we have discovered something about the nature of the blue notes:

1. The higher blue note, B-flat, is derived from the 7th harmonic of the natural harmonic series, and tends therefore to be slightly lower than the minor seventh in the Western tonal system. Introduced with slurs and glissandi it tends to fluctuate around the value of 969 cents. Measurements to that effect, however, are only conclusive if this note, B-flat↓, occurs in sections over a tonic chord. If it occurs over a dominant chord, it may be a *transposition* of the lower blue note to the G level. Accordingly it tends to have a different value, roughly between 969 and 1088 cents.

2. The lower blue note, E / E-flat, correctly described in the literature as a "neutral third," is derived from an interference pattern that forms if two columns of partials are adjoined at the distance of a fifth, the higher one representing a tonic level, the lower one a subdominant level. The lower blue note can be understood as a pitch area covering the distance between a natural third (386 cents) and a lowered minor third (at 267 cents). It tends to fluctuate between these two values according to context and is greatly used as an expression of a wailing sound in a highly melismatic singing style. If the fundamental is C (tonic) as, for example, in the first line of a twelve-bar blues (cf. Charley Patton's "Banty Rooster Blues"), the lower blue note can be raised with a glide to reach a value around 386 cents. If the fundamental changes to F (subdominant) it will tend to be intoned between approximately 267 and ± 300 cents and sound to a Western ear like a minor third. It is important, however, to understand that all these pitch modifications of the lower blue note do not encroach upon its primary conceptualization as one and the same toneme.

Researchers who draw up "blues scales," therefore, are advised *not* to distinguish between E and E-flat in their pitch counting exercises.

3. According to harmonic contexts established by the accompaniment (guitar, etc.), the blue notes can appear in *transposition,* if the underlying chord has changed to suggest a different root. This means that notations of a blue note as B-flat or E-flat are not conclusive as such to ascertain its identity. One has to find out in each case *to which fundamental* the particular blue note is related.

To provide more clarity, I am showing in Figure 1.5 the results obtained from Figure 1.4 in staff notation. The notes that form the scaffolding of the merger scale are written with rings; all other notes, including E = 386 and E-flat = 267 forming together one toneme, are written with black dots. I am confident that this is perhaps the most accurate blues scale we can obtain by abstraction.

My central thesis concerning the blue notes B-flat and E-flat can now be summarized: Many blues singers operate from a mental template (pitch memory) originated in a west-central Sudanic merger model between two scalar sections adjoined at the interval of a fifth, both sections derived from the use of partials 6 to 8 (sometimes to 9) of the natural harmonic series. This tonal material is obtained from speech-produced formants, not from any instrumental experience. Singers are aware of the roots of these two patterns, each with its own set of lower partials and its own fundamental. From the blending of the two columns, conveniently represented as based on fundamentals C and F, there results an interference pattern that determines the overall framework of pitch perception not only in the west-central Sudanic cultures concerned, but also in their New World derivatives, particularly in the blues. The west-central Sudanic tonal heritage is reinterpreted there within the scalar framework of the Western diatonic scale, while its basic functions and concepts are maintained. The C fundamental is identified with the *tonic,* the F fundamental with the *subdominant* degree. The hub of the two scalar patterns, that is, where they overlap (the note written as G),

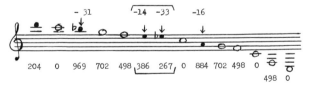

Fig. 1.5. The results of Figure 1.4 in staff notation.

is vaguely associated with the Western *dominant* degree, but without its accompanying dominant chord, due to the absence of the note B in the west-central Sudanic pattern. The west-central Sudanic auditory template conflicts with the Western tonal system particularly in two places whose pitch areas have been described as "blue notes." It also conflicts with Western functional harmony in that the dominant *chord* is predictably difficult to accommodate in the blues, while the subdominant chord can be interpreted as a shift from the fundamental C to the secondary, ancillary center F.[40]

Skip James's "Devil Got My Woman"

Not all melodic themes in the blues tradition are pentatonic. One famous theme that incorporates *six* different pitch-values spread across one and a half octaves is Skip James's "Devil Got My Woman" (Paramount 13088, recorded February, 1931), mentioned earlier. Nehemiah "Skip" James (1902–69) has been recognized as one of the most extraordinary Mississippi bluesmen. After his rediscovery in 1964 and a brief second recording career, he became widely known and his legendary status was reconfirmed with the publication in 1994 of Stephen Calt's probing study of his life and personality.[41]

The analysis of Skip James's music is particularly important, because it might give us clues for solving one of the trickiest problems in the tonality of the blues: the presence in so many early blues, by Bessie Smith and many others, of a third blue note called "the flatted fifth" in the literature. The term "flatted fifth," however, is a misnomer, because the blue note in question is neither a fifth "flattened" nor its derivative, nor is it in any other way related to the fifth of 702 cents. In our scheme, Figures 1.3, 1.4, and 1.5, we have not accounted for this autonomous entity, and the question is into what kind of scheme does it fit?

What is the nature of this blue note? Although it gained prominence in bebop with the "flatted fifth chord," assuming there a function somewhat different from that which it had in the early blues, its prominence in the early blues cannot be denied. For simplicity we can call this blue note ± F-sharp in the key of C. One theory, proposed by David Evans,[42] can perhaps explain several cases in which it occurs. Evans thinks that it is a blue third on top of another blue third, that is, superimposed blue notes that add up to bring about a value close to F-sharp. In this case, the ± F-sharp blue note is a transposition of the lower blue note area, E / E-flat↓ in close to its narrowest interval expression; for example, two times 267 cents would bring it to a value around 534 cents (that is, between F and F-sharp), which I think is realistic.

In actual practice, the singer usually sounds a higher tone, around 300+ cents, which then is doubled to yield a tone of 600++ cents. The frequent use of diminished chords in early jazz could possibly be an expression of such tendencies. This theory probably works for a number of blues, but we are, of course, aware of the fact that blues are not a homogeneous tradition. What explains the tonal material in one item might not be applicable to another.

What other clues do we have? My preliminary impression has been that the ± F-sharp, or third blue note, occurs with particular frequency in blues with a very strong tonal center (C), in vocal lines that develop over a virtual bourdon, while it is less frequent in those blues in which the vocal line adapts easily to progressions into subdominant and dominant chords. Lacking a comprehensive blues sampling project, I cannot support my impressions statistically, but it is worthwhile to try to follow this lead. If the ± F-sharp blue note and the presence of a bourdon-like tonal center, as in the music of many "Delta" blues artists including Robert Belfour, constitute an inter-related *trait cluster,* then we can try to examine what kind of relationship there is between the ± F-sharp blue note and the drone-like awareness of a central reference tone (C).

Can Skip James help us? Unfortunately in Skip James's blues there is no *obvious* presence of the "flatted fifth" in a position within the scale that would compare to Charley Patton's "Banty Rooster Blues" and many other blues where a note around ± F-sharp is most certainly a distinct tonemic unit, and most often resolved downwards into the E-flat ↓ blue note or C. On the other hand, Skip James's blues transcend significantly the ubiquitous pentatonic scalar framework that is familiar from so many other blues, while in no way sounding more "Western." What kind of place then do these additional tones have in Skip James's music? I do not intend to present here a comprehensive analysis of tonal patterns in Skip James's music. But I think it is worthwhile to examine blues that clearly go beyond pentatonism, with the caveat that my results will be limited to this particular blues artist, Skip James, even only to the particular song analyzed.

In Stephen Calt's book there is a transcription by Woody Mann of the guitar introduction and the first verse of "Devil Got My Woman" in Western staff notation, including a tablature notation of the guitar part accompanying the voice.[43] To facilitate comparison I am pointing to this transcription as a reference, but will give below a short notation of my own of Skip James's verse 1 in relative notation (that is, in the key of C) (Ex. 1.3). My objective is to test out a non-Western interpretation of the very same pitch-lines transcribed by Mann.[44]

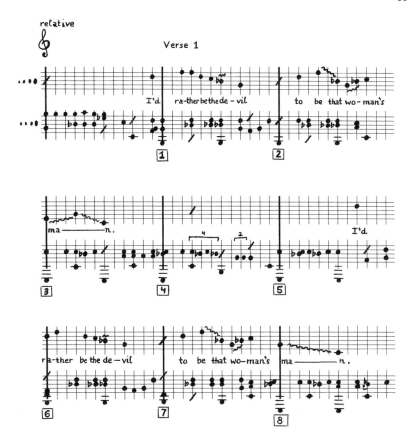

Ex. 1.3. Verse 1 of Skip James's "Devil Got My Woman," vocal and guitar lines. (Transcription by G. Kubik from Paramount 13088, rec. Grafton, Wisconsin, February 1931.)

Pursuing the method proposed earlier, I will now abstract from Skip James's vocal theme (Ex. 1.3) the underlying scalar pattern. The pitch-values are counted from the basic note C and laid out along a graphic scheme (Fig. 1.6). The last note in Skip James's verse 1 transcribed by me as a C′ (by Woody Mann as D′) is the central reference tone of the whole song and will therefore be represented in my graph as the pitch of 0 cents. All the other tones are laid out in relation to this pitch. Since the singer's intonation oscillates in several places, expressed in the transcription (Ex. 1.3) with the sign /~/ over some notes, I prefer to mark all pitch values by shades in their approximate places along the scale, rather than dots.

With regard to verse 1 (Ex. 1.3 and Fig. 1.6), three important observations are to be made: (a) the melody transcends the range of an octave; (b) in the

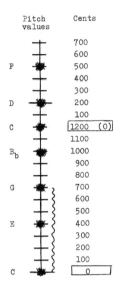

Fig. 1.6. Skip James's tonal material in verse 1 ("I'd rather be the devil to be that woman's man").

lower octave, that is, from 0 to 1200 cents, the singer uses only *four* different pitch values; and the three lowest are connected by melisma and glissandi; and (c) in the upper octave two more tones appear which are *not* duplications of any tones that constitute the lower octave. I think this displays unmistakable leads. If six pitch-values in a vocal theme that is clearly based on a central reference tone are spread out as they are (Fig. 1.6) in disjunct intervals across the range of almost one and a half octaves, with a tendency of the intervals to become narrower as one moves up the scale, then such a scalar arrangement is *likely to be derived* from upper harmonics over a single fundamental.

To check this idea we now consider the *order* of the tones in the scalar arrangement of verse 1. Allowing for slight adjustments of the vocal intonation to the guitar tuning, Skip James's theme looks suspiciously like a projection of an extract of the natural harmonic series from partial 4 to 11, skipping only partial 10, which would have been a mere duplication of partial 5 (Fig. 1.7).

Of course, the natural harmonic series is slightly off-pitch to the (artificial) European tempered system (and Skip James's guitar tuning for that matter); the E-386 is 14 cents flat, the B-flat↓-969 blue note is 31 cents lower than its tempered "namesake," and the F-sharp↓-551 representing partial 11 is exactly halfway between a Western tempered F and F-sharp. Moreover, to the listener's ear the highest tone in Skip James's theme sounds like a perfect fourth (498 cents) rather than a pitch value between F and F-sharp, except perhaps in

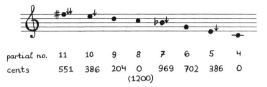

Fig. 1.7. The natural harmonic series from partial 4 to 11.

one repetition of the theme—and about mid-way in the recording—where it seems to be significantly higher. Skip James's customary intonation could be a powerful argument against my thesis, but even with his scalar pattern based on a partials-derived African tonal system, his intonation need not correspond exactly to the cents values of the natural harmonic series (Fig. 1.7). One can expect that some accommodation of pitch with the Western fret-induced guitar tuning must have been made. It is the *order* of Skip James's pitch material in his theme that suggests a mental template proceeding from partial 4 (as a reduplication of the fundamental C two octaves higher) up to partial 11. This idea also has circumstantial support from the fact that there are no Western-style harmonic progressions between tonic, subdominant, and dominant chords in this music.

All pitch-lines in the theme appear to be ultimately connected to a central reference tone or bourdon. For this reason, the underlying guitar patterns cannot be interpreted, in my opinion, in terms of harmonic progressions between dominant seventh and tonic seventh (an A^7 chord to a D^7 chord in Mann's notation), although the guitar bass note patterns may mistakenly suggest such a structure. The notes of the upper lines of the guitar accompaniment clearly match the scalar pattern of the vocal theme.

Obviously, there is tonal opposition between bars 1-2 and bars 3-4 in verse 1. This is not surprising. It often happens in African musical styles, when a theme is based on a single fundamental, that oppositional melodic-harmonic clusters are created by first selectively using a section of higher harmonics for melodic formation to be followed by a section of lower harmonics. Translated into Skip James's verse 1, this means that there is an alternation between a partial 4-5-6 melodic cluster (measures 3-4) and a partial 6-7-8-9-11 melodic cluster (measures 1-2).

In contrast to some Caribbean-influenced African American styles, as exemplified by some of Bo Diddley's guitar patterns of the 1950s, Skip James's music is definitely not based on mouth-bow derived harmonics over two fundamentals, for example, B-flat–D–F and C–E–G (with B-flat and C as the two fundamentals), common for example among the Fang' of Gabon and Guinea Ecuatorial. Such music is strictly organized as a cyclic shifting between these two chord clusters. It is common in some Caribbean styles, and occasionally even in "modal" jazz, but not in Skip James's music. But then, on which African tonal heritage might it be based? Are there any particular areas in Africa where tonal systems over a *single* fundamental with usage of the harmonic series up to partial 11 can be found?

In my continent-wide sample there is one large area that stands out: northern Moçambique with ethnic groups such as the -Shirima, -Meto, -Lomwe, -Makua, -Yao, -Makonde, etc., who incidentally were affected not only by the Arab slave trade across the Indian Ocean[45] but also, especially in the late eighteenth and early nineteenth centuries, by the Atlantic slave trade. *Mangwilo* xylophone players, as I studied them in that area in 1962, and also Yao xylophone players, studied in 1983 and later by Moya Aliya Malamusi and myself,[46] often tune their instruments to scales derived from higher partials of a nonobjectified single fundamental. The harmonic series is definitely used up to the 11th partial as a model for the emerging intervals, possibly in some cases also to the 13th partial, jumping harmonics that are merely simple duplications of lower partials,[47] just as partial 10 is not represented in the pattern forming Skip James's theme.

It is characteristic of this xylophone music (and also of much of the music for stringed instruments such as the *sese* flat-bar zither and the *takare* one-stringed fiddle, all of which are old Asian imports) that it is always based on a prominent bourdon-like central reference tone that the two (xylophone) players sitting opposite each other obtain by a rapid alternation of interlocking strokes on the same key. But the most stunning characteristic of this system is the type of simultaneous sounds that emerge from it. On a xylophone tuned in this way *any note* can be struck together with any other note, and as a result one often gets seconds, sometimes even parallel seconds, and complex sound-clusters without any impression of dissonance. This is so, and even desirable, because any two notes hit together with some emphasis emit a very deep tone that can be faintly heard and which is identical with the fundamental of the series. Such deep tones are called *difference tones* in acoustics, because they can be defined mathematically as the difference between the Hertz values of the two higher notes struck together.

For example, if one hits on a northern Moçambique log xylophone the slat tuned to a pitch representing the 11th partial (at 551 cents) together with its neighboring note tuned to the 10th partial (at 386 cents) and continues these bi-chords in a downward direction (Fig. 1.8), the auditory impression

Fig. 1.8. Bi-chords and difference tones in northern Moçambique xylophone music (schematic illustration). Relative notation.

will be that of a very acceptable sequence of tones, because each bi-chord reinforces, by the effect of the difference tones, the fundamental common to all the notes of this partials-derived scale.

This can also be shown mathematically. If, for example, we take the fundamental to be 170 Hertz (c.p.s.) and calculate the Hertz values up to partial 11, we can then subtract any two neighboring Hertz values from each other, and the difference will always be 170 (Table 1.1).

Table 1.1. How difference tones form: example based on a fundamental of 170 Hertz (c. p. s.).

Partial no.	Notation	Hertz	Difference	Cents values
11	F-sharp↓	1870		551
			170	
10	E↓	1700		386
			170	
9	D	1530		204
			170	
8	C	1360		0
			170	
7	B-flat↓	1190		969
			170	
6	G	1020		702
			170	
5	E↓	850		386
			170	
4	C	680		0
			170	
3	G	510		702
			170	
2	C	340		0
			170	
1	C	170		0

Fig. 1.9. Prominent simultaneous sounds in Skip James's guitar accompaniment to his voice in verse 1 (transcribed in *relative* notation, in the key of C).

I see the memory of some of these backgrounds lingering on in Skip James's blues. We should, therefore, consider some of the guitar chords that accompany his voice not as "chords" in the Western sense with functions, but as *sound clusters* in strategic positions that reinforce the drone in the singer's mind through difference tones. Why, for example, are certain simultaneous sounds on Skip James's guitar so prominent in the accompaniment of the voice-line? (Fig. 1.9).

Figure 1.9a *looks* like a fragmented C⁷ chord, 1.9b like a major-third interval, and 1.9c like a G-minor chord. That is highly deceptive. If we interpret each tone as representing a partial of the harmonic series, a totally different but no less coherent picture emerges. The clash between the C″ and B-flat′ in Figure 1.9a, for example, supported by a very deep C takes on a totally different meaning if we regard it as representing partials 8, 7 and 2. Their difference tones reinforce the fundamental. And if the notes in Figure 1.9b are seen as representing partials 9 and 7, their relevance in relation to the bourdon becomes evident, because their difference tone will reinforce partial 2. The notes in Figure 1.9c, representing partials 9, 7, and 3, create the same effect. All these sound clusters resolve mathematically by reinforcing the fundamental that is common to them.

How does Skip James develop his vocal lines further on? Does their melodic material confirm our findings? He sings a total of four verses:

1. I'd rather be the devil to be that woman's man. (2x in var.)

2. Ah, nothing but the devil changed my baby's mind.
   Oh, nothing but the devil changed my baby's mind.

3. I lay down last night, lay down last night, I lay down last night, tried to take my rest.
   My mind got to ramblin' like the wild geese from the west, from the west.

4. The woman I love, woman that I love, the woman I love, stole'd her from my best friend.

But he got lucky, stole'd her back again.
And he got lucky, stole'd her back again.

It is the first part of the third verse that displays different, and apparently incompatible melodic material. While its second part, "I lay down last night, tried to take my rest," is in line with the melody of verse 1, the first part of this verse reaches up to G″, and in the beginning of verse 4 even up to A″, both times in falsetto voice, and it also introduces a new tone, the E-flat″ blue note (Ex. 1.4).

How can we account for these new elements? Do they represent an expansion even into higher areas of harmonics over the same drone? Or is a more Western interpretation of the G → F → E-flat → C melodic line as a section of a "minor scale" appropriate?

We will certainly not propel ourselves up to the 19th harmonic in order to explain the E-flat″. Actually, the solution to this problem is quite simple and in line with my central thesis concerning the nature of the common blue notes B-flat↓ and E / E-flat. The descending sequence G → F → E-flat → C sung to the words "I lay down last night" is a melodic transposition up a fourth of an identical pattern, D → C → B-flat → G sung to the words "be the devil" in the scalar pattern–determining verse 1 (see Ex. 1.3). This is corroborated by the fact that the line "I lay down last night" is itself transposed downward in measure 4 of verse 3 so that the key words "down last night" are melodically represented as D → C → B-flat → G.

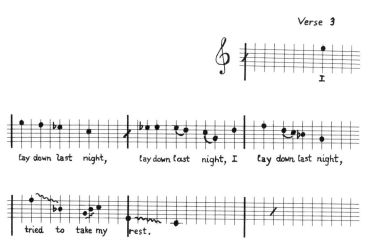

Ex. 1.4. Verse 3 in Skip James's "Devil Got My Woman." (Transcription by G. Kubik from Paramount record 13088.)

Fig. 1.10. Skip James's tonal resources in "Devil Got My Woman": two scalar patterns, both derived from harmonics, but built up over two different fundamentals, C and F, and integrated to form one merger scale.

The explanation of this process in terms of audio-psychological behavior can only be that Skip James's mental reference scheme activates, at the beginning of verse 3, a hidden, secondary fundamental a fourth higher, which is F. His alternation from natural to falsetto voice could also be seen in this context. Due to the strength of the bourdon on C, the F never appears as a bass note in the guitar part, a fact that is reinforced in a technical sense by the guitar's open tuning (relative, from low to high: C, G, C, E-flat, G, C). But in a higher duplication the F appears sporadically in various contexts, characteristically always in the melodic neighborhood of G' in the guitar accompaniment, even in verse 1, and throughout the piece. This simmering presence of the F and its derivative, an A, throughout the guitar accompaniment (see Ex. 1.3, measures 1–3, 6–8)—though never assuming any subdominant function—accounts a great deal for the harmonic ambiguity of "Devil Got My Woman" and also some other songs of Skip James. In a sense, it suggests a bitonal merger with a strong bourdon-like fundamental C and an ancillary fundamental with its own column of partials that is F.

Results of the investigation: Skip James's total melodic resources, that is, voice lines and guitar accompaniment, in "Devil Got My Woman" *derive from the interface, merger, and interference between partials over two fundamentals a fourth apart.* In contrast to the pentatonic scheme presented in Figure 1.4 earlier in this article, however, his awareness of harmonics extends to areas higher than partial 9, in the lower column I (over fundamental C) up to partial 11, in the higher column II (over fundamental F) up to partial 10 (Fig. 1.10). The interference pattern can be shown mathematically much more accurately in a scheme comparable to the one in Figure 1.4 (Fig. 1.11).

The rectangles drawn in Figure 1.11 visualize the pitch resources of Skip James's vocal lines in "Devil Got My Woman"—a heptatonic blues scale—and they delineate where its constituent elements come from. The scheme shows that these tones are derived from two integrated columns of partials over fundamentals a fourth (498 cents) apart. Here, the "male" column—alluding to our allegory in Figures 1.3 and 1.4—is based on C, while the

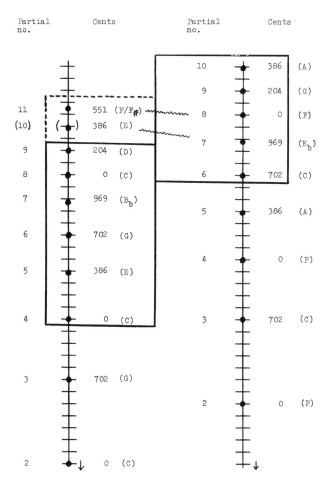

Fig. 1.11. The acoustics of Skip James's tonal resources in "Devil Got My Woman."

"female" column is based on F. So the relationship is inverted as it probably is in many blues.

Pitch interference takes place between partial 11 (in column I) and partial 8 (in column II). Extreme pitch difference (119 cents) exists between partial 10 in column I and partial 7 in column II. But the latter tone, E-flat-969 is closer to D-204 in column I than it is to E-386. This might explain why the upper E is omitted in the melodic formation of Skip James's theme (verse 1). The singer seems to react to the pronounced difference between the two pitch values by suppressing in his mind the interference relationship and avoiding E-386 (partial 10 of column I) altogether in favor of the "blue" E-flat-969 value of column II.

The proximity of the F / F-sharp-551 value (partial 11 in column I) to F (partial 8 in column II) and the fact that the F reduplicates the fundamental, thereby exerting a powerful force, could also be one of the causes of why Skip James adjusts his intonation down to an F. The scalar order of the partials in column I would call for the F / F-sharp-551 intonation, but interference from column II prevents it. The lowering was perhaps also facilitated by influences from the guitar tuning and by the fact that this pitch value at the top end of column I is in an extreme position.

What I have tried here is perhaps a somewhat audacious look at Skip James's mind, but I hope not devoid of an inherent logic. Skip James's "Devil Got My Woman" and some of his other songs (not analyzed here) demonstrate a fascinating expansion of tonal resources beyond the usual pentatonism of the blues. His acute ear apparently processed the experiences of harmonics up to partial 11 over column I (C) and up to partial 10 over column II (F). While my analysis of this particular song has not solved the mystery of the "flatted fifth" blue note in general terms, it has helped us to discover other things that are worthwhile to know. While it is possible, therefore, that the note ± F-sharp in many blues constitutes an octave transposition downwards of a value representing partial 11 over a single fundamental, we must be aware, as suggested by David Evans, that "it may function in a variety of ways in the blues because of problems of fitting it into a Western harmonic scheme as well as its proximity to the perfect fifth and fourth. In some cases it may function as an alternative fifth, for example, John Lee Hooker's 'Hobo Blues,' where the melody rises from tonic to blue third to blue fifth. In other cases it may function as an alternative fourth, where it usually begins a melody line or drops off from a perfect fifth, descending (sometimes through the blue third) to the tonic."[48]

From my analysis emerges a new set of issues to be pursued in the future. In African music there are two very different usages of partials-based materials derived from a single fundamental. In some cultures composition of melodic and harmonic patterns strictly preserves the original layout of the order of tones within the natural harmonic series. This is the case, for example, of melodic-harmonic patterns among the Wagogo of Tanzania with their pentatonic system incorporating a projection of partials 4 to 9. The other usage is that higher partials (for example, partial 9) transcending the scope of an octave are transposed downward by one octave to form the melody-generating scalar pattern, foe example, among the -Makua of the Republic of Congo.[49]

Partials-Based Scales and Blues Texts

Finally, with the tones in Skip James's vocal themes of "Devil Got My Woman" assumed to be a partials-derived scalar pattern, we discover an interesting relationship between the sound values of the partials and *symbolism in the text*. Characteristically, the word "man" that was without doubt central to the singer's identity, coincides with the bourdon tone (partial 4), thereby obtaining additional weight. The "man" is the text's central concern, and in the music this word goes with duplications of the fundamental. It is the cognitive point of departure in the song's patterns. Its importance radiates from the deepest note in the vocal part to tones representing partials 5 and 6 connected by a glide. The centrality of that concept is reinforced by the guitar accompaniment with the sound cluster incorporating partials 8 and 7, reconfirming once again the fundamental as a difference tone. The blue note representing partial 7 carries both the start of the word "devil" and a syllable of the word "woman," underlining perhaps a notion of identity in Skip James's perception. Split into two halves, the word "wo-man" is set in a way that the first syllable identifying the female idea moves up to the blue note representing partial 7, while the second syllable "-man" coincides with a duplication of the basic reference tone, represented by partial 8. Skip James's song starts on a tone representing the 9th partial in the underlying scalar template. Most interestingly, it expresses a condition, a possibility ("I'd").

While the fundamental and its duplications (partials 4, 8) in Skip James's "Devil Got My Woman" most obviously carry the ideas "man," virility, etc., the 7th partial seems to be the negative counterpart expressing both the ideas "devil" and "woman" from the singer's viewpoint. The 6th partial could have a supporting function that enables these words to be completed. The 9th partial is used to express conditional feelings and ideas, while the 11th partial seems to allude to more affirmative and demonstrative patterns of thought.

I consider the distribution of the words and their ideas across the scale of upper partials to be an interesting discovery in sound symbolism—an area of research that has received new impetus recently with the work of Kenichi Tsukada on phonaesthetic systems in Ghana and Zambia.[50] To check whether these findings might have wider significance within the blues tradition, I

examined Titon's sample of forty-eight "downhome blues" themes for associations of two key words, "man" and "woman," with certain tones. Titon's
sample includes mostly male singers, but there are also some well-known
and some lesser-known female singers in the sample. Not all blues texts incorporate these two words, of course. But in those which do, the stunning
result was that the word "man" is indeed regularly associated with the central
reference tone (C) (cf. nos. 1, 23, 24, 26, 30, 31, 40, 45, and 48), and so are, significantly, two other words: "me" and "mine." In one song by Ed Bell, "Mean
Conductor Blues," the word "man" *also* falls in the first line on F bound to
an E by a slur, and in the last line of Charley Patton's "It Won't Be Long" the
word "man" is part of a downward glissando from G into the blue-note area
E-flat and E. The only significant exception where the word "man" is allo-
cated to several other notes, F, G and D, besides C, is a song by a *female* blues
singer, Bessie Smith, "Poor Man's Blues" (no. 27).

This result seems to confirm my suggestion that ego-symbolism as expressed in words such as "man," "me," "mine," etc., as concepts of the *self* of
a male singer, is represented *musically* by association with the central reference tone in the blues. Most stunning, however, are the results I have obtained by scrutinizing the distribution of the word "woman" across Titon's
sample of forty-eight blues themes. "Woman" almost never falls on a C, but
in most cases is musically expressed by either the upper or the lower blue
note (B-flat or E-flat) (cf. nos. 2, 7, 12, 13, 22, 31, 34, 36, 39, 43). There are very
few exceptions to this rule (cf. no. 34 by Son House and no. 48 by Alger "Texas"
Alexander).

"Downhome" blues being predominantly a male tradition, my conclusion
is that this pattern reflects a sound symbolism associated with a harmonics-
based scalar framework that expresses male ideas of *centrality* ("man," "mine,"
"me") and *uncertainty* and *doubt* in relation to females. The basic reference
tone (fundamental C) and the two common blue notes can therefore also
be seen as oppositional tone categories.

Notes

1. Cf. Moya Aliya Malamusi, "*Nthano* Chantefables and Songs Performed by the
Bangwe Player Chitenje Tambala," *South African Journal of African Languages* (Contributions in Honour of David Kenneth Rycroft), 10 (1990): 222–38; Gerhard Kubik
and Moya A. Malamusi, *Opeka Nyimbo—Musician Composers from Southern Malawi*, Double LP, MC 15, Museum Collection Berlin: Museum für Völkerkunde, Ab-
teilung Musikethnologie, 1989.

2. *The Spirit Lives On: Deep South Country Blues and Spirituals*, recorded by David
Evans, Hot Fox HF-CD-005, Pfullendorf, Germany, 1994.

3. Cf. notes by David Evans to *The Spirit Lives On.*

4. Our journey to Memphis materialized thanks to an invitation for the two of us by the Center for Black Music Research (Samuel A. Floyd Jr., director), Columbia College, Chicago, on a joint Rockefeller Residence Fellowship from July 1 to August 31, 1997. Our trip to Tennessee and Mississippi was part of a brief fieldwork period within the program. In Memphis, both of us and Moya's two children were hosted by David and Marice Evans. We take this opportunity to express our thanks to these and other colleagues in the United States too numerous to be named here, for their generous reception and guidance.

5. For performances, see the CD record *Concert Kwela: Donald Kachamba et son ensemble en concert,* Le Chant du Monde LDX 274972 CM 212, "Buluzi" (blues), "I Was a Baby" and "Chipiloni Chanjamile" (items 3, 11, and 14). For an autobiographical account, see Moya A. Malamusi, "Rise and Development of a Chileka Guitar Style in the 1950s and 1960s," in *For Gerhard Kubik: Festschrift on the Occasion of His 60th Birthday,* ed. Dietrich Schüller and August Schmidhofer (Frankfurt: Peter Lang, 1994), 7–72.

6. See Moya's performance in the video *African Guitar,* ed. G. Kubik, Vestapol 13017, 1995.

7. Andrew M. Cohen in "The Hands of Blues Guitarists," printed in this volume, has distinguished three broad stylistic regions in the blues: Eastern or "Piedmont" (Virginia, North and South Carolina); Delta or "Deep South" (encompassing Mississippi and Alabama and parts of neighboring states); and Texas (the area roughly between Houston and Dallas, over to Texarkana and to Shreveport in Louisiana).

8. On subjective illusion patterns, see also Gerhard Kubik, "Subjective Patterns in African Music," in *Cross Rhythms: Papers in African Folklore,* ed. Susan Domowitz, Maureen Eke, and Enoch Mvula, African Studies Program, Vol. 3 (Bloomington, Ind.: Trickster Press, 1989), 129–54. Recently, illusion patterns emerging from timbre structures have been studied in *inanga* (zither) solo performances in Burundi. See Cornelia W. Fales, "Issues of Timbre: The *inanga chuchotée,*" in *Africa,* The Garland Encyclopedia of World Music, vol. 1, ed. Ruth M. Stone (New York and London: Garland, 1998), 164–207.

9. Cf. recordings of Marcel Mogaya with *kembe,* B 8753, July 1964/Kubik, Phonogrammarchiv Vienna.

10. Bradford Robinson, "Blue Note," in *The New Grove Dictionary of Music and Musicians,* vol. 2, ed. Stanley Sadie (London: Macmillan, 1980), 812.

11. Pie-Claude Ngumu, "Les mendzan des Ewondo du Cameroun," *African Music* 5, no. 4 (1975–76): 6–26.

12. Erich Moritz von Hornbostel, "Abschnitt XX: Musik," in Günther Tessmann, *Die Pangwe,* 2 vols. (Berlin: Ernst Wasmuth A.-G., 1913), 2:345–46, 353.

13. A. M. Jones, "Blue Notes and Hot Rhythm," *African Music Society Newsletter* 1, no. 4 (June 1951): 9–12.

14. For Moçambique, see Hugh Tracey, *Chopi Musicians: Their Music, Poetry and Instruments* (London: Oxford University Press, 1948; 2d edition, London:

International African Institute, 1970); Andrew Tracey, "Kambazithe Makolekole and His *valimba* Group: A Glimpse of the Technique of the Sena Xylophone," *African Music* 7, no. 1 (1991): 82–104.

15. For Guinée, see Gilbert Rouget, "Sur les xylophones equiheptaphoniques des Malinké," *Revue de Musicologie* 55, no. 1 (1969): 47–77, and LP record *Musique d'Afrique Occidentale* by Gilbert Rouget, MC. 20.045, Musée de l'Homme, Paris, especially items I/1 and I/2.

16. Cf. recording CD, item 41, *tuwema*, women's association, eastern Angola, in G. Kubik, *Theory of African Music* (Wilhelmshaven: Florian Noetzel, 1994), vol. 1; and *Mukanda na Makisi* by G. Kubik, MC 11 (Berlin: Museum für Völkerkunde, 1981), double LP.

17. Cf. LP record *Pondo Kakou* by Gilbert Rouget, MC 20.141, Musée de l'Homme, Paris, item I/1.

18. Cf. G. Kubik, *Theory of African Music,* 1:188–91.

19. Cf. recordings of "Jovial" by Maurice Djenda and Gerhard Kubik, at Oyem, Phonogrammarchiv Vienna, nos. B 10950 (1966), and G. Kubik, B 17106-17117 (1969).

20. Peter van der Merwe, *Origins of the Popular Style: The Antecedents of Twentieth-Century Popular Music* (Oxford: Clarendon Press, 1989), 127–28.

21. Jeff Todd Titon, *Early Downhome Blues: A Musical and Cultural Analysis* (Urbana: University of Illinois Press, 1977), 67–137 (2d edition, Chapel Hill: University of North Carolina Press, 1994).

22. A. M. Jones, "'Stretched Octaves' in Xylophone Tuning," *Review of Ethnology* 6, no. 16 (1987): 121–24.

23. Gerhard Kubik, *Natureza e estrutura de escalas africanas* (Lisbon: Junta de Investigaçoes do Ultramar, 1970); Kubik, *Theory of African Music,* 1:396–403.

24. Kubik, *Theory of African Music,* 1:87–168.

25. David Evans, *Big Road Blues: Tradition and Creativity in the Folk Blues* (Berkeley and Los Angeles: University of California Press, 1982), 24.

26. Robert Palmer, *Deep Blues* (New York: Viking Press, 1981), 102–4, 260.

27. Paul Oliver, *Savannah Syncopators: African Retentions in the Blues* (London: Studio Vista, 1970).

28. Eric Charry has given a detailed historical account and distribution map of these types of instruments in "Plucked Lutes in West Africa: An Historical Overview," *The Galpin Society Journal* 49 (1996): 3–37.

29. David Ames pointed out: "The muslim scholar, macho and mosque head never plays an instrument or sings secular music or dance. They consider many kinds of Hausa music to be wicked, particularly *goge* music which is called the music of the devil" ("A Sociocultural View of Hausa Musical Activity," in Warren L. d'Azevedo, ed., *The Traditional Artist in African Societies* [Bloomington: Indiana University Press, 1973], 141).

30. Recordings in the Phonogrammarchiv Vienna, nos. B 8903, 8905, 8908-9. These and other recordings have been published on a CD (Neatwork AB 101, 2001)

meant to illustrate my book, *Africa and the Blues* (Jackson: University Press of Mississippi, 1999). For extensions in Texas, see John Minton, "West African Fiddles in Deep East Texas," in *Juneteenth Texas: Essays in African-American Folklore,* ed. Francis E. Abernethy, Patrick B. Mullen, and Alan B. Govenar, Publications of the Texas Folklore Society, no. 54 (Denton: University of North Texas Press, 1996), 291–313.

31. Titon, *Early Downhome Blues,* 155.

32. Ibid., 76, 100, 130.

33. Alan Lomax, *Folk Song Style and Culture* (Washington: American Association for the Advancement of Science, 1968), 314.

34. Cf. recordings B 8602, 8598-9, 8624-5, 8910-11, Nigeria/Cameroon 1963/Kubik, Phonogrammarchiv Vienna.

35. See map, "The Development of African Agricultural Systems," in Jocelyn Murray, ed., *Cultural Atlas of Africa* (Oxford: Phaidon, 1981), 43.

36. The inclusion of a tone representing the 9th partial is evident, for example, in the millet-grinding work song I recorded from a Tikar woman in a remote area of the Cameroon grassland in 1964 (rec. no. B 8645, Phonogrammarchiv Vienna).

37. Cf. Philip D. Curtin, *The Atlantic Slave Trade: A Census* (Madison: University of Wisconsin Press, 1969), 251–57, 291–98.

38. See LP record by Paul Oliver, *Savannah Syncopators,* CBS 52799 (1970).

39. Rec. no. B 8645, Phonogrammarchiv Vienna.

40. For a comprehensive discussion of my new theory on blue notes and their origins, see Kubik, *Africa and the Blues.*

41. Stephen Calt, *I'd Rather Be the Devil: Skip James and the Blues* (New York: Da Capo, 1994).

42. Personal communication, Evans, June 25, 1997, citing "Hobo Blues" by John Lee Hooker (Modern 20-663, Detroit, February 18, 1949) and "Rolling Stone—Parts 1 and 2," by Robert Wilkins (Victor 21741, Memphis, September 7, 1928), as examples.

43. Calt, *I'd Rather Be the Devil,* 366–67.

44. The transcription system employed here is an adapted form of staff notation I have used for many years in transcribing African music. The five lines of the staff have the same meaning as in Western music, but the notation is relative, that is, related to C. The vertical lines, crossing the staff, represent the elementary pulsation, that is, the smallest rhythmic units of orientation in African *and* African American music. A dot in the appropriate place on the line or between indicates the (relative) pitch to be sung or played; but since this is a *nondurational* notation system, all tones are held on until their validity is revoked by the stop sign "/". Further explanations and notational examples can be found in G. Kubik, "Aló-Yoruba Chantefables: An Integrated Approach towards West African Music and Oral Literature," in *African Musicology: Current Trends, Volume 1: A Festschrift Presented to J.H. Kwabena Nketia,* ed. Jacqueline Cogdell DjeDje and William G. Carter (Los Angeles: University of Calfornia, 1989), 129–82.

45. See the southeast African diaspora in Iraq documented by Ulrich and Mary Wegner in Ulrich Wegner, "Afrikanische Musikinstrumente im Südirak," *Baessler-Archiv,* N.F. 30 (1982): 395–442.

46. Instructive recordings can be found on the double-album *Opeka Nyimbo,* Kubik / Malamusi, MC 11, Berlin: Museum für Völkerkunde, 1989, items C-1, C-2, and C-3.

47. Gerhard Kubik, "Recording and Studying Music in Northern Moçambique," *African Music* 3, no. 3 (1969): 77–100; Corrigenda in *African Music* 4, no. 4 (1970): 136–37; Gerhard Kubik, Moya Aliya Malamusi et al., *Malawian Music: A Framework for Analysis* (Zomba: Department of Fine and Performing Arts, 1987).

48. David Evans, letter to author, March 7, 1998.

49. Cf. Kubik, *Theory of African Music,* I:176–81, 184–86.

50. Cf. Kenichi Tsukada, "Drumming, Onomatopoeia and Sound Symbolism among the Luvale of Zambia," in Junzo Kawada, ed., *Cultures Sonores d'Afrique* (Tokyo: Institut de Recherches sur les Langages et Cultures d'Asie et d'Afrique, 1997), 349–93.

2

"They Cert'ly Sound Good to Me"

SHEET MUSIC, SOUTHERN VAUDEVILLE, AND THE COMMERCIAL ASCENDANCY OF THE BLUES

LYNN ABBOTT AND DOUG SEROFF

The era of popular blues music was not suddenly set into motion by Mamie Smith's 1920 recording of "Crazy Blues." By the time Mamie Smith was allowed to walk into a commercial recording studio, the blues was an American entertainment institution with an abounding legendary and a firmly established father figure, W. C. Handy. The history of the commercial ascendancy of the blues is partially preserved in sheet music and, although this field has been well plowed, new insights still crop up in the furrows. A more important but far less explored platform for the blues' commercial ascendancy was the African American vaudeville stage, the history of which is embedded in the entertainment columns of black community newspapers. As soon as there was a visible network of black vaudeville theaters in the South, the first identifiable blues pioneers appeared before the footlights. Working through disparate cultural impulses, these self-determined southern vaudevillians gave specific direction to new vernacular forms, including the so-called classic blues heard on the first crashing wave of race recordings.

Blues in its various twentieth-century expressions was shaped by the historical interaction of two separate impulses and the dynamic tension between them, all under the influence of a confounding outside force—commercialization in a racist society. The first impulse was to perpetuate the indigenous musical and cultural practices of the African American folk heritage, which eventually formed the cornerstone of an independent black cultural image. The second, countering impulse was to demonstrate mastery of standard Western musical and cultural conventions. Through this impulse came the necessary formalizing structures without which there could have been no composition, development, dissemination, and widespread popularization of ragtime, blues, and jazz.

Blues and jazz made their popular ascendancy through the door opened by ragtime and as the fruition of in-group musical expressions extending from slavery. Research in African American community newspapers of the early 1890s reveals diverse musical activity in a wide geographic sampling of black communities in every social stratum.[1] This activity generally reflected trends and phenomena in the dominant culture. Vague rumblings of an independent force affecting the music gradually surfaced from deep within the black communities. Eastern Kansas, the land of John Brown and place of refuge for freedmen escaping the increasingly violent white southern reaction to radical reconstruction, appears to have been a primordial breeding ground for such developments. Witness this rather sheepish commentary from the "Literary and Musical" column of the November 17, 1893, edition of the *Kansas City American Citizen*:

> Now as to Kansas City's musical world we can say but little this week. However, something is to be done this season to maintain interest in this art, for which Kansas City has made herself somewhat noted. We have a number of real professional musicians here, who, so far as talent is concerned, would be creditable to Boston; but it appears that something has diverted the exercise of their powers into channels remote from society's path. Whether this is due to the proper amount of perseverance in a certain direction, or a lack of a proper appreciation on our part, deponent saith not. *But so it is.*

Precisely what was diverting Kansas City's local musicians was spelled out in the April 13, 1895, edition of the *Leavenworth Herald*: "If the present 'rag' craze does not die out pretty soon, every young man in the city will be able to play some kind of a 'rag' and then call himself a piano player. At the present rate, Leavenworth will soon be a close second to Kansas City as a manufacturer of piano pugilists."

The emergent "rag craze" was firmly entrenched in neighborhood saloons, of which there were reported to be "thousands" in eastern Kansas during the 1890s.[2] On April 27, 1895, the *Topeka Weekly Call* announced: "At the next meeting of the Leavenworth city council an ordinance prohibiting piano playing and other music in saloons is to be passed. The ordinance has been drafted by request of the police department. Music in Leavenworth saloons has become an almost indispensable feature." To the editor of the *Leavenworth Herald*, the new music was a reflection of deteriorating social standards: "If you are a crapshooter and a 'piano pugilist' in Kansas City, it is a sign that you are a 'society' man."[3]

Of course, piano rags are "semiclassical" in many of their structural formalities, their division by movements or variations, and their well-developed melodies; they may have grown out of neighborhood saloons but they were also rooted in the culturally bourgeois environment of home parlor entertainment, where ownership and knowledge of the piano were badges of social refinement. The "City Items" column of the *Leavenworth Herald* for August 18, 1894, noted, "It's a mighty poor colored family that hasn't got some kind of tin pan called piano nowadays." It is not hard to imagine how ragtime style could have gravitated from the saloon to the salon and back again.

Although ragtime style was most readily identified with piano players, the 1890s witnessed a similar reorientation within the broad spectrum of community-based singers and players throughout black America. In the face of institutional Jim Crowism, brass bands, string bands, and vocal quartets all began to look inward, less intent on aspiring to outdo white musicians at "the white man's music" and more eager to explore possibilities latent in folk music themes and vernacular music fashions.

Within the immensely popular black vocal quartet tradition of the 1890s, the litmus test of this new, independent musical sensibility was the "barbershop chord." Just as any song could be "ragged," so could it be "barbershopped." Ostensibly complaining about the "musical slang" of barbershop style, a turn-of-the-century black newspaper critic noted, "The chief aim is to so twist and distort a melody that it can be expressed in so-called 'minors' and diminished chords."[4] A distinctively African American invention,[5] the barbershop chord was well ingrained in the incipient ragtime hotbeds of eastern Kansas by 1894, when the *Leavenworth Herald* casually noted, "Although Emporia [a little town about fifty miles southwest of Leavenworth] has a Haydn club it is not above singing 'I found a horseshoe,' with a 'barber-shop chord' on the second horseshoe."[6]

The evolution of this distinctive approach to improvising close harmonies was integral to the crystallization of the famous "blue note." On the authority of his own early quartet-singing experiences,[7] blues father figure W. C. Handy ventured to define the blue note as a "scooping, swooping, slurring tone," the product of "a deep-rooted racial groping for instinctive harmonies."[8] Purveyors of the Western canon warned that barbershop style "violates—at times ruthlessly—the exacting rules and properties of music."[9] Regardless, black vocal quartets embraced the barbershop chord en masse and made it a cornerstone of vocal ragtime and blues.

Ragtime was popularized in the worldwide musical mainstream during the last four years of the nineteenth century. These were trying times for

African Americans, especially in the South, where the white racist backlash from Reconstruction was at its savage zenith. Within the black communities the development of an independent musical sensibility expressed the urge for an effectively self-directed African American cultural life. This did not indicate any sort of yearning for an insular music form outside the purview of the dominant culture; rather, it was an attempt to reconcile cultural aspirations with an expanding black commercial potential in the broader entertainment business.

The two main, intersecting avenues to commercial success in the broader entertainment business were sheet music and the vaudeville stage. Without the requisite institutions in place—publishing companies that looked out for black composers and vaudeville theaters that catered to black performers and audiences—there was little hope for commercial success except in terms dictated by the mainstream, and those terms were decidedly unfavorable to black artists. To realize a fully self-directed black culture, African Americans would have to work out for themselves the measure and direction of their artistic expressions, secure proper credit for their creative output, and retain legal control of opportunities for commercial exploitation and financial reward.

Against this backdrop of contradictions, a trail of blues sensibilities was blazed in popular ragtime sheet music leading up to the blues-publishing explosion of 1912.[10] One conspicuous marker is Antonio Maggio's "I Got the Blues," published in New Orleans in 1908 and "Respectfully Dedicated to all those Who have the Blues." In no way linked to Chris Smith and Elmer Bowman's 1901 "Colored Complaint" by the same title,[11] Maggio's simple little piano piece was billed as "An Up-to-Date Rag." What made it up-to-date was its opening strain in a twelve-bar blues form, a strain that would crop up again in W. C. Handy's 1913 effort "The Jogo Blues" and his 1914 masterpiece "St. Louis Blues."

The shared melodic strain in "I Got the Blues," "Jogo Blues," and "St. Louis Blues" has been described by the scholar who first made note of it as a "stock commercial blues motive."[12] This description seems to imply that commercial prospects for blues publishing managed to reach assembly-line proportions during the 1908–14 period. A better bet is that Handy and Maggio were coincidentally attracted to similarly irrepressible "snatches"—Handy's favorite term—of floating folk melody. Handy claimed to have lifted his variation of the strain from a repetitive chant employed by an A.M.E. preacher in his Florence, Alabama, hometown neighborhood during the early 1890s.[13]

Antonio Maggio's "I Got the Blues" is the earliest published composition known to link the condition of *having* the blues to the musical form that would become popularly known as "the blues." White New Orleans "Dixie-lander" Johnny Lala remembered Maggio as a local mainstream music instructor.[14] A note on the cover of "I Got the Blues" identifies Maggio's "Headquarters" as the Cable Piano Company on Canal Street. There is an implication, at least, that the Cable Piano Company functioned as a racial crossroads for New Orleans musicians; its long-time manager, J. V. Dugan, eventually took over the business and renamed it the Dugan Piano Company,[15] and in 1915 the Dugan Piano Company became "Special Agents" for the publication of Clarence Williams's earliest commercial sheet music efforts.[16]

Another historical landmark of blues in sheet music is "I'm Alabama Bound,"[17] claimed by Alabama-born, New Orleans-based mainstream theater pianist Robert Hoffman.[18] It was originally published in 1909 by Robert Ebberman, a clerk at the D. H. Holmes Department Store on Canal Street.[19] The cover of the original Ebberman edition notes that, although Hoffman adapted it as a "rag time two step," "I'm Alabama Bound" was also known as "The Alabama Blues" (Fig. 2.1). The implication is that by 1909 the term *blues* was known to describe a distinctive folk-musical genre from which Hoffman extracted his melody.

Paul Oliver notes that "*Alabama Bound* was one of a song cluster which included *Don't You Leave Me Here* and *Elder Green's In Town*." Oliver cites exemplary race recordings of it by Papa Charlie Jackson, Harvey Hull, Charley Patton, and Henry Thomas,[20] and there are others as well. Jelly Roll Morton claimed to have originated the tune when he "hit Mobile in 1905,"[21] and the relationship of Hoffman's composition to the blues Morton later recorded as "Don't You Leave Me Here" is obvious.

"I'm Alabama Bound" was also published in 1909 by the legendary African American concert pianist Blind Boone as one of three melodies constituting "Boone's Rag Medley No. 2—Strains from Flat Branch."[22] Robert Hoffman's version appears to have enjoyed the better measure of commercial success. Shortly after that version's initial publication, the copyright was transferred to the Music Shop, another Canal Street operation, which put out a new edition with a garish coon-song-style cover illustration.[23] At the end of 1909 Prince's Band made a commercial recording of it,[24] and in 1910 a vocal edition appeared with lyrics attributed to the Music Shop's proprietor, John J. Puderer. The lyrics include such blues-ready couplets as:

> I'm Alabama bound, I'm Alabama bound,
> I've tried you out, I've got to turn you down.

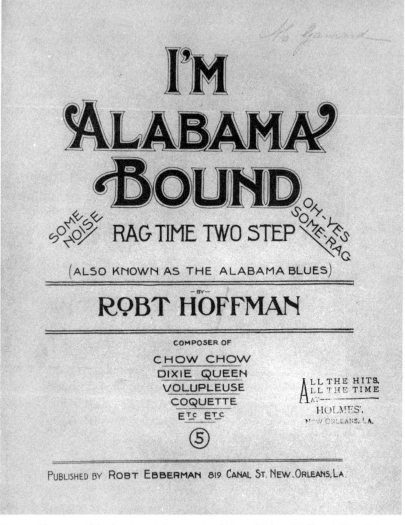

Fig. 2.1. The cover of the first (1909) sheet music edition of Robert Hoffman's "I'm Alabama Bound" (Hogan Jazz Archive, Tulane University).

I done told you, nigger, for to be like me,
Just drink good whiskey, let your cocaine be.[25]

According to the cover of the vocal edition, Hoffman's "I'm Alabama Bound" was being "sung with great success" in mainstream vaudeville by the white

Rag Trio. By 1910 the title was also turning up in newspaper reports from African American entertainers. On a bill with Ma Rainey at the Belmont Street Theater in Pensacola, Florida, in February 1910, "Watkins and Watkins" were "featuring a new act written by themselves entitled 'I'm Alabama Bound.'"[26] A couple of months later a member of Richards & Pringle's Minstrel Band complained: "We would like to know what to do when a band of fifteen pieces under the leadership of able Fred Simpson renders standard overtures from 'Il Trovatore,' 'William Tell,' etc., and some admirer of classic music shouts, 'Play us Alabama Bound.' Well, it must be the way of the world."[27]

Three years after Robert Hoffman's ragtime arrangement of "The Alabama Blues" appeared on the market, W. C. Handy introduced his first blues composition, "The Memphis Blues." It was one of at least four blues titles published or registered for copyright during the fall of 1912; others were "Baby Seals Blues," "Dallas Blues," and "The Negro Blues." Like the two earlier blues-influenced publications from New Orleans—"I Got the Blues" and "I'm Alabama Bound"—"Dallas Blues" and "The Negro Blues" were claimed by white composers.

"Dallas Blues" was self-published in Oklahoma City as a simple piano score by Hart A. Wand, "Composer of 'Tangoitis' & 'Ready Money.'"[28] Wand grew up in Oklahoma City, where he played violin and "led a little dance orchestra."[29] Although he claimed to have "made up" the melody to "Dallas Blues," he also associated it with a "colored porter" at his father's store who whistled along while he rehearsed it and remarked, "That gives me the blues to go back to Dallas."[30] It may have been through Wand's publication of it that "Dallas Blues" was taken up by African American road-show bands. At an afternoon parade in Springfield, Missouri, during May 1914, the famous Rabbit Foot Minstrels Gold Band played "Poet and Peasant" and then "by special request . . . played the 'Dallas Blues' which set 'em wild. A bystander remarked 'Dey sho do punish dem blues.'"[31]

In 1915, a white folklorist published an "African Iliad" comprising thirty-three blues stanzas, each consisting of two rhymed couplets, that he had collected from a singer in Beeville, Texas, as "sung to the tune of 'The Dallas Blues.'"[32] In 1918, a vocal edition of Wand's "Dallas Blues" was published in Chicago.[33] Abbe Niles cited a "beautiful variant" that he had heard "sung by a white American, in an English public house, in 1920" and that he reconstructed in his introduction to W. C. Handy's *Blues: An Anthology.* Among the verses he recalled were the following:

If de river was whiskey and I was a mallard, I said a mallard, I mean duck,
If de river was whiskey and I was a mallard duck,
I would dive right down an' never would come up.

Oh, de Mississippi River am so deep an'—so wide an' deep, an', so deep an'
    wide, an'—
De Mississippi River am so deep an' wide
An' de lights buhn low, on de udder side.[34]

Niles's "variant" of "Dallas Blues" is more closely related to "The Negro Blues,"
which was registered for copyright on November 9, 1912, as by Le Roy White.
Not to be confused with black southern vaudevillian Leroy White, this was
Leroy "Lasses" White, a white minstrel performer who later achieved fame
on the Grand Ole Opry. On the original manuscript submitted to the copyright office, White noted his association with the Happy Hour Theater in
Dallas. The manuscript runs to fifteen verses, a monument to early folk-
blues literature:

I've got the blues but I'm too mean to, I said mean to, I mean cry.
I've got the blues but I'm to mean to cry.
I feel so bad I could lay myself down and die.

The Blues ain't nothing but a good man feeling, I said feeling, I mean bad,
The blues ain't nothing but a good man feeling bad.
That's a feeling that I've often had.

When a man gets blue he takes a train and, I said a train and, I mean rides.
When a man gets blue he takes a train and rides.
But when a woman gets blue she hangs her head and cries.

When I leave I'm going to leave on the Cannon, I said cannon, I mean ball.
When I leave I'm going to leave on the cannon ball,
Carries fourteen coaches there ain't no blinds at all.

There's a big freight train backed up in the, I said in the, I mean yards,
There's a big freight train backed up in the yards,
I'm going to see my Baby if I have to ride the rods.

Yonder comes the train coming down the, I said down the, I mean track.
Yonder comes the train coming down the track.
It's going to take me away but it ain't going to bring me back.

Honey, don't you weep and, I said weep and, I mean moan,
Honey, Honey, don't you weep and moan.
I'm going to build you a house cut out of marble stone.

I cried last night also the night be, I said the night be, I mean before,
I cried last night also the night before.
I raised my hand I took an oath I wouldn't cry no more.

Honey, Honey when I die don't you wear no, I said wear no, I mean black.
Honey, Honey when I die don't you wear no black,
Cause my ghost, it's going to come sneaking back.

I'm going to lay my head down on some railroad, I said railroad, I mean line.
I'm going to lay my head down on some railroad line.
Let the Santa Fe, satisfy my mind.

My home ain't here it's a light house on the, I said on the, I mean sea.
My home ain't here it's a lighthouse on the sea.
I'm going back to my used to be.

Wish I had wings like Noah's, I said Noah's, I mean dove.
Wish I had wings like Noah's dove.
Then I'd fly home to the little girl I love.

Wish I'd died when I was, I said young, I mean a kid,
Wish I'd died when I was quite young.
Then I wouldn't have this hard old race to run.

I'll meet you honey when your heart's going to ache like I said ache like, I
    mean mine.
I'll meet you honey when your heart's going to ache like mine.
I'll meet you honey when you can't change a dime.

People, People, my head ain't made of, I said made of, I mean bone.
People, People, my head ain't made of bone,
'Cause I've sang what I have, I'm not a Graphophone.

Obviously, Lasses White did not *compose* these floating verses; for the most part, at least, he had to have *overheard* them, "collected" them in the streets and vaudeville theaters of Dallas's emerging African American entertainment community. The title of the song identifies, in generic fashion, the original source of the words and music.

Other than by subjecting it to musical notation, Lasses White made no apparent effort to develop "The Negro Blues," that is, lend it any sort of thematic unity or make it conform to the standing rules of popular song construction. Some of the lyrics must have puzzled white audiences and even Lasses himself. The "lighthouse on the sea" verse, for example, probably evolved as an in-crowd abstraction of black songwriter Gussie L. Davis's 1886 ballad hit by that title.

About a year after White submitted "The Negro Blues" for copyright, it was published—as "Nigger Blues"—through a small outfit in Dallas.[35] The revised title immortalizes the contradictions inherent to the commercialization of black cultural inventions in a racist society. For this particular exploit, the original fifteen verses were pared to six, one of which had not been included in the prototype:

> You can call the blues, you can call the blues, any old thing you please,
> You can call the blues any old thing you please,
> But the blues ain't nothing but the doggone heart disease.

In 1916, Lasses White's "Nigger Blues" was commercially recorded by George O'Connor,[36] a successful white Washington, D.C., attorney whose musical sideline—Negro dialect humor and song—made him "the favorite White House entertainer of every President from McKinley through Franklin D. Roosevelt."[37] O'Connor brought stylistic conventions of 1890s minstrelsy to bear on his twentieth-century recordings, at least a few of which were openly mean-spirited.[38] Of the thirty-five titles he recorded between 1914 and 1918,[39] "Nigger Blues" was his bestseller,[40] and it came closest to the original source of African American humor he professed to delineate.

About a year after O'Connor's "Nigger Blues" came out, a related recording, labeled "Dallas Blues," was issued by white vaudeville star Marie Cahill.[41] Composer credit for the song on this recording was claimed by white vaudevillians Bert and Frank Leighton of Long Island, New York, whose copyright submission was registered on May 23, 1916, simply as "The Blues." According to the *ASCAP Biographical Dictionary,* the Leighton brothers were known for their "new versions of traditional songs, blending blues and ragtime." Most of the titles they claimed—"Ain't Dat a Shame," "I Got Mine," "Casey Jones," "Steamboat Bill," "Frankie and Johnny"—are either more commonly considered to be folk songs or are more popularly associated with other composers. To compose "The Blues" the Leightons simply combined the melody of Hart Wand's "Dallas Blues" with the stuttering effect—"I'm going to leave on the cannon, I said cannon, I mean ball"—of Leroy White's "Negro Blues." Their manuscript came to eleven verses, of which Cahill recorded nine. One of the discards is an early document of the well-known "peaches" metaphor:

> If you don't like my peaches, you don't like my peaches, well, then don't
> you shake my tree,
> If you don't like my peaches, don't you shake my tree.
> For I'm a free-stone peach and nothing clings to me.[42]

Marie Cahill's recording of "Dallas Blues" is likely the source of that "beautiful variant" Abbe Niles collected in Great Britain in 1920. It begins with a pseudo-folkloric acknowledgment: "I want to sing to you-all a 'blues' song I heard a darkey sing, down in Dallas, Texas." The recording is echoed—to the extent that two verses, the stuttering effect, and the same "lilting dance time"[43] are shared—in a 1928 race recording inexplicably titled "Banjo Blues," sung and played on guitar and fiddle by Peg Leg Howell and Eddie Anthony.[44] Other race recordings that utilize the stuttering effect include William Harris's "Bull Frog Blues"[45] and Lena Wilson's "Michigan Water Blues."[46]

The creative process of southern folk-blues song construction was initially guided by the capacity for unrestricted recombination of commonly shared ingredients. Within the tradition ownership of a song might be claimed by demonstrating a singular *approach* to, or treatment of, otherwise floating verses and phrases.[47] This offered no practical application for commercial composers; "approach" was not a copyrightable commodity.

On the other hand, the unprotected raw material of blues construction was ripe for exploitation. In recounting his early adventures in blues composition, W. C. Handy openly acknowledged his "frequent custom of using a snatch of folk melody in one out of two or three strains of an otherwise original song."[48] Assessing Handy's work in a 1917 article entitled "The Negro's Contribution to American Art," James Weldon Johnson went even further: "I have spoken of 'The Memphis Blues' as a composition. Strictly speaking, it is not a composition. The name of the composer printed on the copies is Handy, who is a negro musician of Memphis; but 'The Memphis Blues' is one of those negro songs which, like Topsy, 'jest grew.'"[49]

One particular environment in which the blues "jest grew" was the network of culturally independent African American vaudeville theaters that started cropping up in the South and Midwest just after the turn of the century. By 1910 almost every black community in every city in the South had a little vaudeville theater. It was nothing more than *black commercial entertainment for a black audience,* but once this dynamic context was firmly established, the stage was set for a cultural revolution. These little theaters provided the principal platform for the concrete formulation of popular blues and for the subsequent emergence of blues from its rural southern birthplace; a culturally distinctive brand of vaudeville emerged, with the blues as one of its primary components.

The pathbreakers of southern vaudeville were also the cultural outriders of up-to-date, in-crowd African American folk wit, humor, song, and dance.

There were strong generational overtones to this new theatrical movement. Many of its star performers were teenagers, runaways[50]—the toughened urban progeny of Paul Laurence Dunbar's humble cabin dwellers. Heirs to the sensitivities and folk idioms of their rural forebears, they were childhood witnesses to, and victims of, the widespread brutality that characterized the turn-of-the-century South. They possessed a driven creativity, the expression of a furious cultural and social rebelliousness that, like so many of the artists themselves, came right off the streets and into the theaters.

The rise of southern vaudeville was candidly portrayed in the entertainment columns of the African American press, especially *The Indianapolis Freeman,* a nationally distributed paper that catered to black entertainers and featured regular correspondence from various theaters and road shows. Reports from southern theaters started filtering in around 1901, and by 1908 there was evidence of blues in the air. That year at the Lincoln Theater in Knoxville, Tennessee, George Centers and Robert Joplin—Scott Joplin's brother[51]—sang something called "I'll Be a Low Down Dog."[52] In 1909, at the Pythian Temple Theater in New Orleans, Joe Simms sang "Don't Dog Me Around."[53] When Clarence Williams published a version of this same title in 1916, he advertised it as "The Original Blues Song."[54]

The earliest known published account of blues singing on a public stage has it coming from the mouth of a ventriloquist's dummy. Southern vaudevillian John W. F. "Johnnie" Woods grew up in Memphis, where he performed in rough-and-ready theaters such as the Gem and Tick's Big Vaudeville before 1909.[55] That year he toured with the Plant Juice Medicine Company as a "buck and wing dancer, female impersonator and ventriloquist."[56] His "little wooden-headed boy" sang "Trans-mag-ni-fi-can-bam-dam-u-ality."[57] By the spring of 1910 Woods was back on the southern vaudeville routes; particular news from the Airdome Theater in Jacksonville, Florida, was reported in the April 16, 1910, edition of *The Freeman:* "This is the second week of Prof. Woods, the ventriloquist, with his little doll Henry. This week he set the Airdome wild by making little Henry drunk. Did you ever see a ventriloquist's figure get intoxicated? Well, it's rich; it's great; and Prof. Woods knows how to handle his figure. He uses the 'blues' for little Henry in this drunken act. This boy is only twenty-two years old and has a bright future in front of him if he will only stick to it."

After closing in Jacksonville, Johnnie Woods and his blues-singing dummy played five weeks in hometown Memphis.[58] By late 1911 they were appearing in the showcase African American theaters of Chicago and Indianapolis; Woods reflected on his apparent success:

I have been pressed by many theater-goers and newspaper writers to write or explain something of how I came to be a ventriloquist. Now, really, I have been studying and wondering the same thing, for when I first noticed that I was possessed with this peculiar power I did not know what it meant, and it was some years later that I saw a Punch and Judy show in a church. I set about at once and produced a similar attraction, and it was not until the colored picture houses began to spring up through the South that I began to earn any money for my work.... And when I was landed by a medicine show I thought then I had reached the limit, but later, however, I came in contact with [successful black, northern-based producers and performers] Bob Russell, Marion Brooks and Tim Owsley, who were playing through the South with their stock company, and with a short association with them I have learned that I haven't begun.[59]

When called on to account for Woods's popularity, *The Freeman*'s Crown Garden Theater correspondent noted: "He studies the public and consequently has succeeded greatly because he gave what was wanted."[60] Clearly it was at the insistence of southern vaudeville audiences that the blues, a previously submerged aspect of African American folk culture, ascended the stage to be recognized and more fully elaborated. During the spring of 1912 African American vaudeville veteran Paul Carter submitted the first piece of "antiblues" commentary to appear in *The Freeman,* laying "blame" for the by-then rampant vaudeville blues phenomenon at the feet of "The Colored Audience":

The blame for smutty sayings and suggestive dancing in theaters lies with the patrons. There is no class to the vaudeville stage now, and it is getting worse every day. There are a great many acts doing things away out of their line in order to please the patrons and manager. When a performer meets another that has played the theater he intends playing the next week, he will ask how things are over there. This will be the answer: "Oh, they like a little smut, and things with a double meaning. If you don't put it on you can't make it there." He then says to himself, "I guess I'll have to frame up some junk for that bunch." He then lays aside his music for his regular opening, and when he gets to the theater for rehearsal he will say to the piano player, "When I come on just play the 'Blues.'" He opens and starts singing in the wings, "I had a good gal, but the fool laid down and died," and to hear the audience scream one would think the show was closing with a very funny after-piece. When he gets off after the show the crowd is waiting to greet him. You will hear them say, "There's that guy; he sure can sing 'Dem Blues.'" "Did you see him take that 'trip?' Boy he's a cat." Now on the same bill were singers of such class as Abbie Mitchell . . . [and] Lizzie Hart, and no one says a word regarding their classy numbers. But just let a soubrette on the bill, that some comedian has taken from home, because she looked good to him, and showed her how to "fall off the log" and sing any old ragtime song, and she will receive a bunch of flowers and a few cards with prominent names of amusement lovers of the town. She then goes big all the week and gets a return date in the house in three weeks' time for a four weeks' run.[61]

When southern vaudevillians embraced folk-blues concoctions in their stage repertory, the audience shouted loud in recognition; if the southern public was prepared to celebrate the singing of "any old" ragtime or blues song, it was simply celebrating itself—its own uncompromised pride of identity.

The southern vaudeville movement was a manifestation of cultural and economic self-determination. Consider the vulnerability of a thriving and visible new black entertainment industry in the American South; conditions for African American performers tended to amplify the erratic and volatile circumstances of everyday life in the South. This was a movement with an active intellectual component, calling for thoughtful and calculated action. Perhaps no one addressed that aspect of southern vaudeville more forthrightly than did H. Franklin "Baby" Seals, piano player, all-around comedian and straight man, and composer of what is arguably the earliest published vocal blues song, "Baby Seals Blues."

Through open letters in *The Freeman,* Baby Seals established himself as a spokesman for the southern entertainer. He realized the enormous creative potential latent in his southern cultural heritage, and he forthrightly defended it and identified himself with it. In response to the initially cold reception that northern theatrical critics gave to blues-ready southern vaudevillians, Seals asked in 1912, "Why all this criticism about your own sister and brother performers from the South? . . . They did not come up here to get canceled. . . . So let my brothers and sisters of the North wait until we fall, frost or prove otherwise. Then jump on us with both feet. One race of people on top of us is enough for the present."[62]

Originally from Mobile, Alabama,[63] Seals was touring in southern vaudeville by the spring of 1909, when he was identified as the pianist at the Lyric Theater in Shreveport, Louisiana.[64] Based in New Orleans during the early months of 1910, he published his first sheet music hit, a crap-shooting ragtime song called "Shake, Rattle and Roll."[65] By the spring of 1910 Seals had made his way to Texas;[66] playing in the little roughhouse theaters of Houston and Galveston, he was said to "put so much juice in your song that you will sing even when you don't feel like singing."[67]

Baby Seals's main competitor in Houston during this time was H. "Kid" Love, who had spent most of 1909 in Memphis. In 1910 Houston's black entertainment world was centered in two neighboring theaters, the People's, at 211 Milam Street, and the Palace, just a couple blocks up on the other side of the street, at 514 Milam.[68] Baby Seals was often seen at People's during 1910, whereas Kid Love played at the Palace. Correspondence from the Palace in the July 16, 1910, edition of *The Freeman* declared, "Mr. Kid Love is cleaning with his 'Easton Blues' on the piano. He is a cat on a piano."[69] Kid Love's death in Atlanta in 1913 cut short the life and career of one of the world's first professional bluesmen.[70]

While sojourning in Texas Baby Seals joined hands with Miss Floyd Fisher, "The Doll of Memphis,"[71] and they headed back east as a team. For nearly five months beginning in November 1910, they ran the Bijou Theater in Greenwood, Mississippi.[72] The question has been raised whether Seals was inspired to write "Baby Seals Blues" during this stay in the Mississippi Delta: "It is tempting to think so, but the direction of influence between rural/folk and urban/theatrical phenomena had been mutual for some time in the Delta already."[73]

That there was an ongoing history of this mutual influence is irrefutable. However, there is nothing to indicate that Seals's Greenwood experience inspired him to compose his "Blues." Seals had already heard and probably played blues in Texas. In Greenwood Seals was compelled to insulate the Bijou Theater from its racially charged Delta surroundings; he built a self-contained theatrical enclave, complete with "nice rooms for my people" on the second floor: "Now they don't have to go out of the house."[74] Baby Seals and his band of Bijou "Fun Promoters" probably influenced Greenwood's musical sons and daughters more than they influenced him.

By the end of 1911 Seals and Fisher had crossed the Mason-Dixon line and conquered the black theaters of Chicago and Harlem.[75] At the Olio Theater in Louisville, Kentucky, during the spring of 1912, they were "living up to their reputation of the past few months. Seals features 'Blues.'"[76] That fall "Baby Seals Blues" invaded the marketplace. Seals and Fisher sold copies from the stage,[77] and they struck an enterprising arrangement with the editor of *The Freeman* to use the paper as a base for mail-order distribution. An eye-catching ad in the October 19, 1912, edition invited dealers to "write for special terms. Single copies 15 cents. Address E. C. Knox, care The Freeman" (Fig. 2.2).

If the "Stage" columns of *The Freeman* are any indication, "Baby Seals Blues" found special favor with fellow southern vaudevillians. In January

Fig. 2.2. This advertisement for "Baby Seals Blues" first appeared in the October 19, 1912, edition of the *The Indianapolis Freeman* and ran intermittently through January 10, 1914.

1913, "Daddy Jenkins and Little Creole Pet" were at the Elite Theater in Selma, Alabama, with their accompanist, Jelly Roll Morton: "Little Pet takes the house when she sings 'Please Don't Shake Me Papa, While I'm Gone' and 'Baby Seals Blues.'"[78] A few months later at the New Lincoln Theater in Galveston there was a "hailstorm of money caused by Hapel [*sic*] Edwards and Vivian Wright, putting on one of their clever singing, dancing and talking acts, featuring Baby Seals' 'Blues.'"[79] Other southern vaudevillians who featured "Baby Seals Blues" during 1913 included future race recording artists Edna Benbow (Hicks),[80] Laura Smith,[81] Gonzelle White,[82] and Charles Anderson.[83]

When Baby Seals was inducted into the Order of Elks at Richmond, Virginia, in 1913, he was identified as the "Famous Writer of 'Blues.'"[84] In many ways Seals embodied the unprecedented development and upheaval in black entertainment during 1909–13. In that remarkable brief span of time he and his southern "brothers and sisters" managed to rise from the roughneck little theaters of Houston, Greenwood, Mobile, and Memphis to the premier African American vaudeville emporiums of Chicago and New York and to the portals of the white theater establishment. Blues and other timber hewn from rural southern folk culture had served as their battering ram. Had he not died in Anniston, Alabama, on December 29, 1915,[85] Baby Seals might have become a contender for the title "Father of the Blues."

In its earliest commercial manifestations, the blues appeared as a transitional mixture of referential jargon and musical riffs derived from folk blues; the 12-bar AAB structure was not yet a rigid consideration. The stylistic element that appears to have most noticeably distinguished early published blues songs from their up-to-date ragtime cousins was a markedly retarded tempo. Purchasers of the sheet music for "Baby Seals Blues" were advised to play it "Very Slow." W. C. Handy's instructions for playing "The Memphis Blues" indicated "Tempo di Blues," the implication being that everyone already knew that a blues song had to be played "Very Slow." The original sheet music for Hart A. Wand's "Dallas Blues" left no margin for doubt about how a blues tune should be played: "Tempo di Blues. Very Slow."

When "Baby Seals Blues" first appeared on the market in 1912, *The Freeman*'s perceptive Crown Garden Theater correspondent made a point to distinguish it from the generic run of blues songs being performed in black vaudeville: "This song is not the 'Blues' one hears so much of, but is of a clever nature."[86] Apparently, the critic found it to be more consciously developed than were most blues presentations of the time. The trend toward cleverness and development in blues composition and stage performance was not perceived as a significant break from folk tradition. When a "delight-ful little brown skin" named Baby Brown appeared at the Crown Garden during the fall of 1913, the critic noted, "Her last number is the 'Chinese Blues.' Not greatly different to the colored folk blues, but they are the blues just the same."[87]

"Baby Seals Blues" can be seen as a deliberate attempt to reconcile the two historical impulses in African American music, an artful demonstration of the popular saying of the time that the blues was "colored folks' opera." Ref-erences to "colored folks' opera" appeared in the "Stage" columns of *The Freeman* throughout 1910–20. Salem Tutt Whitney's Smart Set Company re-ported in 1917 that "'The Weary Blues,' sung by Moana [Juanita Stinette] and others, passed right on to opera—regular opera—having the touch of one of Wagner's compositions. It was the very height of blues singing."[88] That same year a correspondent for Wooden's Bon Tons allowed that their "Miss Ethalene Jordan . . . deserves much credit for her rendition of popular and classy numbers and remember, she sings the colored folks opera too (The Blues)."[89] Finally, at the Washington Theater in Indianapolis that year, blues composer and future race recording kingpin Perry Bradford was "successful in his pianologue . . . doing what he calls the colored folks opera."[90]

There was a long chain of precedents to this notion of "colored folks' opera." Certain blackface minstrel productions of the mid-1830s were de-scribed as "Ethiopian Operas."[91] Eventually, the concept took on philosoph-ical proportions and a black perspective. In 1893, while serving as head of the National Conservatory of Music in New York City, the famous European composer Antonín Dvořák arrived at this "settled conviction": "I am now satisfied . . . that the future music of this country must be founded upon what are called the negro melodies. This must be the real foundation of any serious and original school of composition to be developed in the United States. . . . These are the folk songs of America and your composers must turn to them. . . . In the negro melodies of America I discover all that is needed for a great and noble school of music."[92]

While the "Dvořák Statement" was emotionally contested by various white American musicians, historians, and critics,[93] many African Americans felt that it merely stated the obvious. The same observation had been made over twenty years earlier, when the Fisk Jubilee Singers introduced slave spirituals to the American concert stage. After hearing them sing in January 1872, a New York clergyman pronounced the Jubilee Singers "living representatives of the only true, native school of American music . . . the genuine soul music of the slave cabins."[94]

With the advent of ragtime, black secular music began to attract a level of intellectual consideration that had previously been reserved for spirituals. "It's a rather curious thing," noted *The Freeman* of March 24, 1894, "that we needed Dvork [*sic*] to tell us what we have known very well during the past 40 years. Negro music is the sweetest music in the world. If you don't believe it, go and see some of the success made by the singing pickaninnies in the various theatres in New York at the present time, to say nothing of the Negro quartets in the 'Uncle Tom's Cabin' shows."

When Dvořák died in 1904, *Freeman* columnist Sylvester Russell took the opportunity to emphasize the influence of the "Dvořák Statement" on African American composers of popular ragtime music. Russell was condescending, but his point was still valid: "Stepping down now to a lower grade of Negro catchy music; what a promise of encouragement he [Dvořák] has set in Rosamond Johnson, Sidney Perrin, Shepard Edmonds and others of the folk-lore race of American song writers."[95]

In 1911, as the initial shock waves of blues and jazz were reverberating from southern vaudeville, Sylvester Russell wrote:

> Dvořák, the great European composer, who first firmly established the procedure of Negro folklore as the only genuine original American music, which he had extracted from the Slavonic melodies of the jubilee and syncopated two-step of the guitar and banjorine, so skillfully used in early stages of buck dancing, was hardly aware that he had handed his name down to posterity sacred to the memory and gratitude of the Negro race in the annals of American musical history. And in Dvořák's contention of the past, the present argument waxes strong, re-enforced by the recent declaration of Signor Giacomo Puccini, grand opera composer in London, England, when he said: "There is no such thing as American music. What they have is Negro music, which is almost the savagery of sound." . . . Puccini's mind had probably wended its way back toward the jungles of Africa. He had probably forgotten that the American Negro, like the Indian, is living in a day when the war cry has ceased and the natives live quiet on the reservation. . . . The only thing that can be said to be savage in the classical development of American (Negro) music, is when composers migrate from the treatment of jubilee, back to the raw dispassionate theory of ragtime lore.[96]

The "Dvořák Statement" had importance as an inspiration and a prediction. The prediction came to pass in a manner that the European maestro might never have imagined. A new American music that drew its vitality in large part from the sources Dvořák espoused did arise to guide the world's aesthetic vision through the twentieth century. Nonetheless it was achieved not through the agency of any sort of presumed-superior, "uplifting" Western classical music but through channels remote from society's path, in the continued development of the folk music by the musical sons and daughters of those who had spawned it. It was in the evolution of popular ragtime, the blues, and jazz that Dvořák's vision of an American national music was realized.

"Colored folks' opera" was black vaudeville's response to the "Dvořák Statement." Its most definitive stage exponent was Charles Anderson, the "yodeler blues singer."[97] Originally from Birmingham, Alabama, Anderson was active in southern vaudeville by 1909, when he surfaced at the Lyric Theater in Memphis.[98] On at least two occasions during 1911—first in Jackson, Mississippi, and then in Birmingham—he shared billings with fellow southern vaudevillian and aspiring blues singer Bessie Smith.[99]

By the summer of 1913 Anderson was performing his trademark combination of blues songs and lullaby yodels. It took a special voice and a keen appreciation of the nature of absurdity to juxtapose these seemingly opposite musical phenomena. To accomplish this feat Anderson costumed as a "colored mammy" and featured "Baby Seals Blues." Under the heading "Charles Anderson, Female Impersonator, Character Actor, Yodler," *The Freeman* reported:

> Charles Anderson does a splendid colored mammy. Everyone likes this creation of his. This kind of portrayal of character does not give offense. This mammy is just a mammy. . . . She does things that are amusing and witty, as many real mammies do. She gets the blues. Then she puts on Baby Seals' well-known song, making a tremendous hit. The part including the song makes for the best character of the kind seen here.[100]

During the summer of 1916 a critic noted, "Anderson calls the blues, a phase of ragtime, grand opera. If it were grand opera, then he was its Caruso. Perhaps he leads the procession in that kind of singing. Last Saturday night he put the house in motion like a boat at sea, when he put over his own blues creation."[101] A review in 1917 stated simply, "His opera, the blues, wins as usual."[102] In 1923, a full decade after he started singing it on stage, Charles Anderson made a commercial recording of "Baby Seals Blues"—labeled "Sing 'Em Blues"—with piano accompaniment by Eddie Heywood.[103] Capturing the full range of Anderson's folk-operatic tenor voice in a remarkable rendition of the first published vocal blues song, this record survives to demonstrate an unabashedly comical resolution of "high" and "low" art, a positive realization of "colored folks opera."

Another staple of Charles Anderson's early vaudeville blues repertory that he also later recorded was W. C. Handy's "St. Louis Blues."[104] Indeed, Sylvester Russell identified Anderson in the October 31, 1914, issue of *The Freeman* as the "artist who introduced Handy's St. Louis Blues," and this was confirmed by Ethel Waters, who claimed to be the "first woman—and the second person—ever to sing professionally that song"; the first, she said, was "Charles Anderson, a very good female impersonator."[105] A report from Chicago's Monogram Theater in 1915 said "Anderson's rendition of 'St. Louis Blues' was Southern perfection that others can't approach."[106]

With its "tango introduction, breaking abruptly then into a low-down blues,"[107] the "St. Louis Blues" is arguably Handy's most artfully crafted blues composition. It was also his first blues to be published with lyrics. Handy was determined that the emotions it expressed "were going to be real. Moreover, it was going to be cut in the native blues pattern."[108] In the tradition of Scott Joplin's classic rags, Handy's "St. Louis Blues" represents a logical extension and practical application of the "Dvořák Statement."

Like Baby F. Seals, W. C. Handy established himself as an intellectual arm of the blues. Unlike Seals, he lived to enjoy wide recognition as a spokesman for the blues, indeed as the "Father of the Blues." Of course the notion that the blues or any other folk-musical style or form could have been spawned by a single composer is anachronistic at best. Nevertheless Handy's image as a blues father figure was in place before 1920. When his Memphis Blues Band appeared in concert at the fashionable Manhattan Casino in Harlem during the summer of 1919, *The Chicago Defender* noted, "W. C. Handy . . . is well known over the world as the 'Daddy of the Blues.'"[109]

The related notion that Memphis, Tennessee, is the birthplace and proper ancestral home of the blues was also well ingrained by 1920. It was during 1915 that Handy's Memphis-based publishing company started advertising itself as the "Home of the Blues."[110] Hard-earned business acumen and effective self-promotion helped to sustain the upward trajectory of Handy's professional fortunes over successive decades. Behind these entrepreneurial skills, though, the operative measure of Handy's success was his ability to bring his recognized "knowledge of the art, science and literature"[111] of music to bear on selected examples of African American folk-musical expression.

In 1918, Handy noticed a statement in a Victor advertisement for spirituals recorded by the Tuskegee Institute Singers: "To the Negro must be given the honor of having originated what is perhaps the most distinctive type of music yet produced in the United States." In response Handy let it be known that the Pace & Handy Music Publishing Company was also "preserving the characteristic melodies of these spirituals and adding to our wonderful store of Negro music a modern Orchestration and scoring which gives us a secular style of music all our own and known to the world now as BLUES."[112]

In a well-circulated article from 1919, Handy pondered "The Significance of the Blues":

> It was Beethoven who said, "Music moves us and we know not why. We feel the tears," etc. Had he lived in America today he would say, "BLUES music moves our feet and we know not why. We feel no tears."
>
> "Blues" music was created to chase away gloom. It is of negro origin and must pertain to negro life. There have been many explanations of the word "Blues." One musician explained to a judge recently that "Blues is Blues." And to the average mind that is a fair explanation.
>
> I am a Southern negro by birth and environments and it is from the levee camps, the mines, the plantations and other places where the negro laborer works that these snatches of melody originate. The negro laborer does his best work while he sings. I have heard on the Mississippi plantation the negro plowman, after a day's work which began at sunrise, sing just these little snatches, "Hurry, sundown, let tomorrow come," which means that he hopes tomorrow will be for him better than today. It is from such sources that I built my "SAINT LOUIS BLUES," which begins, "I hate to see the evening sun go down."
>
> The record for driving rivets is held by a negro. It was held years ago by a man called John Henry, who wagered that he could drive more rivets than the compressed air drill and won, but the effort killed him. To this day wherever the negro laborer uses the hammer you will hear him sing:
>
> "This is the hammer that killed John Henry, Killed him dead, killed him dead." This melody is a typical "Blues" and it is from such sources that I got my material for my "BLUES."
>
> Most "Blues" are ambiguous. They are modeled after the Negro spiritual of slave days. The slaves would sing, "Go down, Moses; tell old Pharaoh let my people go." He had no interest in Pharaoh or Moses, but was thinking about his own freedom. But he dared not sing about himself so he sang of Pharaoh. One man has said, "It is not inconsistent with the constitution of human mind that avails itself of one and the same method of expressing opposite emotions."
>
> The songs of the slaves represented their sorrows rather than their joys. Like tears, they were a relief to an aching heart. The sorrow songs of the slaves we call Jubilee melodies. The happy-go-lucky songs of the Southern Negro we call "Blues."[113]

W. C. Handy was born in 1873 to a stable, socially conservative family in Florence, Alabama, where he learned middle-class values and managed to obtain a well-rounded musical education. He also got some firsthand knowledge of the "levee camps, the mines, the plantations and other places where the negro laborer works"; his early job experiences included a stint on the "shovel brigade" at the McNabb Furnace in Florence.[114]

Unlike Baby Seals and so many others in the first generation of African American blues composers—including Clarence Williams, Perry Bradford, and Jimmie Cox—W. C. Handy was not a product of the southern vaudeville theater tradition. Some ten to twenty years older than most of his blues-composing contemporaries, Handy came of age in a turn-of-the-century minstrel show. En route with Mahara's Mammoth Minstrels in 1899, he was identified as the secretary of a literary club formed among members of the troupe:[115] "Mr. Handy has been three seasons with this company and has become quite popular as a cornet soloist; due to the 'soul' he puts into all he plays. . . . He is a lover of his race and wishes to do something for it besides adding to the harmony of its characteristic songs."[116]

Except for the 1900–1901 season, which he spent "teaching in the band, orchestra and vocal music departments at the A. and M. College at Normal, Ala.,"[117] Handy was with Mahara's Minstrels from 1897 through 1903, touring not only in the South but throughout the nation and as far as Cuba. As director of Mahara's concert band, Handy conducted his earliest-known experiments with vernacular music. During February 1899 the program of the band's evening concerts included "Ragamuffin Characteristic—Handy."[118] Later that year, Handy "added his fantasia, 'At a Georgia Camp-meeting' to his long list of selections. The above piece being Handy's own arrangement; it has plenty of that cake walk stirring qualities about it."[119]

Frank Mahara acknowledged the other side of Handy's work: "Prof. Handy's concert band of 16 picked soloists is the great feature of this company. . . . The high grade of classical music including that beautiful selection 'The Holy City' places Prof. Handy in my estimation, by all odds the greatest musically educated colored person of to day and on a par with the late Gilmore and Sousa."[120] Mahara depicted Handy as a reformer:

Of all the races the negro is most musical; but there has been much criticism (from white musicians who expect the Negro to play in forty years what it has taken the white man 2000 years—yes more—to play) that Negro bands play too uneven, loud and roughly. Prof. Handy is correcting these conditions and after careful study has reached the conclusion that the Negro's music when he is at himself is sweet, passionate, fervent, but when his worst enemy—strong drink—and that desire to out-do in dress, to be the loudest in conversation get a hold on him then you hear the 'who but me' playing so common in our bands.[121]

When he left Mahara's Minstrels at the close of the 1902–3 season,[122] Handy had offers to instruct a white municipal band somewhere in Michigan and a Colored Knights of Pythias Band in Clarksdale, Mississippi. He recalled the "Michigan thing" offered more money and opportunity, "Yet, for no good reason that I could express, I turned my face southward and down the road that led inevitably to the blues."[123]

Handy's nine-piece Clarksdale-based Knights of Pythias band was a pre-jazz territory band doing "yeoman duty in the Delta."[124] In an often-quoted passage from *Father of the Blues*, Handy recalled a dance one night in Cleveland, Mississippi, where the band was upstaged by a downhome string band whose "over-and-over strains" inspired the patrons to shower them with coins: "Then I saw the beauty of primitive music. . . . Art, in a high-brow sense, was not in my mind. My idea of what constitutes music was changed by the sight of that silver money cascading around the splay feet of a Mississippi string band."[125]

In fact, art "in a high-brow sense" was a guiding force in Handy's early experiments with blues composition, and it is at the heart of his claim to the title "Father of the Blues." An unsigned article in the December 22, 1917, edition of *The Freeman* said Handy "Gave the Go to the Blues Idea—A Distinct Musical Creation, Which Has Won High Favor":

> Mr. W. C. Handy . . . is known the world over for his success in writing a number that was destined to set everybody dancing or trying to refrain from making an effort to dance. This dance success is The Memphis Blues. But he did more than write a dance. He ushered into musical composition a new FORM. A style to which no man can lay earlier claim—the BLUES style. At first his numbers were rejected by the leading publishers, who did not understand Negro life down South, and now, since he has made his work go, they are trying to imitate.
>
> This should be convincing to the most skeptical that there is merit in the Blues, as he writes. . . .
>
> To understand Handy, you must not be satisfied with the music as played and sung in the cabarets alone. You must buy his work and play it over and over as you read Dunbar. That is just what the Southern whites did. And when they were convinced that merit was found therein they pressed their convictions wherever they went.

Mr. Handy wants his work looked into more seriously by those of his race who have had the advantages of a musical education. Not viewed by what Liszet [sic] or Wagner did, but by what they would have done if they had been American negroes, living in the times in which we live and suffer.

Around 1907, Handy shifted his base of operation from Clarksdale to Memphis,[126] moving there to instruct the local Colored Knights of Pythias Band.[127] Memphis harbored a long-standing tradition of competitive community-based bands.[128] The city also harbored a deep African American vaudeville theater tradition. At least three black Memphis theaters—the Rialto, Church's Auditorium, and Tick's Tivoli—were active at the turn of the century. In May 1901, as W. C. Handy was preparing to leave his teaching post in Alabama to go back on the road with Mahara's Minstrels,[129] the Rialto Theater was beginning its "summer season in Ragtime Opera"; its roster included Nettie Lewis, "soubrette instigator of ragtime"; Ed Hill, who played "nothing but ragtime"; Bessie Gilliam, "inimitable in ragtime"; and Ora Criswell, "Memphis' own ragtime."[130]

The Rialto appears to have operated under the wing of Memphis's "colorful" white Kinnane family,[131] which included reputed Memphis underworld figure and political boss James Kinnane. As proprietor of the notorious Blue Goose Saloon, Jim Kinnane was immortalized on race recordings. Veteran southern vaudevillian Willie Jackson's 1926 recording "Old New Orleans Blues" advised: "You ever go to Memphis, stop down at Jim Kinnane's / That's a place where monkey women will learn just how to treat a man."[132] Louise Johnson mentioned "Jim Kinnane's," as well as "Church's Hall," in her 1930 recording "On the Wall,"[133] and Robert Wilkins added to the legend with his 1935 recording "[I wish I was down at] Old Jim Canan's."[134]

The Rialto Theater's black manager was Lew Hall and the musical director was J. Ed Green, from Chicago.[135] Green would eventually return to Chicago to direct the original Pekin Theater Stock Company. While in Memphis he resided in the Alhambra Hotel at Beale and Hernando Streets[136] and directed the Rialto's Ragtime Opera Company in "African Princess,"[137] "Uncle Eph's Dream,"[138] and other basically plotless musical comedies geared to meet the increasing popular demand for what Ernest Hogan termed "vaudevillized minstrelsy."[139]

In July 1901, after six successful weeks at the Rialto, a faction of the Rag Time Opera Company was dispatched to the Colored Attraction Park in Birmingham, Alabama, under the direction of Lew Hall.[140] After a month or so Lew Hall's Rag Time Opera Company returned to Memphis and took up residence at Church's Auditorium on Beale Street,[141] where Handy would eventually play for "our elite."[142] Toward the end of the year Lew Hall took stock of his efforts at Church's Auditorium: "I am satisfied I have done something that no other man of colored has did [sic]. I have created substantially the first of its kind in the United States, a colored vaudeville house, and there is more to follow I think."[143]

On December 20, 1901, the Tivoli Music Hall was opened at 81 DeSoto Street. Alfred "Tick" Houston was the proprietor, and the manager was J. Ed Green, late of the Rialto.[144] The Tivoli's early weeks of operation saw the production of the "popular sketches . . . 'Mr. Johnson Turn Me Loose' and 'Mrs. Johnson's Rent Rag Ball.'"[145] Among the featured singers were Estelle Harris, who "donned male attire" and "made a hit with 'Zulu Babe,'"[146] and Rosa Payne, late of Mahara's Minstrels,[147] who "opened a successful engagement singing 'The Ragtime Millionaire.'"[148]

During a visit to Memphis that lasted from January until March of 1902, well-known Chicago cabareteers Poney Moore and Teenan Jones were frequent callers at the Tivoli Music Hall.[149] They were still in town when J. Ed Green announced, "The Tivoli Music Hall is well established in the city. . . . Continuous vaudeville is the attraction."[150] Around 1905 the Tivoli Music Hall was relocated to the corner of South Fourth and Gayoso Streets,[151] where it became known as Tick's Big Vaudeville.

By the time W. C. Handy settled in Memphis, an exquisite cultural stew was simmering on the local African American vaudeville scene. Memphis had become a magnet for the restless new generation of southern talent that was shaping the future of American entertainment. By 1909, the year Handy claimed to have worked out the original "musical setting" for "The Memphis Blues,"[152] the city's black entertainment universe was clustered around two particular street corners in two separate sections of the city. Around the intersection of Main and Market Streets in North Memphis, three theaters were operating within half a block of one another: the Royal Theater occupied 269 North Main, the Gem Theater was at 258 North Main, and the Amuse U was at 253 North Main.[153]

The Royal Theater was in operation from early 1908[154] until some time in 1911.[155] Until his death in 1910, Jim Kinnane's father, Tom Kinnane, owned the theater.[156] The house pianist was Alice McQuillen, known as "Teddy Bear" and reputed to be "as large as any elephant. The piano stool had to be made larger, so one was made to order, all constructed of steel. It was built by the Chickasaw Iron Works. Please don't blow up, Miss Gasoline."[157] Accompanying her was trap drummer Walter James Reid, a veteran of P. G. Lowery's Concert Band and brother of Barnum & Bailey Circus sideshow band manager William H. Reid.[158] Future race recording artist Trixie Colquitt (Butler) played the Royal, as did Charles Anderson and child dancing wonder Little Cuba Austin,[159] who went on to play drums on late-1920s recording sessions with McKinney's Cotton Pickers, the Chocolate Dandies, and Jean Goldkette.[160]

The Gem Theater was operating as early as 1908, when the house pianist was Cornelius Taylor, "better known as 'Old Folks.'"[161] One of the Gem's most noteworthy distinctions was its early association with Memphis's premier husband-and-wife comedy team, Willie Perry and Susie Johnson, known as Long Willie and Little Lulu (or Lula), the "Too Sweets" (or "Two Sweets"). Willie Too Sweet was the Gem's stage manager from 1908 until 1910, and Lulu Too Sweet wrote most of the musical farces that he produced during that time.[162]

The Too Sweets were a highly accomplished, multitalented team. As performers they specialized in comic portrayals of children; apparently this was a genre. In a saucy baby-doll outfit Lulu was the prototypical "baby soubrette," all childhood innocence one moment and then shamelessly manipulating her audience with a double-entendre blues. To her impish stage persona Willie played "the booby, permitting all sorts of pranks to be played on him. He stands for it all."[163] Their "grotesque" humor was further exaggerated by their contrasting physiques: "The lady member . . . looks to weigh about sixty pounds on the stage and Willie looks like [boxing champion] Jack Johnson."[164]

From their excellent vantage point at the Gem Theater, Willie and Lulu Too Sweet were able to observe the ferment of southern vaudeville and the direction it was taking at the turn of the decade. Under Long Willie's aegis the Gem showcased a wide variety of singing and dancing soubrettes, novelty acts, comedians, and buck dancers. Among these performers were pioneer blues singer-composer Jimmie Cox,[165] blues ventriloquist Johnnie Woods, and southern soubrette Floyd Fisher,[166] soon to become the professional partner of Baby F. Seals. When the Too Sweets took their Memphis experience north in 1911, an in-crowd critic noted flatly that Willie appeared to have come "direct from the field to the stage."[167]

In January 1909, the Amuse U Theater opened its doors across the street from the Gem. Its proprietor was twenty-five-year-old Fred A. Barrasso,[168] who proved to be an entrepreneur of a sort that Memphis's ephemeral black theater world had not seen before. Fred Barrasso had the financial resources and hands-on commitment to establish an African American vaudeville enterprise with lasting impact not only in Memphis but throughout the region.

Barrasso's earliest business experience was probably in connection with one of his parents's enterprises. Genoroso and Rosa Barrasso had immigrated to Memphis from Naples in 1893; it was said that Genoroso "had owned considerable property in Italy and brought a large amount of cash to Memphis with him."[169] The Barrassos made several American investments, including the purchase of "a movie theater on North Main . . . when movies first came to Memphis."[170] Before opening the Amuse U Theater, Fred Barrasso was running a saloon at 146 North Main Street.[171]

The "musical director of the Amuse U orchestra" was pianist H. "Kid" Love.[172] It was at the Amuse U Theater in February 1909 that Kid and Gussie Love "celebrated their two years of married life by giving a party to the performers of the Stroll. There was singing, dancing, good music and plenty of refreshments. Every one had a good time until time to go to their respective theaters."[173]

About a mile across town from Main and Market, another storm center of vaudeville activity was radiating from the corner of Gayoso and South Fourth Streets—just one short block north of Beale, on the outer fringe of what is presently touted as the "Beale Street Historic District." Between 1908 and 1912 at least five little theaters operated within a two-block radius of this pivotal location: Tick's Big Vaudeville, the Dixie Theater, the Lyric, the Pekin, and the Savoy.

Until it closed without warning in the spring of 1909,[174] Tick's Big Vaudeville was the bright light of the Gayoso Street theater district. Its "orchestra" was composed of James Osborne, pianist; Joseph Hall, cornetist; and Harry W. Jefferson, trap drummer.[175] During the fall of 1908 Tick's was mixing its vaudeville with comic one-act "afterpieces" produced by, and often featuring, stage manager Happy John Goodloe,[176] who also did a team act with his wife, Ella. In January 1909 Goodloe and Goodloe staged Happy John's latest one-act farce, "Scenes on Beale Street."[177]

Because the husband-and-wife comedy team format was so perfectly suited to give the audience what it wanted—confrontational humor, vernacular dancing, and blues singing—it became southern vaudeville's predominant performance vehicle. From the standpoint of blues history, the most important husband-and-wife team to hold the boards at Tick's Big Vaudeville was Kid and Gussie Love. During the fall of 1908, they "left the house in an uproar" singing "Greasy Greens."[178] Said to be an original composition by Texas vaudevillian George Centers,[179] "Greasy Greens" also turned up in folklorist Howard Odum's pioneer field transcriptions of "Negro secular songs" collected in rural Mississippi around 1908,[180] and it found its way to race re-cordings by Amos "Bumble Bee Slim" Easton[181] and perhaps others.

When Love and Love concluded their engagement at Tick's in January 1909, they went to the newly opened Lyric Theater, just a block and a half away at 313 1/2 Beale Street[182]—practically next door to Pee Wee's Saloon, 317 Beale, the "headquarters for musicians" where W. C. Handy recalled hanging out.[183] Unfortunately, just a week or so later the Lyric "had to close down . . . on account of the manager not being able to pay his employees and per-formers,"[184] and within the next few months Tick's Big Vaudeville followed the Lyric Theater into insolvency.

During the summer of 1909, the Pekin Theater opened for business at 98 South Fourth Street,[185] between Union and Gayoso Streets. Initially it drew most of its staff from performers displaced by the closing of Tick's Big Vaude-ville. Happy John Goodloe was the Pekin's first stage manager.[186] The pit band featured Ed Walker, pianist; Walter Williams, cornetist; and ex-Tick's trap drummer Harry Jefferson.[187] On October 26, 1909, the Hi Jerry Barnes Trio opened at the Pekin Theater with Laura Smith as one of its members. This was Laura Smith's introduction to Memphis, and it was reportedly "nothing but curtain calls."[188] Although she barely appears in the annals of blues literature, Laura Smith was a true pioneer; when she made her first commercial recordings in 1924, she was backed by more than a decade of professional blues-singing experience.

Following the sudden closure of Tick's Big Vaudeville, the prime location at South Fourth and Gayoso was acquired by rising theatrical magnate Fred Barrasso, who remodeled the place and opened it in January 1910 as the Savoy Theater. For the "grand opening" he brought in former members of J. Ed Green's famous Chicago Pekin Stock Company, including Charles Gil-pin, J. Francis Mores, and basso John C. Boone, a graduate of Black Patti's Troubadours.[189] These veteran showmen stayed in Memphis for extended engagements. Gilpin, the future star of Eugene O'Neill's play *The Emperor Jones,* became the Savoy's producer and stage manager, Mores served as chorus director, and J. C. Boone was the business manager.[190] The Savoy was quick to exert itself as a particular hot spot on the Memphis theater scene, and it ultimately became the flagship of an expanded theatrical empire. By the spring of 1910 Laura Smith, Willie and Lulu Too Sweet, Estelle Harris, and other "southern specialists" had combined with the auspicious Chicago contingent to form the strongest stock company Memphis theatergoers had yet seen.[191]

Estelle Harris became one of the Savoy Theater's prime luminaries, and she remained consistently in the forefront of female vaudevillians employing the new blues and jazz idioms throughout the decade. At the Savoy in 1911 she was "featuring her new song successes, 'That's My Man' and 'The Blues in the Indian Style.'"[192] When she headed north in 1913, Estelle Harris was singing "If You Don't Like My Peaches, Don't Shake My Tree."[193] When jazz came up for recognition in Chicago in 1916, Estelle Harris was on the front line as "The Sister that Shouts,"[194] assisted by her "'Jaz' singers, dancers and players," singing W. Benton Overstreet's "New Dance That Everybody's Talking About,"[195] which was published and recorded by at least two African American bands in 1917 as "The 'Jazz' Dance."[196]

In addition to presenting its powerful stock company, the Savoy Theater boasted a five-piece house orchestra under the direction of Estelle Harris's husband, pianist H. P. "Buddy" McGill.[197] A *Freeman* report from the summer of 1910 noted, "Prof. Buddy McGill is still doing funny stunts on the ivory and taking the house nightly with his overture. . . . His latest stunt on the piano is playing 'Home, Sweet Home' with his left hand and 'Nearer My God to Thee' with his right."[198] In addition to working at the Savoy during this time, McGill became one of the "regulars of the Handy syndicate" of band musicians.[199]

By mid-1910 Savoy Theater proprietor Fred Barrasso had established himself as Memphis's prince of black vaudeville. Setting his sights on regional expansion, Barrasso organized a touring party from his Savoy Stock Company to test the waters for prospective theater locations in outlying cities. The first excursion left Memphis for Vicksburg, Mississippi, in June 1910, precipitating an evocative series of reports to *The Freeman*.

> June 25, 1910:
> All is well that ends well. But the package that our manager, F. A. Barrasso, of the Savoy Theater, Memphis, got handed to him by the management of the attraction park in Vicksburg, Miss. was a bird, and the park and theater there is a joke. Why, when the performers saw the dump they thought it was a livery stable, and it looked the part. Well, rehearsal was called at once. The plot was "Back to Memphis by Foot," or "Will We Get Our Money?" Well, we did not get our money, and all that kept us from walking back to Memphis was our manager, who pawned his "socks," which were a swell pair of red cotton hose that he had on for three weeks, to the park manager. . . . But at that we made good and to show you just how well our manager thinks of the town, he has made all arrangements to open a first-class house for colored people only in the heart of the town. . . .

Poor Laura ("Little Ginger") Smith sings herself hoarse every night responding to encores.

The Merry Howards—Edward and Nettie—that high class sketch team, are doing nicely, but their Class of work don't go very big in the South, the patrons of the Southern theaters think that all colored performers must be black face artist and do comedy only. They can't see straight, well dressed, high class singing and talking artists. Every male performer must black up and be a dancer, and a female performer must be just a little barrel house to be a scream in the South.

July 2, 1910:
American Theater, Jackson, Miss.—Well, things are still going big with the Barrasso Big Colored Sensation Company. The company was to have left for Memphis on the 25th, but word came to us to hold the boards, as the No. 2 company was a little weak to follow the No. 1 company, so the big noise, No. 1 will have to play Jackson for another week, closing July 2. Likewise, the Merry Howards, that versatile sketch team, that was to have closed with the company on June 28, they have re-engaged to Manager Barrasso for several weeks longer.

The management is trying very hard to get a special wire put in to the theater for the Fourth of July, to get the returns from the Jeffries-Johnson battle. If all is well that will be our last night in Jackson, Miss., as the town will not support a summer stock company. The theater is a first-class house in every way, but the people will not turn out. To make the matter plainer, the better class of people are kept away by the tougher element.

What a pity! Miss Laura Smith is still with the company, though very homesick. . . . Miss India Allen received a lovely bouquet over the footlights, and it was so small that the sender wrapped it in a sheet of writing paper, with a note enclosed, which read: "I sho dus lub you, an I lik to met yo dis eben."

The members of the company were out joy riding . . . the other afternoon and spent quite a few hours fishing in Pearl River.

Jackson, Miss., is a swell town to live in after a hard rain.

July 9, 1910:
The Savoy Stock Company No. 1 closed a successful three weeks' engagement at the American Theater here and departed Monday, July 4, for Yazoo City for a three nights' stand.

They will play several towns en route to the home of the Savoy Stock Company, Memphis, Tenn.

The company left a great reputation behind them and will ever be remembered by the people of Jackson as being the best colored show that has played the American Theater in years. That's going some, with an entire change of program every night for three weeks.

Miss India Allen, Mrs. May Ransom and Mrs. Nettie Howard are the only females now with the company as our leading soubrette, Miss Laura Smith closed with the road show Saturday night, July 2, and left for Memphis where she can get some "tatoes" raised in Mississippi. She will be missed very much, as she was the life of the company on and off.

As things turned out, Barrasso's "Big Sensation Company" played just one week in Yazoo City and then moved by train to Greenville, Mississippi, where Barrasso leased the Royal Palm Theater for the remainder of the summer.[200] He recruited a few new acts, and to round out the show he installed pianist Murray Smith and trap drummer Joe White in the orchestra pit.[201]

Barrasso was attempting to forge a chain of vaudeville theaters and groom a stable of touring parties to occupy them. To this end he secured the talents of experienced producers and performers who could be depended upon to stage the kind of shows the public would support. He brought in John H. Williams and William Benbow, two men with exceptionally broad stage experience and proven ability as performers and producers.

Known as the "Original Blue Steel," John H. Williams specialized in the comic adaptation of the up-to-date southern folk idioms from which blues was gleaned. He arrived in Memphis in August 1910, following a ten-week engagement in Greenville, South Carolina.[202] Taking the Savoy Theater stage that month, he introduced Baby F. Seals's premier composition, "Shake, Rattle and Roll."[203] Over the next few years Williams started featuring blues songs of his own devising, including "The Sanctified Blues"[204] and his signature "Blue Steel Blues."[205]

William Benbow and his wife, Edna Landry Benbow, arrived at the Savoy on July 27, 1910, following an extended engagement in Oklahoma.[206] William Benbow was a central figure in the ascendancy of southern vaudeville. Born in Montgomery, Alabama, he had been performing in parks, theaters, and tent shows throughout the South since 1899.[207] In 1905 his Old Plantation Minstrels included a ten-piece band from New Orleans.[208] Originally from New Orleans, Edna Landry was Lizzie Miles's half-sister. After joining hands with Benbow in 1909, she quickly established a place among the first generation of popular blues singers. She would record extensively during the early 1920s under the name Edna Hicks.[209]

On September 24, 1910, Barrasso ran this ad in *The Freeman*:

Performers wanted for F. A. Barrasso Tri-State Circuit—Savoy Theater, Memphis, Tenn.; American Theater, Jackson, Miss.; Amuse Theater, Vicksburg,

Miss.; Royal Palm Theater, Greenville, Miss.—Single acts, sister teams, novelty acts. Can also use two more A 1 producers. Fifteen weeks at the best salary
that the South can afford. But you must have the "goods" or there's "nothin'
doin'." Good time to follow this. Salary sure. Prize fighters, see Jack Johnson;
Boozers, see Carry Nation. I pay all transportation over my circuit after joining. Write or wire. Wardrobe must be A 1. Fred A. Barrasso, Sole Owner and
General Mgr. 121 to 123 South Fourth Street, Memphis, Tenn.

The Tri-State Circuit was still gathering momentum when Fred Barrasso died
unexpectedly, on June 25, 1911.[210] From a commercial standpoint Barrasso's
Tri-State Circuit was not particularly impressive, but it was an important
achievement for the African American entertainment profession and a cultural watershed in the evolution of southern vaudeville and blues. Preceding
the often-mentioned Theater Owners' Booking Association (T.O.B.A.) circuit by more than a decade, it was the first attempt to establish a black theater
chain or vaudeville booking agency in the South. Reaching out from its hub
at the Savoy Theater, Fred Barrasso's Tri-State Circuit was the first outward
manifestation of Memphis's identity as the "Home of the Blues."

In *Father of the Blues* W. C. Handy took time to recall some of Beale Street's
"blue diamonds in the rough,"[211] local street-corner and barroom folk
musicians who inspired his blues compositions. However, he conspicuously
avoided mentioning the continuous barrage of professional blues-based
activity that was ringing from the little vaudeville theaters within earshot
of his Beale Street office. If Beale Street really could talk, it would speak not
of a single father figure but of a groundswell *movement* in which commercial
possibilities for the blues were explored by a host of aspiring entertainers.

As William Grant Still recalled it, Handy did in fact comb the Gayoso
Street theater district for musical "ideas," and his successful outings inspired
the "Dean of American Negro Composers" to follow suit:

> Back in the days when America became aware of the "Blues," I worked with
> W. C. Handy in his office on Beale Street in Memphis. This certainly would
> not seem to be an occupation nor a place where anything of real musical
> value could be gained. Nor would nearby Gayoso Street, which was then a
> somewhat disreputable section. But, in searching for musical experiences that
> might later help me, I found there an undeniable color and a musical atmo-
> sphere that stemmed directly from the folk.
>
> Any alert musician could learn something, even in that sordid atmosphere.
> W. C. Handy listened and learned—and what he learned profited him finan-
> cially and in other ways in the succeeding years. He, of course, belongs in
> the popular field of music. But if a popular composer could profit by such

contacts with folk music, why couldn't a serious composer? Instead of having a feeling of condescension, I tried to keep my ears open so I could absorb and make mental notes of things that might be valuable later.[212]

One southern vaudevillian Handy had to have been aware of and probably went out of his way to see was Butler "String Beans" May, a luminous phantom of primal blues lore. Whereas Baby Seals embodied the purposive intellect of the blues in southern vaudeville, String Beans personified the unadulterated instincts of the blues. Among those who professed to having been directly influenced by him are Jelly Roll Morton,[213] Ethel Waters,[214] and Butterbeans and Susie.[215]

Born in Montgomery, Alabama, on August 18, 1894,[216] String Beans was the young lion of African American vaudeville. A full-blown star before he turned sixteen, he was the first black star whose professional success in no way depended on approval from the mainstream. By the time of his tragic death in 1917,[217] "Beans" was known throughout black America for his streetwise humor, contortive vernacular dancing, and outrageous blues piano playing. One contemporary critic went so far as to call him the "blues master piano player of the world."[218]

Beans's trump card was his utter originality. Eulogizing him in 1917, Salem Tutt Whitney readily conceded, "Many of the funny sayings we hear and laugh at in colored vaudeville found their origin in the angular one's think tank."[219] It was noted in September 1911 that one of Beans's compositions, his "new song of 'High Brown Skin Girl,' will make a rabbit hug a hound."[220] Over the next few years he was credited with originating, among others, "The Whiskey Blues,"[221] "Low Down Jail House Blues,"[222] "I Loves My Man Better Than I Loves Myself,"[223] and "Hospital Blues."[224]

Popularly known as "The Elgin Movements Man,"[225] Beans may have also originated the blues metaphor of "Elgin movements (in my hips)," which he was singing as early as 1910[226] and which found its way onto numerous race recordings, including Eva Taylor's 1924 interpretation of "Everybody Loves My Baby"[227] and Robert Johnson's "Walking Blues" from 1936.[228]

Some time before the end of 1913, String Beans combined his metaphor of "Elgin movements" with the theme of the sinking of the Titanic to produce his irreverent tour de force "Titanic Blues."[229] The following description of Beans performing his "Titanic Blues" is based on eyewitness testimony from African American teacher and folklorist Willis Laurence James: "As he attacks the piano, Stringbeans' head starts to nod, his shoulders shake, and his body begins to quiver. Slowly, he sinks to the floor of the stage. Before he sub-

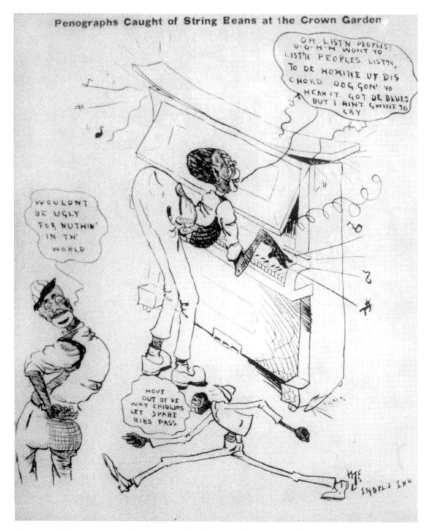

Fig. 2.3. This "penograph" of Butler "String Beans" May, which appeared in the May 16, 1914, edition of *The Indianapolis Freeman*, was inspired by one of his performances at the Crown Garden Theater.

merges, he is executing the Snake Hips . . . , shouting the blues and, as he hits the deck still playing the piano, performing a horizontal grind which would make today's rock and roll dancers seem like staid citizens" (Fig. 2.3).[230]

It seems that W. C. Handy was another eyewitness to this riveting spectacle. Discussing "Titanic songs" in 1928, Abbe Niles brought in "a specimen, remembered for me by the Father of the Blues, W. C. Handy, and which used to be sung at the Monogram Theater, Chicago, by 'String Beans,' a Negro entertainer of high and odoriferous fame":

> I was on dat great Titanic
> De night dat she went down;
> Ev'rybody wondered
> Why I didn't drown—
> I had dem Elgin movements in ma hips,
> Twenty years' guarantee![231]

Niles had already identified String Beans as a "blues pioneer." In his introduction to the first edition of Handy's *Blues: An Anthology,* he allowed that Beans "would improvise verses to his own blues tunes throughout his turn" at the Monogram. Again, it must have been Handy himself who fed Niles this example:

> If any one asks you, has String Beans been along,
> If any one asks you, has String Beans been along,
> Jus' tell 'em String Beans been here, done got his, an' gone.[232]

The one southern vaudeville act that would have been just about impossible for W. C. Handy or any one else in black Memphis to ignore was that of Willie and Lulu Too Sweet. Not only were they a fixture in the local theaters; the Too Sweets resided at 92 South Fourth Street,[233] just three doors down from the Pekin, in the heart of the district.

As was the case with String Beans, the Too Sweets' original songs were an especially important element of their appeal. In September 1912, as Handy was going to press with "The Memphis Blues," the Too Sweets publicly warned that they would "prosecute anyone using our original songs," including "Mama Don't Allow No Easy Talking Here" (see Fig. 2.4).[234] One year later, when they introduced their newest southern vaudeville hit, "I'm So Glad My Mamma Don't Know Where I'm At," the Too Sweets issued a second warning: "Miss Two Sweet has had this song copyrighted in order to keep it from the pirates. She says she will prosecute anyone who sings it. Her other song 'Mamma Don't Allow No Easy Talking,' was stolen from her."[235]

The accusation regarding "Mama Don't Allow" may well have been specifically aimed at Handy, who allowed that the original lyrics of his "Memphis Blues" were inspired by topical verses heard throughout black Memphis, as they were "sung, impromptu," during the 1909 mayoral campaign: "Mister Crump don't allow no easy riders here."[236] Although his original 1912 sheet

Fig. 2.4. This advertisement for Willie and Lulu Too Sweet's original songs appeared in the September 12, 1912, edition of *The Indianapolis Freeman,* one week before W. C. Handy published his first edition of "The Memphis Blues."

music edition of "The Memphis Blues" informed that it was "better known as 'Mister Crump,'" Handy did not combine the "Mister Crump" refrain with "The Memphis Blues" in print until *A Treasury of Blues* came out in 1949.

The earliest and most straightforward account of the historical relationship between Handy's "Memphis Blues" and the folk song "Mister Crump" may be the one given in a 1923 press release heralding the Handy Orchestra's commercial recordings of that year: "One of the most recent issues by Handy's orchestra on Okeh records is 'Memphis Blues.' . . . 'Memphis Blues' was known for two years prior to its publication as 'Mr. Crump,' and is well known to all Colored folks in the South. A little song that the Southerners used to sing about, 'Mr. Crump don't 'low no easy riders, but we don't care what Mr. Crump don't 'low, we're gonnta Barrel House anyhow,' furnished the theme for its composition by Mr. Handy."[237]

In 1927 "Mr. Crump Don't Like It" was recorded by country blues singer-guitarist Frank Stokes,[238] who reportedly started playing in the streets and saloons of South Memphis before the turn of the century.[239] During 1909, the year of E. H. Crump's celebrated mayoral campaign, Frank Stokes, W. C. Handy, and Willie and Lulu "Too Sweet" Perry must have all been familiar faces on Beale Street.

"Mister Crump" was a topical variation of the broader, probably older "Mama Don't Allow" theme, which also took on a life of its own. During the spring of 1914 Madge Clinton treated black vaudeville audiences in Chicago and St. Louis to "Poper Don't Want No Easy Talking and Mama Won't Allow It Here."[240] Several versions of "Mama Don't Allow" appeared on race records, starting with Papa Charlie Jackson's "Mama Don't Allow It"[241] in 1925 and continuing with efforts by William Harris,[242] Frankie "Half Pint" Jaxon,[243]

Washboard Sam,[244] and others. When pianist Charles "Cow Cow" Davenport recorded "Mama Don't Allow" in 1929,[245] he took the initiative to claim the copyright, and he is now generally considered to be its author.

When white composer-entrepreneur Theron C. Bennett took possession of "The Memphis Blues" from W. C. Handy in 1912, he contracted a mainstream lyricist to give it a storyline. The result was touted on the cover of the sheet music as "George A. Norton's Song Founded on W. C. Handy's World Wide 'Blue' Note Melody." Published in 1913, it told of going "down to Memphis town" and hearing Handy's band play "The Memphis Blues":

> I seem to hear it yet,
> Simply can't forget
> That blue refrain,
> There's nothin' like the Handy Band
> That play'd the Memphis Blues so grand.
> Oh them blues.[246]

Norton's lyrics proved to be extraordinarily popular. Handy himself was quick to put them to use.[247] In southern vaudeville "Memphis magnet" Laura Smith probably sang them at the Park Theater in Dallas during the fall of 1913: "Say, she has the whole town whistling 'Them Memphis Blues.'"[248] Handy recalled the Blanks Sisters, a well-respected African American vaudeville team of the time, singing Norton's lyrics "all over the country,"[249] and a note from Indianapolis's Crown Garden Theater in 1914 confirms that "The Blanks Sisters, Arsceola and Birleanna, . . . feature 'Amazon Land' and 'The Memphis Blues.' . . . They wore green and gold for the 'Amazon' number, then the quick change for 'The Memphis Blues' revealed the ladies in satin and lace."[250]

During July 1914 instrumental recordings of "The Memphis Blues" were issued by both Prince's Band[251] and the Victor Military Band.[252] Then, in January 1915, Victor issued a vocal rendition by white minstrel-show performer Morton Harvey, who noted in later years: "Although the orchestra that accompanied me in 'The Memphis Blues' was composed of symphonic players, it wasn't their fault that they didn't get a 'blues' quality into the record. The 'Blues' style of singing and playing, which became so familiar later, was just about to be born. Even the dance records of 'The Memphis Blues' made during that time were played as straight one-steps. However, there were a few good old-fashioned 'trombone smears' in the orchestral effects of my 'Memphis Blues' record."[253]

Harvey could also have apologized for not getting much of a "blues quality" into his reading of George A. Norton's lyrics. Esther Bigeou sang Norton's lyrics on her 1921 race recording of "The Memphis Blues,"[254] and Louis Armstrong dusted them off in a remarkable interpretation on his 1954 LP release *Louis Armstrong Plays W. C. Handy.*[255]

Handy may have lost money by selling off his rights to "The Memphis Blues," but he gained a certain immortality. Norton's lyrical endorsement instantly raised Handy's profile and gave momentum to his decision to establish a publishing company of his own. In *Father of the Blues* Handy recalled Salem Tutt Whitney telling "how he had heard the folks yell in delight after the first four bars and the 'break'" of "Memphis Blues" were played.[256] In 1914 Whitney made this observation in *The Freeman*:

> Not many persons outside of Memphis and vicinity may have a personal acquaintance with Mr. Handy, but who has not been moved and thrilled by the peculiar rhythm and minor strains and cadences of the "Memphis Blues." Mr. Handy wrote the "Memphis Blues" just to please the people of Memphis. He sold it. Since then it has brought thousands of dollars to its purchaser. An enviable reputation to Mr. Handy and added publicity to the city of Memphis. . . .
>
> When Mr. Handy wrote the "Memphis Blues" he builded better than he knew. He was censured by many for writing what they claimed was an inferior piece of music and greatly below his standard as a composer. It is a unique composition; having but twelve measures to a strain instead of sixteen. Its rapid increase in popularity everywhere makes it a psychological study and it is bound to become a classic of its kind just as the real Negro compositions of Will Marion Cooke [*sic*], Scott Joplin and other negro composers who are now considered to be the only real expression of the Negro in music and the only genuine American music.[257]

While appropriately ringing in the "Dvořák Statement," Salem Tutt Whitney's evaluation of "The Memphis Blues" also bore what may be the first published commentary on the twelve-bar structure as a characteristic building block of the blues. Chances are that Handy was more than vaguely aware of how well he "builded" his "Memphis Blues." It was Handy's *mission* as an artist and composer to "make a classic of its kind."

By late 1913 Handy was a fixture in Memphis, with the Pace and Handy Music Company as his centerpost. *The Freeman* of November 15, 1913, reported, "W. C. Handy of the Pace and Handy Music Company, is at the head of one of the most complete music systems in the South. He is doing the dance work for the best people within a radius of 150 miles around Memphis." An advertisement in that same edition of *The Freeman* introduced Handy's second blues composition, "The Jogo Blues."

"The Jogo Blues" failed to fulfill Handy's hope for a "success to compensate" for the loss of "The Memphis Blues," but it did get some play in the commercial mainstream,[258] and it earned him the continued respect of his peers. One week during the spring of 1914 the Rabbit Foot Minstrels "Sundayed at Memphis" and "enjoyed a rare treat in the afternoon, when we all assembled down on the levee to witness an open air concert by the Handy & Bynum Orchestra." At their next engagement, in Newport, Arkansas, the Rabbit Foot's Gold Band closed its evening concert "with Beale Ave's opera, 'Jogo Blues.'"[259]

Like "The Memphis Blues," "The Jogo Blues" was published without lyrics. However, it appears to have merited a vocal treatment on the vaudeville stage from Handy's old Memphis-based songwriting contemporaries and possible adversaries, Willie and Lulu Too Sweet, the original claimants to "Mama Don't Allow." When the Too Sweets performed "Jogo Blues" in Philadelphia during the spring of 1914, it was described as a "new composition by Mr. Sweets."[260] In March 1916 a report from the Douglass Theater in Macon, Georgia, noted: "The Two Sweets are going big with their opening 'Jelly Roll Blues.' Two Sweet himself is an excellent comedian. . . . His parody on, 'Keep It Up All the Time,' is indeed good. The closing number, 'Jogo Blues,' is a scream."[261]

In spite of Willie Too Sweet's apparently prolific output, the only song he is known to have published or registered for copyright is "I'm So Glad My Mama Don't Know Where I'm At." It first hit the marketplace in 1915;[262] in 1918 the copyright was transferred to Tin Pan Alley publisher Leo Feist, who promoted it through mainstream vaudeville star and recording artist Dolly Connolly.[263] Later that year a recording of it was released by another white vaudeville act, the Farber Sisters.[264]

While "I'm So Glad My Mama Don't Know Where I'm At" ascended to the mainstream, its author remained behind the curtain, following the black vaudeville routes into the TOBA era.[265] Meanwhile, an advertisement in *The Freeman* of April 24, 1915, introduced the Pace and Handy Publishing Company's catchy new slogan: "Home of the Blues." A few months later Pace and Handy ran an advertisement for "The Bluest Blues ever published by 'The Home of the Blues'—'The Hesitation Blues.'"[266] According to oral history gathered in Louisville, Kentucky, "Hesitation Blues" was originally "written by Louisville pianist Thomas 'Hop' Hopson and stolen from him, only to be published later by W. C. Handy."[267] At the same time that Handy's version was published, another version of "Hesitation Blues" was made available from the Billy Smythe Music Company of Louisville.[268]

Abbe Niles has suggested that W. C. Handy and Billy Smythe were both inspired by the same folk source. In conversations preparatory to the publication of *Blues: An Anthology,* Niles heard that the Pace and Handy version was originally "played and sung to Handy by a wandering musician" who sang the ubiquitous "If the river was whiskey" verse, as well as one about "Silk stockin's an' ruffled drawers / got many-a po' man wearin' overalls,"[269] a variant of which surfaced in Robert Johnson's 1937 recording "From Four until Late."[270]

"Hesitation Blues" may also have circulated in southern vaudeville before hitting the marketplace; at the Dreamland Theater in Waco, Texas, during the early months of 1913, George and Nana Coleman were "featuring their own composition, 'How Long Must I Wait.'"[271] Both published versions of "Hesitation Blues" were commercially successful. In September 1916 P. G. Lowery's circus annex band acknowledged it was "featuring another number by Pace and Handy 'The Hesitation Blues' and it is quite a hit."[272] That same month the Victor Military Band recorded the Billy Smythe version.[273] A wide range of interpretations, including parodies and topical adaptations of "Hesitation Blues," can be heard on 1920s and 1930s race and hillbilly recordings by Sara Martin and Her Jug Band,[274] Fiddlin' John Carson,[275] and numerous others.

The success of Pace and Handy's "Home of the Blues" translated into attractive job opportunities for Handy's Memphis-based stable of bands, and this precipitated an influx of top-flight musicians to Memphis. In May 1915 *The Freeman* reported, "P. I. [*sic*, P. L.] Jenkins, trombonist, late of A. G. Allen's Minstrels, is now connected with the Handy and Eckford bands at his home town in Memphis, Tenn., where they sing, talk, play, dance and even dream those 'Memphis Blues.'"[276] It was also noted that Jasper Taylor "resigned his position as trap drummer for the Booker Washington Theatre, St. Louis, and will leave for Memphis, Tenn., August 2 [1915], to play at the Alaskan Roof Garden with Handy and his band."[277] A local correspondent summarily noted that "according to the brand of music that we are getting from Memphis, the Tennessee metropolis must have invented blue Monday."[278]

On the evening of May 12, 1916, Handy presented his number-one band at a special concert in Atlanta,[279] "on the stage where Caruso had sung."[280] Handy recalled having given Clarence Williams and A. J. Piron a spot on that program: "They . . . had come to Memphis in the interest of their catalogue, plugging in particular *Brown Skin* and *I Can Beat You Doing What You're Doing Me.* Williams cut capers with the piano stool and played and sang superbly. Piron contributed his fancy fiddling."[281] An original product of New Orleans's rough-and-ready cabaret and vaudeville theater scene, Clarence Williams had gone into partnership with A. J. Piron during the fall of 1915 to form the Williams and Piron Publishing Company; taking off on Pace and Handy's identity as the "Home of the Blues," they eventually dubbed their operation the "Home of Jazz."[282]

Handy claimed to have helped Williams and Piron "get a listing with the five-and-ten cent stores, a difficult assignment at that time."[283] Advertisements in *The Freeman* show that by July 1916, both Pace and Handy and Williams and Piron were distributing their products through Woolworth's, Kress, and other dime-store chains.[284] Handy attributed much of his early success to this arrangement. He was not the first black composer to cut such a deal; it was noted in February 1913 that southern vaudevillian W. M. Stovall's "own songs . . . 'I Have So Much Troubles' and 'I Know You When You Wasn't' are on sale in the five and ten-cent stores."[285] Handy appears to have made the best long-term use of dime-store distribution, however. In 1920 he wrote:

> It is not always the publisher who has the finest list who succeeds most, but the one who finds the best market for his product. One of the best markets for music is the Woolworth Stores, which numbers more than a thousand in America, besides many in Europe and Canada.
>
> There are many publishers who can not get their numbers listed with the Woolworth Stores and at one time last year twenty-nine publishers were dropped from the Woolworth lists at the same time, Pace & Handy were allowed to add more numbers to the Woolworth list, and herein reflected the broadness of the manager of the music buying department who never lose an opportunity to converse with Mr. Pace or Mr. Handy, thereby keeping posted as to their output as well as plans for future production, and it is for these reasons that we request the readers of our paper to call for all music published by Pace & Handy at the WOOLWORTH Stores.[286]

It was intimated during the spring of 1917 that Pace and Handy would relocate to Chicago,[287] and by November of that year there was a Pace and Handy office in that city at 4427 Evans Avenue.[288] Chicago was the capital of the independent African American entertainment world. Its bustling State Street theater district had been dubbed "Broadway in Dahomey."[289] One particular State Street landmark was the Monogram Theater. After Butler "String Beans" May brought the full force of southern vaudeville to bear on the Monogram in 1911,[290] it became the particular destination and jumping-off point for downhome vaudevillians in search of golden opportunities above the Mason-Dixon line.

The pianist and musical director of the Monogram Theater was William H. Dorsey. Born in Louisville, Kentucky, around 1878,[291] Dorsey came to the Monogram in 1908,[292] following several years of apprenticeship in various southern theaters. To supplement his income Dorsey "opened an office at 3159 State Street and went into the business of arranging songs."[293] An advertisement in the November 26, 1910, edition of *The Freeman* described his full range of services: "Music arranged for piano, band and orchestra. Vaudeville artists in need of music of any description for their acts, can be accommodated with bright and catchy music. Words set to music and music set to words." Dorsey's "song shop" was immediately successful. One of his first clients was Shelton Brooks, for whom he arranged "Some of These Days."[294] In 1912 Dorsey hired an assistant, H. Alf Kelley, and incorporated as the Chicago Musical Bureau.[295]

In 1913 the Chicago Musical Bureau expanded its services to include a musical employment agency through which violinist J. Paul Wyer was "imported" from Pensacola, Florida, to fill a position with Chicago's Lincoln Theater orchestra.[296] W. C. Handy recalled having hired the same J. Paul Wyer to play in his "original blues band" after meeting him on the levee in Memphis, around 1908.[297] According to Handy, it was Wyer's free-spirited interpretations of "Mister Crump" during the 1909 Memphis mayoral campaign that gave birth to the "first jazz break" to appear in a printed score—Handy's original 1912 edition of "The Memphis Blues."[298]

J. Paul Wyer's historic tenure with Handy's Memphis band appears to have been a brief one, wedged between stints in southern vaudeville. A report in *The Freeman* said that Wyer was the stage manager of Pensacola's Belmont Street Theater during 1908.[299] In October 1909 Wyer and southern vaudeville pioneer Will Benbow announced plans to open a new theater in Pensacola.[300] When heard from again during the spring of 1910, Wyer was at the People's Theater in Houston, Texas, with Benbow's Alabama Chocolate Drops Company.[301]

After Wyer moved to Chicago in 1913, he and H. Alf Kelley started writing songs together. Their first collaborative effort, "The Long Lost Blues," was arranged by Will Dorsey and published by the Chicago Musical Bureau in 1914.[302] Included on the cover was an inset photograph of Ben Harney, by whom the song was said to have been "Successfully Introduced" in mainstream vaudeville.

In 1915, Wyer and Kelley published their second effort, an instrumental medley entitled "A Bunch of Blues."[303] It strung the chorus of "The Long Lost Blues" together with three additional blues strains—"The Weary Blues," more commonly recognized as "Keep a-Knockin' but You Can't Come In," "Ship Wreck Blues," and the evocative "String Beans Blues," which Wyer and Kelley must have identified with the king of first-generation southern vaudeville piano bluesmen, String Beans May. The same strain can be heard in Cow Cow Davenport's signature "Cow Cow Blues."[304]

When Handy's band made its first commercial recordings in New York City during the fall of 1917, "A Bunch of Blues" was one of the featured compositions.[305] Shortly after the recordings came out, Handy relocated the "Home of the Blues" to New York City; in a matter of just five years he had managed, quite literally, to "blaze a path from Beale Street to Broadway."[306] This specific accomplishment can be seen as an allegory for the commercial ascendancy of blues in African American vaudeville. By the time W. C. Handy got to Broadway, the raw material of southern vaudeville had been rounded into a black national entertainment medium in which blues was a full-fledged institution.

Southern vaudeville had drawn most of its strength and vitality from grassroots sources; some of its most notable exponents had come directly "from the field to the stage." String Beans, Baby Seals, Johnnie Woods and Little Henry, Willie and Lulu Too Sweet, Laura Smith— these were some of the first "blue diamonds in the rough" to rise above the anonymous street corners, barrelhouses, juke joints, railroad depots, and one-room country shacks of folk-blues literature. They were fathers and mothers of the blues on the American stage. From the strategic platform of southern vaudeville, they made fundamental contributions to the development of America's "great and noble school of music." Their work came forth bristling with originality, characterized by self-determination and pride of regional and cultural identity, and driven by insistent demands from the audience to do as Baby Seals had instructed in his anthem:

> Oh sing 'em, sing 'em, sing them blues,
> Cause they cert'ly sound good to me.

Notes

We gratefully acknowledge the cooperation and assistance of Wayne D. Shirley, Betty S. Carter, Dr. David Evans, Dr. Bruce Boyd Raeburn and staff members of the Hogan Jazz Archive at Tulane University, the Fisk University Library Special Collection, and the Center for Popular Music at Middle Tennessee State University.

1. See Doug Seroff, "100 Years from Today," *78 Quarterly* 1, no. 5 (1990): 56–62; Doug Seroff and Lynn Abbott, "100 Years from Today," *78 Quarterly* 1, no. 6 (n.d.): 51–63, and 1, no. 7 (1992): 79–95.

2. *Leavenworth Herald,* July 14, 1894.

3. Ibid., December 29, 1894.

4. "Tom the Tattler," *The Indianapolis Freeman,* December 8, 1900, quoted in Lynn Abbott, "'Play That Barber Shop Chord': A Case for the African-American Origin of Barbershop Harmony," *American Music* 10, no. 3 (Fall 1992): 308.

5. See Abbott, "'Play That Barber Shop Chord,'" 289–325.

6. *Leavenworth Herald,* February 17, 1894.

7. W. C. Handy, *Father of the Blues* (New York: Da Capo, 1969 [1941]), 17–18, 23–26.

8. W. C. Handy, "The Heart of the Blues," *Etude,* March 1940, quoted in Eileen Southern, ed., *Readings in Black American Music* (New York: Norton, 1971), 204.

9. "Tom the Tattler," December 8, 1900, quoted in Abbott, "'Play That Barber Shop Chord,'" 308.

10. See Trebor Jay Tichenor, *Ragtime Rarities* (New York: Dover, 1975); idem, *Ragtime Rediscoveries* (New York: Dover, 1978); and David Lee Joyner, "Southern Ragtime and Its Transition to Published Blues" (Ph.D. diss., Memphis State University, 1986).

11. Chris Smith and Elmer Bowman, "I've Got De Blues" (New York: Lyceum, 1901).

12. Joyner, "Southern Ragtime," 162.

13. Abbe Niles, "Notes to the Collection," in W. C. Handy, ed., *Blues: An Anthology* (New York: Albert and Charles Boni, 1926), 31–32.

14. Richard B. Allen and William Russell, interview with Johnny Lala, September 24, 1958 (Hogan Jazz Archive, Tulane University).

15. *Soards' New Orleans City Directory,* 1908–15 (New Orleans: Soards' Directory).

16. Clarence Williams, "You Missed a Good Woman When You Picked All over Me" (New Orleans: Dugan Piano, 1915); Clarence Williams and A. J. Piron, "Brown Skin (Who You For)" (New Orleans: Dugan Piano, 1915).

17. Robert Hoffman, "I'm Alabama Bound" (New Orleans: Robert Ebberman, 1909).

18. Tad Jones, interview with Mrs. Robert Hoffman, January 25, 1975 (Hogan Jazz Archive, Tulane University).

19. *Soards' New Orleans City Directory,* 1908–12.

20. Paul Oliver, *Songsters and Saints: Vocal Traditions on Race Records* (Cambridge: Cambridge University Press, 1984), 115–17.

21. Alan Lomax, *Mister Jelly Roll* (New York: Duell, Sloan and Pearce, 1950), 121.

22. Boone identified the three strains as "Carrie's Gone to Kansas City," "I'm Alabama Bound, So They Say," and "Oh, Honey, Ain't You Sorry." See Rudi Blesh and Harriet Grossman Janis, *They All Played Ragtime* (New York: Oak, 1971 [1950]), 109.

23. Robert Hoffman, "I'm Alabama Bound" (New Orleans: The Music Shop, 1909).

24. Prince's Band, "I'm Alabama Bound," Columbia A-901, 1909.

25. John J. Puderer, words, and Robert Hoffman, music, "I'm Alabama Bound" (New Orleans: The Music Shop, 1910).

26. "The 'Unknown' Theater Becomes Well Known," *The Freeman*, February 12, 1910, p. 6.

27. "Richard [*sic*] and Pringle's Minstrels," *The Freeman*, April 16, 1910, p. 5.

28. Hart A. Wand, "Dallas Blues" (Oklahoma City: Wand, 1912). Neither "Tangoitis" nor "Ready Money" appears to have been registered for copyright.

29. Samuel Charters, *The Country Blues* (New York: Rinehart, 1959), 35.

30. Ibid.

31. Freddie Pratt, "A Rabbit-Foot Company," *The Freeman*, May 23, 1914.

32. W. Prescott Webb, "Notes on Folk-Lore of Texas," *Journal of American Folk-Lore* 28 (1915): 291–96. Also see David Evans, *Big Road Blues: Tradition & Creativity in the Folk Blues* (New York: Da Capo, 1987 [1982]), 37–38.

33. Lloyd Garrett, words, and Hart A. Wand, music, "Dallas Blues" (Chicago: Frank K. Root, 1918).

34. Abbe Niles, "The Story of the Blues," in W. C. Handy, ed., *A Treasury of the Blues* (New York: Charles Boni, 1949), 12–13.

35. Le Roy "Lasses" White, "Nigger Blues" (Dallas: Bush & Gerts, 1913).

36. George O'Connor, "Nigger Blues," Columbia A-2064, 1916; reissued on a 1978 LP anthology compiled and annotated by David Evans, *Let's Get Loose: Folk and Popular Blues Styles from the Beginnings to the Early 1940s*, New World NW 290.

37. Jim Walsh, "Favorite Pioneer Recording Artists: George H. O'Connor, Part One," *Hobbies* (January 1955): 27.

38. Witness O'Connor's "They May Call You Hawaiian on Broadway (but You're Just Plain Nigger to Me)," Columbia A-2441, 1917.

39. Brian Rust, *The Complete Entertainment Discography* (New Rochelle: Arlington House, 1973), 514–16.

40. Jim Walsh, "Favorite Pioneer Recording Artists: George O'Connor, Part Three," *Hobbies* (March 1955): 32.

41. Marie Cahill, "Dallas Blues (Preceded by Mose's Baptism)," Victor 55081, 1917.

42. Bert Leighton and Frank Leighton, "The Blues" (unpublished copyright submission, 1916, Library of Congress).

43. Paul Oliver, liner notes to *Peg Leg Howell and Eddie Anthony: Complete Recordings in Chronological Order, Volume 2*, Document MBCD 2005.

44. Peg Leg Howell, "Banjo Blues," Columbia 14382-D, 1928.

45. William Harris, "Bull Frog Blues," Gennett 6661, 1928.

46. Lena Wilson, "Michigan Water Blues," Vocalion 14651, 1923.

47. For a broader discussion of these issues, see Evans, *Big Road Blues*.

48. Handy, *Father of the Blues*, 146.

49. James Weldon Johnson, "The Negro's Contribution to American Art," *The New York Evening Post*, quoted in *The Literary Digest*, October 1917; and in Sylvester

Russell, "The Misconception of American Folklore Music," *The Freeman,* December 29, 1917, p. 7.

50. The "Stage" columns of *The Freeman* often carried notices from parents of runaways. The following example appeared in the May 6, 1911, edition: "Any one knowing the whereabouts of Stella Lee Taylor will please notify her mother, Mrs. Mollie Taylor, 706 S. State St., Chicago, Ill." This particular runaway appears to have been Jelly Roll Morton's girlfriend during his ca. 1910–11 exploits with southern vaudevillians. See Alan Lomax, *Mister Jelly Roll,* 143–144; and Lawrence Gushee, "A Preliminary Chronology of the Early Career of Ferd 'Jelly Roll' Morton," *American Music* 3, no. 4 (Winter 1985): 389–412.

51. *Sedalia Sentinel,* December 13, 1899, quoted in Edward A. Berlin, *King of Ragtime: Scott Joplin and His Era* (New York: Oxford University Press, 1994), 77.

52. "Lincoln Theatre, Knoxville, Tenn.," *The Freeman,* March 7, 1908, p. 5.

53. "The Pythian Temple at New Orleans," *The Freeman,* October 16, 1909, p. 5.

54. Clarence Williams, "If You Don't Want Me, Please Don't Dog Me 'Round" (New Orleans: Williams & Piron, 1916).

55. "Plant Juice Medicine Company," *The Freeman,* July 24, 1909, p. 5.

56. "The Stage," *The Freeman,* March 20, 1909, p. 5.

57. "Muskogee, Okla.," *The Freeman,* August 14, 1909, p. 5.

58. "The Stage," *The Freeman,* June 11, 1910, p. 5.

59. "How Woods Became a Great Ventriloquist," *The Freeman,* December 23, 1911.

60. "The Crown Garden Theater, Indianapolis," *The Freeman,* December 2, 1911, p. 5.

61. Paul Carter, "The Colored Audience," *The Freeman,* April 27, 1912, p. 6.

62. Baby F. Seals, "Why Criticism Helps the Profession," *The Freeman,* January 13, 1912.

63. Sylvester Russell, "Baby F. Seals at the Monogram," *The Freeman,* March 2, 1912.

64. "Lyric Theater, Shreveport," *The Freeman,* May 8, 1909, p. 5.

65. Baby F. Seals, "You Got to Shake, Rattle and Roll, or My Money Ante [*sic*] Gwine" (New Orleans, L. Grunewald, 1910). Also see "'You've Got to Shake, Rattle and Roll, or My Money Ain't a-Gwine,'" *The Freeman,* February 12, 1910, p. 6.

66. "People's Theater, Houston," *The Freeman,* February 26, 1910.

67. "Ruby Theater, Galveston, Tex.," *The Freeman,* May 28, 1910, p. 5.

68. People's Theater advertisement in *The Freeman,* March 12, 1910, p. 6.

69. "Palace Theatre, Houston, Texas," *The Freeman,* July 16, 1910.

70. "Gossip of the Stage," *The Freeman,* August 23, 1913, p. 5.

71. "The Stage," *The Freeman,* August 6, 1910, p. 6.

72. Baby F. Seals, "Bijou Theater, Greenwood, Miss.," *The Freeman,* January 21, 1911, p. 5.

73. William W. Westcott, "City Vaudeville Classic Blues: Locale and Venue in Early Blues," in *Ethnomusicology in Canada,* ed. Robert Witmer, 135–41 (Toronto: Institute for Canadian Music, 1990), 140.

74. Baby F. Seals, "Bijou Theater, Greenwood, Miss.," *The Freeman,* January 21, 1911, p. 5.

75. "Gossip of the Stage," *The Freeman,* December 16, 1911, p. 6.

76. Jas. H. Price, "The Olio, Louisville, Ky.," *The Freeman,* April 27, 1912, p. 5.

77. "The New Crown Garden," *The Freeman,* October 12, 1912.

78. "The Team of Jenkins and Jenkins," *The Freeman,* February 1, 1913, p. 5.

79. "New Lincoln Opera House, Galveston, Tex.," *The Freeman,* April 12, 1913.

80. "Galveston, Tex.," *The Freeman,* September 6, 1913.

81. "Alcazar Theater, Galveston, Texas," *The Freeman,* December 20, 1913.

82. *The Freeman,* December 27, 1913.

83. Walter S. Fearance, "St. Louis, Mo.," *The Freeman,* August 23, 1913.

84. "With Sprouting Horns Baby Seals Becomes a Full Fledged Elk," *The Freeman,* March 7, 1914, p. 6.

85. "Baby Seals, Passed Away," *The Freeman,* February 5, 1916.

86. K. C. E., "New Crown Garden," *The Freeman,* October 5, 1912, p. 5.

87. "The New Crown Garden Theater," *The Freeman,* September 27, 1913, p. 5. Perhaps Baby Brown's "Chinese Blues" informed Fred D. Moore, words, and Oscar Gardner, music, "Chinese Blues" (New York: Tell Taylor, 1915).

88. "Smart Set Show Notes," *The Freeman,* April 21, 1917, p. 4.

89. "Wooden's Bon Tons Captured Charlotte by Overwhelming Majority," *The Freeman,* October 6, 1917, p. 3.

90. Billy Lewis, "Vaudeville Still Holding at the Washington Theatre, Indianapolis," *The Freeman,* November 17, 1917, p. 5.

91. Hans Nathan, *Dan Emmett and the Rise of Early Negro Minstrelsy* (Norman: University of Oklahoma Press, 1962), 67–68.

92. "The Real Value of Negro Melodies," *New York Herald,* May 21, 1893, quoted in John C. Tibbetts, ed., *Dvořák in America, 1892–1895* (Portland: Amadeus, 1993), 355–56.

93. Note, for example, Rupert Hughes, *Famous American Composers: Being a Study of the Music of This Country, and of Its Future, with Biographies of the Leading Composers of the Present Time* (Boston: L. C. Page, 1900), 22–23.

94. Theo. L. Culyer, letter to the editor, *New York Herald,* January 17, 1872, quoted in G. D. Pike, *The Jubilee Singers, and Their Campaign for Twenty Thousand Dollars* (New York: AMS, 1974 [1873]), 117–19.

95. Sylvester Russell, "The Great Dvořák Dead," *The Freeman,* June 4, 1904.

96. Sylvester Russell, "Musical and Dramatic," *The Freeman,* February 11, 1911, p. 5.

97. Seymour Jones [James], "Pittsburgh Theater News," *The Freeman,* February 23, 1918, p. 6. For a more detailed account of Charles Anderson's pre-1920 stage ca-

reer, see Lynn Abbott and Doug Seroff, "America's Blue Yodel," *Musical Traditions* 11 (1993): 2–11.

98. "Memphis Theater Notes," *The Freeman*, January 23, 1909.

99. "The American Theater, Jackson, Miss.," *The Freeman*, March 18, 1911, p. 6; "The Show Is a Success," *The Freeman*, December 9, 1911, p. 6. For an account of Bessie Smith's early career in vaudeville, see Doug Seroff and Lynn Abbott, "Bessie Smith: The Early Years," *Blues & Rhythm* 70 (June 1992): 8–11.

100. "The Crown Garden Theater," *The Freeman*, September 13, 1913.

101. "Columbia and Dunnick Theaters, Indianapolis—James L. Nicholson, Manager," *The Freeman*, July 29, 1916.

102. "Washington Theater, Indianapolis," *The Freeman*, February 17, 1917.

103. Charles Anderson, "Sing 'Em Blues," Okeh 8124, 1923; reissued on *Eddie Heywood and the Blues Singers, 1923–1926*, Document DOCD-5380.

104. It is one of the unissued titles from his final, 1928 Okeh session; see R. M. W. Dixon and J. Godrich, *Blues & Gospel Records, 1902–1943* (London: Storyville, 1982), 43.

105. Ethel Waters, *His Eye Is on the Sparrow* (New York: Da Capo, 1992 [1951]), 73.

106. Sylvester Russell, "Chicago Weekly Review," *The Freeman*, April 24, 1915, p. 5.

107. Handy, *Father of the Blues*, 122.

108. Ibid., 119.

109. "Memphis Blues Band," *The Chicago Defender*, June 14, 1919, p. 8.

110. The earliest documented reference to Memphis as "Home of the Blues" is in a Pace and Handy advertisement in *The Freeman* of April 24, 1915.

111. From a blurb on W. C. Handy in "The Stage," *The Freeman*, February 27, 1904, p. 5.

112. *The Freeman*, September 7, 1918, p. 5.

113. W. C. Handy, "The Blues," *The Chicago Defender*, August 30, 1919; idem, "The Significance of the Blues," *The Freeman*, September 6, 1919.

114. Handy, *Father of the Blues*, 139–40.

115. "The Stage," *The Freeman*, January 7, 1899.

116. "William C. Handy," *The Freeman*, February 4, 1899.

117. "Stage," *The Freeman*, September 15, 1900.

118. "The Stage," *The Freeman*, February 18, 1899.

119. "The Stage," *The Freeman*, September 23, 1899, p. 5. The title was originally published from Tin Pan Alley by F. A. "Kerry" Mills in 1897. Sigmund Spaeth identified Mills' "At a Georgia Camp Meeting" in *A History of Popular Music in America* (New York: Random House, 1948), 284, as the "cake-walk classic" that Mills wrote "as a protest against the artificial 'coon songs' of the day." It was immensely popular and extensively recorded.

120. "The Stage," *The Freeman*, October 25, 1902.

121. Ibid., November 22, 1902.

122. Correspondence from Mahara's Minstrels in the August 29, 1903, edition of *The Freeman* noted that their 1903–4 season began in Elburn, Ill., on August 6, 1903, with James H. Harris as the new band director. The February 27, 1904, edition found Handy "now teaching a band of full instrumentation at Clarksdale, Miss."

123. Handy, *Father of the Blues*, 72.

124. Ibid., 73.

125. Ibid., 76–77.

126. The first year Handy was listed in the *Memphis City Directory* was 1907.

127. Handy, *Father of the Blues*, 94.

128. "The Stage," *The Freeman*, September 29, 1900; "Stage," *The Freeman*, February 9, 1901; ibid., February 23, 1901.

129. The May 25, 1901, edition of *The Freeman* carried this announcement: "Wm. C. Handy, cornet soloist, Instructor of band, orchestra and vocal music at the A. and M. College. At liberty after June 1st."

130. *The Freeman*, May 25, 1901.

131. "Stage," *The Freeman*, July 6, 1901; ibid., August 31, 1901.

132. Willie Jackson, "Old New Orleans Blues," Columbia 14136-D, 1926.

133. Louise Johnson, "On the Wall," Paramount 13008, 1930.

134. Robert Wilkins, "Old Jim Canan's" (originally unissued Vocalion), 1935.

135. *The Freeman*, May 25, 1901; ibid., June 8, 1901.

136. "Stage," *The Freeman*, June 1, 1901.

137. Ibid., June 15, 1901.

138. Ibid., July 6, 1901.

139. Ernest Hogan, letter to the editor, *The Freeman*, March 9, 1901.

140. "Stage," *The Freeman*, June 29, 1901.

141. *The Freeman*, July 27, 1901; ibid., September 7, 1901.

142. Handy, *Father of the Blues*, 179.

143. "Stage," *The Freeman*, November 9, 1901.

144. *The Freeman*, December 14, 1901; ibid., December 28, 1901.

145. "Stage," *The Freeman*, January 18, 1902.

146. Ibid.

147. Ibid., April 19, 1902.

148. Ibid., March 1, 1902.

149. Ibid., January 18, 1902; ibid., March 1, 1902.

150. Ibid., February 22, 1902.

151. An advertisement in the September 16, 1905, edition of *The Freeman* placed Tick's at 121 DeSoto Street. City directories from this period indicate that until 1906 or 1907, Fourth Street below Madison was called DeSoto Street.

152. Handy, *Father of the Blues*, 93–94, 125.

153. *Memphis City Directory*, 1909.

154. "The New Royal Theatre, Memphis, Tenn.," *The Freeman*, April 11, 1908, p. 5.

155. The Royal Theater disappears from the *Memphis City Directory* after 1911.

156. "Royal Theater, Memphis, Tenn.," *The Freeman*, December 19, 1908; ibid., April 9, 1910, p. 5; "Jim Kinnane Is Dead after Colorful Life," *Memphis Commercial Appeal*, November 12, 1930.

157. "Royal Theater, Memphis, Tenn.," *The Freeman*, April 9, 1910, p. 5.

158. "The Royal Theater Memphis," *The Freeman*, November 21, 1908, p. 5; "Royal Theater, Memphis," *The Freeman*, December 26, 1908, p. 5.

159. "Royal Theater, Memphis," *The Freeman*, January 8, 1910, p. 5.

160. Brian Rust, *Jazz Records, 1897–1942* (Essex: Storyville, 1975), 337, 624, 1093–95.

161. "Theaters at Memphis, Tenn.," *The Freeman*, October 10, 1908, p. 5.

162. "Gem Theater, Memphis, Tenn.," *The Freeman*, November 28, 1908, p. 5; ibid., December 19, 1908, p. 5; ibid., November 27, 1909, p. 5.

163. "At the New Crown Garden Theater," *The Freeman*, October 11, 1913, p. 5.

164. "The Profession at Jacksonville, Fla.," *The Freeman*, May 14, 1910, p. 7.

165. James Edw. Simpson, "Memphis Stroll," *The Freeman*, March 6, 1909, p. 5.

166. "Gem Theater, Memphis, Tenn.," *The Freeman*, November 6, 1909, p. 5.

167. W. L., "Crown Garden Theater," *The Freeman*, September 23, 1911, p. 4.

168. "The Stage," *The Freeman*, January 9, 1909, p. 5.

169. "Genoroso Barrasso Is Taken by Death," *Memphis Commercial Appeal*, July 8, 1935.

170. "Mrs. Rosa Barrasso, 79, Dies At Home," *Memphis Press Scimitar*, December 26, 1938.

171. *Memphis City Directory*, 1908.

172. James E. Simpson, "Memphis Stroll," *The Freeman*, February 6, 1909, p. 5.

173. Jae. [*sic*] Edw. Simpson, "Memphis Stroll," *The Freeman*, February 20, 1909, p. 5.

174. The last mention of Tick's Big Vaudeville in *The Freeman* was on March 6, 1909.

175. "Theaters at Memphis, Tenn.," *The Freeman*, October 10, 1910, p. 5.

176. "Fick's [*sic*] Vaudeville Show," *The Freeman*, November 14, 1908, p. 5.

177. "Tick's Theater, Memphis," *The Freeman*, January 9, 1909, p. 5.

178. "Tick's Big Vaudeville," *The Freeman*, December 19, 1908, p. 5.

179. Ibid.

180. Howard W. Odum, "Folk-Song and Folk-Poetry as Found in the Secular Songs of the Southern Negroes," *Journal of American Folk-Lore* 24, no. 94 (October–December, 1911): 365.

181. Amos Easton, "Greasy Greens," Vocalion 1719, 1932.

182. *Memphis City Directory*, 1908.

183. Handy, *Father of the Blues*, 91.

184. James E. Simpson, "Memphis Stroll," *The Freeman*, February 6, 1909, p. 5.

185. *Memphis City Directory*, 1910.

186. "Pekin Theater at Memphis, Tenn.," *The Freeman*, July 3, 1909, p. 5.

187. "The Pekin at Memphis," *The Freeman*, September 25, 1909, p. 5.

188. "The Pekin Theater, Memphis, Tenn.," *The Freeman*, November 13, 1909, p. 5.

189. "Profession at Memphis," *The Freeman*, January 29, 1910, p. 5.

190. "Amuse U Theater, Memphis, Tenn.," *The Freeman*, February 19, 1910, p. 5.

191. Ibid.

192. "Gossip of the Stage," *The Freeman*, December 9, 1911, p. 5.

193. "The New Crown Garden Theater," *The Freeman*, June 28, 1913, 5.

194. *The Freeman*, September 30, 1916, p. 5. Estelle Harris may be the person known to have made race recordings in 1923 as "Sister Harris."

195. Sylvester Russell, "Chicago Weekly Review," *The Freeman*, October 7, 1916, p. 5.

196. W. Benton Overstreet, "The 'Jazz' Dance" (Chicago: Will Rossiter, 1917); Handy's Orchestra of Memphis, "That Jazz Dance," Columbia A-2419, 1917; Blake's Jazzone Orchestra, "The Jazz Dance," Pathe 20430, 1917.

197. "Amuse U Theater, Memphis, Tenn.," *The Freeman*, February 19, 1910, p. 5; "Savoy Theater, Memphis, Tenn.," *The Freeman*, April 30, 1910, p. 5.

198. "Savoy Theatre, Memphis," *The Freeman*, June 18, 1910, p. 6.

199. Niles, "The Story of the Blues," 25.

200. "The Royal Palm Theater, Greenville, Miss.," *The Freeman*, July 23, 1910, p. 5.

201. "Barrasso's Big Colored Sensation Co., Greenville, Miss.," *The Freeman*, August 6, 1910, p. 5.

202. "The Stage," *The Freeman*, August 20, 1910, p. 6.

203. "The Savoy, Memphis, Tenn.," *The Freeman*, August 20, 1910, p. 5.

204. "Notes from the Florida Blossoms Company," *The Freeman*, January 1, 1916, p. 6.

205. J. L. Williams, "The Florida Blossoms Show," *The Freeman*, August 14, 1915, p. 6.

206. "Notes from Savoy Theater, Memphis, Tenn.," *The Freeman*, August 13, 1910, p. 6.

207. "The Airdome Theater at Guthrie, Okla.," *The Freeman*, June 25, 1910, p. 5.

208. "The Stage," *The Freeman*, December 30, 1905, p. 5.

209. See Lynn Abbott and Doug Seroff, "Lizzie Miles: Her Forgotten Career in Circus Side-Show Minstrelsy, 1914–1918," *78 Quarterly* 1, no. 7 (1992): 57–70.

210. Fred A. Barrasso obituary, *Memphis Commercial Appeal*, June 26, 1911.

211. Handy, *Father of the Blues*, 137–56.

212. William Grant Still, "Horizons Unlimited," lecture delivered at the University of California at Los Angeles, November 21, 1957, published in Robert Bartlett Haas, ed., *William Grant Still and the Fusion of Cultures in American Music* (Los Angeles: Black Sparrow, 1972), 114. According to Eileen Southern, *Biographical Dictionary of African and Afro-American Musicians* (Westport, Conn.: Greenwood, 1982), 359, Still "was an arranger for W. C. Handy during the summer of 1916."

213. Notes from unrecorded portion of Alan Lomax's Library of Congress interviews with Jelly Roll Morton, as copied from the files by William Russell.

214. Waters, *His Eye Is on the Sparrow,* 75.

215. Billy Lewis, "At the Washington Theater, Indianapolis," *The Freeman,* January 26, 1918.

216. Certificate of Death, Butler May, State Board of Health of Florida.

217. Sylvester Russell, "Untimely Death of String Beans," *The Freeman,* November 24, 1917, p. 5.

218. Billy Lewis, "String Beans and His Future," *The Freeman,* October 14, 1916.

219. Salem Tutt Whitney, "Seen and Heard While Passing," *The Freeman,* June 23, 1917.

220. "Lyre Theatre, Louisville, Ky.," *The Freeman,* September 30, 1911, p. 5.

221. Advertisement for String Beans in *The Freeman,* September 5, 1914, p. 5.

222. H. Woodard, "See the Attractions at the Douglass, Macon, Ga.," *The Freeman,* September 18, 1915, p. 5.

223. "Big Times at the Crown Garden, Indianapolis, This Week," *The Freeman,* November 13, 1915, p. 5.

224. Advertisement for String Beans in *The Freeman,* February 5, 1916, p. 5.

225. Advertisement for String Beans in *The Freeman,* September 2, 1911, p. 5.

226. "Luna Park Theater, Atlanta, Georgia," *The Freeman,* July 16, 1910, p. 5. The metaphor refers to the popular and reputedly dependable Elgin watch.

227. Clarence Williams' Blue Five (Eva Taylor, vocal), "Everybody Loves My Baby," Okeh 8181, 1924.

228. Robert Johnson, "Walking Blues," Vocalion 03601, 1936.

229. Walker W. Thomas, "Pensacola, Fla., Theatrical News," *The Freeman,* November 1, 1913, p. 6.

230. Marshall Stearns and Jean Stearns, "Frontiers of Humor: American Vernacular Dance," *Southern Folklore Quarterly* 30, no. 3 (September 1966): 229.

231. Abbe Niles, "Ballads, Songs and Snatches," *The Bookman* 67, no. 3 (May 1928): 290–91.

232. Abbe Niles, "Sad Horns," in Handy, ed., *Blues: An Anthology,* 23.

233. Entries in the *Memphis City Directory* identify "Willie Perry (c)" as the resident at this address from 1910 through 1912.

234. Advertisement for Willie and Lulu Too Sweet in *The Freeman,* September 21, 1912, p. 5.

235. "The New Crown Garden Theater," *The Freeman,* September 27, 1913, p. 5.

236. Handy, *Father of the Blues,* 93.

237. "Handy's Band," *The Chicago Defender,* August 11, 1923.

238. Beale Street Sheiks, "Mr. Crump Don't Like It," Paramount 12552, 1927.

239. See Bengt Olsson, *Memphis Blues* (London: Studio Vista, 1970), 15–20.

240. Sylvester Russell, "Chicago Weekly Review," *The Freeman,* April 4, 1914, p. 5.

241. Charlie Jackson, "Mama Don't Allow It (And She Ain't Gonna Have It Here)," Paramount 12296, 1925.

242. William Harris, "Hot Time Blues," Gennett 6707, 1928.

243. Frankie "Half Pint" Jaxon, "Mama Don't Allow It," Vocalion 2603, 1933.

244. Washboard Sam, "Mama Don't Allow No. 1," Vocalion 03275, 1935; idem, "Mama Don't Allow No. 2," Vocalion 03375, 1935.

245. Cow Cow Davenport, "Mama Don't Allow No Easy Riders," Vocalion 1434, 1929.

246. George A. Norton, words, and W. C. Handy, music, "The Memphis Blues" (New York: Theron C. Bennett, 1913).

247. Handy, *Father of the Blues,* 128.

248. "Park Theater, Dallas, Tex.," *The Freeman,* September 13, 1913, p. 5.

249. Handy, *Father of the Blues,* 110.

250. "The Blank [*sic*] Sisters," *The Freeman,* April 18, 1914, p. 4.

251. Prince's Band, "Memphis Blues," Columbia A-5591, 1914.

252. Victor Military Band, "The Memphis Blues," Victor 17619, 1914.

253. Morton Harvey, letter to Jim Walsh, August 30, 1954, quoted in Jim Walsh, "The First Singer Who Made a 'Blues' Record: Morton Harvey (Continued from the November Issue)," *Hobbies* (December 1955): 30.

254. Esther Bigeou, "The Memphis Blues," Okeh 8026, 1921.

255. Louis Armstrong, *Great Composers Series: Louis Armstrong Plays W. C. Handy,* Columbia LP CL 591, 1954.

256. Handy, *Father of the Blues,* 102.

257. Salem Tutt Whitney, "Seen and Heard While Passing," *The Freeman,* September 26, 1914, p. 6.

258. Handy, *Father of the Blues,* 117.

259. "Notes from a Rabbit Foot Co.," *The Freeman,* April 18, 1914, p. 4.

260. "The Stage," *Philadelphia Tribune,* April 4, 1914.

261. L. B. Maund, "Macon, Ga.," *The Freeman,* March 4, 1916, p. 5.

262. Willie Toosweet [*sic*], "I'm So Glad My Mamma Don't Know Where I'm At" (St. Louis: Syndicate Music, 1915).

263. Willie Toosweet [*sic*], "I'm So Glad My Mamma Don't Know Where I'm At" (New York: Leo Feist, 1918). Dolly Connolly's photograph is inset on the cover.

264. The Farber Sisters, "I'm So Glad My Mama Don't Know Where I'm At," Columbia A-2573, 1918.

265. See "Champion Parody Writer Heads Lyric Bill," *Houston Informer,* September 19, 1925, p. 5. Willie "Too Sweet" Perry is probably the same person who made race recordings in 1928 and 1931 as "Papa Too Sweet."

266. *The Freeman,* August 14, 1915, p. 5. Although the song was originally advertised in *The Freeman* as "The Hesitation Blues," Handy's sheet music title was "The Hesitating Blues."

267. Brenda Bogert, liner notes to *Clifford Hayes and the Louisville Jug Bands: Volume 1 (1924–1926),* RST Records JPCD-1501-2, 1994.

268. Scott Middleton and Billy Smythe, "Hesitation Blues" (Louisville: Billy Smythe Music, 1915). The *Catalogue of Copyright Entries* indicates that Handy's "Hesitating

Blues" and Middleton and Smythe's "Hesitation Blues" were both logged at the copyright office on May 5, 1915.

269. Niles, "Notes to the Collection," 34.

270. Robert Johnson, "From Four until Late," Vocalion 03623, 1937.

271. "Waco, Tex.," *The Freeman*, March 1, 1913.

272. "Notes from P. G. Lowry's [*sic*] Band with H. & W. Circus," *The Freeman*, September 23, 1916, p. 4.

273. Victor Military Band, "Hesitation Blues," Victor 18163, 1916.

274. Sara Martin Acc. by her Jug Band, "I'm Gonna Be a Lovin' Old Soul," Okeh 8211, 1924.

275. Fiddlin' John Carson, "Georgia's Three Dollar Tag," Bluebird B-5401, 1934.

276. "Stage Gossip," *The Freeman*, May 8, 1915, p. 5.

277. Ibid., July 31, 1915, p. 5.

278. "Stageoscope," *The Freeman*, June 5, 1915.

279. Lynn Abbott, "'Brown Skin, Who You For?' Another Look at Clarence Williams's Early Career," *The Jazz Archivist* 7, nos. 1–2 (December 1993): 9–10.

280. Handy, *Father of the Blues*, 127.

281. Ibid.

282. This slogan first appeared in Williams and Piron's *Freeman* advertisements during the fall of 1919. See Abbott, "'Brown Skin,'" 13–14.

283. Handy, *Father of the Blues*, 127.

284. Williams and Piron advertisement in *The Freeman*, July 15, 1916, p. 5; Pace and Handy advertisement in *The Freeman*, July 15, 1916, p. 5.

285. "Stovall and Stovall," *The Freeman*, February 1, 1913, p. 5.

286. "Call for Pace and Handy's Song Hits," *The Freeman*, July 17, 1920, p. 5.

287. Sylvester Russell, "Chicago Weekly Review," *The Freeman*, May 26, 1917, p. 5.

288. *The Freeman*, November 24, 1917, p. 6.

289. Juli Jones [William P. Foster], "Chicago Show Items," *The Freeman*, August 1, 1908.

290. Sylvester Russell, "May and May Thrill at the Monogram," *The Freeman*, May 27, 1911, p. 5.

291. "Will H. Dorsey Is Dead: Was an Exceptional Musician," *The Freeman*, March 20, 1920, p. 2.

292. Cary B. Lewis, "At the Chicago Theaters," *The Freeman*, September 17, 1910, p. 5.

293. Ibid.

294. Ibid.

295. Sylvester Russell, "Chicago Weekly Review," *The Freeman*, August 24, 1912, p. 5.

296. Ibid., October 4, 1913, 5.

297. Handy, *Father of the Blues*, 95, 279.

298. Niles, "The Story of the Blues," 14, 22–25.

299. "The Florida Blossoms Minstrels," *The Freeman,* December 23, 1911, p. 14.

300. "Managing New Vaudeville House," *The Freeman,* October 16, 1909, p. 5.

301. "People's Theater at Houston, Tex.," *The Freeman,* April 30, 1910, p. 5.

302. H. Alf Kelley, words, and J. Paul Wyer, music, "The Long Lost Blues" (Chicago: Chicago Musical Bureau, 1914).

303. H. Alf Kelley and J. Paul Wyer, "A Bunch of Blues" (Chicago: Will Rossiter, 1915).

304. Cow Cow Davenport, "New Cow Cow Blues," Paramount 12452, 1927.

305. Handy's Orchestra of Memphis, "A Bunch of Blues," Columbia A-2418, 1917.

306. Clifford McGuiness, "Blazed a Path from Beale Street to Broadway," *The Louisiana Weekly,* March 1, 1930.

3

Abbe Niles,
Blues Advocate

ELLIOTT S. HURWITT

One day in the spring of 1925 a young Wall Street attorney walked into the Times Square office of Handy Brothers Music Company. He had an appointment to interview W. C. Handy, the fifty-one-year-old songwriter who had penned a string of blues hits between 1912 and 1922. The lawyer's name was Abbe Niles, and he was visiting Handy not on a business matter but out of curiosity and for his own pleasure. Handy, who had enjoyed a period of great prosperity half a decade earlier, was now struggling to re-build a company that lay in ruins. Any publicity a journalist could offer him was welcome, and Niles intended to write Handy up for the *Wall Street Journal.* Niles had an unquenchable fascination with American musical folklore; Handy was already known as the "Father of the Blues." The two had much to offer each other and they hit it off immediately. Their thirty-three-year friendship would prove both productive and influential.

Niles played a crucial role in W. C. Handy's career, providing him with legal services at a reduced fee, helping him protect his copyrights, editing and annotating his books, and promoting him in the press from 1925 until the songwriter's death in 1958. While newspaper columnists introduced Handy to the masses, Niles explicated him for the intelligentsia in the pages of the better magazines, in books, even in the *Encyclopaedia Britannica.* Up to now, Niles's role in shaping Handy's image has gone largely undiscussed, although his work as an early jazz and blues authority has received some attention.[1]

Edward Abbe Niles was born in the northern New Hampshire village of Berlin in 1894. He was raised in the state capital of Concord, where his father, attorney Edward Cullen Niles, was head of the State's Public Service Commission. Edward C. Niles's father, the Right Reverend William Woodruff Niles, was the Episcopal Bishop of New Hampshire from 1870 to 1914.[2] Young Abbe's mother was musical, and he received piano lessons from Milo Benedict, a Liszt pupil living in Concord. He was then sent to the Hoosac Preparatory School, where he studied piano for four years with Frank Butcher, former assistant organist at Canterbury Cathedral. This Anglo-Episcopalian upbringing was continued at Trinity College, Hartford, where Niles followed in the footsteps of his redoubtable father and grandfather. He won a Rhodes Scholarship in 1917, interrupted his education to serve as a flying instructor in Texas during World War I, spent 1919–20 at Oxford, and received his law degree from Harvard in 1921. Admitted to the New York bar in 1922, Niles was associated with the venerable Wall Street firm of Cadwalader, Wickersham, and Taft from 1925 until his death in 1963.[3]

Niles was a man of exceptionally broad interests. He collected early American tunebooks and maintained an abiding interest in many kinds of music; literature, especially fiction, was an equally strong passion. Niles was an avid tennis player, nationally ranked in the amateur division as a young man. He died while serving as a linesman at Forest Hills on September 2, 1963, having played a match himself earlier in the day.[4] Somehow Niles also found time to maintain a law practice in the financial district, although it is difficult to imagine his attending to corporate law with the same zeal he showed for his avocations. In fact, Niles was never made a partner at Cadwalader. Judging by what he was able to achieve in the pursuit of his hobbies, it appears that a legal partnership was not one of his central goals in life.

Niles and Handy

Abbe Niles's first awareness of W. C. Handy can be dated to the appearance of "The Memphis Blues" in its second published version, a song with added words by George Norton. This edition of the song, published by Theron Bennett in New York, became an enormous hit, and its lyrics praising Handy's band gave the songwriter his first wave of national fame. As Niles himself put it at the beginning of his foreword to Handy's autobiography, *Father of the Blues*, "To me in Connecticut in 1913, came the *Memphis Blues*, an olive among the marshmallows of that year's popular music."[5]

Niles turned nineteen in 1913 and was already at Trinity College, Hartford, when the vocal version of "The Memphis Blues" appeared (Handy turned forty that same year). A 1954 *Trinity College Bulletin* alumnus profile credits student tastes at school with turning Niles's musical activities toward the vernacular: "This extralegal interest, which claims only his leisure moments, had its start at Trinity. He arrived on campus with a musical acquaintance limited to the classic and soon found his repertoire 'didn't go over too well.' To increase the usefulness of his talented piano to the Mandolin and Glee Clubs, he began to accumulate a library of popular sheet music—a start on the extensive collection, dating from the first publication of sheet music in America in 1790, which now fills his Forest Hills home."[6]

When Niles contacted Handy for the 1925 interviews that quickly grew into their first book, he had been an admirer for over a decade. Niles soon became Handy's unofficial legal advisor as well as his friend. Inevitably, this relationship, which lasted from the 1920s to the 1950s, reflected the racial mores of its time. Niles and his wife socialized with Handy and his family, and Niles sometimes had Handy to his home. But while Niles called Handy "Bill" and referred to him as "Bill," "W. C.," or "Mr. Handy," depending on whom he was addressing, the Handys always called Niles "Mr. Niles." In a brief undated memoir in the Niles Papers, Katherine Niles, a southerner recently arrived in the north, described her new husband and his black friends at the release party for *Blues: An Anthology* in 1926:

> The test for me came when the publishers gave a party at the Cotton Club to celebrate the release of the book. Fresh up from Texas, I had not been to Harlem or to any other place as a guest except with people of my own race. But with some misgivings I went. It took me some years to wear down the habit of over-compensating. . . . I noticed that like Mr. Handy, the others of his race did not come forward but waited for guests to come to them. As the evening progressed, the Handys, Mr. and Mrs. and several of their grown children, drew apart. Abbe sought out Katharine and danced with her. I was hardly prepared for this, but Abbe's behavior was in all ways that of a gentleman.[7]

Niles's choice of a dancing partner was hardly accidental. Of the songwriter's five children, Katharine Handy was the one to whom he was closest. She was the first to sing "St. Louis Blues" in public, with Handy's band in 1914 (she was only twelve at the time). She became a mainstay of the family business in the 1920s, and was a key figure in the enterprise in the first two decades after Handy's death. Katherine Niles's vignette offers a glimpse of race relations in the most socially advanced circle of New York society in 1926. This book party, thrown by the politically progressive, intellectually adventurous Greenwich Village publishers Albert and Charles Boni, was a very rare occasion on which black people were admitted to the Cotton Club as guests.

Niles was not an especially frequent visitor to Harlem nightclubs, to judge from his writings. In a footnote to his June 1928 column in *The Bookman* Niles defined "race records" for his readers, adding, "Most dealers haven't them, but all can obtain them. Listening to race records is nearly the only way for white people to share the Negroes' pleasures without bothering the Negroes."[8]

Niles made no effort to insinuate himself into the Harlem community, as Carl Van Vechten and Nancy Cunard did.[9] Dancing with Katharine Handy was one thing; there remained a tacit line of respect that Niles would not have crossed. His deep love of music was its own reward and not an excuse for "slumming." Niles was an avid theatergoer, and it is striking that we find no references to him in the segregated nightclubs of the 1920s and 1930s.[10]

While Niles was not above using words like "darkey" and "nigger" in his writings, at least in quotes from song lyrics, his preferred term was "Negro," capitalized, as Handy and other "race men" stipulated.[11] His special insight and respect for others saved Niles from many of the common cultural blinders of his era. Niles's love of the rough and raw styles of folk music was not race-determined; he favored the same qualities in blues as in "hillbilly" music. Niles had no need to admire a "Noble Savage," and essentialist cant about the "primitive" or "exotic," so prevalent in the work of Van Vechten and virtually all their peers, is conspicuously absent from Niles's criticism.

At first glance it might seem unlikely that Alabama-bred Handy and quintessential Yankee Niles should have formed a close personal bond. In fact, the songwriter and the lawyer had important things in common. Handy's father and grandfather had been preachers and Niles was the grandson of a prominent churchman. Both families were proud and well established, leading the two men to share a certain *noblesse oblige*. Handy was sometimes overgenerous with his money; Niles showed a near indifference to professional success, if not to his standing as a music and folklore pundit. Both Handy and Niles were highly intelligent, educated, curious, and notably good at retaining information. They shared a sense of humor; Handy's earthy, even "blue," while Niles's dry, understated wit, cutting at times, was more often harmlessly whimsical. The most important of their common qualities, however, was a fascination with folk music and folklore. The two men identified with each other's connoisseurship and boundless enthusiasm for old tunes and lyrics.

Apart from their common interests, Handy and Niles clearly liked and admired each other. Of Handy's indomitable spirit, Niles wrote, "He tells of

Fig. 3.1. W. C. Handy with Abbe and Katherine Niles. Edward Abbe Niles Papers. Courtesy of the Watkinson Library, Trinity College, Hartford.

having been worried. I have seen him troubled, but never scared. He is an expansionist at heart, and he would retain the grand manner in jail or in the poorhouse; but he won't have to. As he remarked (at about sixty-six) in the face of a threat: 'I don't think anything can stop me now.'"[12] Elsewhere, Niles expressed his appreciation in less heroic but equally affectionate terms, "He is a poet, composer, musician, humorist, a natural born folklorist and a lot of fun."[13]

Handy's Books

BLUES: AN ANTHOLOGY

Blues: An Anthology, edited by W. C. Handy and embellished with an introduction and notes by Abbe Niles, originated in a series of 1925 interviews
between its co-authors.[14] The anthology was created swiftly, appearing little
more than a year after Niles and Handy's first meeting. They must have
begun discussing such a project almost from the beginning of their conversations. The result was a publication that was revolutionary in every respect.

Blues: An Anthology was the first collection to emphasize blues (primarily
vaudeville or commercial blues) at a time when other folklorists were issuing primarily folk-song anthologies or else folk blues texts without music.
The quantity of music in *Blues: An Anthology* was in itself unusual. Fifty
compositions were listed in the table of contents, most of them being complete songs printed with piano accompaniments. These included most of
Handy's best-known blues, plus a wealth of songs by others. In addition to
the listed songs, other bits of old folk blues, work song and spiritual, some
quite brief, were also introduced, "all drawn from the memory of W. C.
Handy."[15]

Niles was passionate in his literary interests and knew all the best novels
of the day. He wanted very badly to establish Handy's reputation as a central
figure in the culture of his time. Thus, the original title of his Introduction,
"Sad Horns," was taken from *The Great Gatsby.* If F. Scott Fitzgerald was
going to "plug" a Handy product, Niles would make the most of it: "orchestras which set the rhythm of the year, summing up the sadness and sugges-
tiveness of life in new tunes. All night the saxophones wailed the hopeless
comment of the 'Beale Street Blues' while a hundred pairs of golden and silver slippers shuffled the shining dust. At the gray tea hour there were always
rooms that throbbed incessantly with this low, sweet fever, while fresh faces
drifted here and there like rose petals blown by the sad horns around the
floor."[16]

Abbe Niles's Introduction to *Blues: An Anthology* was a curious amalgam;
one of the first serious attempts at blues scholarship, it was also sophisticated
publicity for Handy. Niles's Introduction and his critical notes ("Notes to
the Collection") are consulted regularly by blues scholars to this day. The
book has been reissued repeatedly with new introductions and updated
material, but the original text is irreplaceable. It is unfortunate that the currently available version of the anthology is so at variance with the original.[17]
A facsimile of the 1926 edition should be made available.

Niles's commentary in *Blues: An Anthology* served several purposes at once. There were a reasonably accurate history and description of blues, first as text (an area that others were addressing at the same time), then as music, *terra incognita* for many of his readers. The introductory chapters were followed by one on Handy himself, a foretaste of the autobiography that would follow fifteen years later. Indeed, much of *Blues: An Anthology* is either about, or even by, Handy himself.

Handy obviously gave the biographical material in *Blues: An Anthology* to Niles, and the lion's share of information on the music as well. However, Niles was very much his own man, reading and listening to virtually everything with any relevance to his topic, including books and records that Handy was unfamiliar with. Any suggestion that Niles was simply a mouthpiece for Handy propaganda would be a serious misunderstanding of their relationship.

A section of *Blues: An Anthology* entitled "The Modern Blues" followed the general introduction. Curiously, Niles began this passage with a considerable discussion of the blue note. Although this was hardly a modern characteristic of blues, Niles was specifically interested here in blue notes as an element in Handy's compositional method. On the way to his "blue note" definition, Niles digressed long enough to commend and correct his peers. He was impressed with Virgil Thomson's 1924 article "Jazz," but quibbled with his definition of the "blues formula."[18] Niles reserved more serious censure for folklorist Dorothy Scarborough, for the chapter entitled "Blues" in her book *On the Trail of Negro Folk-Songs*.[19] Although Niles did not name Scarborough or her book, there can be no doubt about whom he meant: "[O]ne regrets to find in a chapter on the subject by a generally acute observer—a chapter of which half is given over to an interview with Handy—six examples, of which six exhibit no musical characteristic of the blues, old or new, whatever."[20]

The six music examples in Scarborough's "Blues" are not in fact blues but folk songs, loosely related to blues, given to her by informants in Texas. Critic Edmund Wilson, sensing that Scarborough's discussion of blues was deficient, was tougher on her than Niles. (Yet Wilson, also, in a show of stunning naiveté, upbraided Scarborough for not getting Handy to reveal to her the ultimate origins of "Frankie and Johnny.")[21] It is nonetheless curious that Scarborough made the errors she did, since she had been given several good examples of blues by Handy, notably "Joe Turner." Possibly Handy confused her by also discussing folk songs he had adapted, such as "Careless Love" and "Long Gone." There is no evidence in the Niles Papers that he ever met or corresponded with Scarborough. This is striking given that Scarborough, like Niles, was living in New York in the mid-1920s. Earlier, Niles had been stationed in Texas during World War I, at a time when Scarborough was already the leading folklorist in the state.[22] Moreover, Niles's wife was from Texas, and she specifically recalled that Niles had learned some Texas blues during his military service there.[23]

It was hardly unusual for folklorists of the 1920s to take an interest in W. C. Handy. John Jacob Niles also credited Handy with assistance for his book *Singing Soldiers* (1927). (Handy is identified in the Introduction as "W. H. Handy.")[24] Abbe Niles found things to dislike in the Kentucky Niles's book as well. (The two were not related.) Niles's singling out of Scarborough and John Jacob Niles for criticism might appear self-serving, given that Abbe Niles was in the process of supplanting them as experts on Handy, indeed, on blues and folklore generally. However, these attacks should also be seen in the light of Niles's background. He was generally more critical of the southern folklorists than of midwesterners like Carl Sandburg and Carl Van Vechten, with whom he had more in common culturally.

A later section of *Blues: An Anthology,* entitled "Adoption and Influence of the Blues," acts as a reception history of the music and includes a few observations on Gershwin's use of blues in his work. The following chapter, "The Pioneers," credits Wilbur Sweatman, Ma Rainey, Butler "String Beans" May, and other seminal figures but gives pride of place to Handy's Memphis band members and early interpreters. This is the most subjective part of Niles's text, the most obvious in its emphasis on the Handy coterie. Finally, in "Notes to the Collection," Niles discussed some of Handy's and other contributors' songs, most briefly, a few warranting a full paragraph. Here, too, Handy and Niles were concerned with the origins of the Handy repertoire. Handy, through Niles, identified folk sources for "Loveless Love," "St. Louis Blues," "Joe Turner Blues," and other songs. They took pains to declare the simultaneous appearance of Handy's "Hesitating Blues" and Billy Smythe and Scott Middleton's "Hesitation Blues" in 1915 a coincidence.[25]

The bulk of *Blues: An Anthology* is taken up by the songs themselves, a selection that changed over time, with pieces added or dropped from edition to edition depending on changing tastes and the availability of material. Most significantly, *Blues: An Anthology* could not include "The Memphis Blues," which only appeared in the revised version of the anthology, *A Treasury of the Blues* (1949), nine years after Handy had recaptured the copyright.

The final section of *Blues: An Anthology,* conspicuously separated from the rest of the table of contents, comprised excerpts from John Alden Carpenter's ballet *Krazy Kat* and from Gershwin's *Rhapsody in Blue* and *Piano Concerto in F.* These were concert pieces in which Niles found traces of blues influence. For good measure, the anthology included Gershwin's "The Half of It, Dearie, Blues." Handy and Gershwin had a mutual professional regard;[26] this must have eased the way when it came time to ask permission to use the latter's music in the collection.

Clearly, in his commentary for *Blues: An Anthology,* Niles was inventing a history for the blues in which a central place was reserved for Handy. In two passages from his Introduction, Niles was quite precise about how important Handy was to the establishment of the blues in American culture. Of the blues generally, Niles wrote in his Introduction, "Its possibilities were appreciated by W. C. Handy, a colored musician with creative as well as analytical powers, and he wrote the first (and many more) published blues, commencing a revolution in the popular tunes of this land comparable only to that brought about by the introduction of ragtime."[27] A still more forceful statement of this theme can be found ten pages later. Niles, having defined the blues as a simple form, essentially an empty vessel waiting to be filled, wrote, "It remained for a musician to take it up, to attempt to put into it something of value: and but for one man, the blues might not yet have penetrated the national consciousness."[28]

These passages show Niles giving in to the temptation to turn the anthology into a manifesto. Simultaneously, he was clearing a space for himself as the undisputed expert on the blues, brushing aside older and better-established competition. It can hardly have escaped the attention of the book's readers that it opened with forty pages of text by Edward Abbe Niles, only partially acting as Handy's amanuensis. *Blues: An Anthology* established Niles as the leading authority on his subject, in which capacity he was very active through the end of the 1920s.

Handy took a keen interest in Niles's remarks in *Blues: An Anthology* during the book's production, and in letters he sent Niles in January 1926 his concerns were varied but always deeply felt. Niles included a few excerpts from these letters in his foreword to *Father of the Blues.*[29] In the passages quoted there Handy sought to deemphasize his reputation as a drinking, gambling roustabout, to heighten Niles's sensitivity to racial terminology, to give credit to his peers and to straighten out a few matters of musical folklore.[30]

However, no subject so concerned Handy as the importance of giving a proper account of himself and his achievements, and cutting the right sort of figure for his public. He took particular pride in his considerable musical skills. In the following passage, which was not used in Niles's *Father of the Blues* foreword, Handy reminds his co-author that the songwriter is also a band arranger of speed and prowess:

Re, Ability to write one's own musical thoughts and SCORE THEM.

Dear Mr. Niles:
Just as I started to dictate my wife asked me a question, which is very important "whether or not that we are going to say that I write every note of my music for all instruments"? . . .

The orchestration of "AUNT HAGAR'S BLUES" was written on my knee in Brownlee's Barber Shop, Chicago, Ill. and tried out in the Vendome Theatre the same evening with Tate's Vendome Orchestra with pronounced success. When I turned this song over to Robbins-Engels [*sic*], Inc.,[31] we had seventeen hundred orchestrations in stock for which they paid and destroyed and brought in an expert arranger paying a considerable price for his arrangement. . . .

As an arranger of popular songs this could not be criticised [*sic*], but the essentials in Blues, the simplicity in most cases is destroyed by the average Broadway arranger and the melody is so distorted that to me it is like seeing a farmer plowing in evening dress.

The following underscored sentence was inserted between the two preceding paragraphs as an afterthought: "(*They later on learned that the original orchestration was the best.*)"[32]

Blues: An Anthology was a triumph for all three of its creators: Handy, Niles, and the illustrator, Miguel Covarrubias, a Diego Rivera protegé barely in his twenties.[33] The triumvirate responsible for the collection elicited the following remark, attributed by Niles to "a Texan lady": "*My Lord, a Mexican, a Yankee and a nigger!*"[34] There was some more pertinent criticism in one corner of the musical press. Henry Osgood, writing in *Modern Music*, questioned aspects of Niles's analysis. He also opined that Gershwin's "The Half of It, Dearie, Blues" outclassed any of the other blues in the volume.[35]

Among those whose opinions mattered most to Handy and Niles, the reaction was highly positive. James Weldon Johnson, Carl Van Vechten, and other arbiters of taste in black culture saw the importance of *Blues: An Anthology* at once. Johnson compared Niles's analysis with Van Vechten's 1925 and 1926 *Vanity Fair* articles on blues. Both men, in his view, had surpassed the recent work of Dorothy Scarborough and the team of Odum and Johnson.[36] Langston Hughes, whose own first volume of poetry, *Weary Blues*, came out in the same year, had the generosity of spirit to praise Albert and

Charles Boni as well as the authors and illustrator.[37] The most laudatory review of Niles's commentary was by Edmund Wilson, who at this time was writing with great enthusiasm on American folklore and popular culture in *The New Republic*, "There is an introduction by Mr. Abbé [*sic*] Niles,[38] who, standing outside the university tradition, has written an excellent critical essay full of literary and musical appreciation and based on an exhaustive study of his subject. . . . Mr. Niles has supplied a history, not merely of the blues, but of the whole growth of modern jazz, with an analysis of its nature, both intelligent and scholarly, and an account of its principal exponents."[39]

A volume like *Blues: An Anthology,* however thorough, could hardly hope for comprehensiveness, and the book had an afterlife, as Niles and Handy continued collecting, trading and inventing new verses, especially for the greatest blues songs. Their revised publication, *A Treasury of the Blues* (1949), reflected their continuing interest in this process, with changes in Niles's text as well as in the selection of songs. There was an intimate side to their verse-trading as well. The flyleaf in the front of Abbe Niles's copy of *Blues: An Anthology* was partly turned over to the purpose of collecting blues verses. (It also bears dedications from Handy and Covarrubias, a beautifully written measure of music by the former and an extraordinary little self-caricature by the latter, dated May 10, 1926.) Some of the added blues lyrics in the Niles copy's flyleaf were clearly written in a few years later, and all of them are in Abbe Niles's hand:

SUNG TO ST. LOUIS BLUES BY COON-SANDERS ORCHESTRA,
CHICAGO, 1930:

Tell me Grandma—Grandma, why do you love Grandpa so?
Tell me pretty Grandma,
why you love poor old rheumatic broken-down Grandpa so?
Why, 'cause he's got the same sweet thing
he had forty years ago.[40]

Directly above this bit of ribaldry, written with a blunter pencil and probably at an earlier date, is the inscription "*A song of String-beans*" and the famous lyrics to "String Beans's 'Titanic song.'"[41] Niles was fascinated with this song, printing a slightly different version of it in his column in *The Bookman* in May of 1928. Citing Handy as his source, Niles placed "'String Beans,' a Negro entertainer of high and odoriferous fame" (a very early reference to a performer as "funky") in the Monogram Theater in Chicago.[42] While Handy was based in Memphis during 1905–17, he went to Chicago frequently. When he left Memphis it was his original intention to settle there, and Chicago was his second (sometimes first) home from about the end of 1916 until June or July of 1918.[43] Handy was sometimes in Chicago for extended visits in the 1920s, and visited often in later years.[44] On at least one occasion in the early 1930s, Handy and some young musicians drove to Chicago from Memphis, a considerable distance, simply to hear music.[45] Considering how much time he spent in Chicago, it is possible that Handy never saw "String Beans" May perform in Memphis, seeing him only in Chicago in 1916–17.

Whether in Memphis or Chicago, Handy must have known "String Beans," by reputation, if not personally. Yet whatever he told Niles about the performer was somehow garbled in the telling. Another of Niles's annotations in his copy of *Blues: An Anthology,* this one in the margins of the text proper, reveals a misidentification of the performer: "String-beans was Butler May, also known as Sweetie May."[46] There was a "Sweetie May" in black vaudeville during Butler May's heyday, they were married for a time, and she was still active after his death.[47] Apparently by the mid-1920s, even the most vivid black vaudeville stars of the World War I era were fading from memory. There had been a lot of changes in the decade since "String Beans" died, and novelty reigned in popular culture. Even so, we can be certain from Niles's error that he never saw "String Beans" on the stage.

The delight Handy and Niles took in the collecting and creating of song lyrics eventually found expression in a Handy song with some Niles lyrics. In November 1929, three years after the appearance of *Blues: An Anthology,* the Handy–Margaret Gregory song "Wall Street Blues" was published with "extra stanzas contributed by Spencer Williams, E. Abbe Niles and Arthur Neale." Most of the verses refer to bad investments and general money woes:

> There's static in the Radio, Atlas Powder has exploded,
> I'd have kept away from Remington Arms
> If I'd thought that it was loaded.
> Wailin' Wall Street if you win you lose.
> I've been gold-bricked, I've got the Wall Street Blues.[48]

FATHER OF THE BLUES

If it is self-evident that Abbe Niles played a significant role in establishing the "Father of the Blues" legend, it is also certain that he did not coin the songwriter's sobriquet. Handy was already generally known as "Father of the Blues" or "Daddy of the Blues" in the 1930s, judging from Memphis newspaper columns of the period, but precisely when the moniker was first used is not currently known. The concept, if not the phrase, went back to at least 1917.[49] Abbe Niles was not the only author promoting the "Father of the Blues" legend in the 1920s and 1930s. George Washington Lee, who knew Handy in Memphis, contributed to Handy mythology in his own writings, including the popular book *Beale Street Where the Blues Began.*[50] However, Lee seldom used the "Father of the Blues" phrase in his famous 1934 work or in his other writings of the period.

In 1941, Handy's autobiography, *Father of the Blues,* was published. Niles was instrumental in this project, writing a brief but insightful foreword that provides a look behind the scenes unlike anything in the autobiography proper. The early working title of *Father of the Blues* was *Fight It Out,* a phrase that had great resonance for Handy personally.[51] He was dissuaded from using the title by his friend James Weldon Johnson. Perhaps Johnson bears some responsibility for the "Father of the Blues" name as well: "I do not think you have chosen a good title. *Fight It Out* is an old-style, worn-out title. It is the kind of title that belongs on the boys' stories of the Algier [*sic*] school,[52] or it might be the story of an agitator, but you are a composer and an artist. It seems to me that the logical title for your book, the title that would attract the attention of the country, and make for the sale of the book is—*The Life of W.C. Handy, Father of the Blues.*"[53]

Handy responded to Johnson's forceful letter four days later, placing the blame for the "Fight It Out" title on John Rosamond Johnson, James Weldon's brother. Handy and Rosamond Johnson were spending a great deal of time together during this period, touring with Joe Laurie's nostalgic "Memory Lane" show beginning in 1933, "I had originally planned this work under the title, 'Father of the Blues,' but your brother suggested the title, 'Fight It Out.'"[54] Whether or not James Weldon Johnson accepted this story, it seems highly improbable. Possibly Handy invented both phrases—"Fight It Out" and "Father of the Blues."

Whatever the origins of its title, *Father of the Blues* is a classic American autobiography, almost unique in its firsthand account of black show business at the turn of the century.[55] The Harlem Renaissance writer Arna Bontemps was enlisted in the project to guarantee stylistic elegance and continuity. Although Handy described the genesis of *Father of the Blues* in his own "Author's Acknowledgment," it is sometimes held that Bontemps actually wrote the book. In fact, the process began with Handy dictating several autobiographical chapters, probably the entire early portion of the book, which his secretary typed for him in his office, probably beginning in 1933. Handy showed this work in progress to friends who visited his apartment from the late 1930s to around 1940.[56]

A late typescript of *Father of the Blues* in the James Weldon Johnson Papers demonstrates that Handy insisted on having the last word on his life story as well as the first. This copy came from Arna Bontemps himself, and on the front page he wrote the following note: "'Father of the Blues'—W. C. Handy. Here is a part of my version of Mr. Handy's autobiography. Compare this with the first part of the book to see how Mr. Handy *revised the revision!* Arna Bontemps"[57] (emphasis in the original).

Handy-Bontemps disputes over the text of the autobiography seem to have involved primarily the poetic, evocative early chapters, by far the most interesting sections of the book. The later chapters of *Father of the Blues*, largely a dry recitation of events and honors, ca. 1937–40, feel like another book entirely. Further research will tell us more about the relative responsibility Handy and Bontemps bore for the disparate sections of *Father of the Blues.*[58]

The Bontemps typescript at Yale is a late-stage copy of the book, but not every variance between versions can be explained by differences of opinion between Handy and Bontemps. Certain names and other particulars were apparently removed from the autobiography *after* Handy and Bontemps had their struggle over the content and style of *Father of the Blues,* that is, shortly before the book saw print. Since the deletions include the names of the two men who relieved Handy of "The Memphis Blues" in 1912, and possibly some other sensitive matters, it appears likely that Abbe Niles, with an eye toward avoiding lawsuits, was involved in editorial decisions toward the end.

Niles had mentioned Theron Bennett in his discussion of "The Memphis Blues" in *Blues: An Anthology,* but was elaborately polite about what Bennett had done.[59] Niles was more direct in the revised text for *A Treasury of the Blues* in 1949, where he named both Bennett and his confederate L. Z. Phillips in a less circumspect description of the transaction in which Handy lost "The Memphis Blues."[60] Yet only eight years earlier, when *Father of the Blues* was published, it was still considered prudent to be discreet in the matter.

The publication of *Father of the Blues* was the apotheosis of Handy's career, and has colored his image to this day. Ultimately, Niles used his pull at Cadwalader, Wickersham, and Taft in consummating publication of the book. When it came time to deliver the final manuscript of *Father of the Blues* to Macmillan, it was borne uptown by Walbridge S. Taft, a senior partner at Cadwalader and a scion of the leading Republican family in Ohio.[61]

Niles's Legal Work for Handy

W. C. Handy called Abbe Niles his "friend, attorney and benefactor." By "benefactor" Handy referred to the varied services Niles performed for him, including publicity work in the press, much of it conducted in prominent levels of public discourse. But Handy's debt to Niles went considerably beyond that. In a 1942 letter accompanying an autographed copy of *Father of the Blues,* Handy testified to his reliance on Niles, "who helped me considerably in my autobiography and many other items pertaining to music, and above all things has been my counsellor for about sixteen years and . . . during this time, I haven't had to look inside of a jail, nor even a court room."[62]

Niles, it should be noted, was only one of Handy's attorneys. He represented Handy personally, in music business affairs and personal matters, not Handy Brothers Music Company.[63] Handy was also represented by the smaller firms of Champe and Zaun, and later Swords, Crockett, Wells, and Petite, only becoming a formal client ("office client") of Cadwalader as late as 1953.[64] As Niles put it, "I have done this or that for him these many years, and he has long known the way to C. W. & T. . . . Things were tough in the 20s and 30s, and I still have a Handy file entitled 'Sup. Pros and Garnishments.'[65] Later . . . there was another: 'Automobile Matters & Accidents.'"[66]

Niles was scrupulous in giving legal advice to Handy at a greatly reduced pay scale. He provided discounted legal services to at least one other important black musician of the 1920s and 1930s as well. Katherine Niles, Abbe's widow, recalled that choir director Eva Jessye had also been among her husband's special clients: "Eva Jessye, whose choir sang in Gershwin's folk opera, *Porgy and Bess,* became Abbe's friend and client as had Mr. Handy. Like many other gifted people, W. C. Handy and Eva Jessye were too naïve and trusting to protect themselves from the business world and often found themselves in legal and business troubles. Family problems and responsibilities were large. Abbe suffered with them and never had the heart to charge a fair amount."[67]

Niles's archive includes a letter to Eva Jessye from George Gershwin, discussing her payment for preparing the chorus of *Porgy and Bess:*

> You must understand that in order for an undertaking of this kind to run, expenses must be brought down to a minimum. As you know there is not a lot of money in opera for anyone. We are trying to do something artistic & new for negroes who are musicians, & if we succeed we will have something to feel proud of.

> The $150 salary you speak of in your letter is I believe a bit high, unless you
> played some other part in the opera as well as coach. I feel the Eva Jessye choir
> is right for this opera & hope the price of the ensemble is made reasonable.[68]

Jessye apparently sent this letter to Niles for his comments. It would be difficult to explain the presence of the letter in the Niles archive in any other
way. Jessye's papers are housed elsewhere,[69] and apart from this item and an
autographed score of *Porgy and Bess,* there is only a brief note from Gershwin in the Niles Papers.[70] Niles also did what he could to get Jessye work,
judging from a letter to him from Robert Simon of the Judson Radio Program Corporation, and he mentioned her in print as well.[71]

Niles's primary client in the music world, however, was W. C. Handy, and
Handy was in business difficulties again and again, beginning long before
he met Niles. Handy and his original songwriting partner, Harry Pace, were
"fleeced" (Handy's own word) by a "song-shark" on their first song in 1907.[72]
Falling victim to a far more costly 1912 miscalculation, Handy had sold the
rights to "The Memphis Blues" to Theron C. Bennett and L. Z. Phillips for
$50. Pace and Handy started their own publishing company the following
year and, by 1918, when the company moved to New York, they had reason
to expect success on Tin Pan Alley.

In early 1921, Harry Pace left the Pace & Handy Music Company to found
Black Swan Records. Pace retained a stake in Handy's company for another
decade and the two conducted business together in the early 1920s, but
Handy was not on the board of Black Swan nor was he a company share-
holder. Black Swan Records would last only a few years.[73] Harry Pace returned to the insurance business, where he became wealthy and influenced
the course of African American enterprise more than almost any other man
of his generation.[74]

W. C. Handy experienced a terrible crisis on Pace's departure. A combination of factors beyond Handy's control led to dramatic business reverses.
Sales of sheet music plummeted in 1920, on the heels of a paper shortage
and a printers' strike. Records had sold extremely well in 1919, leading to
overproduction in 1920. A general economic downturn made 1921 a bad year
for sheet music, although some recordings still sold well.[75] However, in 1922
the sudden viability of home radio created a national fad. Royalties from
records had provided most of Handy's income since at least 1919, and their
sales now declined precipitously.[76] Finally, most of Handy's vaudeville or
commercial blues were temporarily regarded as passé by 1921, when commercial blues that were closer to their folk roots were gaining favor. Several

of his best songs would again become profitable later on, but in the early 1920s this would not have been apparent.

Harry Pace had been a steadying influence at Pace & Handy, and following his withdrawal Handy had a great deal of difficulty adjusting to new realities that grew harsher day by day. Under terrible emotional strain and facing certain economic ruin, he simultaneously suffered dental problems that left him with nerve damage in his face. The combined stresses of deepening debt and health problems caused Handy to go temporarily blind in 1922.[77] He spent much of that year in a state of forced inactivity.

W. C. Handy showed remarkable resilience during his period of recovery, 1922-23. Medical attention restored part of his sight; he would lose it again, completely and permanently, following an accident in 1943. Handy's older son, W. C. Jr., his daughters and his brother Charles all did what they could to preserve the much-reduced business, now known as Handy Brothers. Family members filled sheet music orders and did paper work at night after working all day at salaried jobs. Charles, who worked in a financial district stockroom, and his wife Ruth, a public school teacher, were particularly crucial to the firm's survival.[78]

Handy took other measures in the early 1920s, selling his town house on Harlem's Striver's Row and assigning the copyrights of some of his best songs to other publishers. He made recordings in 1922 and 1923,[79] and went out on tour promoting the 1923 OKeh discs with blues star Sara Martin. These appearances should be viewed, at least in part, as elaborate song-plugging expeditions.[80] Beginning in the late 1920s several of Handy's songs came back into vogue, albeit often in irreverent hopped-up swing arrangements.[81] But slower, more "bluesy" recordings, such as Bessie Smith's 1925 Columbia discs of "St. Louis Blues," "Yellow Dog Blues," and "Loveless Love" also sold well. Handy was not the only one who benefited from the release of these recordings; Columbia badly needed a boost at the same time.[82]

Such was the situation as Abbe Niles found it in 1925. Handy Brothers Music Company was by this time very much a family operation, for better and for worse. Non-family members, black and white, were involved in the company over the next few decades, but they were seldom part of the inner circle of the business, which was closely guarded after the retrenchment of the early 1920s.

Over the thirty-three years of their relationship Handy and Niles formed a considerable personal and professional bond, and Handy knew Niles had his interests at heart. Even so there were times, with Handy preoccupied with a large family and immense circle of acquaintances and associates, when he neglected to inform Niles of his business dealings, often to his great disadvantage. Niles vividly described the goings-on in the Handy Brothers Music Company office, "Between storms [Handy] reigns supreme, solving old and insoluble difficulties by sheer force of character and personality, laying the firm foundations of new and worse ones, doing justice, spending money, borrowing more, paying other people's debts, planning good works, buying songs in magnificent haste, repenting at leisure, . . . *soliciting advice upon contracts after allowing them to become binding*" (emphasis added).[83] Handy's reverses were not all attributable to bad luck, prejudice, or the machinations of greedy business rivals. Given the moneymaking songs he wrote, and the durability of at least one of them, Handy might have become rich. Over time Handy did become more consistent in the application of sound business practices. Even so, he always fared better when he had an able advisor, such as Harry Pace or Abbe Niles, at his side.

Without question, the most important work Abbe Niles did for Handy pertained to the area of copyrights. Once Niles began attending to these matters he made frequent contact with Handy and his family members and staff regarding the copyrights on pieces old and new, and received a steady stream of communications from the Handys about these matters.[84] One indication of how keenly Niles attended to copyright matters can be found in the deposit of sheet music in his archive in the Watkinson Library, Trinity College, Hartford. While most of the song sheets traceable to Niles bear no annotations apart from an occasional dedication from Handy, a copy of "The Basement Blues," 1931 edition, bears the following typed note, stapled to the first page of music:

THE BASEMENT BLUES

> Copies mailed to Register of Copyrights April 8, 1952, with application for registration in published form. Deposited copies were identical with the attached except lacking the erroneous notice "Revised Edition Copyrighted 1931."
> A. A. N.[85]

This was a routine copyright renewal on a twenty-eight-year-old song ("The Basement Blues" appeared in 1924), one no longer of much commercial value. The available Handy-Niles correspondence contains several mentions of copyright matters, particularly renewals of copyrights on older material, and most especially toward the end of the Handy-Niles relationship, 1940–58, when all of the most important Handy tunes came up for renewal.

The high point of Handy-Niles copyright activity was the recapture of the copyright to "The Memphis Blues" in 1940. Niles was actually with Handy at the Library of Congress when the songwriter reclaimed "The Memphis Blues" in person in 1940.[86] For most of the 1940s Handy could reap the rewards of his favorite piece in all its versions. Then Jerry Vogel Music Company sued Handy, claiming to have acquired the rights to the 1913 song version from the son of George Norton, the lyricist.[87] After several years' litigation, Handy was able to claim victory, sharing the proceeds from the song evenly with Vogel. Handy also kept sole ownership of the original instrumental, various instrumental arrangements, and the newer song version by his sometime office colleague J. Russel Robinson.[88]

Handy's letters to Abbe Niles reveal his yearning to claim "The Memphis Blues," his first hit and always his sentimental favorite. Handy chafed at the sight of others making money from it during the song's "captivity," 1912–39. The following passage describes a visit to Joe Morris, the publisher who had acquired the rights to "The Memphis Blues" from Theron Bennett. Handy was trying to get permission to include "The Memphis Blues" in *Blues: An Anthology.* (This is from one of two letters dated January 26, 1926. The right margin of the original of this letter was apparently damaged, hence, the occasional bracketed letters and question marks in the copy):

> Mr. Boni was in today and we went to see Joe Morris who practically ignored us until I insisted on a conference. He was brutally frank almost to the verge of insulting. We finally got his price, which was $500.00 to include "Memphis Blues".
>
> When Mr. Boni told him that other publishers were giving their f[ull?] Consent and inasmuchas [*sic*] I had never received anything but the $10[o?] that Bennett gave me they ought to strain a point even if nothing but for sentiment to include it at a smaller figure. His answer [was?] so blunt that Mr. Boni told him that he would capitalize this inte[rview] for the basis of his publicity, which might act to his disadv[an-tage] and embarrassment.[89]

It is interesting that Handy was *reporting* this event to Niles. He and Boni (probably Albert, who took a more active part in this project than his brother Charles) also may have handled the permissions for songs by Handy's colleagues that were included in *Blues: An Anthology.* Niles, as we have seen, was not yet acting as Handy's attorney, although he took a lawyer's interest in their joint writings when he thought it necessary. Perhaps Handy and Boni spared Niles the mundane chore of applying for permissions to reprint songs, especially since Handy was friendly with several of the songwriters whose works he drew on, and Niles had a lot of writing to do. It is unlikely that the hard-boiled Joe Morris would have been cowed by Niles's presence in any case, given his unambiguous ownership of "The Memphis Blues" in 1926.

HANDY VERSUS MORTON

During the later years of their relationship, Abbe Niles spent a considerable amount of energy on behalf of W. C. Handy's reputation. Handy had a positive image for the most part; he began receiving press coverage in the 1930s in national magazines like *Time*, and was becoming a national icon.[90] Yet an undercurrent of doubt began building in 1938, following a March 26 feature on Handy on the "Ripley's Believe It or Not" radio program. This aroused the wrath of Jelly Roll Morton, an avid Ripley's fan, who wrote a denunciatory letter about Handy and sent it to Ripley's offices. On April 23, the *Baltimore Afro-American* ran an article in which Morton's letter was quoted and paraphrased. That summer, a lengthy Morton letter, apparently the original sent to Ripley in its entirety, was printed in *Down Beat*, which gave Handy an opportunity to reply in the September issue.[91]

Among other things, Morton claimed that "Jogo Blues" and, by extension, the final strain of "St. Louis Blues," had been written by one of Handy's guitarists, Guy Williams, who failed to copyright it. He also claimed that "St. Louis Blues" had gone out of favor by the 1920s and had to be turned over to Melrose (Morton's publisher) to be rearranged and made viable. Morton further charged that Handy had stolen "The Memphis Blues" from three composers, including Tony Jackson, Morton himself, and a more obscure figure Morton called "Black Butts." More damagingly, he pointed out that Handy could not play blues, jazz, or any of the other modern styles.[92]

Morton's charges were a strange mixture of fact, conjecture, and fantasy. He was certainly correct about Handy's lack of performing prowess by this time, whether as cornetist, singer or conductor, and his outdated aesthetic. Handy was born in 1873, Morton in 1890; the former was a contemporary of Bob Cole and J. Rosamond Johnson, the latter a contemporary of James P. Johnson and Cole Porter. Thus, to some extent, the conflict between Handy and Morton was a generational one. In fact, given the age gap, it is striking that Morton's recordings of the late 1930s are so similar to Handy's in at least one respect. Like Handy, Morton relied on younger, Swing-generation sidemen to give his band recordings some stylistic currency, but Morton's instrumental and vocal style by this time was barely less anachronistic than Handy's. To some extent Morton was still playing 1918 piano in 1938. His style was ideal for the Dixieland revival that would erupt in the early 1940s. The coincidence of this movement with Morton's demise, following a prolonged career slump, would make him the perfect jazz martyr for the revivalists. He had embodied the "correct" career trajectory for a jazzman.

Not surprisingly, Morton completely failed to mention that his career was in a prolonged downturn in 1938. Deriding Handy's musical style, he described it as consisting of "folk songs, hymns, anthems, etc." Morton is disappointingly imprecise here, as if feigning indifference. He should have written "marches, spirituals, minstrel music, cakewalks, ragtime, etc." Perhaps this would have been too close to home as well as closer to the mark. Morton did not want to write anything that reminded his readers of Handy's broad experience and considerable career in music in the late nineteenth century. This would have drawn attention to the fact that Handy received praise for his playing in the 1890s, forty years before Morton's attacks, when the younger man was a mere child.[93]

Morton also made Handy's honorific of "Professor" into cause for derision: "Who ever heard of anyone wearing the name of Professor advocate ragtime, jazz, stomps, blues, etc.?"[94] The trouble with this question is that the nickname "Fess," short for Professor, was a common one in popular music throughout the early decades of the twentieth century, and piano players were commonly referred to as "professors." Perhaps the real problem was that Handy was using the word differently, boasting of his teacher's certificate and brief teaching career. This did give him more right to the honorific "professor" than the other musicians he knew in show business. For that matter, few of them could arrange and write out the parts for a large military or concert band with numerous transposing instruments, as Handy was able to do.[95] None of this would have struck Morton as appropriate behavior for a blues musician.

Other aspects of Morton's charges are more serious. Plagiarism was one of the most frequently voiced criticisms of Handy, and remains so to this day. While Handy was always forthright about his folk sources, he acknowledged no borrowings from the commercial blues and vaudeville orbits. A great many country blues phrases percolated into popular entertainment during the years around 1910–30, and Handy was only one of many songwriters who adapted and published them. He also invented, like his commercial blues competitors, some of what he used. Like many of them, he likewise stands accused of appropriating some of these phrases from others. Who stole what from whom will never be ascertained. There are now a great many proposed origins for the different strains of "The Memphis Blues," and also more than one for the final strain of "St. Louis Blues," which Handy adapted from his earlier "Jogo Blues."[96] In this latter instance we should not forget Handy's own claim that he first heard the melody in church as a child in Alabama, sung by an elder as an offertory tune, "come along, come along, come along."[97]

Handy defended his legend against Morton's blasts, although in his usual way he did this in part by changing the subject. Morton's taunts elicited a few cutting remarks from Handy about Morton's preferring attacks on his brethren to protecting his own interests.[98] However, nothing Handy could write in his own defense would change the fact that he was unable to *perform* jazz or blues convincingly in 1938, and probably had not been at his peak as an instrumentalist since about 1900. Although this fact had nothing to do with his claim to being "Father of the Blues," it has always been used to undermine his legitimacy.

Some of the matters raised by Morton can never be fully resolved, but the damage to reputations over six decades has been entirely one-sided, with Handy's legend eroding inexorably while Morton's grows steadily over time. Only in recent years has it become known to scholars what an inveterate fabulist Jelly Roll Morton was, and this knowledge has not impressed itself upon the general public during the current Morton boom. A new biography of Morton is called for, particularly one that deals forthrightly with his business affairs.[99]

Be that as it may, Handy overreached in claiming to be "Father of the Blues" and the creator of the first jazz "break," and in doing so left himself open to attack. He surely knew that he had been only one of four songwriters to copyright a blues in 1912, but he conveniently "forgot" this and repeatedly returned to the "first" claims. These claims were *commercial* claims in the ragtime era and many musicians and songwriters made them. It is striking how many of the early Handy "manifestos" are advertisements in newspapers, magazines and trade journals. In Handy's case this salesmanship was turned into something big, and the consequences were large as well. This, however, cannot obscure his seminal achievement in turning elements of country blues into something that would gain worldwide acceptance at the dawn of the Jazz Age.

The earliest document in the Niles Papers bearing on the Handy-Morton dispute dates from about a dozen years after the fracas in *Down Beat*. Alan Lomax's biography *Mr. Jelly Roll* had appeared in 1950, excerpting the old *Baltimore Afro-American/Down Beat* letter, with some commentary by Lomax.[100] Handy, or perhaps Niles on his behalf, demanded a retraction. The following memorandum was duly released to the press:

Duell, Sloan and Pearce, publishers and Alan Lomax, author of the current biography, Mister Jelly Roll, announce their regret that by inadvertance, this book reprints an unfounded statement by the late New Orleans jazz pianist and composer, Ferdinand "Jelly Roll" Morton, which insinuates that W.C. Handy's famous "St. Louis Blues" and "Jogo Blues" were not his own work but one of his bandmen's. This action followed upon Mr. Handy's protest and emphatic denial, and he announces his acceptance of the amends.

As to the other unfriendly comments on Handy by Jelly Roll, quoted in the Lomax book, Mr. Handy has stated his preference that these be allowed to stand as reflecting Jelly Roll's attitude toward others' success in what he considered his own domain.

February 28, 1951

At the bottom of the Duell memorandum is a handwritten note that reads, "For the sake of a fine man and a good musician, Mr. Handy, I am willing to sign this—Sorry he took offense. Alan Lomax. All regards to him."[101]

By this time the damage to Handy had been done; Niles even began to hear the Morton version of events from members of his own peer group. Here is Niles's reply to one such discomforting communiqué:

I assume your impression about the origin of "St. Louis Blues" comes from Jelly Roll Morton, namely about the world's most unreliable source. Mr. Handy holds the signed apologies and retractions of the publisher and writer of the Lomax biography of Jelly Roll for repeating that particular libel. The "Jogo Blues," from which one of the three strains of "St. Louis" was indeed taken in 1914, was also Handy's own composition, published and copyrighted by him in 1913. Incidentally, Guy Williams himself has yet to be heard from with any claims, and long before the jealous Jelly first published his blast in 1938, Handy had been the houseguest of Williams out in St. Louis or Kansas City—I forget which. From what I have heard of Williams,[102] anyone who had ever gotten away with a nickel of his (let alone a since-famous composition) had better keep a Continent's width away from him.

As to your impression that "Summer Time" was borrowed from "St. Louis", I have never heard any complaint about it from Handy (who does not like to have his pieces borrowed from), and I am familiar with and fond of both these pieces and still don't see your point.* Explain it to me sometime when we meet, and meanwhile thanks for the explanation about the Alumni Fund.[103]

The asterisk refers to a handwritten note at the bottom of the page, which reads: "Three notes don't make a Summer-Time!"

Niles in the Magazines

Throughout his life Abbe Niles read fiction eagerly and, in 1924, he began contributing book reviews to a magazine called *The Independent*. He had a weakness for historical romances, and a special fondness for the now forgotten English novelist E. R. Eddison, corresponding with him and trying to promote his work. But Niles could also be an astute judge of literary talent; his review of *A Passage to India* predicted that the novel would become a classic.[104] Not surprisingly, given his advanced attitudes in such matters, Niles did not ignore the racial and colonial aspects of Forster's great novel.

During 1924 and 1925 Niles was primarily a book reviewer, but from 1926 on he was almost exclusively a music critic. Niles entered music criticism by way of his literary interests, the turning point, as he acknowledged, being the positive reaction to his review of Alexander Woolcott's *Life of Irving Berlin* in *The New Republic* in 1925.[105] It is highly appropriate that Niles's brief career as a music critic began with this thoughtful and thorough appreciation of Berlin's oeuvre. Niles was a great fan of Berlin's; in his 1925 article he called him the first among equals in a trinity that included Gershwin and Jerome Kern. This enthusiasm for songwriters reached its peak with his work with Handy. From Niles's point of view, Handy had the advantage, over the white Tin Pan Alley giants, of being a living transmitter of musical folklore.

Abbe Niles was fascinated with ballads, campaign songs, drinking songs, minstrelsy, and American popular song of the 1870s to 1890s (and any other era). As we have seen above, any book or article by Carl Sandburg, John Jacob Niles, Sigmund Spaeth, Dorothy Scarborough, indeed by any of his peers, was devoured, reviewed in a magazine if possible, and returned to again and again if found valuable. Niles opposed the position of Newman White, who, in a famous article, argued for white origins for black folk traditions.[106] For Niles, unless proven otherwise, the influence was more likely to run the other way, and he did not exclude cowboy songs from his search for traces of black musical sources.

In an essay in *The Nation* in late 1926 Niles made one of his strongest statements regarding the power and originality of America's black musical culture. The occasion was an offer to several writers to discuss influences on American culture from "other than Nordic sources," in the words of the magazine's editors. Niles chose this forum to defend the spirituals both against those who undervalued them and those who felt they had to be made more respectable or improved by symphonic development, in this case including James Weldon Johnson: "More can be asked from no body of folk-song than may be found among the spirituals . . . it is difficult to appreciate Mr. Johnson's concern that Negro themes should be commonly employed in this country as material for music in the larger forms."[107]

Niles pointed out that Johnson's "anxiety" ultimately led, "in grosser form," to Paul Whiteman's egregious rhetorical question: "What folksong would have amounted to anything if some great writer had not put it into a symphony?" Niles had an answer for Whiteman, and it shows his usual independence of mind, "Dvorak's use of Negro themes doubtless helped the spirituals toward recognition, but the weaving of an integral living thing like a folksong into the structure of a symphony may . . . invigorate the latter only at the expense of the former; it is by no means written that the 'New World Symphony' will outlive 'Go Down, Moses.'"[108]

Elsewhere, Niles expressed repeated impatience with fellow folklorists for emphasizing lyrics over melodies in their publications, in this case referring to a collection edited by Newman White: "*American Negro Folk Songs . . .* seems to me to be not the richest collection in its field but easily the most thorough and scientific. Although it contains the words of more than eight hundred actual examples, so many are mere fragments or are variants of others already in print, as to imply that the uncollected material is thinning out; and that the neglected and almost unknown *musical* side of the *secular* folksong will yield the most interesting and important discoveries in the future"[109] (emphasis in the original).

Niles's disapproval of White centered on this question of texts versus melodies, rather than on White's somewhat negative assessment of blues, although this can hardly have pleased Niles either. Howard Odum and Guy Johnson's *Negro Workaday Songs* similarly focused on blues lyrics and folklore, and printed only texts, albeit some valuable blues lyrics.[110] Niles was mild in his criticism this time, despite his irritation at having no musical notation to look at.[111]

Abbe Niles was definite about what he expected in folk or blues anthologies: not just texts but melodies, preferably skillfully harmonized, printed with as many verses as possible, plus a searching and wide-ranging analysis, or at least a few entertaining comments. This he provided in his coproduction *Blues: An Anthology,* and he knew it could be done. He also felt more of a personal kinship with his fellow amateur enthusiasts than with the academic folklorists. Carl Sandburg's *American Song Bag* met with his enthusiastic approval, not surprisingly, as it contained so much music, including a version of the blues "Joe Turner," a song Handy had also adapted and published.[112] Niles referred to Sandburg affectionately in one of his magazine columns as "the American song-bug," and Sandburg's letters to Niles were friendly and informal.[113]

Between 1925 and 1927 Niles wrote a handful of remarkable articles on music for *The New Republic*. The columns of February 3 and September 29, 1926, and June 8, 1927, were particularly valuable for their discussions of blues issues. "Blue Notes," the first of these three columns, included an excellent definition of the blues, paralleling much of what Niles was concurrently writing in the commentary to *Blues: An Anthology*.[114] With these two publications Niles suddenly became the leading authority on his subject. Perhaps Niles's most remarkable insight of all was into meaning in the blues, and especially the existential aspect of the blues tradition. He had the best informants in the field when he wrote these lines characterizing blues in general:

> The essence of most is found in the traditional common-property line:
>
> Got the blues, but too dam' mean to cry.
>
> No one sentence can sum up more completely than this, the philosophy between the lines of most of these little verses. Yet in them the forgotten singers did not always amuse themselves with their troubles; nearer universal was the element of pure self: one sang of one's feelings, thoughts and interests, and if the subject was generally painful, that was the result, not of convention, but of racial history. This personal and philosophical tinge distinguishes the blues from such three-line ballads as Frankie and Johnny, leaving them a secular counterpart of the spirituals.[115]

Niles was still interested in this subject sixteen months later, when he reviewed two books, including Langston Hughes's second collection of poems, *Fine Clothes to the Jew*. Niles bypassed the poems in his commentary, although they included such evocative lyrics as these:

> Play it,
> Jazz Band!
> You know that tune
> That laughs and cries at the same time,
> You know it.[116]

If he failed to engage with Hughes's poetry, Niles at least quoted the poet's own prose introduction approvingly, "The *Blues*, unlike the *Spirituals*, have a strict poetic pattern: one long line repeated and a third line to rhyme with the other two. Sometimes the second line in repetition is slightly changed and sometimes, but very seldom, it is omitted. The mood of the *Blues* is almost always despondency, but when they are sung people laugh." Niles then continued where he felt Hughes left off:

> The last sentence is remarkable for what it leaves unsaid, for commentators on the blues, including the reviewer, have expressed overdefinite conclusions on the state of mind they represent. Their psychology, or their philosophy, if any, is in fact too complex to fit into any single pigeon-hole such as that of bravery, humility, optimism, "making the best of things," or, since they presuppose no audience, exhibitionism or appeal to sympathy. Although the gusto in their best phrases is unmistakable, even the comfort of having well stated one's grievance will not invariably explain them.[117]

Insights of this order into the meaning of blues were available to only a handful of white writers and intellectuals in the 1920s. Only direct access to sources in the black community like W. C. Handy and Langston Hughes could give someone of Niles's background this understanding, and he had thought carefully about what his sources were telling him. It would be another five decades before the existential questions in black music would be more cogently addressed, most remarkably in the work of James Cone.[118]

Niles's journalistic career reached a peak in 1928, when his regular column, "Ballads, Songs and Snatches," appeared in a magazine called *The Bookman*. Niles's work soon caught the eye of people in the music business, and major record companies like Victor began sending him everything they released in the pop music field. He was also sent books, sheet music, and other materials.[119] Before long, Niles and his wife became overwhelmed by the sheer volume of records and other items arriving at their door.[120] His regular column was discontinued a year after it began, and after early 1929 Niles's reviewing and similar activities were much reduced.

Niles's first *Bookman* piece introduced him to his readers and consisted primarily of a discussion of early American tunebooks and their collectors. Subsequent articles usually focused on contemporary pop music. Niles allowed himself great latitude in his choice of subject in the *Bookman* column. He occasionally indulged in asides on politics and the mores of society, but these were brief and of a humorous nature. His real passion was the music, and whether by black or white musicians, the more unvarnished it was the better Niles liked it. This from his first regular column following the introductory essay:

> On the Columbia record 14250-D the Negro Empress of the Blues, Bessie Smith, raises her immense voice, and, in tones of great bitterness and haunting sadness . . . and to the accompaniment of the strangest sounds known to the banjo, she sings in part:

> A bedbug sure's evil, he don't mean me no good
> Yeah, a bedbug sure's evil, he don't mean me no good
> Ain't he a woodpecker—and I'm a chunk of wood![121]

Niles followed praise for Smith with a statement describing the scope of his column, analysis of some recent books and articles attempting to define jazz, brief opinions on dozens of new shows and pop tunes, and finally an attack on the more insipid song styles of the day (the "vo-do-de-o-do" songs of Rudy Vallee and his imitators). This gives some idea of the range of Niles's pieces. He even provided a sidebar listing the biggest song hits of the day.

Niles's next column continued this same mix. He had just received a new piece of sheet music by veteran black songwriter Chris Smith, and he quoted from the lyrics of "Rabbit-Foot Man" with evident relish:

> I've got a tub full of lizards, mosquitoes and fleas,
> My back yard is full of goopher-dust trees,
> I make love-powders from a slippery-ellum limb,
> An' when my roots starts a-workin', it's too bad, Jim! . . .
> I can fix him so he can't quit, 'deed I can—
> But you gotta grease the mitt of the Rabbit-Foot Man.[122]

In the columns that followed Niles repeatedly plugged pianist/singer/songwriter Willard Robison, a white performer so immersed in spirituals and blues that listeners of all colors were often confused about his racial identity. In two separate columns Niles discussed James P. Johnson's *Yamekraw,* one of the first extended compositions by a black jazz musician. Niles gave favorable mention to numerous jazz and blues musicians of both races, although he singled out some, like Clarence Williams, for special praise: "If Handy is Father of the Blues, Williams is their uncle. He writes his own words and music, sings, plays the piano, and leads two distinctive orchestras, the Washboard Five and the Jazz Kings. His clear and engaging voice is upraised this month in 'My Woman Done Me Wrong (So Far as I Am Concerned)'—a noble title—and the somewhat reprehensible 'Farm Hand Papa,' both with Jimmy Johnson's elegant piano accompaniment (*Columbia*)."[123]

Niles also mentioned many of the other blues or commercial blues artists of the period, including Clara Smith ("the World's Greatest Moaner, in 'Jelly, Look What You Done Done' (Col.) What a Song!"),[124] Bessie Brown, Rabbit Brown, Lillian Glinn, Lonnie Johnson, Elizabeth Johnson, Spencer Williams, Wilton Crawley, and Victoria Spivey. After the passage of seventy years one is struck by how keen Niles's aesthetic judgments were. Records like Jim Jackson's "Old Dog Blue" and "Minglewood Blues" by Cannon's Jug Stompers, both reissued on the Folkways *Anthology of American Folk Music* in 1952, became cornerstones of the folk and blues revival of the next two decades.[125] Niles was also interested in white country music, and in the interactions between the black and white traditions. In reviewing the Jimmie Rodgers recording of "Blue Yodel No. III" and "Never No Mo' Blues" he established the special category "*White man gone black.*"[126]

Niles generally agreed with W. C. Handy about performers and song-writers, but he followed no party line. Handy befriended the popular white blackface vaudevillian Al Bernard in 1919, published some of his songs, and wrote appreciatively about him in *Father of the Blues.*[127] Niles praised Bernard at times, but also took the "boy from New Orleans" to task: "Al Bernard's record of 'St. Louis Blues' and 'Beale Street Blues' (Brun.) is worth knowing, though I don't hold with all this singer's devices; white people when singing Negro character songs almost universally become roguish, causing, if the roguishness is carried far enough, severe pains in the neck. . . . A real blues-singer, Alberta Hunter, has recently sung 'Beale Street Blues' and Pinkard's 'Sugar' to 'Fats' Waller's organ-jazz accompaniment (Vic. r.)."[128]

The time would come when Handy would have cause to rue his association with Al Bernard. After Bernard's death, his widow got the notion that his songs were worth something (hardly likely; his sort of blackface routine had been passé for decades). Gertrude Bernard began to pester Handy for any Al Bernard materials in his possession, culminating in the following letter, which Handy copied and included in an in-house memo:

> Dear W.C.:
> Your letter of January 27th, 1955 does not meet with my approval.
> My letter to you of January 12th, 1955 is still my decision.
> I want all of Al. Bernard's songs, books, plates, etc.
> Please give me an appointment so that I can bring my lawyer up with me, and we can get this matter settled.
>
> Sincerely, Gertrude Bernard

Below her signature and above his own, Handy added the following: "Now we can't play with matters like this." Katharine Handy Lewis added the following note in the margin of the letter: "We didn't hear anymore from Mrs. Bernard that I know of."[129]

Niles's work at *Bookman* coincided approximately with the release of the first genuine country blues records, and he greeted several of these with great enthusiasm and with an awareness that there was something uncommon about their style:

A few unusual singers should be mentioned: . . . Blind Willie Johnson's violent, tortured and abysmal shouts and groans and his inspired guitar in a primitive and frightening Negro religious song "Nobody's Fault But Mine"; . . . Barbecue Bob . . . , whaling his guitar and singing "Motherless Chile Blues", which commences:

Ef I mistreat you, gal, I sho' don' mean no hawm,
I'm a motherless chile, an' don' know right f'um wrong.[130]

Niles loved blues, but in his *Bookman* column he also had fun with the ribaldry that vies with other blues moods such as melancholy, irony and defiance. He let his readers know which black records had sexual *double entendres* and referred to Bessie Smith's famous disc of "Empty Bed Blues" as a "celebrated pornograph record."[131]

Niles's final *Bookman* piece was partly devoted to a summing-up of the jazz, blues and hillbilly music he had reviewed in the previous eleven months. The list was provided for amusement value, but it gives some idea of how broad, and how overworked, Niles was:

During the year 1928, I have, for The Bookman, listened to . . . the dance-music . . . not only of the more polished orchestras that lurk, Tuxedo-clad, beneath the potted palms, but of Boyd Senter and his Senterpedes; Jelly Roll Morton's Red Hot Peppers; The Dixieland Jug Blowers; Curtis Mosby's Dixieland Blue Blowers; Wilson's Catfish String Band; Gid Tanner's Skillet Lickers; Joe Foss's Hungry Sand Lappers; Frank Blevin's Tar Heel Rattlers; Peg Leg Howell and his Gang; Clarence Williams's Washboard Five; Creath's Jazz-O-Maniacs; The Whoopee Makers; The New Orleans Bootblacks; Dad Blackard's Moonshiners; and The Goofus Five. From the mass of American music, or something, that has been thus passed through my ears, I select a few examples as the richest in the strangeness, the bitter, salty wit and humor, and the flashes of defiant, unwilling beauty which characterize good jazz.[132]

Carl Van Vechten had been the most perceptive critic of blues in the magazines in 1925. R. D. Darrell wrote much of the best jazz criticism published between 1927 and 1932. But nothing written by either man surpasses Niles's writings on blues and spirituals in *The New Republic* and *The Nation* in 1926, or his 1928 work for *The Bookman*, which encompassed everything from operetta to fox trot to the grittiest blues and hillbilly records. Readers of Niles's columns also got bonuses in the form of asides about nineteenth-century American song, minstrelsy, the collecting of old songbooks, and other matters. It is high time Niles got his due as a critic.

The 1929 *Encyclopaedia Britannica*

By the late 1920s Abbe Niles's reputation as a blues and jazz authority was yielding some extraordinary results. Essentially untrained as a scholar and writer, he was selected to write the first article on "Jazz" ever to appear in the *Encyclopaedia Britannica.* Correspondence from editors at Britannica shows that Niles was approached by letter on February 16, 1928, and was offered $25 for a maximum of 1500 words due April 15. Niles was very busy with his *Bookman* column and additional work in other magazines throughout 1928. He immediately accepted the Britannica assignment, but requested more time, judging from a letter, dated February 18, granting him an extension until May 1.[133]

There was also a short article on "Blues" in the fourteenth edition of the *Britannica.* Niles made inquiries about this, and was invited to come to the offices and look at the piece, which was in page form by that time. The article was described to him as being by a member of the editorial staff and about four hundred words long. The final two paragraphs of this letter can hardly have given Niles confidence:

> The article describes the motif as originating in the contest in Memphis in 1909, which gave rise to the "Memphis Blues"; discussed in Mr. Carpenter's "Krazy Kats" Blues [*sic*] in 1922, and of Mr Gershwin's "Rhapsody in Blues" [*sic*] in 1924.
>
> There is no bibliography and the article is not to be signed.[134]

Niles probably declined to visit the *Britannica* offices, then in the Canadian Pacific Building at 342 Madison Ave., New York, although if he had examined the article there would have been nothing he could do to prevent its inclusion so late in the production process. The "Blues" article in the fourteenth edition of the *Encyclopaedia Britannica* is precisely as described in the letter. *Krazy Kat* and *Rhapsody in Blue* are the only two pieces mentioned aside from "The Memphis Blues." Both pieces had been excerpted in *Blues: An Anthology,* quite possibly at Niles's suggestion. This is probably where the anonymous contributor to the *Britannica* got the unfortunate idea to use these jazzy orchestral works as examples of blues; the irony is both cruel and somewhat amusing.

However, in his "Jazz" article, Niles does discuss blues and acknowledges blues as an essential component of jazz. Out of eight music examples, two are by black composers, "Banjo Blues" by Spencer Williams and "The Memphis

Blues."[135] Both are used to demonstrate the jazz "break" and, to a lesser extent, "blue" notes. Niles drew a distinction between Memphis-style jazz (blues and "breaks") and New Orleans style, with its characteristic instrumental polyphony. To a degree, Niles's entire argument is built around the idea that the "break" in "The Memphis Blues" provided a fundamental impetus for the creation of jazz generally. This is certainly not the view held today. However, it should be remembered that both James Reese Europe and Irene Castle claimed that the fox trot was invented when Europe played "The Memphis Blues" on the piano for the Castles during a rehearsal.[136] If "The Memphis Blues" is not the original jazz composition (or the first published blues), it apparently provided the foundation for the ubiquitous dance music of the Jazz Age.

Niles's brief history of jazz is primarily interesting for its stress on the importance of blues as an *element,* or *building block,* of jazz, and a necessary part of the transition to jazz from ragtime.[137] This was innovative historiography for the time, and it should hardly be surprising if Niles at the same time exaggerated Handy's importance in the development of jazz in his article. Ultimately, Niles's "Jazz" article is less satisfying than the best of his magazine work. Even so, the *Encyclopaedia Britannica* article provided a better definition of jazz than one was likely to find in other reference books in 1929, and it was a fitting coda to Niles's brief but extraordinary career as a critic.

Niles's Correspondence

Niles received some remarkable letters in response to his magazine work, his radio appearances and his association with Handy. Irving Berlin wrote following Niles's review of the Woolcott biography,[138] but so did less eminent persons, especially college and prep school students and recent graduates of his own social class. These included such future luminaries of the jazz world as John Hammond and R. D. Darrell, along with a number of others who never made a mark in music. One fan was a young Canadian woman who had recently arrived at *Bookman* as secretary to the advertising manager. Her name was Ruth Barr and she wrote an enthusiastic letter to Niles after reading the galleys of his famous "Jazz 1928" column: "I like my blues heavy and I like orchestrations in which one clarinet runs away up while another runs down and all the instruments seem to be running wild except for loose links of rhythm, but thru which a pattern is discernible to the experienced listener. In fact, I enjoy jazz not only emotionally, but also intellectually. Now laugh that off."[139]

Not all the letters Niles received were thanks from songwriters and performers, nor were they all fan letters. Niles appeared on the radio in the 1930s, sometimes playing piano to illustrate talks by his friend Sigmund Spaeth. Niles's initial fame, gained through his writings in the late 1920s, had been somewhat limited. However, radio was enormously popular during the 1930s, when Niles appeared on it. Thus Niles gained a far broader audience than the intelligentsia who read *The Bookman*. Ultimately Niles received letters from several songwriters in distress. A poignant message arrived from a would-be lyricist in California who had heard Niles on the radio:

> I wrote some words for songs and sent them to a company, to look over for me, they wanted to service those songs and put them on the market. But they wanted $50 dollars. Since this depression hit the country we have had to struggle along to keep our home. As I have 5 little one's to care for am not able to go out side. But am sure I can make a go of writing and songs. I had a little money in the bank, and was trying to get some one to go 50-50 with me, then the [?illegible] closed.
>
> I feel, I would, like, to try and have some thing, to help, my children, to receive, an education, some thing, I was deprived, off [*sic*] on account, of my fathers death. I would like to have a little more advice on this, and wonder, if you would please look my music & song over. . . .
>
> Wish you much success in life
>
> Sincerely, an anxious Mother.[140]

Nor was this unsuccessful aspirant the only songwriter to approach Niles about problems with publishers, especially with song-sharks and other con artists. The following excerpt is from a letter, the date and first page of which are unfortunately missing. As in the previous example, the original orthography and grammar have been retained:

> but after making a contract with this so called Music pub. co. is stop selling the Song, i all so hold a copywrite for the song, all so letters from them stating that they rec. the $60.00, so please let me know if you Take hold of cases of this king [*sic*], or Refer me to some one that do.
>
> and oblige
> Paul Carter
> #118 Jackson St.
> Bainbridge Ga

In the lower-right-hand margin of this page, Niles wrote the following parenthetical note to himself: "(Writer of Weeping Willow Blues)."[141]

Lacking Niles's side of the correspondence with these parties, we have no way of knowing how, or if, he responded to such entreaties. But a collection of papers that recently surfaced in New York indicates that, at least in some instances, Niles took the hard luck cases that came his way seriously. In 1936, Handy sent Niles a letter he had just received from a woman named Frankie Baker (1877–1952) who claimed to be the subject of the song "Frankie and Johnny." She wanted part of the proceeds from the movie *She Done Him Wrong*. (Indeed, Baker would go on to sue Paramount Pictures, and Mae West personally, in 1939.) Niles certainly knew that this woman had no chance of gaining anything by her claim, but he diligently took legal notes on the subject, tried to find some way of making a case, and probably contacted several other people for advice.[142] He was clearly intrigued by all manner of folklore and intellectual property rights, but also sympathetic toward lost causes and underdogs. His response to the Frankie Baker matter is typical of Niles's character. Most attorneys would have laughed her off; Niles was too curious and too humane for that.

Conclusion

Abbe Niles was an exceptional character: an upper-class Yankee whose business was the law, and whose passion was the blues. Niles seems preternaturally suited to the office of blues advocate, able defender, at law and in print, of the music he loved, and of W. C. Handy, the man who, for Niles, personified that music. Niles singlehandedly contributed as much to the building of the Handy legend as the entire puff press of the day, while giving it a more serious and permanent form in his articles, and his work on Handy's books. He had the wit to grasp Handy's seminal role in transmitting the blues to the American mainstream, and the eloquence to convey his excitement over Handy to the general public.

An early and key authority on the blues, Abbe Niles had an unusual feeling for the form *as music* as well as folklore, and a rare understanding of blues as a cornerstone of jazz and dance music. His sensibility and extraordinary knowledge made him one of the most important white figures in the blues scene in the 1920s. Niles's empathy and humanism set him apart, and uniquely qualified him for his historic role as W. C. Handy's counselor and protector. In this capacity Niles helped ensure the survival of a black family-owned music publishing business that, after eight decades, has proved of immense and lasting importance in America's cultural history.

Notes

This chapter is respectfully dedicated to Mr. Samuel Charters, who understood the importance of Abbe Niles long ago.

A preliminary version of this paper was presented at the Northeast Chapter meeting of the College Music Society, Trinity College, Hartford, Connecticut, April 5, 1997. For their assistance with the paper in the course of its creation, my thanks to Lynn Abbott, David Evans, Elizabeth Ellis Hurwitt, Peter Muir, and Charles G. Price.

1. Samuel Charters, "Abbe Niles, a Pioneering Jazz Critic of the 1920s," *Jazz Review* (May 1959): 25–26, the only previous article devoted to Niles, is an excellent introduction to his work in the magazine *The Bookman.* Charters also discusses Niles's pioneering blues criticism in *The Country Blues* (1959; New York: Da Capo, 1975). David Evans mentions Niles in his *Big Road Blues* (1982; New York: Da Capo, 1987). James Lincoln Collier discusses Niles in: *The Reception of Jazz in America: A New View,* ISAM Monographs No. 27 (Brooklyn: Institute for Studies in American Music, 1988); and *Jazz, The American Theme Song* (New York: Oxford University Press, 1993).

2. Bishop Niles's tenure was not without controversy. He was the addressee of a respectful but heated polemic, "Was the Revised Constitution of the Diocese legally approved? Or is it null and void? A Letter to the Right Reverend William Woodruff Niles" (Boston: A. Williams & Co., c. 1879), New York Public Library. The author, one Hall Harrison, was Assistant Master, St. Paul's School, Concord, and Rector of St. Andrews, Hopkinton.

3. The biographical details in this essay derive primarily from three sources: a one-page autobiographical typescript dating from the mid-late 1920s; the article "Edward Abbe Niles' 16: New York Lawyer Is Off-hours Boswell of the Blues," in the feature "Alumni Portraits," *Trinity College Bulletin* (March 1954): 9; and a two-page, unsigned, typed announcement of the donation of the Abbe Niles Papers by Niles's widow Katherine. This document, entitled *Niles Music Collection,* dates from around 1975. All three courtesy of the Edward Abbe Niles Papers, Watkinson Library, Trinity College, Hartford (hereinafter abbreviated, by permission, to "Niles Papers, Watkinson, Trinity").

My research on Abbe Niles was aided considerably by the fine staff of the Watkinson Library, Trinity College, Hartford. I particularly wish to thank Alesandra Schmidt, Assistant Curator for Reference and Manuscripts.

4. *New York Times,* September 3, 1963, p. 33. W. C. Handy clipping files, Institute of Jazz Studies, Rutgers University, Newark. For further biographical details, *New York Herald Tribune,* September 3, 1963, 20.

5. Abbe Niles, Foreword to W.C. Handy's *Father of the Blues* (New York: Macmillan, 1941), v.

6. Trinity College Bulletin, March 1954, 9, Niles Papers, Watkinson, Trinity.

7. Katherine Niles, "Notes on Abbe Niles and W. C. Handy," unpublished typescript, n.d., 2, Niles Papers, Watkinson, Trinity.

8. Abbe Niles, "Ballads, Songs and Snatches," *The Bookman*, June 1928, 422.

9. Ann Douglas, *Terrible Honesty* (New York: Farrar Straus and Giroux, 1995), 272–82, 287–92. Douglas is sympathetic to both Van Vechten and Cunard, and her discussion highlights their social activities. Niles liked Van Vechten and favorably reviewed two of his novels, *The Tattooed Countess,* and *Nigger Heaven* (*The Independent,* September 27, 1924, p. 201; and *The New Republic,* September 29, 1926, p. 162, respectively). Van Vechten was one of Niles's few peers among white critics in his love of, and genuine understanding of, blues.

10. Niles's club-going days seem to have come later. Around 1940 Niles developed a mania for boogie-woogie piano and he became a regular at Café Society, where he could hear Albert Ammons, Pete Johnson, Meade Lux Lewis, and Hazel Scott. Katherine Niles, "Notes on Abbe Niles and W. C. Handy," 4, Niles Papers, Watkinson, Trinity.

11. Niles included "darkey," "Dixie" and "Uncle Remus" in a list of words he disliked, although probably for aesthetic as much as political reasons. "Ballads, Songs and Snatches," *The Bookman,* April 1928, p. 170. However Niles, like most Americans of his time, used the word "colored" casually and without self-consciousness.

12. Abbe Niles, Foreword to *Father of the Blues,* vi.

13. Abbe Niles, "William C. Handy," *The Labellum News* (Cadwalader, Wickersham and Taft house publication), November 7, 1957, p. 270, Niles Papers, Watkinson, Trinity. This was a special issue largely written by Niles and devoted to Handy.

14. *Blues: An Anthology,* edited by W. C. Handy, with an Introduction by Abbe Niles, illustrations by Miguel Covarrubias (New York: Albert & Charles Boni, 1926), 1. Niles gave the date of his first interview with Handy as Spring 1925. The year is sometimes given as 1924, but the version in the Introduction to *Blues: An Anthology* should be considered authoritative. Niles may have taken notes during his interviews with Handy. If they survived, their location has not been disclosed.

15. Niles, "Notes to the Collection," *Blues: An Anthology,* 25.

16. Niles, Introduction to *Blues: An Anthology,* 1, quoting Fitzgerald, *The Great Gatsby* (New York: Scribner, 1925), 133.

17. *Blues: An Anthology,* edited by W.C. Handy, with an Historical and Critical Text by Abbe Niles, revised by Jerry Silverman, new Introduction by William Ferris (1972; New York: Da Capo, 1990). The 1972 and 1990 editions are based on *A Treasury of the Blues,* Handy and Niles's 1949 revision of *Blues: An Anthology.* While the Ferris introduction is a notable addition, it remains preferable for scholars working on Handy to return to the original 1926 text. Subsequent references herein, unless otherwise specified, are to the 1926 edition.

18. Virgil Thomson, "Jazz," *The American Mercury,* August 1924, pp. 465–67. Reprinted in *A Virgil Thomson Reader* (Boston: Houghton Mifflin, 1981), 15–18. Thomson was exceptionally perceptive about the dance music that was played in hotel

ballrooms, if not about blues. He seldom incorporated blues into his own composi-tions, although "Blues (Speculation)" from *The Plow That Broke the Plains* (1936) is a skillful evocation of the sleaziest blues-inflected jazz of the 1920s.

19. Dorothy Scarborough, "The `Blues' as Folk-Songs," *Texas Folklore Society Pub-lications,* no. 2 (1923): 52–66. Reprinted as "Blues" in her book *On the Trail of Negro Folk-Songs* (1925; Hatboro, Pa.: Folklore Associates, 1963), 264–80.

20. Abbe Niles, *Blues: An Anthology,* 15. This is only one of several controversial passages deleted from subsequent editions of the anthology.

21. Edmund Wilson, "American Ballads and Their Collectors," *The New Republic,* June 30, 1926, p. 169. The fact that a man of Wilson's intelligence would think Handy had the answers to such mysteries is a tribute to the songwriter's growing stature at the time. It also reminds us how little the intelligentsia knew about blues in the 1920s.

22. Sylvia Ann Grider, "Scarborough, Emily Dorothy (1878–1935)," *Encyclopedia of American Folklore,* Jan Harold Brunvand, ed. (New York: Garland, 1996), 651. Scar-borough was elected president of the Texas Folklore Society in 1914. She taught at Barnard College in the 1920s.

23. "In Houston during the War, Abbe had played on the piano and danced to Texas Blues—Rice Hotel Blues and Dallas Blues." Katherine Niles, "Notes on Abbe Niles and W. C. Handy," 1, Niles Papers, Watkinson, Trinity.

24. John Jacob Niles, *Singing Soldiers* (New York: Scribner's, 1927); Abbe Niles, "Real and Artificial Folk-Song" (book review), *The New Republic,* June 8, 1927, pp. 76–77.

25. Niles, "Notes to the Collection," *Blues: An Anthology,* 34.

26. Henry Levine, "Gershwin, Handy and the Blues," *Clavier,* October 1970, pp. 10–20, reproduces the inscription on the copy of *Rhapsody in Blue* given to Handy by Gershwin on August 30, 1926: "To Mr. Handy, whose early 'blue' songs are the forefathers of this work. With admiration and best wishes, George Gershwin."

27. Niles, Introduction to *Blues: An Anthology,* 1.

28. Ibid., 10.

29. Copies of three letters Handy sent Niles in January 1926 are preserved in the Niles Papers. Dated January 25 and January 26 (two letters), they are not on Handy Brothers stationery. Each has the words "*COPY* (line for line)" typed at the top. They appear to be scrupulously accurate in every detail, including spelling errors. These copies were probably made by Niles's secretary; the custom of making such exact transcripts, sometimes known in the trade as "Chinese copy," continues in corporate law to this day.

30. Abbe Niles, Foreword to *Father of the Blues,* x–xi.

31. The company was actually known as Richmond-Robbins, Inc., when Handy assigned the "Aunt Hagar's Children Blues" copyright to them in October 1922. In later years, the firm was known as Robbins, Engel, then as Robbins Music Co.

32. This passage is from one of two letters dated January 26, 1926, Niles Papers, Watkinson, Trinity, Hartford.

33. Covarrubias (1904–57) headed straight to Harlem on arriving in New York, and in short order he was one of the most fashionable artists in the city. In March 1926, the year of *Blues: An Anthology,* Covarrubias was nominated to the *Vanity Fair* Hall of Fame. In this occasional feature, the magazine printed photographs of notable figures in the arts, with capsule descriptions of their achievements. In March 1926 the other nominees were Rudyard Kipling, Arturo Toscanini, Anita Loos (author of *Gentlemen Prefer Blondes*) and the now-forgotten Spanish painter Lopez Mesquita.

34. Niles, Foreword to *Father of the Blues,* ix. The "Texan lady" failed to remark on the fact that the Boni Brothers were Jews.

35. Henry O. Osgood, review of *Blues: An Anthology, Modern Music* 4/1 (November–December 1926): 25–28. Osgood accepted the idea that Handy had single-handedly fathered the blues, a popular notion among those whose knowledge of the subject derived entirely from Handy and Niles. Osgood's 1926 book *So This Is Jazz* was largely an appreciation of the Paul Whiteman organization, but included a short chapter on Handy. On the whole, Osgood did not think much of black music and musicians.

36. James Weldon Johnson, "Now We Have the Blues" (review of *Blues: An Anthology*), *Amsterdam News,* July 7, 1926. Reprinted in *Selected Writings of James Weldon Johnson,* Sondra K. Wilson, ed. (New York: Oxford University Press, 1995), 2:388–91.

37. Langston Hughes, review of *Blues: An Anthology, Opportunity,* August 1926, p. 259.

38. Niles never used the accent on his first name. "Abbe" was Niles's middle name, and his mother's maiden name. Her brother, James Abbe, was a successful fashion and portrait photographer of the 1920s, and his work appeared regularly in *Vanity Fair.* The erring accent has turned up regularly over the last seven decades, in some of the best sources, and the error was even made by people who actually knew Niles.

39. Edmund Wilson, "Shanty-Boy Ballads and Blues," *The New Republic,* July 14, 1926, p. 228.

40. The Coon-Sanders version of "St. Louis Blues" is not listed in Brian Rust, *Jazz Records, 1897–1942,* 4th ed. (New Rochelle, N.Y.: Arlington House, 1978). Possibly Niles transcribed these lyrics from the radio. Coon-Sanders was a white dance band that enjoyed a following around 1930. Niles favorably reviewed some of their records in his "Ballads, Songs and Snatches" column, *The Bookman,* June 1928, p. 422.

41. "*A song of String-beans*," handwritten annotation by Abbe Niles in his presentation copy of *Blues: An Anthology,* Niles Papers, Watkinson, Trinity. The career of vaudevillian Butler "String Beans" May (1894–1917) was first discussed in Lynn Abbott and Doug Seroff, "'They Cert'ly Sound Good to Me': Sheet Music, Southern Vaudeville, and the Commercial Ascendancy of the Blues," *American Music* 14, no. 4 (Winter 1996): 435–37; reprinted as Chapter 2. Abbott and Seroff quote the version of the Titanic lyrics that Niles reproduced in *The Bookman.*

42. Abbe Niles, "Ballads, Songs and Snatches," *The Bookman,* May 1928, pp. 290–91.

43. *Father of the Blues,* 177; Sylvester Russell, "Chicago Weekly Review," *The Freeman,* June 1, 1918, p. 5; Certificate of Incorporation of Pace & Handy Music Company, New York, July 10, 1918.

44. *Chicago Defender,* March 22, 1924, p. 6; Handy, letter to Carl Van Vechten, August 20, 1941, James Weldon Johnson Papers, Beinecke Rare Book and Manuscript Library, Yale University. In 1941, Handy visited Pittsburgh, Cleveland, and Detroit, as well as Chicago, in a caravan that included Eubie Blake and Andy Razaf, promoting their patriotic "race" song "We Are Americans Too" (a Handy publication), and Handy's autobiography.

45. Rozelle Claxton, telephone interview by author, November 3, 1994. Handy was appearing with the Clarence Davis Band in Memphis at the time. He particularly wanted these young musicians to hear Earl Hines and his orchestra.

46. Abbe Niles, handwritten annotation in his presentation copy of *Blues: An Anthology,* 23.

47. "Sweetie May" appearing with "Klein's Jass Girls," was described as a "dainty, versatile soubrette," *The Freeman,* December 1, 1917, p. 5. The "four Jazz Girls, headed by Billy Young and Sweetie May," were still active the following year, *The Freeman,* August 17, 1918, p. 6.

48. "Wall Street Blues," music by W. C. Handy, words by Margaret Gregory and others, was published by Handy Brothers on November 30, 1929. It is difficult to imagine many people finding this song amusing in the early months of 1930.

49. See Abbott and Seroff, "'They Certl'y Sound Good To Me,'" pp. 72–73, this volume, quoting an anonymous article, "Gave the Go to the Blues Idea—A Distinct Musical Creation, Which Has Won High Favor," in *The Freeman,* December 22, 1917.

50. George Washington Lee, *Beale Street Where the Blues Began* (New York: Robert O. Ballou, 1934). Lee's book was a national success, even a Book-of-the-Month-Club selection.

51. In interviews as late as the 1950s Handy used expressions such as "I decided to fight it out" in recalling his response to repeated adversity. Handy described the autobiography's origins, and the original "Fight It Out" title, in his Author's Acknowledgments to *Father of the Blues,* xiii. More tellingly, the phrase can be found on page 203 of the book, in Handy's description of his greatest challenge, the business and personal reverses of the early 1920s.

52. Johnson's reference is to the rags-to-riches stories of Horatio Alger (1832–99), author of over 120 works of popular fiction. James Weldon Johnson knew Handy fairly well, but less well than his brother did. In fact the Alger model of achievement must have been part of Handy's cultural background, and the "Fight It Out" motto suited both him and his book.

53. James Weldon Johnson, letter to W. C. Handy, March 15, 1935, James Weldon Johnson Papers, Beinecke Rare Book Library, Yale University.

54. W. C. Handy, letter to James Weldon Johnson, March 19, 1935, Johnson Papers, Beinecke, Yale.

55. Tom Fletcher's *100 Years of the Negro in Show Business* (New York: Burdge, 1954) is the other great memoir to deal extensively with late-stage minstrelsy and other aspects of this era. Fletcher's memoir resembles Handy's in its frequent maddening imprecision and elision, and also contains more errors than Handy's.

56. W. O. Smith, *Sideman* (Nashville: Rutledge Hill Press, 1991), 111.

57. W. C. Handy, *Father of the Blues,* typescript, with annotation by Arna Bontemps, James Weldon Johnson Papers, Beinecke Rare Book Library, Yale University.

58. The oldest known manuscript of the autobiography, bearing the original title "Fight It Out," is in the W. C. Handy Home and Museum in Florence, Alabama. A slightly later typescript is in the Countee Cullen Papers, Atlanta University. Comparison of these early versions, the one at Yale and the published version, will prove highly instructive.

59. *Blues: An Anthology,* 14. It is certainly possible that Handy only later took to characterizing the "Memphis Blues" transaction as a swindle. An active commercial publisher like Theron Bennett would have purchased many songs as potential investments. Most of these would not have paid off, and it could well be that $50 was at the high end of what Bennett was willing to pay in one of these speculative deals.

60. *Blues: An Anthology* (1990 edition), 26. (The text of the modern reprint reflects the 1949 version, *A Treasury of the Blues.*)

61. Abbe Niles, "William C. Handy," *Labellum News,* November 7, 1957, p. 270, Niles Papers, Watkinson, Trinity.

62. W. C. Handy, letter to Morris E. Dry, April 1, 1942, Niles Papers, Watkinson, Trinity. This letter was clearly written at the instigation of Niles himself. Dry was among his few peers in the small fraternity of serious sheet music collectors.

63. The distinction is an important one. Handy had begun to copyright some of his songs in his own right rather than in the Company's name long before Niles came on the scene. It was useful to have two parallel sets of commercial properties, particularly in times of problems with creditors, and Niles strongly urged Handy to continue this practice.

64. Abbe Niles, "William C. Handy," *Labellum News,* 270, Niles Papers, Watkinson, Trinity.

65. Subpoenas, prosecutions, and garnishments.

66. Niles, "William C. Handy," *Labellum News,* 270, Niles Papers, Watkinson, Trinity.

67. Katherine Niles, "Notes on Abbe Niles and W.C. Handy," 2, Niles Papers, Watkinson, Trinity.

68. George Gershwin, letter to Eva Jessye, Niles Papers, Watkinson, Trinity. The letter bears no date, but the envelope survives, postmarked "Palm Beach, Feb. 8, 1935." In fairness to Gershwin, production costs were a major concern in the original production of *Porgy and Bess,* and Gershwin had to invest some of his own money

in the enterprise (Hollis Alpert, *The Life and Times of Porgy and Bess* [New York: Knopf, 1990], 98).

69. A part of Eva Jessye's correspondence is in the Leonard Axe Library, Pittsburg State University, Pittsburg, Kansas. There are no letters from Abbe Niles in this archive. The larger deposit of her papers, at the University of Michigan, Ann Arbor, has not been systematically inventoried.

70. The note is scribbled on an undated gallery announcement for Harry Botkin, a painter who was Gershwin's cousin. Niles Papers, Watkinson, Trinity. Harry Botkin's brother, Benjamin Botkin, was a leading American folklorist, and Niles had some familiarity with Botkin and his work, to judge from a letter to Niles from George Milburn, January 28, 1931 (Niles Papers, Watkinson, Trinity). Botkin somehow managed to shed no light on the blues in his one related collection, *A Treasury of Mississippi River Folklore* (New York: Crown, 1955), which, however, concludes with a twice-familiar quote from Handy. Botkin was also editor of *Folk-Say, A Regional Miscellany,* an annual that sometimes included articles Niles would have read, such as Sterling Brown's "The Blues as Folk Poetry" (*Folk-Say* 1930: 324–39). In general, however, Niles would not have cared for Botkin's work on folklore, which was not much concerned with music in any case.

71. Robert A. Simon, Judson Radio Program Corporation, letter to Abbe Niles, October 20, 1930, Niles Papers, Watkinson, Trinity; Niles, "Ballads, Songs and Snatches," *The Bookman,* October 1928, p. 215.

72. Handy, letter to Abbe Niles, January 25, 1926, Niles Papers, Watkinson, Trinity. "Song-sharks" were publishers who took fees from songwriters to publish songs that they never promoted or distributed. These con men were a common scourge in the early decades of the twentieth century.

73. Helge Thygesen, Mark Berresford and Russ Shor, *Black Swan—The Record Label of the Harlem Renaissance* (Nottingham, England: Vintage Jazz Mart Publications, 1996), is a fine introduction to Black Swan. The company was founded (as Pace Phonograph Corporation) in early 1921, and was already in production by the time its Articles of Incorporation were filed in New York on June 17 of that year. Pace's catalogue was leased to Paramount in 1924, and the property ultimately liquidated. A good earlier summary of the entire Black Swan story is a long 1939 letter written by Harry Pace, printed in Roi Ottley and William J. Weatherby, eds., *The Negro in New York* (Dobbs Ferry, N.Y.: Oceana Publications/The New York Public Library, 1967), 232–35.

74. An excellent general introduction to Harry Pace is the entry on him in John N. Ingham and Lynne B. Feldman, *African-American Business Leaders: A Biographical Dictionary* (Westport, Conn.: Greenwood, 1994), 501–17.

75. Roland Gelatt, *The Fabulous Phonograph, 1877–1977,* 3d ed. (New York: Macmillan, 1977), 210.

76. Russell Sanjek and David Sanjek, *American Popular Music Business in the 20th Century* (New York: Oxford University Press, 1991), 26.

77. The details of this situation are complicated. See Handy's description of his troubles, and his recovery from them, in *Father of the Blues,* chap. 15, "All In—Down and Out."

78. I owe this information to Handy's oldest grandchild, Minnie Handy Hanson, and to his great-granddaughter Edwina Handy Da Costa. Although Ms. Da Costa is too young to have known Handy well, she spent many hours talking with Charles Handy, the composer's much younger brother and business partner (1889–1980).

79. It is unclear how Handy participated in the January and March 1922 recordings, since he was blind at the time, apparently due to nerve damage from an infected tooth. He could hardly have conducted or played the cornet under these circumstances. Perhaps the recordings were simply issued under his name.

80. Tours of this kind were covered by the music trade press, since the record companies that promoted them had influence (often financial influence) with the magazines. In this instance see, for example, *Talking Machine World,* August 15, 1923, p. 80, and September 15, 1923, pp. 51 and 96.

81. Brian Rust, *Jazz Records, 1897–1942,* reveals a marked increase in new recordings of Handy songs in the later 1920s and 1930s.

82. Columbia went into involuntary receivership in 1921. Sanjek and Sanjek, *American Popular Music Business in the 20th Century* (New York: Oxford University Press, 1991), 20. It was years before Columbia was again competitive with Victor, which had better management and a more lucrative catalogue, including the enormously popular Caruso records, in the early 1920s.

83. Abbe Niles, Foreword to *Father of the Blues,* vi. Langston Hughes described Handy's office as resembling George S. Kaufman and Moss Hart's madcap 1936 comedy *You Can't Take It with You* in his article "Maker of the Blues," *Negro Digest,* January 1943, p. 38 (condensed from the *Chicago Defender,* November 28, 1942).

84. All Handy Brothers Music Company business matters, no matter how long ago resolved, are considered confidential by the still-extant company, run by family members. Repeated efforts to gain access to company files have been gently rebuffed. Similarly, Niles-Handy documents preserved in the vaults of Cadwalader, Wickersham, and Taft are privileged and confidential. This deprives us of vast amounts of information preserved in these two repositories. Thus, of necessity, this essay relies on the partial information available in libraries and other public sources.

85. Sheet music deposits, Watkinson Library, Trinity College, Hartford. The sheet music is not part of the Niles Papers, and Niles's deposit of music has not been kept separate from music donated by others. On the whole, it is obvious which pieces in the Watkinson music deposits are from the Niles collection. We will probably never know whether he donated any of the classical scores in the Watkinson music deposits.

86. Abbe Niles, Foreword to *Father of the Blues,* v.

87. Robert Johnson, "Who Owns Noted 'Memphis Blues'? W. C. Handy Faces Legal Fight," *Memphis Press-Scimitar,* July 1, 1949. Clipping in Mississippi Valley Collection, University of Memphis.

88. Handy Brothers Music Co. form letter, headed "Dear Friends: SUBJECT: 'MEMPHIS BLUES' GEO. A. NORTON VERSION," May 29, 1953. These "Dear Friends" messages, essentially press releases, were sent to journalists and others friendly to Handy in the later years of his life. Carl Van Vechten Papers, Beinecke Rare Book and Manuscript Library, Yale University.

89. W. C. Handy, letter to Abbe Niles, "Tuesday" [sic] January 26, 1926, Niles Papers, Watkinson, Trinity. This is the shorter of two letters of this date. Reference has been made to the longer letter above.

90. An image the size of Handy's cannot be constructed by two men working alone. Handy's legend expanded considerably in the 1930s and 1940s, when his personal appearances at events like the dedication of Handy Park in Memphis (1931) garnered increased national attention. For an example of the periodic coverage of Handy's frequent returns to Memphis in the 1930s, see *Time*, May 25, 1936, pp. 54–55.

91. Jelly Roll Morton, "Handy Not Father of Blues, Says Jelly Roll," *Baltimore Afro-American*, April 23, 1938; Morton, "I Created Jazz in 1902, Not W. C. Handy," *Down Beat*, August and September 1938; W. C. Handy, "I Would Not Play Jazz If I Could," *Down Beat*, September 1938. The latter two reprinted in *Down Beat: 60 Years of Jazz*, ed. Frank Alkyer (Milwaukee: Hal Leonard Publications, 1995), pp. 35–37.

92. Morton, "I Created Jazz in 1902, Not W. C. Handy," *Down Beat: 60 Years of Jazz*, 35–36.

93. Handy himself collected and disseminated examples from the following sources: *Sacramento Record-Union*, March 1, 1897; *Rockford, Ill., Republic*, June 25, 1899; *Havana Journal*, [January?] 1900; and *Florence, Ala., Herald*, March 8, 1900. Admittedly, the last of these was Handy's hometown paper. For examples of similar praise in *The Freeman* in the same years, see Abbott and Seroff, "They Certl'y Sound Good to Me," Chapter 2, pp. 71–72, this volume.

94. This and Morton's other quote above both from "I Created Jazz in 1902, Not W. C. Handy," *Down Beat: 60 Years of Jazz*, 35.

95. Handy's (undated) autograph concert band parts for "The Basement Blues," a 1924 composition, are in the James Weldon Johnson Collection (VMS H19 B2), Beinecke Rare Book and Manuscript Library, Yale University. Handy gave this set of parts to Carl Van Vechten for the Johnson collection in 1942. Van Vechten took charge of compiling the archive as a memorial to Johnson, and solicited manuscripts from a number of significant figures.

96. To summarize the controversy over "The Memphis Blues": Jelly Roll Morton claimed that Handy got each of the three strains of the piece from other composers, and named the three, himself included as composer of the second strain and "assembler" of the tune. Abbott and Seroff, in their article reprinted in this collection, suggest that Handy may have stolen "The Memphis Blues" from vaudevillians Willie and Lulu Too Sweet. However, it has long been asserted by fans of country blues that "Mr. Crump," the source (more properly *a* source) of "The Memphis Blues,"

originated with Memphis street singer Frank Stokes, who recorded a version of the song in 1927. We can hardly credit all of these claims.

97. Niles, "Notes to the Collection," *Blues: An Anthology,* 31–32.

98. Handy, "I Would Not Play Jazz If I Could," *Down Beat: 60 Years of Jazz,* 37.

99. Lawrence Gushee, "A Preliminary Chronology of the Early Career of Jelly Roll Morton," *American Music* 3, no. 4 (Winter 1985): 389–412. Gushee reveals that Morton was untruthful about his name, his family background, and his age. This last inaccuracy is important, since it means that Morton claimed to have invented jazz when he was twelve years old. Morton was slow to publish and copyright his works, instead electing to protect his (pianistic) trade secrets from potential rivals. The result, predictably, was that he never realized the financial rewards of his considerable work as a composer. By the late 1930s, the sight of a competitor like Handy reaping both royalties and a steady stream of positive press was too much for Morton to bear in silence. His attack on Handy was a cry of pain, the outburst of a passé entertainer confronted with the spectacle of a still-more passé rival celebrated as a charming anachronism.

100. Alan Lomax, *Mister Jelly Roll* (New York: Duell, Sloan and Pearce, 1950), 236–38.

101. Duell, Sloan and Pearce Memorandum, February 28, 1951, Niles Papers, Watkinson, Trinity.

102. Obviously, whatever Niles knew about Guy Williams must have come from Handy.

103. Abbe Niles, letter to George Malcolm-Smith, February 26, 1953, Niles Papers, Watkinson, Trinity.

104. Abbe Niles, "Oriental Mystery" (review of *A Passage to India* by E. M. Forster), *The Independent,* August 31, 1924, p. 134.

105. Irving Berlin, letter to Abbe Niles, December 21, 1925, Niles Papers, Watkinson, Trinity; Niles, unpublished one-page autobiographical sketch, mid-late 1920s, Niles Papers, Watkinson, Trinity.

106. Newman White, "The White Man in the Woodpile: Some Influences on Negro Secular Folk-Songs," *American Speech,* 4 (October 1928–August 1929): 207–15.

107. Abbe Niles, "Rediscovering the Spirituals," *The Nation,* December 1, 1926, pp. 598–99.

108. Ibid.

109. Abbe Niles, "The Literature of Folk-Song," *The Bookman,* January 1929, p. 709.

110. Howard Odum and Guy Johnson, *Negro Workaday Songs* (Chapel Hill: University of North Carolina Press, 1926).

111. Abbe Niles, "Aunt Hagar's Children" (book review), *The New Republic,* September 29, 1926, pp. 162–63.

112. Carl Sandburg, *The American Song Bag* (New York: Harcourt, Brace & World, 1927); Abbe Niles, "Sandburg's Reliques" (review of *The American Song Bag*), *The*

New Republic, March 21, 1928, p. 170. Niles was unperturbed by Sandburg's inadequate commentary.

113. Abbe Niles, "Ballads, Songs and Snatches," *The Bookman,* February 1928, p. 652; Carl Sandburg, letters to Abbe Niles, November 20, 1929, April 5, 1930, and April 27, 1940, Niles Papers, Watkinson, Trinity, Hartford.

114. An excerpt from this definition was reprinted in James Lincoln Collier, *Jazz: The American Theme Song* (New York: Oxford, 1993), 227, a sign that Niles's seminal work as a blues and jazz critic is finally on the verge of more general recognition.

115. Abbe Niles, "Blue Notes," *The New Republic,* February 3, 1926, p. 292. Niles also remembered to thank W. C. Handy, in a footnote to this article, for all the help he had given him with blues information.

116. Langston Hughes, "Jazz Band in a Parisian Cabaret" (excerpt), *Fine Clothes to the Jew* (New York: Knopf, 1927), 74. Hughes's book was divided into subsections, one entitled "Beale Street Love."

117. Abbe Niles, "Real and Artificial Folk-Song" (review of Carl Van Vechten's *Nigger Heaven* as well as Hughes's second collection), *The New Republic,* June 8, 1927, p. 77.

118. James H. Cone, in *The Spirituals and the Blues: An Interpretation* (New York: Seabury Press, 1972), discusses, from a theologian's vantage point, the individual's sense of self in black music. After more than a quarter century, this book remains unsurpassed. Albert Murray, *Stomping the Blues* (New York: McGraw-Hill, 1976), is, in general, a corrective to the cliché image of blues as monotonously doleful and lugubrious. An earlier article that contributed to understanding of meaning in the blues is Sterling Brown, "The Blues as Folk Poetry," 1930 (cited above; see note 70).

119. There are always exceptions. The house of De Sylva, Brown and Henderson was so formidable in the production of hits at this time that they needed no help from anyone. Their sales manager crisply informed Niles that they would send him some, but not all, of their new issues automatically, and that he should occasionally send them a postcard to remind them. D. M. Winkler, sales manager, De Sylva, Brown and Henderson, Inc., letter to Abbe Niles, October 22, 1928, Niles Papers, Watkinson, Trinity.

120. Samuel Charters, in the one previous article on Abbe Niles, noted the rapid exhaustion of Niles's energies during 1928: "By September he was beginning to sound a little harassed. The flood of Christmas releases and special publications finished him off." Charters, "Abbe Niles, a Pioneer Jazz Critic of the 1920s," *Jazz Review,* May 1959, p. 25.

121. Abbe Niles, "Ballads, Songs and Snatches," *The Bookman,* February 1928, p. 653.

122. Abbe Niles, "Ballads, Songs and Snatches," *The Bookman,* March 1928, p. 68.

123. Abbe Niles, "Ballads, Songs and Snatches," *The Bookman,* November 1928, p. 328. This is an early use of the "Father of the Blues" moniker, although there were earlier ones. Both Williams sides reissued on "Clarence Williams 1927–1928," Classics CD 752 (1994).

124. Abbe Niles, "Ballads, Songs and Snatches," *The Bookman,* August 1928, p. 689.

125. Jim Jackson, "Old Dog Blue," Victor 21387A (February 2, 1928), and Cannon's Jug Stompers, "Minglewood Blues," Victor 21267A (January 30, 1928), both reissued on the *Anthology of American Folk Music,* Folkways, 1952. Reissued on compact disc by Smithsonian Folkways, 1997. Niles, "Ballads, Songs and Snatches," *The Bookman,* October 1928, p. 214 (Jim Jackson review); and both August 1928, p. 688, and January 1929, p. 572 (two mentions of Cannon's Jug Stompers). Readers with an interest in white country music can test Niles's endorsements of records by Buell Kazee, Bascom Lamar Lunsford, and other artists against the corresponding selections in the Folkways Anthology as well.

126. Abbe Niles, "Ballads, Songs and Snatches," *The Bookman,* November 1928, p. 329.

127. Handy, *Father of the Blues,* 196–97.

128. Abbe Niles, "Ballads, Songs and Snatches," *The Bookman,* June 1928, p. 423. (The "r" in such record abbreviations stands for "race record.") Niles tended to prefer Al Jolson to Al Bernard. Today's jazz and blues fan would probably reverse his judgment, but aesthetics also change over seven decades.

129. W. C. Handy, letter to Katharine Handy Lewis, April 19, 1955, including copy of letter to Handy from Gertrude Bernard, April 18, 1955, with handwritten annotation by Katharine Handy Lewis. Katharine Handy Lewis Papers, Schomburg Center for Research in Black Culture, New York Public Library. Office correspondence of this type was a common way for Handy Brothers business to be conducted, especially during the later years of Handy's life.

130. Abbe Niles, "Ballads, Songs and Snatches," *The Bookman,* June 1928, p. 423.

131. Abbe Niles, "Ballads, Songs and Snatches," *The Bookman,* October 1928, p. 214.

132. Abbe Niles, "Ballads, Songs and Snatches," *The Bookman,* January 1929, pp. 570–71.

133. Walter B. Pitkin, Editorial Department, *Encyclopaedia Britannica,* letters to Abbe Niles, February 16 and 18, 1928, Niles Papers, Watkinson, Trinity.

134. William H. Turner Jr., Editorial Department, *Encyclopaedia Britannica,* letter to Abbe Niles, November 22, 1928, Niles Papers, Watkinson, Trinity.

135. Neither would be considered a textbook example of blues today, but the perspective of the 1920s and that of the present differ considerably.

136. Reid Badger, *A Life in Ragtime: A Biography of James Reese Europe* (New York: Oxford, 1995), 115.

137. Abbe Niles, "Jazz," *Encyclopaedia Britannica,* 14th ed. (1929), 12:983.

138. Irving Berlin, letter to Abbe Niles, December 21, 1925, Niles Papers, Watkinson, Trinity.

139. Ruth Barr, letter to Abbe Niles, on *Bookman* stationery, December 6, 1928, Niles Papers, Watkinson, Trinity. Barr also offered to do any odd jobs she could to assist Niles with his work on the "Ballads, Songs and Snatches" column, but her offer came too late.

140. Mrs. Georgia Loveland Noonan, letter to Abbe Niles, February 2[?o], 1932, Niles Papers, Watkinson, Trinity. Mrs. Noonan wrote from Corona del Mar, California. Punctuation retained from the original.

141. Paul Carter, letter to Abbe Niles, n.d., Niles Papers, Watkinson, Trinity. Carter, a veteran of black vaudeville, was mentioned frequently in the entertainment columns of *The Freeman* in the World War I era. Bessie Smith's recording of "Weeping Willow Blues" (Columbia 14042-D, September 26, 1924) shows the song in its best light. However, it is possible that Carter's letter refers to another song entirely.

142. Two pages of legal notes in Abbe Niles's hand, correspondence involving Frankie Baker, Handy, Niles and others, and several newspaper clippings, were offered for sale by Argosy Books, New York, in their Catalogue 817, 1997. The proprietors offered to throw in John Huston's early book *Frankie and Johnny,* inscribed to Niles, but the price was beyond this author's budget. However, a perusal of Niles's notes revealed his serious attempts to find a plausible legal tack and the names and phone numbers of several colleagues he probably called for consultations.

4

The Hands of
Blues Guitarists

ANDREW M. COHEN

In this paper I contend that there was regional clustering to the ways that African American folk and blues guitar players from the early part of the twentieth century held their picking hands and that these postures facilitated certain musical patterns while inhibiting others. The player's picking hand posture therefore serves as an important determinant of the elusive quality called "style." If there is such a thing as regional style, we should see it expressed in visual images showing how different players held their hands, even as we hear it expressed on their recordings.

The Sample

I constructed a sample based on recordings, visual images (photographs and videos), personal observation, and biographical data. The ninety-four black guitar players in this sample are listed with information on their birth year, the place where they learned the guitar, their typical hand position, and their approach to keeping time. In all but one case timekeeping was done with the right thumb on the bass strings of the guitar. A list of the players, along with the relevant information about them, appears in Appendix Table 4.7 below. Statistics (mainly percentages) and tables drawn from these data will appear as I go along.

My sample includes four women, one of whom (Elizabeth Cotten) played the guitar left-handed and upside down. It includes eleven blind men. At least five nonstandard tunings were used. Some players typically played with a slide, some did so rarely, and some never did. Eight National steel guitars

Table 4.1. Distribution of players in the
sample by state.

State	Number of players
Alabama	3
Arkansas	2
Delaware	1
Florida	1
Georgia	10
Illinois	2
Indiana	1
Kentucky	2
Louisiana	3
Mississippi	28
North Carolina	7
Oklahoma	1
South Carolina	7
Tennessee	8
Texas	10
Virginia	7
West Virginia	1
Total	94

(a metal-body guitar with a thin metal resonator inside) plus one wooden Regal guitar with a metal resonator were used, along with a nine-string guitar and a half-dozen twelve-string guitars tuned to several different pitches. Most played one or another version of a six-string guitar, for the most part wooden flattop models. Of the players who survived into the 1960s and beyond, most adopted electric guitars when they could. Most of the guitars cost their owners very little, and many were not very good instruments. Hand positions show consistent patterning through all this.

The sample is not random in any valid statistical sense, but it is broad. Its geographic spread covers the South, thinly in some places and more thickly in others. Table 4.1 shows the distribution of the players by state. The largest number of players are from Mississippi. Adding Alabama, western Tennessee, eastern Arkansas, Louisiana, and Texas, along with some outlier states that were the targets of migrants from this region (Oklahoma, Illinois, Indiana, Kentucky), brings the total to fifty-eight. I call this the "Deep South" region. Although this region divides into two subregions, it is stylistically quite distinct from the East.

Thirty-six examples make up the "Eastern" region (Florida, Georgia, South Carolina, North Carolina, eastern Tennessee, Virginia, West Virginia, Maryland, and Delaware). The sample breaks in Tennessee and Georgia. Players from eastern Tennessee seem to have played Deep South blues with Eastern technique, judging by how they held their hands and their general instrumental agility. Many of the players associated with Atlanta came from elsewhere. I include them in the Eastern part of the sample even though their influences seem mixed. Styles and hand positions for outliers universally correspond to their respective hearth areas.

The word *style* clouds discussion whenever it comes up. One may speak variously of a regional style (analogous to a dialect), a local style (analogous to a patois), or a personal style (analogous to an idiolect). Understanding is impeded when the term is applied to a genre ("blues style") or a format ("string-band style"). In this paper I use the word only to discuss how a player used his or her thumb to keep time, establish rhythm, and articulate bass notes. This allows me to talk about guitar players in general rather than blues or gospel players, songsters, or country-dance musicians, since those roles often overlapped within the same person. Many of the players were exclusively blues performers, but some were not. What seems to be regional, and to vary over time, is whether the bass line alternates between two or more bass strings or involves the continuous or intermittent striking of either single bass strings or adjacent clusters of strings. There are refinements to each approach, of course, and some of those are regional.

Each entry in my database lists the player's name (or a moniker), place of learning, birth year, observable hand posture, and a judgment as to playing style. The players' birth years range from 1874 to 1940. Their initial learning years can be estimated, when not actually known, as being on the average seven to ten years from their birth.

Some of the entries in my working database (118 entries) were incomplete to one degree or another. I could relate what personal and musical data there were to the rest of the sample, but visual images were lacking or useless for some of the players, especially the earliest ones. In some cases (for example, Simmie Dooley), there were no pictures at all. In other cases (for example, Charley Patton and Papa Charlie Jackson), the single known picture did not show the person playing. The birthdates of most of the unusable entries fell before the turn of the twentieth century.

The individuals in the sample were all "fingerpickers." All but a few used the right thumb to play bass notes, while the right index finger responded in some way with treble notes. Of the guitarists who differed from that description, a few used more than one finger to play the treble line, and one (Elizabeth Cotten) played left-handed and with the guitar turned upside down, so that her index finger and thumb switched roles. (It should be noted that although some "right-side-up" players do use the thumb to play high notes, fingers are almost never used to play bass notes except for thumb-finger runs.)

Those who have best explicated black folk and blues guitar styles tend to emphasize individual genius over regionality.[1] Through the data from my sample I will show that individual genius rests on a bed of regional style.

Blues Stylistic Regions

In earlier literature about the blues, two amorphous regions were proposed as stylistic fountainheads, the "Piedmont" and the "Delta" (my "Deep South"). A third region, "Texas" (or, more properly, "East Texas"), is often suggested as a subregion of the Delta or as a separate hearth area.[2] Although there is nothing drastically wrong with the earlier formulations, they are unsupported by anything other than the authors' own (admittedly informed) opinions. These researchers did not attempt to establish precise geographical boundaries or detailed stylistic hallmarks of the different regions. There was also no attempt to account for development within the regions or interaction between them over time. I hope that the descriptive terms I offer here will help investigators to reconstruct at least the outlines of past musical activity.

If we posit that at any given time blues regions were stylistically (and posturally) separate, then an empirical assessment of players' performance techniques and their peak years of performance should more finely draw boundaries around those regions. For now I define the regions as follows:

1. Eastern: I use this word as the equivalent of the more commonly used "Piedmont," the rolling detrital hills that constitute tobacco country south and east of the Appalachians. We can expect black folk-blues guitarists from Delaware to Florida, east of a line connecting Knoxville and Atlanta and extending north and south from there, to extend their right thumbs when they play, and most of them play bass strings with an alternating thumb. A large majority of the black guitar players in the region play with their thumbs extended, as do most white guitarists in the region. The central part of this region—the Virginias and the Carolinas—is the part of the country where blacks and whites have lived side by side the longest. This fact may also help to explain why there is relatively more shared textual material in this tobacco country than in cotton country.[3] If white players such as Sam McGee, Merle

Travis, and Ike Everly were included in the sample, the hills of Tennessee and Kentucky would extend the Eastern approach to music. In fact, black musicians also inhabit those hills: Bill Williams was from Greenup, Kentucky; Elvie Johnson was from Bowling Green, Kentucky; and Howard Armstrong learned not far from Cumberland Gap.

2. Delta: The so-called Delta is not a delta at all but the lush swampy land, cleared of woods in the last century and a half, between the Yazoo and Mississippi rivers from Memphis to Vicksburg. Not to be confused with the delta at the mouth of the Mississippi River below New Orleans, this patch of land is a part, but not all, of the hearth area of Mississippi's blues culture. As a stylistic region the Delta is much larger, encompassing the states of Mississippi and Alabama and extending to eastern Arkansas, western Tennessee, and northeastern Louisiana. In this region thumb use shows little overt patterning; instead, thumbed notes are struck as needed within melodic guitar figures. I call this "utility-thumb" playing.

3. Texas: Another stylistic area can be identified between (roughly) Houston and Dallas and over to Texarkana, Texas, and Shreveport, Louisiana. This area gave rise to players such as Leadbelly (Huddie Ledbetter), Blind Lemon Jefferson, Blind Willie Johnson, Mance Lipscomb, and Black Ace before World War II, and Lightnin' Hopkins, Juke Boy Bonner, and Lil' Son Jackson later on. With the exception of work by Jefferson, who was a true intuitive virtuoso, and some of Blind Willie Johnson's sacred material, most of what the Texas and northwestern Louisiana players do melodically (that is, on the treble side of the guitar) they do in conjunction with a "dead thumb," playing four beats to the measure on the same string.

Hand Postures

At this point I would like to offer definitions of hand postures, using my own terminology and providing illustrations and some preliminary explication of how these positions limit or facilitate playing in one style or another. It should be noted that these positions are points on a continuum and that the players' hands are anything but static. The terms refer to the relative positions of thumb and index finger at the start of the picking cycle, called here the "mean recovery posture."

The pad of muscle at the base of the thumb actually comprises three different muscles: an abductor, an extensor, and an adductor. Thus, in relation to the middle of the hand, the thumb may be abducted (away from the palm, as one holds a tumbler), extended (as if one played a tenth on the piano), or adducted (as when touching thumb and fifth fingertip); or it can sit somewhere inside the triangle bounded by these extreme points.

1. Extended (abbreviated *e* in the tables and appendixes): At full extension, the thumb's metacarpal (that is, the longish bone that anchors the muscles) is extended at the wrist in such a way that the raised short and long extensor tendons outline a little pocket of skin that *Grant's Anatomy* calls the "anatomical snuff box."[4] The index finger is positioned on one of the treble strings at a ninety-degree angle; if flexed slightly, the index finger would be drawn across it. The finger sits far enough toward the guitar's bridge from the thumb so that they would not touch even if either of them swept across all six strings (see Fig. 4.1). In Eastern style playing the thumb's mean recovery posture starts at or near full extension, and bass notes are "pushed" into existence.

The foregoing presumes no muscular tension, proper hang and positioning of the guitar, and no injuries or anomalous interferences. None of this can be expected to occur all the time, of course, but in practice most (all but eight) Eastern players of whom I know or have seen photographs or videos show an extended thumb and plenty of clearance for their index finger at mean recovery, ready to begin a picking cycle.

2. Stacked (abbreviated *s* in the tables and appendixes): In the stacked position the index finger sits directly below the thumb, such that if a straightedge were held against the tips of the two digits, it would cross the strings at a ninety-degree angle. Put differently, the thumb and finger cannot pass each other, but the finger can get out of the way by pulling sideways across the string instead of pulling more or less straight up. This is how Furry Lewis managed his "alternating thumb" style (Fig. 4.2).

Some players cock their wrist and some do not. Those who do this exaggerate the extension of the thumb. Those who do not (for example, Furry Lewis) tend to start the cycle with their thumb and fingertip in opposition ("stacked"), whatever their intention. Cocking the wrist (that is, placing it in "ulnar deviation") involves another muscle, flexor carpi ulnaris, the action of which pulls the body of the hand away from the thumb.

3. Lutiform (abbreviated *l* in the tables and appendixes): In the lutiform position the index finger projects toward the player's left, beyond the thumb, as a lute player's would. To sound the strings the index finger has to sweep sideways across them or pull toward the palm at a steep angle. Because the thumb is already adducted, playing melodic figures against an alternating thumb from this position is nearly impossible, and playing a melodic figure on one string with both thumb and finger is slightly harder than that (Fig. 4.3).

Fig. 4.1. Mrs. Etta Baker, of Morganton, North Carolina, shown playing with her thumb extended. Photo by Dale Galgozy.

Guitar players play different ways at different times, and not everybody looks the same in action as when posing. John Jackson was probably the most agile Eastern-style player in recent years. I had a chance to watch him play from up close and can aver that his typical hand position was lutiform. I have several different pictures and videos of him showing him playing

Fig. 4.2. Furry Lewis, of Memphis, Tennessee, shown playing with his thumb stacked directly over his index finger. Photo by David Evans.

with a lutiform playing position, although a publicity photo clearly shows his index finger tucked behind his thumb at mean recovery.

Most players in the sample were represented by photographs, videos, personal observation (I have met and played with about a third of them over the past forty years), or some combination of these. Even if the player is

Fig. 4.3. Robert "Pete" Williams, of Scotlandville, Louisiana, playing with a lutiform hand posture; note the hyperextensible "hitchhiker" thumb. Photo by Marina Bokelman.

visually well represented, however, images still may be ambiguous. One case that comes to mind is that of Blind Willie McTell, shown in four different pictures playing three different ways on four different twelve-string guitars. No films of him exist, and no one now participating in blues scholarship ever saw him play.

People may play more than one kind of stroke, which would occasion changing positions back and forth. Jim Brewer, for instance, used to make his lead lines sparkle by using what classical guitarists call a "rest" stroke (that is, the picking finger comes to rest on the next adjacent string) in addition to the more common "free" stroke, where the picking finger comes free of the strings. Using the rest stroke entails rolling the wrist out, straightening the index finger out "through" the string, and either recovering and repeating or repositioning the hand for free strokes.

The lone picture of Blind Lemon Jefferson shows his thumb extended, the ulnar edge of his hand resting on the bridge, the guitar sitting more or less flat on his lap. On his records it sounds as if he availed himself of a range of techniques so broad as to encompass most of what is found elsewhere.

Despite all these problematic cases, I believe that when they pose for a photograph, people set their hands exactly as they usually do to play and that the pictures of them posing tend to show their hands at or near mean recovery, ready to begin a picking cycle.

Of course assessing whether a person always holds to this or that position is chancy, especially if there is only one extant photograph. To test whether my judgments of hand positions were correct, I asked Dr. C. Owen Lovejoy to look at a group of photographs. Lovejoy is not a blues scholar; rather, he is the human anatomist who established that "Lucy," the famous proto-human fossil, had been an upright, bipedal, humanlike walker.[5] He is also an avocational guitarist of some skill. I asked him to look at all the pictures of people playing guitar in one of my sources, the book *Nothing but the Blues*. Boris Basiuk, a friend from Toronto who is himself a guitarist and transcriber of blues songs, tabulated Lovejoy's judgments, and I then scored the same photographs. Dr. Lovejoy and I each looked at the same fifty-two pictures; our assessments compared as follows: twenty-five were in complete accord; eleven differed by my making them compound rather than categorical positions (for example, "*s/e*" instead of "*s*"); twelve were one position apart (on the continuum *e-s-l*); and four were two positions apart. If we had looked at the pictures together, the results would likely have been much closer.

There is a potential confound concerning the presence or absence of a hyperextensible, or "hitchhiker's," thumb. Geneticist Michael R. Cummings states that this is an autosomal recessive trait,[6] which means that both the mother and the father must carry the gene for the offspring to be affected, although the trait will not appear if the offspring receives only one such gene. Predicted frequency is one in four in the population at large, and it is a little more than that in my sample: in the sample the trait appeared in twenty-seven of eighty-nine cases, or a little more than 30 percent. Five cases were visually ambiguous.

Because the trait was distributed over the whole study area, my confidence in the fairness, if not the randomness, of the data was increased. Three pairs of brothers had it (the Trices, the McGhees, and the Fodrells); one pair (the McCoys) lacked it. One pair (the Hickses) is uncertain: there are pictures of Barbecue Bob Hicks, who lacks it, but the only one of his brother Charlie is a prison mug shot.

Having neutralized that potential spoiler, I can examine what the relationship is between hand position and picking style, by region and over time.

Thumbing Patterns and Regional Styles

Whether small changes in playing posture result in changes in playing style or regional preferences for a particular rhythmic background ultimately result in regional postural differences is a chicken-and-egg sort of question. Whichever is the case there are systematic differences both in posture and style (taken as a function of timekeeping) between the Deep South and the Eastern players.

The classic Eastern alternating bass consists of four thumb strokes per measure alternating between a low and a high bass string. Melodies, usually played with the index (and occasionally also the middle) finger, fall between or together with the thumb notes, so that a kind of counterpoint is established. The thumb notes form a regular rhythmic and harmonic backdrop against which the melody can syncopate. In addition, as Table 4.3 indicates, there is a strong association between the use of an alternating thumb and the "extended" hand posture. Example 4.1 shows a typical alternating bass both in standard notation and in guitar tablature. In the tablature the horizontal lines represent strings (the highest line representing the highest-pitched string, etc.), and the numbers on the notes indicate frets on which the strings are pressed. A zero indicates a struck open string. Upward stems indicate fingered notes, and downward stems indicate thumbed notes.

There are several patterns that sound like this alternating bass but are nevertheless distinct from it. One could be called the "slow alternating bass," because in 4/4 time the first low bass note is struck as before but is allowed to ring an extra beat, whereupon the higher bass note (octave or fifth) is struck and allowed to ring (Ex. 4.2). This strategy of playing only the first and third beats allows the thumb time to find a way around an index finger often in its way. Skip James's "Hard Time Killin' Floor Blues" (Paramount 13065, 1931) is constructed in this manner. In the style field of the database I call this "sab," for slow alternating bass.

Yet another sound-alike is the t-1 run, in which the thumb and index finger alternate momentarily to play short scalar sequences up and down single strings. The thumb and index finger work together like a plectrum. This

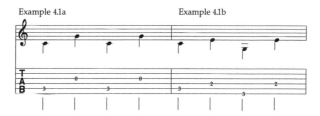

Ex. 4.1a and b. Typical two-string and three-string alternating bass patterns.

Example 4.2

Ex. 4.2. Slow alternating bass (guitar in open E minor tuning), from Skip James, "Hard Time Killin' Floor Blues" (Paramount 13065, 1931).

technique produces a distinctive sound, because normally the thumbed note rings and the fingered note is staccato. Much more common in the East than in the Deep South, the technique requires the picking thumb and finger to be in the extended posture. The musical example here is from (South Carolina guitarist) Reverend Gary Davis's "Get Right Church" (Riverside LP 148, 1956; Ex. 4.3).

Robert "Pete" Williams, a Louisiana bluesman, typically inserted an alternating bass as a time stroke between melodic motifs, but he seems to have bounced back and forth between this by itself and a fingered melodic motif by itself (Ex. 4.4).

The "dead-thumb" bass is the same bass note played four times in a 4/4 measure. Companion to this is a triplet shuffle, four triplets in a measure, the middle note of each triplet being silent (Ex. 4.5). This changes 4/4 time to 12/8.

Example 4.3

Ex. 4.3. T-1 run, from Reverend Gary Davis, "Get Right Church" (Riverside LP 148, 1956).

Example 4.4

Ex. 4.4. Alternating bass, from Robert "Pete" Williams, "I'm Lonesome Blues" (Folk-Lyric LPS A-3, 1959).

Utility-thumb players use the thumb intermittently on one string at a time. I invoke the notion of "utility" because the thumb is used when and where it is needed in the measure. Melodic figures are for the most part carried by the finger. Exemplary players of this kind are Honeyboy Edwards, R. L. Burnside, and Tommy Johnson. Utility-thumb players have a kind of "finger-led" approach to their music: their thumb may start or end a measure, but often it strikes only once per measure. The result is a high-note figure punctuated by a regular bass note, this pattern recurring as a riff throughout the song, whatever else is inserted in terms of bass runs or melodic figures (Ex. 4.6).

With the exception of some of the oldest known players (John Hurt, Robert Wilkins, Sam Chatmon, and Blind Lemon Jefferson, all born in the 1890s), the Delta, Memphis, Texas, St. Louis, and about half of the Atlanta players

Example 4.5a   Example 4.5b

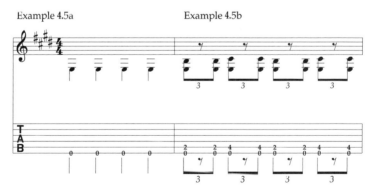

Ex. 4.5a and b. Typical dead-thumb bass and its companion, the triplet shuffle.

Example 4.6

Ex. 4.6. Utility-thumb bass (guitar in open G tuning), from R. L Burnside, "Long Haired Doney" (Arhoolie CD 402, 1967).

tended to play with their thumb and finger either vertically stacked or in the lutiform position. In either case it is difficult for the thumb to cross the finger to play melody notes or for the finger to play a bass string, because thumb and index finger share a track. Using the thumb and finger together (t-1) to play runs seems to disappear somewhere west of Cumberland Gap.

Even though there was a certain amount of variation in each area and for each time period, some clear postural clusters associate positively with regional stylistic traits. These are clear enough to establish trends through the gray areas along a gradient from extended to lutiform and along a continuum from "truly contrapuntal" to "total dead thumb." As noted, years and place of learning have much to do with how a guitarist processes and presents tunes.

I assume that position is culturally carried, preferences for one hand position over another being regionally consistent without there being explicit rules about what constitutes "proper" hand posture in one or another place. There seem to be some clear differences between Eastern and Deep South guitar players, as well as some variation between different areas of the Deep South over time.

Dead-thumb playing occurs in several variants from Atlanta to Texas. Although it was quite common among the players born after 1905, it was less frequent among players born before then, except for the Texas/Louisiana group (for example, Leadbelly and Henry Thomas). It was all but absent from Delaware to Durham and on west to about Knoxville until after World War II. Alternating thumb playing was especially characteristic of the eastern region and remains so, but it was found in such places as Texas and

Mississippi among players born before 1900. After that the use of the alternating-thumb technique dwindled, such that after birth year 1910 almost no one in either the extended Delta or Texas regions used it to organize his or her playing.

The following section lists the possibilities inherent in a guitar style based on a dead-thumb or utility-thumb technique, in contrast to one based on an alternating thumb.

1. MELODY: D/U, RARELY; A, YES

In this context the melody is the tune of the song played approximately as it is sung. Although some Deep South guitar players were interesting melodically, they tended to be rare and of the oldest generation. Normally Deep South bluesmen play a "riff," that is, a repeated figure, against a monotonic bass of some sort. Eastern guitar players tend to play more melodically against an alternating bass.

2. THUMB-CROSS RUNS: D/U, NO; A, YES

"Thumb-cross runs" (t-1) are done on the same or adjacent strings by the thumb and first finger working together, alternately. Films of Gary Davis, whose playing was based on an alternating thumb, show that he did this often; those of Big Bill Broonzy (a dead-thumb player) show that despite his otherwise excellent technique, he did not.

3. BASS RUNS: D/U, YES; A, YES

Bass runs can be done from any position by the thumb. If the hand position is "Eastern," however, with the thumb extended beyond the index finger, the thumb and finger can be used together to "walk" the notes between chords. In essence this is the thumb-cross technique. If the thumb and index finger are opposed, the whole hand must move up and down for both to strike the same string alternately.

Consider Big Bill Broonzy's technique. His "hitchhiker" thumb appears incurvate at the metacarpal joint; it is fully adducted at the end of its travel. In action the tip of his thumb sat directly over the tip of his index finger, its phalanges riding up and down on the rigid metacarpal. His fingers sat slantwise across the treble strings rather than perpendicular to them. It would have been awkward for him to play t-1 runs since his thumb was already adducted and his finger was in the way. Dead thumbers like Broonzy use their thumbs alone for bass runs.

4. SYNCOPATION: D/U, SOMETIMES; A, AUTOMATICALLY

Syncopation results from a melody's stresses being purposely offset from the regular rhythm underneath it, such that normally unstressed beats are highlighted. Dead-thumb players syncopate, but the Eastern players are famous for long syncopated passages.

5. COUNTERPOINT: D/U, NO; A, YES

Counterpoint, the setting of two discrete melodies against one another, is impossible using a monotonic bass, of course; it is just barely possible, with great control and perseverance, in Eastern-style playing. Reverend Gary Davis approached it often enough, and hints of it are found in the playing of John Hurt, Lonnie Johnson, Blind Blake, Brownie McGhee, Etta Baker, and others. True counterpoint is possible as a programmed substitution of the alternating bass line, although the "continuo" provided by a strict alternation has the virtue of supporting the played melody, harmonizing with it while not interfering, simply because it is *not* programmed but automatic.

6. CROOKED STRUCTURE: D/U, OFTEN; A, LESS OFTEN

"Crooked structure" is usually applied to fiddle tunes that for one reason or another do not fit into an even number of bars or whose phrasing is asymmetrical. Since the Eastern style of both folk music and blues is ordered by the alternating bass, it is rare to find a piece that is not "square," except for tags and 6/4 "one-and-a-half" measures separating stanza lines. "Riff" players generally do not have to be exactly on time, unlike melodic players, who must fit the end of their music to the end of a figure. Riff players can get by at a dance playing irregular numbers of bars as long as they keep a steady beat.

7. SLIP GRACE NOTES: D/U, YES; A, YES

"Slip-thumb" grace notes are what Reverend Gary Davis called "rolling the bass." These are especially obvious in Blind Blake's pieces, particularly jazzy ones such as "West Coast Blues" and "Blind Arthur's Breakdown." The "slip" occurs before a stressed downbeat, tying the last quarter- or half-beat from the measure before into the stressed downbeat. Where the notes of shortest duration are sixteenth notes, the grace note's value is a sixteenth; in a slower blues the value is, correspondingly, an eighth.

Strengths of Association

It remains for me to tabulate the players' hand positions by region, generation, and style. I recognized three areas in the first category: Eastern, Delta, and Texas, the last area including northwest Louisiana and Oklahoma. (There are three Louisiana players in the sample, but they are from the southeastern part of the state and are included in the Delta region.)

By breaking the sample at the end of 1905, we catch some of the last members of the generation of guitarists who would be considered "songsters," such as Mance Lipscomb, Leadbelly, and Charley Patton. These individuals played blues among a variety of other song forms. For those born in 1906 and after, such as Bukka White, Robert Johnson, and Blind Boy Fuller, a world of interaction and monetary gain condensed around the blues just as those individuals came of age, reinforced by commercial blues recordings beginning in 1920. These artists, whom I designate as "bluesmen," performed blues almost exclusively. Table 4.2 sorts postures by region between the two age groups, thus approximating this watershed between "songsters" and "bluesmen."

Table 4.3 sorts hand posture against what are identified here as stylistic hallmarks: alternating, utility, and dead thumbing styles. I have simplified

Table 4.2. Region sorted against hand posture.

	Region			
Hand posture	Eastern	Delta	Texas	Total
Musicians born before 1906				
Extended	8	13	3	24
Stacked	3	9	2	14
Lutiform	0	3	1	4
Total	11	25	6	42
Musicians born after 1905				
Extended	21	5	1	27
Stacked	4	10	2	16
Lutiform	1	6	2	9
Total	26	21	5	52

Table 4.3. Hand posture sorted against style.

Thumb style	Hand posture			
	Extended	Stacked	Lutiform	Total
Musicians born before 1906				
Alternating	10	3	0	13
Utility	6	3	1	10
Dead	8	8	3	19
Total	24	14	4	42
Musicians born after 1905				
Alternating	16	0	1	17
Utility	9	8	3	20
Dead	2	8	5	15
Total	27	16	9	52

the style category for clarity by dropping secondary elements in favor of the artist's predominant timekeeping approach. The Appendix Table 4.7 (below) shows more of the elements of each individual's playing style.

The strongest single association is between extended thumb position and alternating thumb style: roughly 87 percent of alternating thumb players extend their thumbs. Extended-thumb players also turn up in the ranks of dead-thumb and utility-thumb players, but the reverse is not true: few stacked or lutiform players use an alternating thumb technique, regardless of region. On the other hand, the utility- and dead-thumb players, taken together, constitute almost 91 percent of the stacked and lutiform players. Although utility-thumb use occurs in roughly a quarter to a third of all players in each position, the dead-thumb technique is especially associated with stacked and lutiform positions, occurring in about half of all such cases but in less than 20 percent of extended-thumb players.

Table 4.4 sorts region against thumbing style. I suggest the following model for the geography of blues thumbing styles: first, what I call "utility-thumb" playing was widespread in the Mississippi Delta and in adjacent parts of Arkansas, west Tennessee, and Louisiana early in the twentieth century (it seems to have crept into the eastern region with the post-1905 birth cohort, so that it shows up among those contemporaneous with Blind Boy Fuller); second, the dead-thumb technique was most common in Texas and northwestern Louisiana players, although some players from the extended Delta region used it in all time periods. Eastern players, on the other hand,

Table 4.4. Region sorted against style

Thumb style	Region			
	Eastern	Delta	Texas	Total
Musicians born before 1906				
Alternating	5	7	1	13
Dead	4	10	4	18
Utility	1	9	1	11
Total	10	26	6	42
Musicians born after 1905				
Alternating	15	2	0	17
Dead	3	8	4	15
Utility	8	11	1	20
Total	26	21	5	52

generally used an alternating bass to keep time, and they kept their thumb and index finger in a line parallel to a single string to make bass runs. These last two techniques are facilitated by the index finger being tucked back toward the bridge, out of the way of the extended thumb.

There are at least two other styles common in the extended Delta region, one older and one a development of utility-thumb playing. The older is an alternating thumb style, remarkably similar to what the Eastern players were doing, that shows up among such older players as Mississippi John Hurt, Sam Chatmon, Furry Lewis, and Robert Wilkins in both picking and postural aspects. The main difference is that in the Delta, runs on single strings using thumb and index finger in combination occurred infrequently. The younger style, present in Mississippi and parts of both Louisiana and Georgia, is shared by Jessie Mae Hemphill, John Lee Hooker, Robert "Pete" Williams, Luther "Georgia Boy" Johnson, and Robert Belfour, among others. It is a "boogie" style, droning and somewhat amorphous, that features few chord changes. Physically it is accomplished primarily through utility- and dead-thumb approaches. Although it sounds primitive (a better word is "minimalist"), it is a construct that emerged largely after World War II.

Dead thumbing is probably as old as alternate thumbing and its contrapuntal elaborations. The Texas region dead-thumb technique and the Delta region utility-thumb technique seem to have emerged around the beginning of this century along with the blues genre, as songster and minstrel material began to disappear from the repertories of black musicians in those areas.[7]

Leadbelly, born in 1888 on the Louisiana-Texas border, was a classic dead-thumb player who used his thumb alone for making bass runs. Henry Thomas, another Texan and the oldest player in the database, born in 1874, also beat the same note four times to the bar.[8]

Age Cohorts and Their Hand Positions

A cohort is in this study a group of people who were born during a particular span of years. One way to check my scheme, assuming the observations are correct in the first place, is to divide the players by birth date to see who played in what way. I divided the sample into five-year cohorts, starting with Henry Thomas (born in 1874) and ending with Robert Belfour (born in 1940), without respect to region (Table 4.5).

Table 4.5 shows a bulge in extended posture, peaking in the 1895–99 group but with its median point occurring ten years later. The jump in stacked position begins in the 1900–1904 cohort. The median point for this group occurs more or less simultaneously with that of the extended-thumb players. A steady rise of lutiform players begins in the 1895–99 group, peaking in the 1915–19 group. Positions peak and then appear to diminish ten years apart, at least in part because the sample thins out.

Table 4.5. Cohorts and hand posture.

| Cohort | Hand posture | | |
	Extended	Stacked	Lutiform
1870–74	1	0	0
1875–79	0	0	0
1880–84	0	0	0
1885–89	2	2	0
1890–94	4	2	0
1895–99	9	3	1
1900–1904	6	5	2
1905–9	7	6	1
1910–14	6	3	1
1915–19	8	2	4
1920–24	1	3	2
1925–29	3	1	1
1930–34	1	1	1
1935–39	3	1	0
1940–44	0	1	0

Table 4.6. The blind players.

Name	State	Year of Birth	Hand Posture	Style
Blind Blake*	Fla.	1893	e	a/d/cp/t-1/st
Gary Davis	S.C.	1896	e	a/t 1/cp
Blind Lemon Jefferson	Tex.	1897	e	d/u/t-1/t
Blind Willie McTell	Ga.	1898	s	d/u/t
Blind Willie Johnson*	Tex.	1902	s	d/a
Daniel K. Womack	Va.	1904	s	a/sab
Sleepy John Estes	Tenn.	1904	s	d
Blind Boy Fuller	N.C.	1908	e	a/u/cp/st
Rev. Pearly Brown	Ga.	1915	s	u/d
Jim Brewer	Miss.	1920	s	d/u
Snooks Eaglin	La.	1936	e	u/d/t-1

Legend: An asterisk after a name = date uncertain; style = most consistent timekeeping predilection; a = alternating thumb; sab = slow alternating bass; t-1 = alternation of thumb and index finger for runs; cp = counterpoint; u = utility thumb; d = dead thumb; st = slip thumb; t = runs made with thumb only.

The Blind Players

Almost as though nature were providing a control group, there are eleven blind players in the sample (Table 4.6). They are especially significant because most were already blind before they learned to play the guitar, meaning that they could not see other players and had to derive their styles and hand positions from the *sound* of the music they wanted to play. This was normally the music of their community and region. Their thumb positions and playing patterns are for the most part consistent with their times and regions. The most anomalous case is Snooks Eaglin, a versatile guitarist from New Orleans greatly influenced by jazz and commercial rhythm and blues music.

Summary and Conclusions

The sample allowed me to draw several conclusions.

1. The Eastern style is posturally conservative. Most players consistently showed an extended thumb position. This position is in turn highly correlated with the alternating thumb style.
2. There are both more positional variety and more stylistic development in the Delta and Texas regions.

3. This variety and development are likely associated with the rise of the blues tradition within the folk music of the Delta and Texas regions and the consequent creative musical ferment there. This tradition appears to have been absorbed into the more conservative Eastern region without much change to that region's patterns of posture and style.

Appendixes

Table 4.7. The Sample of Guitarists

Name	Learn place	State	YoB	Pos.	Style
Henry Thomas	Big Sandy	Tex.	1874	e	d
Frank Stokes	Memphis	Tenn.	1887	e	d
Sam Collins	McComb	Miss.	1887	e	u/d
Peg Leg Howell	Eatonton	Ga.	1888	s	u/d
Huddie Ledbetter	Leigh	Tex.	1888	s	d
Charley Jordan*	Mabelvale	Ark.	1890	e	u/t-1
Jim Jackson*	Hernando	Miss.	1890	e	a
John Hurt	Avalon	Miss.	1893	e	a
Furry Lewis*	Memphis	Tenn.	1893	s	a
Big Bill Broonzy	Chicago	Ill.	1893	s	d
Blind Blake*	Jacksonville	Fla.	1893	e	a/d/cp/t-1/st
Elizabeth Cotten	Chapel Hill	N.C.	1895	e	a
Mance Lipscomb	Navasota	Tex.	1895	l	d/a
Elvie Johnson*	Bowling Green	Ky.	1895	e	a
Cat Iron*	Natchez	Miss.	1896	e	a
Robert Willkins	Hernando	Miss.	1896	e	a
Jesse Fuller	various	Ga.	1896	e	d
Rev. Gary Davis	Laurens	S.C.	1896	e	a/t-1/cp
Walter Phelps	Laurens	S.C.	1896	e	d/sab
Sam Chatmon	Bolton	Miss.	1897	e	u/d/a
Memphis Minnie	Walls	Miss.	1897	s	u/d
Lemon Jefferson	Wortham	Tex.	1897	e	d/u/t-1/t
Sylvester Weaver	Louisville	Ky.	1897	s	d
Willie McTell	Statesboro	Ga.	1898	s	d/u/t
Pink Anderson	Spartanburg	S.C.	1900	e	a/d
Ishmon Bracey	Byram	Miss.	1901	l	u/sab
Skip James	Bentonia	Miss.	1902	e	d/sab
Willie Johnson*	Marlin	Tex.	1902	s	d/a
Peetie Wheatstraw	Cotton Plant	Ark.	1902	l	d/u
Son House	Clarksdale	Miss.	1902	e	d
Barbecue Bob Hicks	Walnut Grove	Ga.	1902	e	d

(*continued*)

Table 4.7. *Continued*

Name	Learn place	State	YoB	Pos.	Style
Big Joe Williams	Crawford	Miss.	1903	s	d
Lum Guffin	Memphis	Tenn.	1903	s	a/d
Scrapper Blackwell	Indianapolis	Ind.	1903	e	d/u
Scott Dunbar	Lake Mary	Miss.	1904	e	u/d
Daniel K. Womack	Roanoke	Va.	1904	s	a/sab
Sleepy John Estes	Brownsville	Tenn.	1904	s	d
Roosevelt Holts	Tylertown	Miss.	1905	e	u
Arthur Crudup	Forest	Miss.	1905	s	u
Joe McCoy	Vicksburg	Miss.	1905	l	d
Black Ace	Hughes Springs	Tex.	1905	e	a/d
Ed Bell	Greenville	Ala.	1905	s	d/a
Curley Weaver	Porterdale	Ga.	1906	e	u
Carl Martin	Big Stone Gap	Va.	1906	e	u
Babe Stovall	Tylertown	Miss.	1907	e	a
Shirley Griffith	Jackson	Miss.	1908	s	d/st
Blind Boy Fuller	Wadesboro	N.C.	1908	e	a/u/cp/st
Henry Johnson	Union	S.C.	1908	e	a/u
Howard Armstrong	La Follette	Tenn.	1909	s	d/u
Henry Townsend	Cairo	Ill.	1909	s	u/d
Bukka White	Houston	Miss.	1909	s	d
Homesick James	Somerville	Tenn.	1910	s	d/u
Ted Bogan	Spartanburg	S.C.	1910	e	a/t-1
Willie Trice	Hillsboro	N.C.	1910	e	a/st
Herman E. Johnson	Scotlandville	La.	1910	e	u/t-1
Nat Reese	Princeton	W.Va.	1911	s	u/d
Robert Johnson	Robinsonville	Miss.	1911	e	u/d
Lightnin' Hopkins	Centerville	Tex.	1912	s	d/u
Etta Baker	Morganton	N.C.	1913	e	a
Buddy Moss	Augusta	Ga.	1914	e	u
Robert "Pete" Williams	Scotlandville	La.	1914	l	u/d/a
Josh White	Greenville	S.C.	1915	e	d/u
Honeyboy Edwards	Shaw	Miss.	1915	e	u
Rev. Pearly Brown	Americus	Ga.	1915	s	u/d
Muddy Waters	Clarksdale	Miss.	1915	l	d
Brownie McGhee	Kingsport	Tenn.	1915	e	u/t
John Lee	Evergreen	Ala.	1915	e	a/d
Lil' Son Jackson	Tyler	Tex.	1916	e	u/st
Frankie Lee Sims	Marshall	Tex.	1917	s	d
Richard Trice	Hillsboro	N.C.	1917	e	a
John Lee Hooker	Clarksdale	Miss.	1917	l	u

Table 4.7. *Continued*

Name	Learn place	State	YoB	Pos.	Style
Archie Edwards	Union Hall	Va.	1918	e	a
Elmore James	Belzoni	Miss.	1918	l	u
Frank Hovington	Frederica	Del.	1919	e	a
Jim Brewer	Brookhaven	Miss.	1920	s	d/u
Pernell Charity	Waverly	Va.	1920	e	a/d
Lowell Fulson	Tulsa	Okla.	1921	s	u
Joe Hill Louis	Memphis	Tenn.	1921	l	d
John Jackson	Rapahannock	Va.	1924	l	a/st
George Bussey	Waverly Hall	Ga.	1924	s	u/d
Maxwell Street Jimmy Davis	Clarksdale	Miss.	1925	l	d/u
R. L. Burnside	Oxford	Miss.	1926	s	u/d/sab
Turner Fodrell	Sheridan	Va.	1927	e	a
Amos Stokes	Macon	Ga.	1928	e	a
John Dee Holeman	Raleigh	N.C.	1929	e	d/u
John Cephas	Bowling Green	Va.	1930	e	a/u/d
Juke Boy Bonner	Bellville	Tex.	1932	l	d/u
Jessie Mae Hemphill	Como	Miss.	1933	s	u
Jimmie Lee Harris	Phenix City	Ala.	1935	s	d/a
Snooks Eaglin	New Orleans	La.	1936	e	u/d/t-1
Larry Johnson	Wrightsville	Ga.	1938	e	a/u
Tom Winslow	N. Central	N.C.	1938	e	a
Robert Belfour	Red Banks	Miss.	1940	s	u/d

Legend: YoB = year of birth (* after name = date uncertain); Pos. = hand posture; Style = most consistent timekeeping predilection; a = alternating thumb; sab = slow alternating bass; t-1 = alternation of thumb and index finger for runs; cp= counterpoint; u = utility thumb; d = dead thumb; st = slip thumb; t = runs made with thumb only.

PRINT

The following printed sources yielded photographs depicting hand positions.

Bruce Bastin, *Red River Blues: The Blues Tradition in the Southeast* (Urbana: University of Illinois Press, 1986): Josh White, Curley Weaver, Buddy Moss, Willie McTell, Willie Trice, Richard Trice, and Brownie McGhee.

Lawrence Cohn, ed., *Nothing but the Blues* (New York: Abbeville, 1993): Honeyboy Edwards, Blind Boy Fuller, Blind Blake, Joe Hill Louis, Blind Lemon Jefferson, Blind Willie Johnson, Big Joe Williams, Robert Johnson, Arthur Crudup, Muddy Waters, John Lee Hooker, Joe McCoy, Skip James, Henry Townsend, Memphis Minnie, and Babe Stovall.

Sheldon Harris, *Blues Who's Who* (New Rochelle, N.Y.: Arlington House, 1979): Barbecue Bob Hicks, Frankie Lee Sims, Robert "Pete" Williams, Huddie Ledbetter, Big Bill Broonzy, Peetie Wheatstraw, and Scrapper Blackwell.

Robert Tilling, *Oh, What a Beautiful City* (Jersey, England: Paul Mill, 1992): Rev. Gary Davis and Larry Johnson.

VIDEOTAPES

Beale Street Blues Museum, Memphis, in-house video: Furry Lewis.

Eleanor Ellis, prod., *House Party:* John Cephas, John Dee Holeman, John Jackson, and Archie Edwards.

Legends of Country Blues Guitar, vol. 1 (Vestapol 13003): Mance Lipscomb, John Hurt, Gary Davis, Son House, Big Bill Broonzy, Brownie McGhee, Robert "Pete" Williams, Josh White, and Henry Townsend.

Legends of Country Blues Guitar, vol. 2 (Vestapol 13016): Houston Stackhouse, Big Joe Williams, Son House, Gary Davis, Leadbelly, Bukka White and Sam Chatmon.

Blues up the Country (Vestapol 13037): Rev. Gary Davis, John Jackson, Pink Anderson, Jesse Fuller, Furry Lewis, Josh White, and Robert "Pete" Williams.

Legends of Delta Blues (Vestapol 13038): Son House, Bukka White, John Lee Hooker, and Honeyboy Edwards.

William Spence, ed., clip from 1984 Old Songs Festival: Jim Brewer.

Lane Wilkins, videotape of her grandfather, Reverend Robert Wilkins.

ALBUM COVERS AND NOTES

The Spirit Lives On, Hot Fox HF-CD-005, notes: Robert Belfour.

Georgia Street Singer, Folk Lyric 108, cover: Rev. Pearly Brown.

Shake Sugaree, Folkways LP 1003, cover: Elizabeth Cotten.

The Virginian, Trix 3309, cover: Pernell Charity.

The Union County Flash, Trix 3304, cover: Henry Johnson.

PHOTOGRAPHS

Dale Galgozy: Etta Baker.

John Jackson publicity photo.

BIOGRAPHICAL SOURCES

Biographical data came from various LP and CD notes; Sheldon Harris, *Blues Who's Who;* and Robert Santelli, *The Big Book of Blues* (New York: Penguin, 1993). Original recordings by most artists are listed in Robert M. W. Dixon and John Godrich, *Blues and Gospel Records, 1902–1943,* 3d ed. (Chigwell, England: Storyville, 1982); Mike Leadbitter and Neil

Slaven, *Blues Records 1943–1970, A Selective Discography, Vol. 1, A to K* (London: Record Information Services, 1987); and Mike Leadbitter, Leslie Fancourt, and Paul Pelletier, *Blues Records 1943–1970, "The Bible of the Blues," Vol. 2, L to Z* (London: Record Information Services, 1994). I listened to most recordings made through the 1950s on reissue LPs and CDs.

Notes

This paper is an outgrowth of my M.A. thesis, "Piedmont Bluesmen: A Tradition of American Griots" (Kent State University, 1994). I wish to thank David Evans for access to his collection of recordings. I wish also to thank Dr. C. Owen Lovejoy of Kent State University's Anthropology Department; Boris Basiuk of Toronto, Ontario; Ed Cabell of Morgantown, West Virginia; Larkin Bryant of Memphis, Tennessee; and Jack DiAlesandro of Ravenna, Ohio, for assistance.

1. Stefan Grossman, *The Country Blues Guitar* (New York: Oak, 1968); idem, *Ragtime Blues Guitarists* (New York: Oak, 1970); idem, *Rev. Gary Davis: The Holy Blues* (New York: Robbins Music, 1970); Woody Mann, *Six Black Blues Guitarists* (New York: Oak, 1973); idem, *Anthology of Blues Guitar* (New York: Oak, 1993); Stephen Calt and Gayle Dean Wardlow, *King of the Delta Blues: The Life and Music of Charlie Patton* (Newton, N.J.: Rock Chapel, 1988).

2. See, for example, Pete Welding, "Stringin' the Blues: The Art of Folk Blues Guitar," *Down Beat* 32, no. 14 (July 1, 1965): 22–24, 56; Charles Keil, *Urban Blues* (Chicago: University of Chicago Press, 1966), 59–68, 217–24; Richard Middleton, *Pop Music and the Blues* (London: Victor Gollancz, 1972), 61–70; David Evans, *Big Road Blues: Tradition and Creativity in the Folk Blues* (Berkeley and Los Angeles: University of California Press, 1982), 167–69, 262–64; and Andrew James Hassard, "The Cultural Diffusion of Blues Music and the Migration of Its Performers" (M.A. thesis, University of Southern Mississippi, 1989). Two books by Samuel Charters treating the history of country blues are organized on a regional basis, *The Bluesmen* (New York: Oak, 1967) and *Sweet As the Showers of Rain* (New York: Oak, 1977). The regional approach has been maintained in more recent histories, such as Bruce Bastin, *Red River Blues: The Blues Tradition in the Southeast* (Urbana: University of Illinois Press, 1986); Robert Palmer, *Deep Blues* (New York: Viking, 1981); Lawrence Cohn, ed., *Nothing but the Blues: The Music and the Musicians* (New York: Abbeville, 1993); and Kip Lornell and Ted Mealor, "A&R Men and the Geography of Piedmont Blues Recordings: 1924-1941," *ARSC Journal* 26, no. 1 (Spring 1995): 1–22.

3. See Tony Russell, *Blacks, Whites and Blues* (London: Studio Vista, 1970).

4. James E. Anderson, ed., *Grant's Atlas of Anatomy,* 8th ed. (Baltimore: Williams and Wilkins, 1983), 6-83, 6-85E.

5. C. Owen Lovejoy, "The Origins of Man," *Science* 211 (December 1981): 341–50.

6. Michael R. Cummings, *Human Heredity* (St. Paul: West, 1988), 65–66.

7. Mack McCormick, in his notes to *Ragtime Texas* (Herwin 209; this is the entire recorded output of Henry Thomas), comments on the passage of the older material: "No arrow points to a birthplace or innovator. But what does seem apparent is that from whatever point or points the blues emerged they quickly gained consent and spread dramatically throughout the South. All of a sudden those songs about possums and raccoons and gum stumps began to vanish."

8. Jack DiAlesandro and I computed the chi-square statistic for Tables 4.2, 4.3, and 4.4. These tables comprise age-matched subsamples from each region. They relate hand position to region, hand position to style, and style to region. The null hypothesis (H_0) was that there was no significant association between the two variables compared in each table, and the experimental hypothesis (H_1) was that there was. In each case the null hypothesis was retained for the older group and rejected for the younger group.

The null hypothesis means that styles of music of the pre-1906 birth group were proportionately (not absolutely evenly) distributed among the three regions, that hand postures were distributed in proportionate ratios within those populations, and that thumbing styles were developed without reference to hand position.

Rejection of the null hypothesis in the post-1905 birth group was very strong. For region correlated with style, there is less than one chance in a thousand that the results obtained could have occurred by random sampling; for region correlated with hand posture, less than five chances in a thousand; and for hand posture correlated with style, again, less than one chance in a thousand. Rejection suggests that there is an association between region, hand posture, and style in the generation born after 1905, that is, in the generation that began to identify itself exclusively with blues music.

5

From Bumble Bee Slim
to Black Boy Shine

NICKNAMES OF BLUES SINGERS

DAVID EVANS

During his fieldwork in the Mississippi Delta in 1967, folklorist William Ferris was impressed by the importance of nicknames of blues singers in their communities. He wrote, "Nicknames such as 'Pine Top,' 'Cairo,' and 'Poppa Jazz' are more important than surnames and often when I inquired after actual names no one recognized the person."[1] In my own fieldwork in the Delta and other regions of the South during the 1960s and 1970s I encountered my share of blues singers with nicknames, including Uncle Snapper, Fiddlin' Joe, Shake 'Em On Down, Peck, Dink, Nig, Babe, Little Sister, Tiny, and Blind Log. In more recent decades I have known and recorded Big Lucky, Chicago Bob, Piano Red, Slop Jar, Chicken George, Boogie Man, Uncle Ben, Blue, Shine, Earl the Pearl, Wolfman, and The She-Wolf.[2] The striking character of some of these names and the personalities that went with them impressed me at the time and they have stayed with me up to now. Like Ferris, I have come to believe that nicknames can express important and fundamental aspects of the identities of blues singers.

The main published work on nicknames of blues singers up to now is a series of articles by James K. Skipper Jr. and Paul Leslie published in 1988 and 1989.[3] Their sample is the 571 artists listed in Sheldon Harris's *Blues Who's Who: A Biographical Dictionary of Blues Singers,* of which 464 were male and 105 female.[4] Of the male artists, 309 (67 percent) had nicknames, while of the females, 28 (27 percent) had them. The authors recognize a number of categories and naming practices, which are discussed below, including the obvious ones of musical associations, geographical terms, and physical characteristics. However, they establish a dichotomy between nicknames related to the blues and those not related to the blues. Furthermore, they split some content categories, such as geographical terms and nicknames indicating age, between these two extremes and sometimes appear undecided about whether to categorize nicknames on the basis of their content and symbolism or their origin, that is, the manner or incident by which singers acquired them. Because of their preoccupation with origins, they wind up with a large number of nicknames with "unknown origins"—44 (13 percent of all artists with nicknames). Some of their interpretations based on origins ignore obvious symbolic referents of the nicknames, and in a few cases they are simply wrong. They also place each nickname in one category only, although many of them clearly have multiple referents or can be understood on several levels of meaning. Two further brief articles, one by Jim Higgs and another by Jim O'Neal, recognize a number of the principles by which blues nicknames are formed, but for the most part they contain anecdotes explaining the meaning or origin of particular nicknames.[5]

The present discussion is an attempt to conduct a larger-scale survey of blues nicknames by using a sample different from that in *Blues Who's Who,* which was based on its compiler's judgment of who were the artistically and historically most important artists. My sample consists of African American artists who made commercial and field recordings of blues between 1920 and 1970. For this sample, which encompasses well over three thousand artists, I shall determine the percentage of blues singers who bore nicknames, the full range of meanings and categories of meaning of the nicknames, and the percentages of each category of nickname. In the course of this investigation, I shall attempt to explain the existence and popularity of the various types of nicknames. The advantage of using such a large sample is that I can avoid the temptation to concentrate selectively on the most exotic nicknames or the most famous bearers of nicknames (for example, Muddy Waters, Howlin' Wolf, B. B. King), as well as the temptation to select the data to fit a preconceived theory. In interpreting the data, I take the point of view that virtually all of the nicknames to some degree have a relationship to blues music or its environment. In my survey, I find few nicknames that would fall into such categories recognized by Skipper and Leslie as "pet names," nicknames based on critical incidents (often in childhood), or "childhood nicknames." Instead, I am concerned with what the nicknames symbolized to other adults who encountered these singers at live performances or through records. Leola B. Grant's nickname of Coot, for instance, was in her explanation a deformation of a childhood term of endearment, Cutie,[6] but in the minds of most listeners a coot is a black aquatic bird and the word would suggest skin color and perhaps other personality traits.

For purposes of this study, I view nicknames as supplements to or substitutes for a person's given name (for example, Big Joe Williams; Bumble Bee Slim for Amos Easton). In almost all cases nicknames consist of ordinary words that describe or suggest one or more attributes of the person. A few nicknames, however, are derived from other names, usually of famous people (including fellow musicians). On first encounter, a nickname may disguise the real name of a person and function as a pseudonym, although most bearers of nicknames are willing to reveal their real names when asked. Actual pseudonyms normally appear as ordinary names and are not intended to call special attention to their bearers. Nicknames, on the other hand, project the attributes embodied in them as some sort of special, essential, or outstanding feature of a person that is worthy of attention. In other words, they project a simplified and focussed *persona* or image that may or may not be consistent with the actual being, appearance, or personality of the bearer. In the case of blues artists, nicknames may be conferred on them by themselves or by family members, friends, audience members, or promoters (including record companies). For our purposes, the giver of a nickname is unimportant. What is significant is that the nickname has one or more recognizable meanings, has been used within a blues musical context, and is, so to speak, approved for use in this context by both artist and audience. Because nicknames consist of words that people also use in everyday speech, they establish a sense of informality and familiarity with the individuals who bear them. This sense is especially useful for blues singers, who may be strangers to their audiences and whose role as entertainers exalts them over an audience that yet wants to be on close terms with them. In referring to an artist by a nickname, members of an audience feel that they know something special and intimate about that artist.

My sample comprises the 3,728 African American blues artists listed in *Blues and Gospel Records 1890–1943* and *Blues Records 1943–1970,* the standard discographies in the field.[7] Since blues songs did not come to be recorded until 1920, this survey covers blues artists who were active between this date and 1970, a time period during which blues music was at a peak of popularity and importance within the African American community. Included in this survey is every artist who recorded at least one blues title or a song in a closely related genre of secular music, such as a folk ballad, a ragtime song, or a dance tune. Artists who recorded only religious material, children's songs, or other secular material clearly originating in a pre-blues era are excluded. Also excluded are artists who sang without instrumental accompaniment, such as the great number who made field recordings of hollers and prison work songs. Blues is essentially a form of song that requires instrumental accompaniment, and for the purposes of this survey I felt that singers who recorded without accompaniment were not performing blues and could not be considered blues singers. Accompanists are included in the survey only if their names are credited on a record label as a singer or other principal artist. Although this policy results in the exclusion of some artists with interesting nicknames who performed accompaniments on blues recordings, many of these artists, in fact, came from the jazz field. It was felt that including them would skew the survey too much toward instrumentalists rather than singers and too much toward jazz, which is another musical realm, although one that is related to blues and that interacted with blues throughout the twentieth century.[8] Names of groups are not considered here (for example, Memphis Jug Band), unless the group name consists of a series of individual names or nicknames (for example, the team of Butterbeans and Susie). Artists who made field recordings in prisons are not included unless they also recorded in the free world (for example, Leadbelly). Although this policy undoubtedly has resulted in the exclusion of a few incarcerated artists who clearly were blues singers, it reduces the possibility that the survey will be skewed by a number of prison nicknames whose meanings are derived from the artists' status as prisoners. For example, Hogman Maxey, a blues singer and guitarist recorded at the Louisiana State Penitentiary, is excluded. His nickname was derived from his job of caring for the hogs at the prison farm. Published surveys of prison nicknames reveal some that are similar to those of blues singers but many others that are formed on very different principles.[9] Perhaps a few blues singers in our survey received their nicknames in prisons and later used them in their musical careers in the free world, but I don't believe they constitute a large number.

It was tempting to include in this survey the nicknames of blues artists who were active during this period but never made recordings, such as the pianists recalled by Little Brother Montgomery named Papa Lord God, Rip Top, Sudan Washington, Red Cayou, Little Dooky, Long Tall Friday, Dehlco Robert, Ernest "Flunky" Johnson (also known as Ernest "44" Johnson), Ragging Willie Wells, Stiff Arm Eddie, Skinny Head Pete, Burnt Face Jake, Game Kid, Boogus, Tuts Washington, Kid Clayton, Drive 'Em Down, Kid Sheik, Frenchman Joe, Blind Jug, Blind Homer, Black Emile (also known as Brown

Mule), Coot Davis, Little Low Friday, Asthma Slim, Little Sammy, and Little Willie.[10] To include them, however, would mean putting no limits on the survey and would open it up to the possibility of picking nicknames because of their exotic quality. One of my purposes is to determine the percentage of blues singers that actually had nicknames during this period, and by limiting the survey to recorded blues singers we impose a more or less unbiased and objective standard. The names supplied by artists at the time of recording and printed on record labels represent individuals who were trying to project their music, personalities, and names to audiences in a clearly musical setting. Other known blues nicknames can be studied later, after some naming principles and statistics have been established for these recorded singers.

There are some inherent problems and necessary cautions in using names and nicknames as they appear on record labels, company files, and notations to field recordings for a survey of this sort. For example, some artists in the survey are known to have had nicknames that did not appear on their records. Charlie Burse was known both as Laughing Charlie and Ukulele Ike, but he is tabulated here as an artist without a nickname because neither of these nicknames appeared on his records. Blind Willie McTell had six different nicknames on his records but the name by which he was best known to family and friends, Doog or Doogie, never appeared on any of his records. Bessie Smith was widely known as Empress of the Blues but this title never appeared on her record labels. These known nicknames are, therefore, not included in this survey. On the other hand, some artists undoubtedly adopted nicknames only for the purpose of making records. Some of these names were probably given to them by their record companies, perhaps without any input from the artist. This might have been the case especially with descriptive phrases that follow an artist's name on record labels. For example, Kansas City Bill Weldon is described on some records as Hawaiian Guitar Wizard, Alice Moore as Little Alice from St. Louis, and Curtis Jones as The Texas Wonder. In most cases these descriptive phrases have been counted as nicknames, although it may not be known whether they were ever used by the singers in person. On the other hand, some nicknames and pseudonyms were given by record companies or even created by artists themselves for the purpose of disguising their identities when their records were bootlegged, when they recorded for one company while under contract to another, when their recordings were licensed to another company at a special low rate of payment, or when they were released on a company's subsidiary "budget" label.[11] In some of these cases the companies avoided paying royalties to an

artist by issuing his or her recordings under a different name. These pseudonyms and pseudo-nicknames are not considered in this survey unless there
is some reason to think that the artist might have used the nickname in other
circumstances or unless such a name is the only one by which an artist is
known. Some artists recorded blues and religious songs under different names.
In such cases the artists' names on blues titles are the ones considered here.
Shortenings and derivatives of standard English names (for example, Jim,
Bill, Joe, Bessie) are not viewed as true nicknames, unless it is known that
they were used as stereotypical names (for example, Robert Brown as Washboard Sam, Gus Cannon as Banjo Joe, or Wilber McCoy as Kansas Joe), in
which case they form a special category of nicknames. In several cases surnames were distorted into words that served as nicknames. For example,
Huddie Ledbetter became Leadbelly, Walter Brown McGhee became Brownie
McGhee, Jesse Cryor became Cryin' Jesse, Andrew Hogg became Smokey
Hogg, and Sam Maghett became Magic Sam. Such distortions have been
viewed here as real nicknames, since their usage falls within the typical patterns described below. Other artists, however, simply had somewhat unusual
given names that nevertheless fall within African American cultural practices of naming. For example, Missouri Anderson and Georgia White were
probably both named after states where they are known to have lived. Glory
Bernard, Hammie Nixon, Eliza Christmas Lee, Romeo Nelson, Star Page,
Classie Ballou, Jewel Brown, and Sax (short for Saxton) Kari also appear to
be real given names. Furry Lewis is probably simply a mishearing or misspelling of a surname used as a given name, such as Feary, Ferry, Furey,
Fury, or Ferree. Although Lewis recorded a "Furry's Blues" and a "Mr. Furry's
Blues," he never made any attempt in his many interviews to explain the
meaning of the name or tried to project any image consistent with it, always
stating simply that his full name was Walter Furry Lewis. Some supposed
nicknames were merely field recordists' misunderstandings of the real names
of artists, such as Cat-Iron for William Carradine or Do-Boy Diamond for
William DuBois Diamond. All of these have been excluded from consideration as nicknames. Even if any of them ever functioned as nicknames for
some listeners, they represent only a small fraction of the total and generally
fall within the established patterns of nicknaming of other blues singers. On
the other hand, a few artists named Royal, Prince, Princess, King Solomon,
Judge, Dolly, and Lovey are viewed as bearing nicknames, although these terms
can fall within African American cultural patterns of given birth names.[12] I
am hopeful that all of these factors and problems balance one another out
in this large sample and that this survey comes close to representing names

and nicknames that were actually in use by recorded blues artists during the period from 1920 to 1970.

My procedure is to analyze the nicknames of recorded blues artists separately for the periods 1920–43 and 1943–70. I do this in part because the standard discographies that form the basis of the sample considered here are split according to these two time periods. There is, however, an actual historical logic for this division. World War II (1941–45) was a disruptive event in the course of recorded blues history. From mid-1942 to the end of the war in 1945 there was very little blues recording due to wartime shellac shortages and a musicians' union strike against recording studios. After the war many new independent record companies sprang up all over the nation, eventually breaking the dominance of the three companies that controlled most blues recording at the outbreak of the war. The new companies recorded mostly new artists in new styles, with the blues becoming more urbanized in the process. The period after the war also saw the rise of the Civil Rights Movement and changes in social attitudes within the African American community and in America as a whole. The division of our sample into these two periods will reveal some changes and dynamics in blues nicknaming patterns that are related to these other changes in the blues recording industry, the sound of the music itself, and social conditions and attitudes. The two periods will henceforth be known by the terms "prewar" and "postwar." Recordings made in the year 1943 fall into both periods, but as previously noted there were very few actually made in that year. Some recording artists, of course, had careers that spanned both periods, but these were not terribly numerous. In any case, a certain amount of overlap of artists is to be expected in any division by time period. It does not obscure the continuities or the changing trends in nicknaming practices. We shall examine blues nicknames in the prewar period first, using the data to establish categories of analysis and interpretation. Following this, we shall examine the postwar data to see how nicknaming practices changed or remained the same. Because of the large number of nicknames surveyed, there will be many interpretations given along the way for individual nicknames and portions of data. We must, however, also look for more general trends and try not to get too bogged down in individual cases, no matter how fascinating the nickname or how important or influential the artist.

Almost all of the nicknames fall easily into a limited number of categories and subcategories based on their meaning and symbolism. There are six major categories. The first is a small group of stereotypical names, such as Joe, Sam, and Mandy, which we know were not the real names of the artists.

The second, much larger, category is familiar terms, usually springing from family relationships and friendship, such as Son, Sister, Buddy, Dad, Baby, and Kid. The third category is musical terms. These fall into five subcategories: (a) terms descriptive of instruments, musical styles, and dances associated with the blues; (b) terms describing the blues environment or context; (c) terms containing or referring to song lyrics or titles; (d) terms referring to other blues artists or, by extension, other famous personalities; and (e) terms suggesting a rank order among musical figures. The fourth category covers nonmusical terms that are descriptive of essential qualities of the person. Again, there are five subcategories: (a) direct descriptions of physical appearance; (b) descriptions of personality or character; (c) terms signifying social, racial, or ethnic status; (d) terms giving the artist's occupation outside music; and (e) geographical terms associated with the artist. The fifth category includes terms that suggest associations with special things and qualities outside the artist's everyday being, usually ones that the artist would like to be associated with, although a few normally have negative connotations. In other words, although these terms might more or less accurately describe the artist's appearance, personality, and propensities, they do so in symbolic or metaphorical ways that also make them significant *projections* of the artist. These fall into six subcategories: (a) terms describing tastes in food; (b) terms describing sexual tastes, abilities, and characteristics; (c) terms describing animals and nature; (d) terms associated with manmade mechanical devices; (e) terms associated with royalty or other exalted status; and (f) terms associated with the supernatural, magic, and luck. The sixth and final category is a small group of nicknames with uncertain or unclassifiable meanings.

I have resisted the temptation always to link a single artist with a single nickname that fits neatly into a single category. Some artists were known by more than one nickname. Guitarist James Arnold first recorded as Gitfiddle Jim and later as Kokomo Arnold. The latter name was derived from his theme song, "Old Original Kokomo Blues," which had an added geographical significance suggesting an association between the artist and the city of Kokomo, Indiana. Floyd Council was known by such diverse nicknames as Dipper Boy, The Devil's Daddy-in-Law, and Blind Boy Fuller's Buddy. Wilber McCoy was known on records as Kansas Joe, The Hillbilly Plowboy, The Mississippi Mudder, Mud Dauber Joe, Georgia Pine Boy, Big Joe, and Hamfoot Ham, as well as the pseudonyms of Bill Wilber and Joe Williams. He even recorded gospel titles as Hallelujah Joe. Willie Samuel McTell recorded as Blind Willie, Blind Sammie, Georgia Bill, Hot Shot Willie, Pig 'n' Whistle Red, and Barrelhouse Sammy (The Country Boy). William Bunch was Peetie

Wheatstraw, The Devil's Son-in-Law, and The High Sheriff from Hell. The female singer with perhaps the most nicknames was Bessie Mae Smith, itself probably a nickname formed by grafting the name of the extremely popular singer Bessie Smith onto this singer's real name of May Belle Miller. She also recorded as Blue Belle, St. Louis Bessie, and Streamline Mae. Sometimes a single nickname has multiple meanings or strings together two or more naming principles. Jelly Roll Anderson's nickname refers to both food and sex, as does Roosevelt Sykes's nickname, The Honey Dripper, with its further suggestion of an animal referent (a honey bee). Nicknames that combine two or more naming principles are ones such as Arkansas Shorty, Memphis Slim, Tampa Red, Black Boy Shine, Black Ivory King, Blues Birdhead, Western Kid, Little Son Joe, Kid Stormy Weather, and Ragtime Texas. Such nicknames are included under any and every category that is applicable to them. This means that the number of nicknames is larger than the number of artists bearing nicknames and that some nicknames are placed in more than one category of interpretation.

My categorization and interpretation of blues nicknames is based on their *cultural meaning* during the time period. Information about the origins of specific nicknames is not ignored, but it does not overrule obvious meanings springing from a term's usual associations within the culture. My judgments are based on familiarity since the early 1960s with African American folklore, folk speech, and music, particularly blues, both through extensive fieldwork and study of the scholarly literature. I have listened to a majority of the 3,728 artists represented in the survey. I don't claim to be omniscient about nicknames and their meanings, however, and others are welcome and encouraged to amplify, modify, or dispute any of these judgments.

The criteria given above yield a list of 1,195 recorded blues artists from the prewar period. Of these, 760 were male, 434 were female, and one (Baby Payne) is of undetermined gender. The males (64 percent) thus outnumber the females (36 percent) by nearly two to one. Female artists were predominant in the earliest years, from 1920 to 1926. From 1927 to 1931 male and female artists were recorded about equally. From 1932 to 1943 male artists were in the great majority. There were 387 artists with nicknames, or 32 percent of the total number of artists. A great disparity, however, exists in the percentages of male and female artists. There were 323 male artists with nicknames, or 43 percent of all male artists, whereas only 63 female artists had nicknames, a mere 15 percent of all female artists.

The category of stereotypical names contains only 11 male and 5 female artists that we know of, 4 percent of all artists having nicknames, although very likely there were more that simply can not be identified on the basis of

Table 5.1. Numbers and percentages of blues artists with nicknames, with breakdown by nickname category.

	m&f #	m&f %	m #	m %	f #	f %
		1920–1970				
Total Artists	3,728	100%	2,870	77%	851	23%
Artists with Nicknames	1,387	37% of all	1,231	43%	153	18%
1. Stereotypical Names	23	2%	18	1%	5	3%
2. Familiar Terms	352	25%	313	25%	38	25%
3. Musical Terms	432	31%	390	32%	42	27%
a. instruments/styles/dances	251	18%	233	19%	18	12%
b. blues context	12	1%	10	1%	2	1%
c. song lyrics/titles	62	4%	57	5%	5	3%
d. other artists/famous people	124	9%	110	9%	14	9%
e. rank order	8	1%	5	0%	3	2%
4. Non-Musical Terms: Essential	716	52%	659	54%	56	37%
a. physical traits	470	34%	431	35%	38	25%
b. personality/character traits	93	7%	91	7%	2	1%
c. social/racial/ethnic status	57	4%	52	4%	5	3%
d. occupation	52	4%	47	4%	5	3%
e. geographical	128	9%	115	9%	13	8%
5. Non-Musical Terms: Projected/Symbolic	328	24%	277	23%	51	33%
a. food	74	5%	63	5%	11	7%
b. sexual	63	5%	44	4%	20	13%
c. animals/nature	91	7%	81	7%	10	7%
d. mechanical	20	1%	14	1%	6	4%
e. royalty/exalted status	79	6%	70	6%	9	6%
f. supernatural/magic/luck	36	3%	36	3%	0	0%
6. Other/Uncertain	32	2%	27	2%	4	3%

Note: m = male; f = female. The male and female numbers combined are sometimes slightly lower than the total number of artists because the gender of a few artists could not be determined. Within nickname categories the percentages are of artists of the same gender bearing nicknames, not of the total number of artists.

our present knowledge. Several of these names, however, may simply have been given by record companies as pseudonyms to disguise the artist's identity for one reason or another. The latter may include Sluefoot Joe (Ed Bell), who recorded for another label as Barefoot Bill, Pinewood Tom (Joshua White), whose real name appeared on his religious records, Hannah May

	1920–1943						1943–1970				
m&f #	m&f %	m #	m %	f #	f %	m&f #	m&f %	m #	m %	f #	f %
1,195	100%	760	64%	434	36%	2,533	100%	2,110	83%	417	16%
387	32% of all	323	43%	63	15%	1,000	39% of all	908	43%	90	22%
16	4%	11	3%	5	8%	7	1%	7	1%	0	0%
98	25%	82	25%	15	24%	254	25%	231	25%	23	26%
107	28%	90	28%	17	27%	325	33%	300	33%	25	28%
56	14%	51	16%	5	8%	195	20%	182	20%	13	14%
6	2%	4	1%	2	3%	6	1%	6	1%	0	0%
17	4%	15	5%	2	3%	45	5%	42	5%	3	3%
28	7%	23	7%	5	8%	96	10%	87	10%	9	10%
5	1%	2	1%	3	5%	3	0%	3	0%	0	0%
193	50%	176	54%	17	27%	524	52%	483	53%	40	44%
106	27%	100	31%	6	10%	364	36%	331	36%	32	36%
16	4%	16	5%	0	0%	77	8%	75	8%	2	2%
29	7%	25	8%	4	6%	28	3%	27	3%	1	1%
13	3%	11	3%	2	3%	39	4%	36	4%	3	3%
56	14%	48	15%	8	13%	72	7%	67	7%	5	6%
102	26%	87	27%	15	24%	225	23%	189	21%	36	40%
24	6%	22	7%	2	3%	50	5%	41	5%	9	10%
24	6%	21	7%	3	5%	39	4%	22	2%	16	18%
39	10%	32	10%	7	11%	52	5%	49	5%	3	3%
8	2%	5	2%	3	5%	12	1%	9	1%	3	3%
12	3%	12	4%	0	0%	67	7%	58	6%	9	10%
13	3%	13	4%	0	0%	23	2%	23	3%	0	0%
12	3%	11	3%	1	2%	20	2%	16	2%	3	3%

(Mozelle Alderson), possibly recording in violation of a contract with another company, and three different singers known simply as Mandy Lee. Among the men there were five Joes and two Sams. These included Sluefoot Joe (Ed Bell), Banjo Joe (Gus Cannon), Little Son Joe (Ernest Lawlars), Kansas Joe (Wilber McCoy), Monkey Joe (Jesse Coleman), Alabama Sam (Walter Roland), and Washboard Sam (Robert Brown). Perhaps the best-known artist with a stereotypical name was Dinah Washington, whose real name was Ruth Lee Jones. Her nickname was given to her by a record producer who liked its sound. Dinah was a stereotypical name found in nineteenth-century minstrel songs, while Washington is a common African American surname vaguely suggesting connections to one-time Negro leader Booker T. Washington and even America's first president. Of the other names in this category, Sam and Mandy were often used as generic names to designate black men and women, and Joe is a common name also among American whites used to designate an ordinary guy, as in "an average Joe," Joe Blow, or Joe Doaks. If white record company executives and producers assigned these names on record labels, they were not only expressing their own stereotyped notions but also may have been trying to create the impression that the singer was no one special and merely a vehicle for presenting the song. Nevertheless, we know that most of these names were actually used by the artists in their ongoing careers, which suggests that they had some positive value to the artists. I think this value was that they seemed to make the artists like every man or woman, particularly black men and women who had been stereotyped. This would have increased the sense of identity that listeners would feel with them. These artists thus absorbed and became absorbed into the stereotypical images of these names, which were magnified through their use as nicknames. They became, in a sense, Super-Sams, Joes, Mandys, and Dinahs. We shall return to this line of thought when we look at nicknames suggesting physical appearance, racial and social designations.

Familiar terms are found among 25 percent of all prewar blues artists with nicknames, 82 males and 17 females. In a number of cases they are combined with other kinds of terms, for example, Blind Boy Fuller, Whistlin' Kid Dockett, and Little Son Joe. Among the males there were 22 named Boy (usually compounds such as Big Boy, Poor Boy, Sonny Boy, or Buddy Boy), 16 named Kid, 13 named Son, Sonny, or Sonny Boy, 8 named Bud, Buddy, or Buddy Boy, 8 named Papa, 4 named Buster, 4 named Uncle, 2 named Dad or Daddy, 2 named Bo, and one each named Mister, Old Man, Junior, Brother-in-Law, Little Brother, Bozo, Baby Doo, and Bubba. Among the females there were 7 named Babe or Baby, 4 named Sis or Sister, 3 named Miss, and 1 each named Girl, Auntie, and Ma or Madame Ma (Rainey). Although many of these nicknames were probably conferred in childhood, one should not assume from this rather high incidence of familiar terms that the world of blues music during this era was infused with "family values" or that the music was "family entertainment." The most popular male nicknames, Boy and Kid, generally signify a young person on his own in the company of adults, while the most popular female term, Babe or Baby, has well-known romantic or sexual connotations. Papa and Daddy can have similar connotations.

Many of the other names suggest members of an age set rather than an inter-generational family. Nevertheless, the substantial percentage of terms describing family relationships demands further explanation. Without contradicting the likelihood that some of these nicknames were acquired in ordinary family and community settings, I believe that they also suggest the idea of the blues community as a family. This family largely existed apart from a society made up of families as we normally view them, and its relationships were usually more transitory. Many blues singers, due to social pressures of poverty and racial discrimination as well as their own personalities and itinerant lifestyles, had very tenuous or broken relationships with their parents, children, and spouses. Troubled or broken relationships with lovers, friends, and family members are also a pervasive theme in blues lyrics.[13] The use of nicknames describing family and other close relationships would therefore at least partly represent a longing to reconstruct actual broken or strained relationships or to construct an idealized "blues family,"[14] an idea somewhat comparable to the frequently expressed wish in the blues to "build me a heaven of my own." I am reminded here of a blues singer I knew nicknamed Uncle Ben. His real name was Ben, and his nickname was, he said, inspired by the familiar brand of instant rice with a black man's face on the box. (We shall overlook here the possibly stereotypical usage of the term Uncle that lies in the background of this brand name, but which is entirely irrelevant to this blues artist and his personality.) He was a tough, irascible former merchant seaman with a string of failed marriages that had produced no children. After the most recent failure he had settled in Memphis, some eight hundred miles from his closest blood relatives in Virginia, and become a street performer on the newly reopened Beale Street. It was here that he reinvented himself as Uncle Ben. He would call various musical partners his Nephews, but most would leave him within a few weeks after a falling-out over money, music, or a clash of personalities. His nickname, therefore, represented an ideal far more than a reality. We shall encounter the use of nicknames as projected desires and ideals elsewhere in this study.

Musical nicknames are relatively easy to understand. They are found among 107 (28 percent) of all prewar artists with nicknames. Males had 90 of these names, and females had 17, making their rate of occurrence roughly equal between the sexes. Descriptive musical terms were by far the most common at 56 or half of all musical nicknames. Of these, 24 described instruments, especially the guitar and piano, although these were sometimes referred to by other words such as Gitfiddle and Ivory. Guitar and piano are the two most common instruments played by blues singers. The banjo, ukulele, stovepipe, fiddle, harmonica, and washboard were also occasionally mentioned. Vocal styles were suggested by 15 names, including such artists as Howling Smith, Talking Billy Anderson, Yodeling Kid Brown, Whistlin' Pete, Cry Baby Godfrey, Laughing Charley, The Mississippi Moaner, Signifying Mary Johnson, and probably Yack Taylor. A specific instrumental style was associated with only two artists. One was pianist James "Steady Roll" Johnson, whose nickname can easily have a sexual interpretation as well. The other was Bill Weldon, known as The Hawaiian Guitar Wizard, referring not to his ethnicity but to his "Hawaiian" slide guitar style. Four artists were associated with dances, all of whose names also have sexual associations, James "Boodle It" Wiggins, Willie "Boodle It" Right, Black Bottom McPhail, and Bob White (The Woogie Man). Three artists were associated with musical genres or music in general. Henry "Ragtime Texas" Thomas, Bill "Jazz" Gillum, and Rhythm Willie, while seven artists simply used the word "Blue" or "Blues." (Blue is sometimes used to designate very dark skin color, but in the present context it is likely to have had primarily a musical meaning.)[15]

A blues context was suggested by the nicknames of only 6 artists, 4 male and 2 female. All of these used the term Barrel House, or in one instance the variant Keghouse. These terms suggest a lowdown saloon environment. Not surprisingly, most of these artists featured song titles and lyrics with lowdown themes, such as Barrel House Annie's "Ain't Gonna Give It Away" and "Must Get Mine in Front," Barrelhouse Frankie Wallace's "I Had to Smack That Thing," Keghouse's "Canned Heat Blues" and "Sock It Blues," and Nolan "Barrel House" Welsh's "Larceny Woman Blues" and "Dying Pickpocket Blues."

Song lyrics and titles were used or suggested in the nicknames of 15 male and 2 female artists. I include here only artists who used titles or lyrics of songs that they did not compose themselves, with the exception of Harry "Freddie" Shayne, who had accompanied singer Priscilla Stewart on piano in 1924. Stewart had a hit with Shayne's composition "Mr. Freddie Blues," and Shayne later adopted the nickname in order to call attention to his role as composer. He recorded his own version of "Original Mr. Freddie Blues" in 1935. This nickname and 7 others came from the lyrics or titles of hit blues recordings, although a number of them have sexual meanings as well. These include George "Oh Red" Washington (from the hit of that title recorded by the Harlem Hamfats), Bumble Bee Slim (from Memphis Minnie's "Bumble Bee"), Mr. Freddie Spruell (from Shayne's hit song), Big Road Webster Taylor (possibly from Tommy Johnson's "Big Road Blues"), Kokomo Arnold (from various recordings of "Kokomo Blues"), Tallahassee Tight (from Tampa Red and Georgia Tom's "It's Tight Like That"), and Too Tight Henry (from Blind Blake's "Too Tight"). Titles of nonblues popular songs accounted for 5 nicknames, most of them coming from the names of characters featured in the songs. These included Sweet Georgia Brown, Sadie Green, Kid Stormy Weather, Whistlin' Rufus, and Little Willie Green. Traditional folksongs accounted for the remaining 4 nicknames in this group, Bo Weavil Jackson, Salty Dog Sam (Collins), Stavin' Chain (Wilson Jones), and Red Hot Ole Mose, the latter from the street cry of a hot tamale vendor. Although these artists represent a fairly low percentage of blues nicknames, we shall see later that a larger percentage of blues artists sang original "signature" songs that contained or explained their nicknames in the titles or lyrics.

Other blues artists and popular personalities lent their names as blues nicknames to 23 male and 5 female artists. Among those drawn from the blues world were Louie Bluie (from Louis Armstrong), Pinetop Burks and Aaron "Pine Top" Sparks (from Pine Top Smith), Leroy Carter and Leroy's Buddy (from Leroy Carr), Floyd Council as Blind Boy Fuller's Buddy, Brownie McGhee as Blind Boy Fuller No. 2, Sonny Terry as Blind Boy Fuller's Harmonica Player, Floyd Council as The Devil's Daddy-in-Law, Jimmie Gordon as Peetie Wheatstraw's Brother, Robert Lee McCoy as Peetie's Boy, and Harmon Ray as Peetie Wheatstraw's Buddy (all after William Bunch, who was known as Peetie Wheatstraw, The Devil's Son-in-Law), Joe Bullum (used by Jimmie Gordon on a recorded version of an earlier blues hit of Joe Pullum), King Solomon Hill as Blind Lemon's Buddy (from Blind Lemon Jefferson), Sonny Boy Williams (from Sonny Boy Williamson), Ernest Lawlars as Mr. Memphis Minnie (from the nickname of his more famous blues singing wife), Merline Johnson as the Yas Yas Girl (from Jimmy Strange, who had earlier recorded as The Yas Yas Man), Bessie Mae Smith and Ruby Smith (from Bessie Smith), and another singer who bore or adopted the same name as the famous Clara Smith. Several of the famous singers so honored died young and tragically, and their names were clearly adopted for nicknames as tributes after their deaths, with the suggestion and hope that the new bearer would carry on the musical legacy and level of success of the original bearer of the name. In other cases the names of more famous artists were adopted for nicknames while they were still living and musically active. The intent was either to fool record buyers or more often to gain a commercial boost through association. A few artists took nicknames from famous historical, biblical, or fictional characters. I have classified them here with the nicknames derived from musical figures, as all are prominent names in popular culture. These include Buster Brown (from a popular brand of shoes),

Jesse James, Jesse James Jefferson, Little David, King David (Crockett), King Solomon Hill, J. T. "Funny Paper" Smith (probably from Snuffy Smith, the stereotyped hillbilly character in the newspaper comics), Flyin' Lindburg (Milton Sparks), and Diamond Lil Hardaway (from a movie character portrayed by sexy actress Mae West). It should be noted that the biblical King David was a renowned singer and harpist and Diamond Lil was an entertainer. The use of these names for their associative value hardly requires further explanation, other than to point out that all of the honored blues artists, historical and biblical figures, and fictional characters were noted for especially flamboyant deeds or personalities. Of the artists who adopted the names of others, only Buster Brown, Leroy's Buddy, and the Yas Yas Girl retained these particular nicknames throughout sustained recording careers. The others either had short careers or switched to different names as their careers progressed.

A final small group of 5 prewar artists bear nicknames that suggest a rank order among blues singers. Original Bessie Brown and Stovepipe No. 1 seem to have adopted their nicknames in order to discourage other artists with the same names or nicknames, whereas Original Victoria Spivey was apparently trying to recall past successes after a slump in her career. Brownie McGhee was briefly called Blind Boy Fuller No. 2 in order to capitalize on Fuller's success and status immediately following his untimely death. Josephine Baker was called L'étoile noire des Folies Bergères (The Black Star of the Folies Bergères) on her French recordings, although perhaps these properly fall outside this survey.

The category of nonmusical nicknames that describe essential qualities of the artists is the largest, covering 193 artists (50 percent of all prewar blues artists bearing nicknames). This type of nickname is twice as prevalent among males as among females. Nicknames offering physical descriptions are the most numerous. There is great disparity between males and females, however, with 100 male artists having such nicknames compared to only 6 females. In some cases physical description is combined with one or more other qualities, as in nicknames like Memphis Slim, Little Buddy Doyle, and Arkansas Shorty. Eighteen male and 2 female artists had nicknames based on skin and/or hair color. These included Red Nelson, Brownie Stubblefield, Speckled Red, The Black Ace (Buck Turner), Black Spider Dumplin', Pink Anderson, Red Mike Bailey (St. Louis Red Mike), Black Boy Shine, Black Ivory King, Bull City Red (Oh Red), Black Byrd (John Byrd), Dusky Dailey, Smoky Harrison, Brownie McGhee, Piano Red, Black Bob, Chocolate Brown (Irene Scruggs), and Josephine Baker as L'étoile noire des Folies Bergères. It can be seen from this list that black and red are the predominant colors, followed by brown. There are no nicknames describing a "yellow" or "bright" complexion. Gradations of skin color and their supposed relationships to personality traits constituted an important theme in blues lyrics of the pre-war era.[16] Some of these names will be discussed below under the subcategory of terms designating racial and social status. An equally important area of physical description is handicapped status. There were 18 artists described as Blind, 4 as Peg Leg, as well as Charlie "Specks" McFadden (also known as Black Patch McFadden), Cripple Clarence Lofton, Sluefoot Joe, and One Arm Slim. Handicapped poor people were especially drawn to musical careers in the first half of the twentieth century, and the incidence of such nicknames here should not be surprising. Another important factor is height, with 12 male and 4 female artists described as Little, Tiny, Wee, Peanut, Half-Pint, and Stump, while 14 male artists are described as Big or Big Boy, 3 as Pine Top, and another as Long. (Pine Top can refer both to height and to a style of upturned hair often worn by musicians.)[17] Eight male artists were Slim, while 4 were called Fat or Fats. Three were called Old or Old Man. Other descriptive nicknames were Pretty Boy, Babyface, Curley, Jelly Jaw (referring to the movement of the artist's jaws while singing but possibly having a further sexual meaning), Egg Shell (bald headed), Flat Foot, Barefoot, Leadbelly, Hound Head, Birdhead, Billiken, Scarecrow, Little Hat, Socks, and Blue Coat. This last term is probably a holdover from a typical costume of minstrel show performers.

Sixteen male artists had nicknames referring to personality, character, or habitual behavior. Some of these were undoubtedly acquired in childhood, such as Skip James and Uncle Skipper (Charley Jordan) and perhaps Scrapper Blackwell, Mooch Richardson, and Sleepy John Estes. (Sleepy could also refer to appearance. This particular artist had lost an eye.) The remaining terms, however, seem fairly closely tied to a blues context or presentational style. These are Lonesome Charlie Harrison, Sloppy Henry, Rambling Bob, Ramblin' Thomas, Bogus Ben Covington (who apparently faked blindness), Hot Shot Willie (McTell), Papa Too Sweet, Tenderfoot Edwards, Sophisticated Jimmy LaRue (who specialized in songs with double entendre lyrics), The Mad Comic (Sam Theard), and Corny Allen Grier.

Twenty-five male and 4 female artists had nicknames referring to racial, social, or ethnic status. I include here the terms listed above denoting black or brown skin color, to which we can add Hi Henry Brown and Coot Grant (Leola B. Wilson). Other nicknames refer directly to racial designations, such as John "Big Nig" Bray, King of Spades (Sam Montgomery), and Cooney

Vaughan, while Wilber McCoy was listed in company files as The Hillbilly Plowboy for a title that was recorded but never issued. A few names referred to regional subcultures within black America, such as Polite "Frenchy" Christian, Creole George Guesnon, Johnnie "Geechie" Temple, and Geeshie Wiley. The remaining nicknames in this subcategory all suggest low social status. These include Shufflin' Sam, Poor Boy Burke, Poor Jab (Jones), Willie "Poor Boy" Lofton, Poor Bill, Poor Jim, Poor Charley (West), and Po' Joe Williams. Although these nicknames pertain to only 7 percent of all artists with nicknames, they can hardly be dismissed. In fact, we might add to the discussion the 22 nicknames that contain the word "Boy," a term commonly applied to black males to suggest inferior status, and stereotyped names such as Sam and Mandy. One might indeed wonder why a blues singer would bear a nickname such as Shufflin' Sam, Big Nig, or Black Boy Shine, which on the surface appear to suggest acquiescence to racial stereotypes. A closer examination, however, reveals that these artists were hardly acquiescent personalities. Shufflin' Sam, who was better known as Washboard Sam, worked at times as a private investigator and often composed and sang blues about bullying, violence, and aggression. John "Big Nig" Bray worked in a lumber camp, had served in World War I, and sang about his encounters with the women in Belgium and France, as well as with German soldiers on the battlefield. Black Boy Shine, whose nickname combines three terms that had negative connotations in the 1930s when he recorded, sang of his independent existence, living for the moment in lowdown dives, flophouses, and hobo boxcars. Black Ivory King, whose nickname contains the startling notion (for 1937) of a black king over something white, sang of a similar existence on the margins of society. I personally knew Brownie McGhee, Poor Jim (Yank Rachell), Johnnie "Geechie" Temple, and Po' Joe Williams and can testify that they never displayed acquiescent or obsequious behavior in my presence. Their bearing of nicknames that superficially seem to suggest a second-class status must therefore serve a more important purpose. Rather than accepting a stereotype, they used these nicknames to break through the stereotype and assert their individuality and independence. It is the same motivation that Richard Wright had in calling his autobiographical novel *Black Boy* and that some modern-day rap performers have in using the word "Nigger" to describe themselves and others in their circle. These artists express solidarity with and appeal to the most alienated, marginalized, uprooted, poor, and lowdown individuals in black American society and serve as spokespersons for them through their songs and recordings.

A small number of nicknames, 11 male and 2 female, describe nonmusical occupations. A few of these were relatively prestigious positions, such as Preacher Thomas (Jesse James Jefferson, whose Preacher nickname could also suggest a singing style), The Cotton Belt Porter (Freeman Stowers), Doctor Clayton, Doctor Higgs, and Doc Dasher, although the preacher and at least one of the doctors were evidently fictitious. Doctor Clayton claimed to have been born in Africa and raised by an American doctor who had worked there and adopted him. Doctor Higgs was an herbalist who evidently worked as a musician in medicine shows. Five of the occupational terms describe rural manual labor that was not especially prestigious, including Floyd "Dipper Boy" Council, The Hillbilly Plowboy (Wilber McCoy), Stable Boy Sam, The Mississippi Muleskinner (Big Road Webster Taylor), and Walter "Cowboy" Washington, although the occupations of cowboy and muleskinner did give their holders a sometimes positive reputation for toughness. Stable Boy Sam was also known as Spark Plug Smith, a nickname taken from the name of a horse in a newspaper comic strip. A few nicknames describe criminal occupations. Among males there was only Peanut the Kidnapper, while the only two females with occupational nicknames were both described as prostitutes, The Tuneful Tramp (Star Page) and Bertha "Chippie" Hill. These nicknames describing low status or outlaw occupations can be understood in the same sense as the racial and social nicknames discussed above.

A rather large group of 48 men and 8 women bore nicknames referring to geographical locations. Almost all of these were states and cities located in the South, with Mississippi leading the way with 9 artists. A number of others were border states and cities, such as St. Louis (4), Kansas (2), and Kansas City. The only northern locations were found in the nicknames of Kokomo Arnold, which was likely derived from a song title, and Montana Taylor, who was actually born in that state. A few other nicknames suggested streets and highways (Broadway Jones, Willie "61" Blackwell, Big Road Webster Taylor), a body of water (Cedar Creek Sheik), regions (Western Kid, Pinewood Tom), and a neighborhood (Oak Cliff T-Bone). The relatively large number of geographical nicknames, 14 percent of all artists with nicknames, might be interpreted as suggesting a "sense of place" among blues artists. This was undoubtedly the case for some artists who remained locally or regionally based, but perhaps just as often there was a sense of estrangement from place. Most of these artists were recorded in the North and many were based there, while many others were itinerant. Most of these place names would have had an exotic ring for audiences and especially for listeners to records. Although some artists like Mississippi John Hurt lived almost their entire lives in a single community, most were well traveled and gave the impression to their audiences of being men and women of the world. At least in their own minds if not in their actual circumstances, most were *from* the places mentioned in their nicknames, rather than located *in* these places. We should not discount the possibility that these nicknames sometimes functioned nostalgically for artists in the way that some terms for family relationships may have done; a place name used as a nickname was usually liberating rather than confining.

We come now to a large category of nicknames suggesting special things and qualities outside the artist's everyday being, usually things and qualities the artist would like to be associated with. Although I have set up this category to contrast with the previous large category of nicknames that describe *essential* qualities of the artist, there are many ambiguous cases. One might consider, for example, that nicknames containing sexual and food imagery and referents would be "essential" and part of the "everyday being" of a person. No doubt this is true in some specific cases and in the general sense that sex and food are a normal part of human life, but clearly these nicknames often contain a significant element of fantasy, boasting, exaggeration, and projection, and it is for this reason that I discuss them here. There are 102 artists with nicknames in this category, or 26 percent of all artists in the prewar period with nicknames. It should be noted as well that some of the nicknames in the "musical terms" category discussed earlier contain considerable projection and fantasy, particularly those derived from other musical and popular culture personalities.

Nicknames describing food and tastes in food have a considerable overlap with sexual nicknames to the point where it is nearly futile to separate them. Students of the human psyche are well aware of the universal close relationship between food and sexual symbolism. Twenty-two male and 2 female artists in the prewar era had nicknames referring to food. A few of these may simply have represented real personal tastes in food, such as Eugene "Dry Bread" Anthony, Barbecue Bob, Hamfoot Ham (Wilber McCoy), Ham Gravy, Chicken Wilson, Cat Juice Charley (for homemade whisky), and Neckbones. It should be noted, however, that "ham" had associations with exaggerated performance style and with "jive" and "hokum" music, which both of the artists so named performed. Chicken was a stereotypical food of gluttons and comic figures, especially comic preachers, although it can also have a sexual meaning with reference to a young or under-aged woman. Dry Bread, Catjuice, and Neckbones would all have had lowdown or low-class associations. All of these associations are in keeping with other observable patterns of nicknaming among blues singers, as discussed above. The remaining food nicknames all have rather obvious sexual meanings as well, referring to sweetness or tenderness, or suggesting sexual anatomy or positions. These include Jelly Roll Anderson, Butterbeans, Pork Chops (Lee Green), Beans Hambone, Honey Hill, Hambone Willie Newbern, Guilford "Peachtree" Payne, Pigmeat Terry, Jaydee "Jelly Jaw" Short, Sugar Cane Johnny, The Honey Dripper (Roosevelt Sykes), Black Spider Dumplin', Sugar Underwood, Aaron "T-Bone" Walker, Pigmeat Pete (Wesley Wilson), and the 2 women, Sweet Pease Spivey and Chocolate Brown (Irene Scruggs). Many of these terms occur in blues lyrics and titles of the period.[18]

I counted 21 sexual nicknames among men and 3 among women, although these include many of the food terms. The sexual terms describe tastes and preferences, sexual activities and movements, and sexual allure and potency. Besides the sexual food terms listed above, these nicknames include Cedar Creek Sheik, Sheik Johnson, Bert "Snake Root" Hatton, Frank "Springback" James, James "Steady Roll" Johnson, Willie "Boodle It" Right, James "Boodle It" Wiggins, The Yas Yas Man (Jimmy Strange), Sweet Papa Stovepipe, Sweet Papa Tadpole, Lovin' Sam (Theard) from Down in Bam, Too Tight Henry, Tallahassee Tight, Pretty Boy Walker, and among women Red Hot Shakin' Davis, Yas Yas Girl (Merline Johnson), and The Za Zu Girl. Since love and sex are the topics of most blues songs, the incidence of sexual nicknames among blues singers should not be surprising. We have seen many nicknames classified in other categories that also have some degree of sexual meaning. The fact that many of these sexual nicknames are somewhat disguised as food, animal, musical, or other types of nicknames gives them an in-group significance that might escape the attention or censure of "squares."

Animals and nature provide nicknames for 32 male and 7 female singers. A few of these are obviously suggestive of human physical characteristics. They include the aforementioned Coot Grant, Black Byrd, Bert "Snake Root" Hatton, Hound Head Henry, Sweet Papa Tadpole, and Black Spider Dumplin', to which we could add Minnow Townsend, Blues Birdhead, Bo Weavil Jackson, and Boll Weavil Bill (from the insect's black color). Others, however, are quite clearly chosen on account of the animal's qualities of wildness, aggressiveness, strength, mischievousness, or abilities to fly, swim under water, bite, sting, or make honey. Many of these qualities have a significant sexual and even magical meaning as well. Such names are The Fox and The Rabbit, Feathers and Frogs (both duos), Richard "Rabbit" Brown, Spider

Carter, Jaybird Coleman, Jaybird (Rajah Evans), Thomas "Jaybird" Jones, Bumble Bee Slim, Buck Franklin, Barrel House Buck McFarland, Buck Turner, Mud Dauber Joe, Monkey Joe, James "Bat" Robinson, The Howling Wolf (J. T. Smith), Kingfish Bill Tomlin (possibly named after the character in the "Amos 'n' Andy" radio show), Skeeter Hinton, and The Lone Wolf (Oscar Woods), along with females Skeet Brown, Skeets Edwards, and Bee Turner. Domestic animals are used as nicknames by Spark Plug Smith (named after a comic strip race horse), Milk Bull (Walter Vincson, with an ambiguous but obviously sexual meaning), and Cow Cow Davenport (from the cowcatchers of trains on which he used to ride as a hobo). Animals live outside the rules of human society and often are thought to have special or magical qualities and powers. It should not be surprising that animal nicknames were used by blues singers, who often both grew up in rural areas surrounded by domestic and wild animals and also operated on the margins of society. Animal imagery is also very prominent in the lyrics and titles of blues from this period. A few representative titles are "I'm an Old Bumble Bee," "Black Snake Moan," "I'm a Rattlesnakin' Daddy," "Rootin' Ground Hog," "Catfish Blues," and "Jersey Bull Blues."[19] On a more abstract level of the natural world, Ozie "Daybreak" McPherson and Kid Stormy Weather were the only two nicknames from this era based on natural phenomena, although it is likely that the latter comes more directly from the title of a popular song.

Far fewer artists drew their nicknames from man-made devices. I count only 5 males and 3 females, and a couple of these are ambiguous cases. All but one have a connection to mechanical devices and vehicles that suggest speed and power. These are Six Cylinder Smith, Spark Plug Smith (although this nickname actually comes from a horse's name), Bobby Cadillac, Side Wheel Sallie Duffie, Streamline Mae (probably from a train), Charles "Cow Cow" Davenport (from the cowcatchers on trains), and George "Bullet" Williams. The only exception is Freezone, whose nickname is apparently derived from a corn remedy. Cars, trains, and guns are common subjects in blues songs and common in the blues environment.[20] Cars and trains are also related thematically to geographical nicknames as symbols of mobility.

Royalty or some other type of preeminence or exalted status is suggested in 12 nicknames, all borne by males. We know that a number of female vaudeville blues singers of the 1920s were known as queens and empresses but these titles were never used on their records. A couple of these examples, King Solomon Hill and Prince Moore, may not be nicknames at all but simply given names. King David, however, is certainly a nickname, connected to a David Crockett who is himself named after a famous historical personality and backwoods folk hero. The other Kings in the group are Black Ivory King and King of Spades (Sam Montgomery), both names having racial connotations. The notion of a black king was a direct challenge to the social and political status quo of the time. Both of these artists recorded in the mid-1930s when the emperor of Ethiopia, Haile Selassie, was in the news. Other more exotic forms of royalty are represented by Kaiser Clifton, Rajah Evans, Prince Budda (Frankie Jaxon), Cedar Creek Sheik, and Sheik Johnson, collectively suggesting an attempt at displaying worldliness by blues singers whose audiences often had limited social and geographical horizons. The Sheiks are undoubtedly based on the popularity of the film *The Sheik,* starring Rudolph Valentino as the desert lover. Champion Jack Dupree drew his nickname from his prior boxing career, while the significance of the designation of Charlie Segar as Key Board Wizard Supreme should be obvious.

The final group within this category consists of nicknames suggesting connections to the supernatural, magic, and luck. Much has been made of these themes in the blues in recent literature, especially connections of the blues or of certain blues artists to the devil.[21] But these themes occur in nicknames only fifteen times in the prewar era, and some of these cases are ambiguous. Three artists are Wizards but only in respect to their musical instruments. Tampa Red was The Guitar Wizard, Bill Weldon the Hawaiian Guitar Wizard, and Charlie Segar the Key Board Wizard Supreme. Bert "Snake Root" Hatton's nickname might suggest a status as a root doctor, but more likely it is sexual symbolism with only a hint of magical power. Curtis Jones was simply The Texas Wonder, while Charley Patton was The Masked Marvel. These nicknames were used on only one each of the many records made by these artists, although they do suggest some sort of superhero status.[22] Asbestos Burns also suggests a magical power but in a comic sense. Three artists took their nicknames from playing cards, presumably denoting luck and success in gambling, Jack o' Diamonds, King of Spades (Sam Montgomery), and The Black Ace (Buck Turner), although the latter two also have significant racial meanings. The only nicknames directly connected with a supernatural being, in all cases the devil, are The Red Devil (Red Nelson), Peetie Wheatstraw (The Devil's Son-in-Law, also known as The High Sheriff from Hell), and The Devil's Daddy-in-law (Floyd Council), the latter obviously inspired by the success of Peetie Wheatstraw. These names all have significant comic overtones, and it is debatable whether listeners thought these artists were serious disciples of Satan.[23] As for African supernatural beings, a subject much discussed in recent blues literature,[24] there are no direct references in blues nicknames, and I can detect no covert or symbolic ones. In a very general sense, however, the limited interest in magic and the supernatural displayed in blues nicknames (3 percent of artists with nicknames) could have an African background. The same could be said for most of the other nicknames in this category that represent projections and symbols. Without denying the trickster-like character of many blues artists or the reports of their pacts made with the devil for the gaining of musical skills and other powers, I find these elements not to be major themes in blues nicknames of this period.

There are only 12 nicknames in the final category of the prewar period, those with uncertain or unclassifiable meanings (3 percent). The category includes three artists whose apparent nicknames may actually be given names or their derivatives. These are the aforementioned Furry Lewis, Scottie Nesbitt, and Son Becky, whose real name was Leon Calhoun. Son Becky may represent a case of a male nickname derived from a woman's name, suggesting a man who has that woman on his mind.[25] Ki Ki Johnson and Popo Warfield probably retained childhood pet names, although the latter could be a variation of Papa. These two names, along with Cow Cow Davenport, may reflect a typically African naming pattern of emphatic reduplication.[26] James "Yank" Rachell also had a childhood nickname given by his grandmother, although its precise meaning is unclear. Ardell "Shelly" Bragg, the only female in this category, also has a nickname that she probably gained in childhood. Blind Blake's apparent surname possibly masks a dialectal form of "bloke." He was from Jacksonville, Florida, or possibly the nearby sea islands, where such a pronunciation of "bloke" would have been in use. Composer credits on his records suggest that his real name was Arthur Phelps. Jab Jones and Jabo Williams may be bearers of African names, probably in their cases used as nicknames. Stovepipe Johnson's nickname could refer either to the stovepipe used as a musical instrument (as it evidently does with Daddy Stovepipe and Stovepipe No. 1), or to a stovepipe hat worn as a costume in a holdover from minstrel shows, or even as a reference to the color black. Finally there is the mysterious nickname Three Fifteen given to a singer named Dave Bluntson. Possibly it represents the number of a train or highway.

We might pause here to comment on the relatively low incidence of blues nicknames among female singers of the prewar period, 15 percent of all female artists as compared to 43 percent of all male artists. In a study of this subject by Skipper and Leslie, who found a much higher 29 percent of female singers between 1890 and 1970 to have had nicknames, the authors attribute the gender disparity to the fact that "women . . . have been expected to be in the home, keeping house and raising children," that they are expected in American society to have "an inward orientation."[27] I would agree with these statements but would also point out that blues singers were known to be out of the home and on their own. This applied to women as well as men, although some of the women singers were clearly attached in their careers to husbands, male partners, accompanists, and managers. It probably was felt within the blues community that it was simply undignified for a woman to have a nickname, since the other main group of women with nicknames was prostitutes. Of the 63 female blues singers with nicknames from this era, only 18 referred in any way to the singer's sexual allure. Seven of these, however, were merely Babe or Baby, and 3 others made reference to sweetness: Chocolate Brown, Sweet Georgia Brown, and Sweet Pease Spivey. None of these nicknames are especially provocative in a sexual sense. Somewhat more provocative are the nicknames based on cars and trains: Bobby Cadillac, Side Wheel Sallie Duffie, and Streamline Mae. This leaves 5 nicknames that are quite overtly sexual: Red Hot Shakin' Davis, Yas Yas Girl, The Za Zu Girl, and 2 occupational nicknames referring specifically to prostitution, The Tuneful Tramp and Chippie.[28] Female blues singers made recordings especially during the era of vaudeville blues, which lasted roughly until 1931. After this they were mostly confined to singing in cabarets, clubs, barrelhouses, and house parties, and they recorded with less frequency for the remainder of the prewar period. The vaudeville stage provided elevation and distance from the audience, and the whole vaudeville scene was infused with symbols suggesting dignity and status, such as elaborate beaded gowns, titles of royalty like "Empress" and "Queen," and sometimes operatic tendencies in the singing. Very few of the female singers connected to this scene had nicknames, and the ones that did generally had relatively sedate ones, such as Ma Rainey, Mandy Lee, Baby Benbow, Original Bessie Brown, and Diamond Lil Hardaway. Bertha Hill was bold indeed in using the nickname Chippie within this context. Of all the nicknames of women blues singers, 17 referred to music and 20 were stereotypical names or familiar terms, for a total of 59 percent. Physical descriptions and geographical designations accounted for another 14 nicknames or 22 percent. These types of nicknames are generally the least threatening to one's dignity and social status.

The discussion of prostitution raises the issue of the relationship of blues nicknames to those of other social groups. It is well known that the practice of nicknaming in America flourishes especially within groups that are socially marginalized or physically isolated, where there is great physical danger or social tension, and where heroic status is attainable, often the status of a rebel or outlaw hero. Groups that fit this description are athletes, soldiers, policemen, sailors, lumberjacks, miners, cowboys, hoboes, entertainers, gamblers, pimps and prostitutes, other criminals, prisoners, children, and marginalized ethnic groups. Certainly the world of blues was a marginal one, even within black American society, which was itself marginalized by American society. Blues furthermore intersected frequently enough with the worlds of other forms of entertainment (acting, dancing, other musical genres), hoboing, dangerous occupations, pimping and prostitution, gambling, criminal activity, and prison, and many blues artists participated in some of these worlds from time to time. These intersecting worlds no doubt contributed to the store of blues nicknames and reinforced their use within the world of blues. Obvious examples include such nicknames as The Mad Comic, Red Hot Shakin' Davis, Black Bottom McPhail, Ragtime Texas (Henry Thomas), Jazz Gillum, Cow Cow Davenport, Walter "Cowboy" Washington, Leadbelly (a prison nickname), Peanut the Kidnapper, Jack o' Diamonds, and Bertha "Chippie" Hill.

Let us turn now to a consideration of blues nicknames in the postwar era (1943–70). We have already noted how World War II and a shellac shortage and musicians' union strike in the wartime years all had a disruptive effect on the blues and its recording industry, and how hundreds of new independent record companies in the postwar years broke the monopoly that a handful of companies exercised in blues recording just before the war. These companies recorded many new, generally more urbanized, styles of blues, mostly by new artists. The rising Civil Rights Movement during this era also led to changing statuses, changing self-image, and changing attitudes toward the blues and blues singers in the African American community. We shall see that these changes, and those in the sound of the music and the blues record industry, are reflected in changes in some of the blues nicknaming patterns.

A significantly larger number of blues artists recorded during the postwar era, 2,533 or more than twice as many as recorded in the prewar era (1,195). This is largely a reflection of the much greater number of record companies, along with growing prosperity and ability to purchase records in the African American community, greater access to records in an increasingly urban population, and the increased radio airplay of records. The growth in popularity of blues among white Americans and Europeans during this period created additional recording opportunities. While the overall number of blues singers increased, the male-female ratio was significantly altered from 64/36 percent in the prewar era to 83/16 percent in the postwar era. (The other 1 percent is the result of not being able to determine the gender of a handful of artists.) The significant drop in the percentage of female artists demonstrates that blues had become a largely male performance genre in the postwar era, with approximately 5 out of every 6 blues recording artists being male. This trend had actually begun to set in at the beginning of the 1930s, following the decline of the female-dominated vaudeville style of blues and the theater circuit that supported it. Female singers from the early 1930s onward increasingly turned toward jazz and popular tunes and later to "soul" material or remained stalwarts in the realm of gospel music.

The percentage of blues artists with nicknames is 39 percent, up from 32 percent in the prewar era. This seems to be due largely to an increase in nicknaming among female blues singers in the postwar era, 22 percent, up from 15 percent in the prewar era, while the percentage of male blues singers with nicknames held steady at 43 percent. Thus, while the profile of women as blues singers diminished in the postwar era, they drew closer to their male counterparts in the percentage who had nicknames. Nevertheless, the male percentage was still almost twice the female percentage, reflecting no doubt the still lingering attitude that it was undignified and potentially scandalous for a woman to have a nickname. The increase in the percentage of female blues singers' nicknames suggests a growing willingness on their part to risk their personal reputations in a professional arena that was increasingly dominated by males.

For both men and women the same categories of blues nicknames that were established for the prewar era are applicable in the postwar era. Some of their percentages of usage change significantly, however, and one can also note sometimes a change in thematic range within a category. It will become clear that these changes can often be explained by the changes in blues and the record industry as well as the changes in social attitudes noted above.

Only 7 artists, all of them male, have stereotypical nicknames, 4 Sams and 3 Joes. These represent only 1 percent of all postwar artists with nicknames, down significantly from 4 percent in the prewar era. This reduction suggests that such names were falling out of favor in a time of rising agitation for civil rights and social equality. Indeed, 6 of these 7 artists had begun their recording careers in the 1940s or even earlier and were thus among the older generation of postwar blues artists. We shall observe a similar reduction in other types of nicknames with stereotypical or negative meanings in the postwar era.

Familiar terms were used as nicknames of 254 postwar blues artists, 25 percent of all artists with nicknames. Of these, 231 (25 percent) were male and

23 (26 percent) female. These percentages were almost exactly the same as in the prewar era: 25 percent of all artists, 25 percent male and 24 percent female. The names include the usual Son/Sonny/Sonny Boy, Bud/Buddy/Buddy Boy, Cousin, Papa, Dad/Daddy, Junior, Babe/Baby, Brother, Bubba, Bo, Buster, Butch, and Kid among the males, and Babe/Baby, Mama, Girl, and Sister among the females. Among the males there were also a few new but essentially unremarkable nicknames, such as Tabby/Tab, Tot, Papoose, Boo/Boo Boo, Goo Goo, Chico, Shep, and Snooks/Snooky/Snookum. The use of the nicknames Boy and Girl, which could sometimes have a demeaning sense when used as terms of address by whites, was down less than one percent in the postwar period. However, it is unlikely that many of these usages would have been considered demeaning in either era since they usually occurred within compound nicknames, such as Sonny Boy, Buddy Boy, Baby Boy, and Blues Girl. Of these compounds, only Big Boy is likely to have had a demeaning sense in some cases, and significantly its usage decreased from 8 in the prewar era (2.5 percent) to 5 in the postwar era (0.6 percent). Even more spectacular was the rise in the postwar era of nicknames containing respectful terms of address, such as Mister (27), Junior (26), Mrs. (2), and Miss (10). During the 1940s civil rights organizations, such as the National Association for the Advancement of Colored People, campaigned vigorously for the use of respectful terms of address for black people, particularly in the press. The overall success of their campaign seems to be reflected in the use of such terms among blues artists in the postwar years. They were virtually absent in the prewar era, which saw only one Mister, three Misses, and one Madame.

The use of nicknames containing musical terms rose somewhat in the postwar era, from 28 percent to 33 percent. Most of this increase was among males, who displayed the same percentages as the overall figures, whereas such nicknames rose only 1 percent among females (27 percent to 28 percent). The main increases were in the subcategories of instruments/styles/dances and other artists/famous people. The subcategory of song lyrics/titles increased by only 1 percent, while the subcategories of blues context and rank order decreased. The overall increase, especially in nicknames related to instruments/styles/dances, may be related to an increase in opportunities for professional careers in blues, particularly among male artists in the postwar era. Such nicknames display a greater variety and specificity than in the prewar era. Besides such familiar terms as Blue/Blues, Guitar, Piano, Harmonica/Harp/Harpo/Harper/Harp Blowin', and Washboard, we find such nicknames as Talking Boy, Whispering, Mushmouth, Two-Voice,

Singer/Singin'/Sing-Sation, Scat Man, Hootin' Owl, Tye-tongue, Screaming, Frogman, Mumbles, and Loudmouth to specify vocal styles; Riff, Choker, Blow It, Blow Top, Hot Lips, Peck, and Shakey to suggest instrumental styles; Man (for mandolin), Dual Trumpeter, One-String, Fender (a brand of electric guitar), Ironing Board (for an electric keyboard), Sax/Sax Man, Sticks, One Man Band/Trio, Fiddlin', and Gabriel/Gabe (for the trumpet blowing angel) to represent instruments; Jazz, Soul, Swing, Jive, Rhythm, Jam/Jammin', Boogie (Woogie), and Rockin'/Rocky/Rocker/Good Rocking/Rockhouse for musical genres; Hop, Jump/Jumping, Bumps, Twist, The Stroll, Boogaloo, Stomp, Cha Cha, Rubberlegs, Hip Shakin', Shake a Plenty, and T-Bone to represent dance and movement; and Hotsy Totsy, Hip, The Cat, and Long Time to indicate general musicality. All but one of the female nicknames in this subcategory suggested vocal genres or styles. They included Blue/Blues/ Good Blues, Soul, Bea Bopp, Rhapsody, and Rock 'n' Roll/Rock-a-way. The lone exception was Hip Shakin'.

In the prewar period 20 of the 28 artists with nicknames derived from the names of famous people took them from the names or nicknames of other blues or jazz artists. The remainder were drawn from characters in the movies, comic strips, popular culture, the Bible, a notorious outlaw, and a flying ace. In the postwar era 58 out of 96 artists took their nicknames from the names of other blues and jazz artists, a ratio lower by 11 percent. The artists who inspired the most nicknames were B. B. King (B. B. Brown, Bee Bee Carn, B. B. Carter, Curtis "C. C." Griffin, B. B. King Jr., Andrew "Blues Boy" Odom, and Bee Bee Queen), Sonny Boy Williamson (two other Sonny Boy Williamsons, two Sonny Boy Williamses, Sonny Boy Johnson, Little Sonny, and Chicago Sunny Boy), Fats Domino (The Fat Man, Fats Jr., Fats Gaines, and Skinny Dynamo), Muddy Waters (Muddy Waters Jr., Eddie Clearwater/Clear Waters, and Muddy Walters), Little Walter (Little Papa Walter and Little Walter Jr.), Piano Red (Memphis Piano Red and Piano "C" Red—"C" for Chicago), T-Bone Walker (Little T-Bone and T-Bone Walker Jr.), Lightnin' Hopkins (Lightnin' Slim and Lightnin' Jr.), and Peetie Wheatstraw (Peetie Wheatstraw's Buddy and Herman "Peetie Wheatstraw" Ray). It is probably of some significance that all of these original inspirations were themselves bearers of nicknames. Other musical figures who inspired namesakes were Johnny Ace (Johnny Acey), Little Milton (Big Milton), Gatemouth Brown (James "Wide Mouth" Brown), Elmore James (Elmer James), Count Basie (Detroit Count), Bo Diddley (Bo Dudley), Guitar Slim (Guitar Slim Green), Hot Lips Page (Hot Lips Johnson), Lionel Hampton (Harmon "Hump" Jones), Nat King Cole (King Kolax), Magic Sam (Magic Slim), Cab Calloway (Cab

McMillan), Jimmy Reed (Jimmy Reeves Jr.), Walter "Shakey" Horton (Shakey Jake), Albert King (Al King), Doctor Clayton (Doctor Clayton's Buddy), Pvt. Cecil Gant (Pvt. Lloyd Thompson), Blind Boy Fuller (Little Boy Fuller), Chuck Willis (Chick Willis), Little Miss Cornshucks (Little Miss Sharecropper), Ma Rainey (Big Memphis Ma Rainey), Country Slim (Miss Country Slim), and Billie "Lady Day" Holiday (Devonia "Lady Dee" Williams). Louis Armstrong, Ray Charles, Smokey Hogg, and Earl King had their names usurped outright by other artists, as did Sonny Boy Williamson noted earlier. Once again, almost all of the original inspirations had nicknames to begin with.

The remaining artists in this subcategory were inspired by biblical, historical, and fictional characters. They display a considerably broader range of inspiration than their prewar counterparts, a fact that can probably be correlated with a rising educational level among postwar blues artists, greater penetration of the mass media, particularly movies and the new medium of television, and a greater awareness of the world in general. Artists with biblical nicknames include four Little Davids, one King David, three King Solomons, Gabriel, Prince Gabe, and Delilah. All of the male biblical figures were known for musical abilities, while Delilah was known for her sexual allure. From films and television come Little Caesar, Casanova Jr., G. L. "Davy" Crockett, Pinnochio James, King Syam, King Tut, Little Mummy, Mr. Calhoun (probably from a character in the "Amos 'n' Andy" television series), Tiny Tim, Mighty Joe Young, and Mitzi Mars (after the sexy singer-actress Mitzi Gaynor), along with western and outlaw figures Wild Bill, Wild Bill Phillips, Billy "The Kid" Emerson, two Jesse Jameses, and Pancho Villa. Tiny Topsy comes from literature and Cordelia de Milo from art. From the general world of popular culture and children's lore come Buster Brown, Good Time Charlie, Tommy Tucker, Jack "The Bear" Parker, Prince Albert (probably from the name of a popular brand of tobacco depicting Queen Victoria's consort on the can), Wee Willie Wayne, Frank "Sweet" Williams, and James "Big Sambo" Young. Two blues artists honored prominent black personalities with their nicknames. Piney Brown took his name from the owner of a famous saloon in Kansas City, whose death in 1940 was commemorated in Joe Turner's "Piney Brown Blues." Leslie Hill honored the heavyweight boxing champion Joe Louis by becoming Joe Hill Louis.

Nicknames derived from song titles and lyrics came mostly from blues sources, in a number of cases from an artist's earlier hit record. The song "Good Rockin' Tonight," a hit in 1947 for both Roy Brown and Wynonie Harris, inspired an extraordinary 7 nicknames, 5 Good Rockin's and 2 called

Mighty Man after a line in the song, "I'm a mighty, mighty man." Eight nicknames came from the titles of jazz tunes or popular songs. Cherokee, Joe "Papoose" Fritz, and two King Porters represented jazz, while popular song inspired J. T. "Nature Boy" Brown, Danny Boy Thomas, Danny "Run Joe" Taylor (from a calypso hit) and Muddy Water (the original nickname of Muddy Waters). The subcategory of blues context contains 3 artists with the nickname Barrel House, one Juke Boy, a Pig 'n' Whistle Red (after the name of a drive-in barbecue restaurant where the artist regularly performed), a Floorshow, and a Blind Street Singer. The subcategory of rank order contains 3 artists who are concerned to let it be known that they are The Original.

Nonmusical nicknames that describe essential qualities of the artists remain the largest category in the postwar era, comprising 52 percent of all artists with nicknames, up from 50 percent in the prewar era. Among male artists there was actually a slight decrease from 54 percent to 53 percent, but among females there was a considerable increase from 27 percent to 44 percent. This increase was especially marked in the subcategory of nicknames describing physical traits, which rose from 10 percent to 36 percent of all nicknames among women and from 31 percent to 36 percent among men. In the prewar era 4 of the 6 female nicknames in this subcategory described small size (Wee, Tiny, Little), and the other 2 described color (Chocolate Brown, Noire). In the postwar era 19 of the 32 women in this subcategory are described as Little, Little Bit, Tiny, and Wee, but 8 women are now described as Big, Chubby, Fatso, or Fatwoman. These statistical increases suggest that female blues singers in the postwar era had become more comfortable with their physicality, including large size. Other descriptive nicknames for women in the postwar era were Glad Rags, Dimples, Angel Face, and The Brown. Among postwar male artists the greatest number of nicknames by far indicated size or strength. These included Little/Li'l/Little Man (102), Tiny (4), Pee Wee (4), Wee (2), Shorty (3), Short Stuff, Stump, Petite, Big/Bigs/Big Boy/Big Daddy (63), Giant, Tall, Long Tall (3), Long/Long Man (2), Treetop (2), Pinetop, Slim (34), Skinny, Thin Man, String Bean, Fats/Fat Boy/Fat Man (14), Chubby, Jelly Belly, Leadbelly, Mighty, and Crusher. Hair and facial features were described in the nicknames Curley (5), Nappy, Bushy Head, Longhair, Baldhead, Cleanhead (3), Meat Head, Baby Face (2), Pretty Boy, Handsome, Smilin'/Smiley (4), Gatemouth (2), Wide Mouth, and Google Eyes. Age was indicated by Old, Young (3), and Teenage, and color by Red (21), Pink, Speckled, Blonde, Brownie, Black (2), and Smoky/Smokey (5). The use of color designations in nicknames was down significantly in the postwar period, particularly those indicating black color. Most of the latter used the more euphemistic term Smokey. This suggests a lowered importance of color distinctions within the African American community as well as a rejection of the term "Black," which had often been used with negative intent in the prewar era. In the 1960s Black would be resurrected and given a positive meaning as an all-embracing term for African Americans, for whom gradations of physical blackness were now of little consequence. Among prewar male artists with nicknames, 8 percent described some sort of physical handicap. This percentage dropped markedly to 2.5 percent in the postwar era, probably reflecting improved health care in the African American community. Blind/Blind Boy occurred 16 times and Peg Leg 5 times, while Nubbit (indicating a missing thumb tip), Shakey, Cripple, and Stick (for a walking stick) occurred once each. Two other artists were described as Lefty or Left Handed. The remaining nicknames indicated general appearance or clothing. They included Dusty (2), Barefoot, Polka Dot, Top Hat, The Hat, Boots, Blazer Boy (2), and Flash.

Nicknames describing personality and character traits were also more prominent in the postwar era, doubling from 4 percent to 8 percent of all nicknames. All but 2 of the 77 artists with such nicknames were males. The 2 women bore the nickname Sweet. This increase probably reflects a shift in male self-image from membership in a generic class ("the Negro") to a greater sense of individuality and personality. The great majority of these nicknames have a positive meaning, suggesting happiness, success, sexual power, or toughness. General happiness was indicated by Happy (5), Happy Wanderer, Gay, Jolly, Peppy, Pleasant, and Skip/Skippy (2). Success was suggested by Fabulous (3), Cool Papa, Frosty, Hepcat, Slick (3), Sly, Handy, and Flash. Sexual success was suggested by Cozy (2), Tender (2), Sweet/Sweets (2), Mustright, Hot Shot, Easy Papa, Playboy (2), Manish Boy, and Tippo Lite (probably from the tiptoeing of a man making a "midnight creep"). Nicknames carrying a sense of toughness, sometimes with a suggestion of cruelty, were Bad/Big Bad (2), Tuff, Scrapper, Joltin' Joe (perhaps derived from the nickname of the baseball player Joe Dimaggio), Shifty, Rockheart, Jealous, Hungry, and Moohah (suggesting loudness). To these we might add a number of nicknames that suggested that the artist was insane or out of control: Wild/Wild Child/Wild Man/Wild Bill (5), Madman, Mad Dog, Krazy, and Loose Wig. These nicknames for toughness or madness, which constitute 2 percent of all male nicknames in the postwar era, are almost entirely absent in the prewar era. The only prewar examples are Scrapper Blackwell, who recorded in both eras, and The Mad Comic, whose madness is immediately neutralized by his humor. The rise of this sort of imagery in the postwar era suggests that black males felt more confident in expressing toughness, "badness," and "wildness" during a time of increasing assertiveness and civil rights agitation. It should be kept in mind that a black person who resisted white harassment or insults, either verbally or physically, was typically labeled a "crazy nigger" or "bad nigger" by the whites and was often a target for severe retaliation, death, or confinement in a prison or mental institution. By the time of the postwar era this pattern of retaliation had begun to weaken, and it became safer to assert one's manhood. Only 15 of the 75 male nicknames in this subcategory describe sadness, weakness, unpopularity, or other negative character traits. These are Sad Head, Square, Lazy (3), Slow, Sleepy (3), Slack, Lonesome/Lone Cat (3), and Shy Guy. A few further nicknames describe an itinerant lifestyle that could be viewed either positively or negatively. These are Ramblin', Suitcase, Driftin' (2), and Walkin'.

The subcategory of nicknames designating social, racial, or ethnic status diminished from 7 percent in the prewar era to 3 percent of all nicknames in the postwar era. As already noted above, terms such as Black (2), Big Sambo, Nappy, and Brownie are rare in the postwar era and are matched in number (5) by the more euphemistic Smokey. The only woman with such a nickname was Cocoa Taylor, and this may be simply a misspelling of her more normal nickname Koko, itself derived from her real name Cora. Poor (4) and Slim Pickens suggest a low social status, and Country (9) suggests a lack of sophistication, although it can also express positive values of authenticity, tradition, and strength. The nicknames Geechie, Cherokee, and Haji Baba suggest special ethnic categories within or on the fringes of African American society.

Nicknames that describe non-musical occupations rose slightly from 3 percent to 4 percent of all nicknames in the postwar era. In the prewar period such nicknames were almost equally divided between occupations that were prestigious and ones that were of low status or outside the law. In the postwar era, however, the occupations described in blues nicknames are overwhelmingly prestigious and exhibit greater variety than those in the prewar era. Although some of these occupations in nicknames probably represent fantasies, this pattern suggests a growth in opportunities for gainful employment beyond farming and unskilled labor. These nicknames include Doctor/Doc (13), Professor, Judge, Lawyer, Pro, Undertaker, Reverend, Preacher (2), Deacon (3), The Flock Rocker, Pvt./G.I. (2), Corp., Soldier Boy, Sailor Boy, Schoolboy (2), Buster Bronco, Chef, Jack of All Trades, and Girl Friday. The only nicknames with negative or illegal associations belonged to Crook Jr., Shoe Shine Johnny, Little Miss Sharecropper, and Bertha "Chippie" Hill.

Hill was a holdover from the prewar recording era, and Shoe Shine Johnny's real name happened to be Johnny Shines. He had actually held a number of good paying jobs, was skilled in photography, and was taking adult education classes when I knew him in the 1980s. Little Miss Sharecropper was used as a nickname by LaVern Baker briefly at the beginning of her career. She later starred in films and on television and ran an officers' club in the Philippines for twenty-two years. These two artists' lives belied the lowly status of their early nicknames.

Geographical nicknames were down considerably from 14 percent to 7 percent of all nicknames in the postwar era. Most of these continued to describe states, cities, regions, neighborhoods, or streets in the South, while a few, such as Dixie, South, Sunnyland, Sunny Rhodes, and Country (9), suggested the South in general. The few northern and western locations were almost all places with substantial African American communities. One artist, Big Maybelle, was dubbed America's Queen Mother of Soul on one of her records. The decline in the use of geographical nicknames in the postwar era, despite a continuing pattern of migration from the South to the North and West, suggests that geographical origins had become a less important part of the self-image of African Americans and perhaps also the fact that southern origins had come to be embarrassing and to represent a not so fondly remembered past of rural hardship and discrimination, something to be left out of one's self-image.

The category of nicknames describing fantasized and projected things and qualities that lie outside the artist's everyday being declined slightly from 26 percent to 23 percent of all artists with nicknames in the postwar era. This change was not equal, however, among male and female blues singers. The male percentage dropped somewhat more steeply from 27 percent to 21 percent, but the female percentage rose substantially from 24 percent to 40 percent. This increase suggests that women blues singers in the postwar era felt more comfortable in expressing projections and fantasies in their nicknames, just as they did in describing their physical characteristics. Among women this increase occurred in the subcategories of nicknames that described food, sex, and royalty or other exalted status, while their percentages declined in the other subcategories. The male percentage increased only in the subcategory of royalty and exalted status.

As in the prewar era, the subcategories of food and sexual nicknames overlap considerably and are best considered together. The male nicknames in these two subcategories are somewhat more varied, imaginative, and provocative than the female. The most common male nicknames referring to food were Sugarman/Sugar Boy/Sugarcane (5) and Honeyboy/Mr. Honey (5). Others suggesting sweetness were Cookie, Cake, Candy/Candyman (2), Peppermint, and Lolly-Pop. A number of these names probably had an additional sexual meaning. Vegetables were represented by Budd Spudd, Potato, Butterbeans, Coleslaw, Peach Tree (probably sexual as well), Mr. String Bean (more likely referring to thinness), Pepper, and Sweet Pea. Meats, often with an obvious additional sexual meaning, were represented by Sirloin Burg, Spam Daggers, Doc Sausage, Chick (2, possibly referring instead to a young woman), Smokey Hogg, Ham, Pig Meat (definitely referring to a taste for young women), Pork Chops (a common slang term for women's thighs), and T-Bone. Other food nicknames were Butter and Daddy Hot Cakes. Five artists' nicknames commemorated alcoholic drinks. These were Drink, Winehead Willie, Thunderbird (a brand of cheap fortified wine), and Sweet Lucy (homemade wine). Most of the nicknames of women in the food subcategory suggested sweetness, sometimes with an added sexual meaning. These included Honey (2), Sugar Pie, Miss Peaches, Cherri, and The Lollypop Mama. The others were Little Miss Cornshucks (more suggestive of a rural background than of food), Mary Sassafras, and Cocoa Taylor (possibly simply a misspelling, as noted earlier). The male and female nicknames representing sweet foods have been enumerated in the sexual subcategory, as have some others with obvious sexual meanings. Further nicknames in the latter subcategory are The Heartbreaker, Lover Boy (2), Cleanhead Cootsie, Hot Lips (2), The Blonde (sic) Bomber, Prince Love, Bunky, and Tang (probably from "poontang") for males, and Baby Doll/Dolly (2), Baby Love, Delilah (the biblical temptress of Samson), Cordelia de Milo (after the classical nude sculpture), Chippie, Fluffy, Bombshell, Hip Shakin', Bunky, and Yas Yas Girl for women. Considering the prominence of sexual themes and frank lyricism in the blues in general, one might be surprised at the rather low percentage of sexual nicknames and the rather mild nature of most of them. The statistics are somewhat deceiving, however, because many nicknames using musical, physical, animal, and mechanical imagery have further sexual meanings.

Nicknames that describe animals and nature declined from 10 percent to 5 percent of all nicknames in the postwar era. This fact is undoubtedly to be correlated with increasing urbanization of the African American population and of blues music. Mammals, reptiles, fish, birds, and insects were represented among the male animal nicknames. These were Cow Cow, Mule, Dr. Horse, The Cat, The Lone Cat, Hound Dog, Mad Dog, Buck (3), The Fox/ The Sly Fox, Howlin' Wolf, The Young Wolf, Bull Moose, Big Moose (2),

Mr. Bear, Jack The Bear, Groundhog, Bunny, Snake, Rattlesnake, Frogman (mainly from the artist's croaking vocal effect), Mudcat (a type of catfish), The Thunderbird, Hootin' Owl, Royal Hawk, Nighthawk, Coot, Boll Weevil, Bee, Bumble Bee, and Stick-Horse (a hobby-horse; alternatively, a horse that must be forced to work). The only female animal nicknames were Little Chickadee, Chicken, and Kitty. Piney Clarke's nickname perhaps indicates his height. One type of nickname within this subcategory that saw an increase in the postwar era was nicknames that described forces of nature, such as storms and floods. There were 16 of these, compared to only 2 in the prewar era. They were Little Mr. Midnight, Lonesome Sundown, Goldrush, Cool Breeze, Hurricane (2), Stormy, Thunder, Thunderhead, Lightning (4), Duke Bayou, Muddy Waters, and Clear Waters (Eddie Clearwater). Such forces of nature are usually not specifically rural in occurrence and could be viewed as being more powerful than anything in the animal world. Their increased usage in nicknames during the postwar era can be correlated with an increased sense of empowerment in the African American community. Nicknames referring to mechanical devices also often suggested very powerful forces. They included H-Bomb Ferguson, TNT Tribble, Railroad Earl, Cow Cow Davenport (from a train's cowcatcher), Hot Rod Happy, Model T Slim, T. V. Slim, B. B. King (actually an abbreviation of Blues Boy), and Little Hatchet among the men, and T. V. Mama, Bonnie "Bombshell" Lee, and Byllye "Jet" Williams among the women.

Nicknames suggesting royalty or exalted status were the only subcategory of those exhibiting fantasy or projection that increased for both men and women in the postwar era. Overall they increased from 3 percent to 7 percent (from 4 percent to 6 percent for males and 0 percent to 10 percent for females). This increase is similar to other increases that we have already noted in terms that suggest greater power and social status. The male nicknames in this subcategory were Royal (3), His Majesty, Emperor, King (26), Prince (9), Crown Prince (2), Duke (6), Earl, Count (4), Silver, Champion, Big Chief, The Great (3), Sir, and Prez. Duke, Count, and Prez may have been influenced by the nicknames of jazz stars Duke Ellington, Count Basie, and Lester "Prez" Young. Among women the nicknames were Queen, Queen Mother, Princess, Duchess (2), The Countess, and Lady (3).

Although nicknames suggesting the supernatural, magic, and luck contain images of power, this subcategory actually decreased somewhat in the postwar era, from 3 percent to 2 percent of all male nicknames. (There were no women with such nicknames in either era.) These included Genius, Wonder Boy, The Mystery Man, Lucky (6), Ace (5), Black Diamond, Voodoo

Man, Doctor (with reference to being a root doctor), Mojo (4), Magic (2), and Poison. The decline in this subcategory can probably be correlated with a decline in the belief in magic and sorcery in the African American community in the postwar era and a growing preference for symbols of real physical power, mechanical power, royal power and forces of nature.

The final postwar category of "other" nicknames includes a few that employ the principle of reduplication (2 JoJo's, Zuzu, Cow Cow, and Koko), Icky Renrut (a play on the artist's real name of Ike Turner), and several names of uncertain meaning (Jick, Hooks, Dupsee, Sandman, Lick, Slide, Ditty, Gip, Tac, Dootsie, Dady, Bixie, and Rally). Several of the latter are probably childhood pet names. The nickname Taj Mahal falls completely outside any of the observable patterns of African American blues nicknaming. It was adopted by an artist who is more properly part of the folk-music revival scene.

In their earlier studies of blues nicknames Skipper and Leslie made a major categorical distinction between "nicknames related to the blues" and "nicknames not related to the blues," pointing out that "nearly four-fifths of the blues artists' nicknames are not directly related to playing or singing blues music."[29] To be precise, they found 21.1 percent of blues nicknames to pertain to music. Although I also make a separate category of musical nicknames and find them to constitute 31 percent of all blues nicknames, it is my contention that virtually all of the nicknames in my survey are in a broader sense "related to the blues." Categorization of nicknames is useful for separating them into thematic groups based on their primary meaning and symbolism, but it should not be an end in itself or the sole basis for drawing conclusions or even statistics. The relationship of most of these nicknames to the blues is seen in their multiple and overlapping levels of meaning and in the consistent picture of a blues world that they paint, one that conforms closely to typical life histories, experiences, lyric themes, and contextual factors.[30] Although some nicknames were undoubtedly suggested or given by executives of record companies, the blues artists themselves largely controlled the presentation and use or non-use of their nicknames in their encounters with these companies. An unflattering or inappropriate nickname, or one that was meaningless outside a small intimate circle, could normally be suppressed by the artist in these encounters. It is for this reason that so few blues nicknames in the present survey, only 32 (2 percent), have uncertain or unclassifiable meanings.

We must not confuse *meaning* with *origin*. Skipper and Leslie placed great emphasis on the origins or actual referents of nicknames and therefore left

13 percent of their nicknames in a category called "unknown origins," even though almost all of them have obvious meanings, such as Smoky Babe, Professor Longhair, Lone Cat, Long Gone, and Son.[31] In another publication, for the purpose of demonstrating the importance of a nickname's origin, they cite the example of a female baseball shortstop nicknamed Venus.[32] She received this nickname by analogy with the famous Venus de Milo statue that is missing its arms, because in one game a ball bounced off her skull into the glove of the second base player, who was able to make a double play. According to Leslie and Skipper, one would have to know about this incident in order to understand the meaning of the nickname Venus. This may be true for anyone concerned with origins, but one must wonder whether the name of the ancient goddess of love was appropriate to the player in any other ways or whether it conveyed a different image to fellow players and especially fans who may not have been familiar with the story of its origin.

Nicknames are worn more or less permanently, long after the incidents that inspired them have passed. An anecdote about the incident may be retold when the bearer of a nickname makes an appearance, but certainly not always. I am reminded here of a blues artist I knew called Slop Jar. He was a pianist of considerable size and strength with a very powerful voice and a thunderous playing style, combined with formidable technique. He liked to curse, boast, and bluster, and frequently stated that he *was* the blues and that others didn't know or were simply false pretenders. He wasn't especially fond of his nickname but didn't try to suppress it and even performed a "Slop Jar Blues." One might say he wore it defiantly. He had received this nickname years earlier when a woman he had somehow offended struck him in the head with a chamber pot while he was seated at the piano. The incident is certainly memorable and was recited whenever someone inquired about the nickname, but it hardly accounts for the full meaning and impact of this term. In view of our larger survey, we can see that Slop Jar fits well with other nicknames that suggest a lowdown social status, and in the case of this particular artist it could easily be taken to mean that he was "full of shit." Like a number of other blues singers who bore nicknames suggesting low status, this artist worked his way through his nickname by always wearing fine suits and having gold in his mouth and a large diamond stickpin in his ear. He backed up his boasts of "being" the blues with superb performances that would have cowed most rivals into submission. The particular incident behind the origin of his nickname was of little importance when Slop Jar appeared for a performance.

In a general survey of nickname scholarship, Theodore J. Holland Jr. has noted that scholars have found that in various cultures nicknames can conceal identity, function as instruments of social solidarity, maintain and ratify specific social relationships, maintain boundaries, exercise social control and ethical condemnation, confer status, call attention to their bearers, and provide compensation for things and statuses that are difficult to obtain.[33] Our survey of the themes of blues nicknames reveals that they display all of these functions, and we can determine this in many cases without having to know the specific circumstances under which the nicknames were first given. I have classified the nicknames by theme or referent and given statistics of their occurrence, but these statistics should be used with great caution on account of the possibility of multiple referents of a single nickname and multiple and overlapping levels of meaning. In a perhaps more meaningful sense, these nicknames could be viewed as related to a number of abstract domains with even greater overlap, which, despite the striking individuality of many of the names, provide a consistent view of the blues world in its physical, social, artistic, spiritual, and psychological dimensions. These abstract domains are music/musical values; location/mobility; family/community; racial/social status; appearance/reputation/image/fame; desires/lusts/hungers; and power/magic/luck.

As an indication of the unity and interrelationship of blues nicknaming practices with blues music and the blues world, I would like to point out the fact that many blues singers bearing nicknames also performed a particular song that contained or even explained or justified the nickname. Merely surveying song titles, without listening to every recorded blues for lyric relationships to nicknames, I have found 83 artists who recorded "nickname blues" in the prewar period and 150 in the postwar period, meaning that as many as 17 percent of all artists with nicknames performed such songs (21 percent prewar; 15 percent postwar). Typical examples are "Black Shine Blues" by Black Boy Shine, "Down in Black Bottom" by Black Bottom McPhail, "Jab Blues" by Jabo Williams, "Yodeling the Blues" by Yodeling Kid Brown, "Moaning Blues" by Moanin' Bernice Edwards, "Street Walker Blues" by Bertha "Chippie" Hill, "Weak Eyed Blues" by Charlie "Specks" McFadden, "Ramblin' Man" by Ramblin' Thomas, "They Call Me Casanova" by Casanova Jr., "Root Doctor Blues" by Doctor Clayton, "Sure Cure for the Blues" by Willie "Doc" Jones, "They Call Me Lazy" by Lazy Lester, "Rampart Street Blues" by Ramp Davis, "Bone Crushin' Man" by Guitar Crusher, "Fat and Greasy" by Walter "Fats" Pichon, "Queen Bee" by Bee Bee Queen, "I'm a Big Man" by Big

Daddy Rogers, and "Moose Is on the Loose" by Johnny "Big Moose" Walker. Keeping in mind that some of these song titles fall into more than one nickname category, and that some artists recorded more than one "nickname blues," I found that they exhibited an interesting pattern in respect to the classification system of the nicknames themselves. Since there was a difference of no more than 4 percent in any single category between the prewar and postwar eras, I will give only the overall statistics. Not surprisingly, there were no "nickname blues" related to the category of stereotypical names and only 6 (3 percent) related to the "other" category. Familiar terms were contained in the song titles of 32 (14 percent) artists, music-related terms in the titles of 56 (24 percent) artists, and terms containing essential qualities in the titles of 103 (44 percent) artists. These percentages are all seven to eleven percent lower than the percentages of artists with nicknames in the same categories. On the other hand, song titles containing terms related to nicknames in the category of projected things and desires numbered 70 (30 percent). This was 6 percent higher than the percentage of blues artists with nicknames in this category. This statistic suggests that these "nickname blues" are especially important in projecting fantasy images of artists, while "nickname blues" in general are important in reinforcing whatever image the nickname suggests. Artists who perform such signature tunes are able to provide a complete visual and musical package tied up with a catchy and memorable nickname.

We have seen in this study that blues nicknames help to build an image of a world that incorporates the music itself, social and family relationships and statuses, and qualities that are desirable, prestigious, powerful, dangerous, or magically charged. Collectively, these terms provide a complex, multifaceted, and multileveled image of blues singers that both masks their everyday, nonmusical identities and magnifies certain traits, relationships, and projections to give them heroic and sometimes mystical stature. Such artists become a kind of "everyman" (or every woman), at least up to the semantic limits of their nicknames. Within their world they represent everyone who has ever been fat or slim, lived in Mississippi, played or tried to play a guitar, fancied himself or herself to be a bumblebee, craved jelly roll, or been called "Black Shine."

Notes

An earlier version of this paper was presented at the annual meeting of the American Folklore Society in Austin, Texas, on October 31, 1997. I am grateful to Dr. Gerhard Kubik for his helpful comments. I also wish to thank my wife, Marice Evans, and Dr.

Guido van Rijn for help in identifying some blues recording artists by gender and interpreting the meanings of some nicknames. Dr. van Rijn solicited the help of blues record collectors Chris Smith, Dave Sax, Hans Westerduijn, Daniel Gugolz, and John Broven, whose aid I also gratefully acknowledge.

1. William Ferris, *Blues from the Delta* (New York: Anchor, 1978), 13.

2. In this study I have avoided the use of quotation marks or parentheses around nicknames unless the nickname occurs within a given name, thus Lightnin' Hopkins but Sam "Lightnin'" Hopkins.

3. James K. Skipper Jr. and Paul Leslie, "Nicknames and Blues Singers, Part I: Frequency of Use 1890–1977," *Popular Music and Society* 12, no. 1 (1988): 37–48; "Nicknames and Blues Singers 1890–1977, Part II: Classification and Analysis," *Popular Music and Society* 13, no. 3 (1989): 29–43; "Women, Nicknames, and Blues Singers," *Names* 36 (1988): 193–202.

4. Sheldon Harris, *Blues Who's Who: A Biographical Dictionary of Blues Singers* (New Rochelle, N.Y.: Arlington House, 1979). The slight disparity between the number of singers in the sample and the total of male and female singers is not explained.

5. Jim Higgs, "Nicknames in the Blues," *Blues News* (Las Vegas Blues Society) 8, no. 2 (March 15, 1995): 20–21 (reprinted from the Sacramento Blues Society's *Blue Notes,* December 1994). Naming principles that Higgs recognized were pet names, physical traits (including physical handicaps), geographical locations, musical performance styles, song lyrics and titles, names of other musicians, personality traits, childhood experiences, supernatural beings, and names of railroads. The other article is Jim O'Neal, "Bo Carter and Boake: Nicknames in the Blues," *Living Blues* 173 (July–August, 2004): 104.

6. Skipper and Leslie, "Part II," 34.

7. Robert M. W. Dixon, John Godrich, and Howard Rye, *Blues & Gospel Records 1890–1943,* 4th ed. (Oxford: Clarendon, 1997); Mike Leadbitter and Neil Slaven, *Blues Records 1943–1970, A Selective Discography, Vol. 1, A to K* (London: Record Information Services, 1987); Mike Leadbitter, Leslie Fancourt, and Paul Pelletier, *Blues Records 1943–1970, "The Bible of the Blues," Vol. 2, L to Z* (London: Record Information Services, 1994). After this essay was written, a new discography for the period 1943–70 was published: Les Fancourt and Bob McGrath, *The Blues Discography 1943–1970* (West Vancouver, B.C.: Eyeball Productions, 2006). It lists more than three hundred artists not included in the earlier discography for the period. Nevertheless, because of the large size of the original sample, it is not likely that these new listings would significantly alter my conclusions.

8. For a survey of jazz nicknames, see James Skipper Jr., "Nicknames, Folk Heroes and Jazz Musicians," *Popular Music and Society* 10 (1986): 51–62.

9. Ruby Terrill Lomax, "Negro Nicknames," in *Backwoods to Border,* Publications of the Texas Folklore Society, 18, ed. Mody C. Boatright and Donald Day (Dallas:

Southern Methodist University Press, 1943), 163–71; Bruce Jackson, "Prison Nicknames," *Western Folklore* 26 (1967): 48–54. See also James K. Skipper Jr., "Nicknames of Notorious American Twentieth Century Criminals and Deviants: The Decline of the Folk Hero Syndrome," *Deviant Behavior* 6 (1985): 99–114.

10. Karl Gert zur Heide, *Deep South Piano: The Story of Little Brother Montgomery* (London: Studio Vista, 1970), 17–39.

11. Frank Owen, "The Name's Not the Same: Guide to Blues Pseudonyms," *Storyville* 1:1 (October 1965): 25–26; 1:2 (December 1965): 15–16.

12. J. L. Dillard, *Black Names*, Contributions to the Sociology of Language #13 (The Hague: Mouton, 1976); Arthur Palmer Hudson, "Some Curious Negro Names," *Southern Folklore Quarterly* 2 (1938): 179–93.

13. Cf. Alan Lomax, *The Land Where the Blues Began* (New York: Pantheon, 1993), 358–422; and David Evans, "Traditional Blues Lyrics and Myth: Some Correspondences," in *The Lyrics in African American Popular Music*, ed. Robert Springer (Bern: Peter Lang, 2001), 17–40.

14. On the concept of the "blues family," see Ferris, *Blues from the Delta*, 11–24.

15. Ruby Terrill Lomax, "Negro Nicknames," 165.

16. Paul Oliver, *Blues Fell This Morning: Meaning in the Blues* (Cambridge: Cambridge University Press, 1990), 69–76.

17. Ruby Terrill Lomax, "Negro Nicknames," 168.

18. Oliver, *Blues Fell This Morning*, 109–14.

19. Oliver, *Blues Fell This Morning*, 104–7; Paul Garon, *Blues and the Poetic Spirit* (London: Eddison, 1975), 112–20.

20. Oliver, *Blues Fell This Morning*, 107–9.

21. Oliver, *Blues Fell This Morning*, 117–37; Garon, *Blues and the Poetic Spirit*, 140–68; Julio Finn, *The Bluesman* (London: Quartet, 1986); Jon Michael Spencer, *Blues and Evil* (Knoxville: University of Tennessee Press, 1993); David Evans, "Robert Johnson: Pact with the Devil," *Blues Revue* 21 (February–March 1996): 12–13; 22 (April–May 1996): 12–13; 23 (June–July, 1996): 12–13.

22. On Patton as a larger-than-life heroic figure see David Evans, "Charley Patton: The Conscience of the Delta," in *The Voice of the Delta: Charley Patton and the Mississippi Blues Traditions—Influences and Comparisons, An International Symposium*, ed. Robert Sacré (Liège: Presses universitaires de Liège, 1987), 109–217.

23. On Peetie Wheatstraw (real name William Bunch) see Paul Garon, *The Devil's Son-in-Law: The Story of Peetie Wheatstraw and His Songs*, rev. ed. (Chicago: Charles H. Kerr, 2003).

24. Finn, *The Bluesman*; Spencer, *Blues and Evil*, 1–34; Samuel A. Floyd Jr., *The Power of Black Music: Interpreting Its History from Africa to the United States* (New York: Oxford University Press, 1995), 72–74.

25. Ruby Terrill Lomax, "Negro Nicknames," 166.

26. Dillard, *Black Names*, 29.

27. Skipper and Leslie, "Women, Nicknames, and Blues Singers," 200.

28. On the term Chippie, see Jean-Paul Levet, *Talkin' That Talk: Le langage du blues et du jazz* (Paris: Hatier, 1992), 60.

29. Skipper and Leslie, "Nicknames and Blues Singers 1890–1977, Part II," 36.

30. For surveys of these topics, see Oliver, *Blues Fell This Morning;* Ferris, *Blues from the Delta;* Barry Lee Pearson, *"Sounds So Good to Me": The Bluesman's Story* (Philadelphia: University of Pennsylvania Press, 1984); and Alan Lomax, *The Land Where the Blues Began.*

31. Skipper and Leslie, "Nicknames and Blues Singers 1890–1977, Part II," 41.

32. Paul L. Leslie and James K. Skipper Jr., "Toward a Theory of Nicknames: A Case for Socio-Onomastics," *Names* 38 (1990): 274.

33. Theodore J. Holland Jr., "The Many Faces of Nicknames," *Names* 38 (1990): 258–63.

6

Preachin' the Blues

A TEXTUAL LINGUISTIC ANALYSIS OF SON HOUSE'S "DRY SPELL BLUES"

LUIGI MONGE

SON HOUSE, "PREACHIN' THE BLUES," PARAMOUNT 13013 (1930)

Part One

Oh, I'm gon' get me religion, I'm gon' join the Baptist Church,
Oh, I'm gon' get me religion, I'm gon' join the Baptist Church,
I'm gon' be a Baptist preacher and I sure won't have to work.

Oh, I'm gon' preach these blues now, and I want everybody to shout,
Mmmmm, I want everybody to shout,
I'm gon' do like a prisoner, I'm gonna roll my time on out.

Oh, in my room, I bowed down to pray,
Oh, I was in my room, I bowed down to pray,
Said the blues come 'long and they drove my spirit away.

Oh, and I had religion, Lord, this very day,
Oh, I had religion, Lord, this very day,
But the womens and whiskey, well, they would not let me pray.

Oh, I wish I had me a heaven of my own [*Spoken:*] Great God Almighty.
Aaaa, heaven of my own,
Then I'd give all my women a long, long happy home.

Yeah, I love my baby just like I love myself,
Oooh, just like I love myself,
Well, if she don't have me, she won't have nobody else.

Part Two

Hey, I'm gon' fold my arms, I'm gonna kneel down in prayer,
Oh, I fold my arms, gonna kneel down in prayer,
When I get up, I'm gon' see if my preachin' suit a man's ear.

Now, I met The Blues this mornin', walkin' just like a man,
Oooooooh, walkin' just like a man,
I said, "Good mornin', Blues; now gimme your right hand."

Now, ain't nothin' now, baby, Lord, that's gon' worry my mind,
Oooh, Lord, that's gon' worry my mind,
Oh, I'm satisfied, I got the longest line.

Oh, I'm got to stay on the job, I ain't got no time to lose,
Hey, I ain't got no time to lose,
I swear to God I've got to preach these gospel blues [*Spoken:*] Great God
    Almighty.

Oh, I'm gon' preach these blues and choose my seat and sit down,
Oh, I'm gon' preach these blues now, and choose my seat and sit down,
When the spirit comes, sisters, I want you to jump straight up and down.

As an introduction to Son House's musical activity, I summarize here what we have come to know about him. Despite some questionable evidence of a much earlier date of birth,[1] it is generally agreed that Eddie James "Son" House Jr., was born on March 21, 1902, on a farm near Riverton between Lyon and Clarksdale in the Mississippi Delta. His father was a musician in a family-run brass band. At the age of eight, Son followed his mother to Tallulah, Louisiana, after his parents' separation. Working in the field was the only daily occupation he could take up from childhood on, but he disliked farming and found refuge in religion. At fifteen he preached his first sermon. Under the influence of strict Puritanism, he started to preach regularly in the Baptist church, but soon the pleasures of the senses turned out to be as strong as his devoutness. In 1924 he married an older woman, Carrie Martin, but their marriage did not last. His musical career started very late, when he returned to Lyon. Inspired by local musicians James McCoy and Willie Wilson, he learned the rudiments of guitar, enabling him to play at parties and picnics. During one of these he killed a man in self-defense and was sentenced to fifteen years' imprisonment, but he spent only a little more than one year, presumably in the notorious Parchman Farm, from which he was released under the compulsion of not coming back to Clarksdale. So

House went to Jeffreys plantation in nearby Lula, Mississippi, where he met Blues recording artist Charley Patton, who suggested that the Paramount Record Company record him. In a now famous 1930 session House made nine recordings, among them "Preachin' the Blues" and "Dry Spell Blues." On that occasion he met Willie Brown. House followed him to Robinsonville, Mississippi, where in the 1930s, the two often played together at house parties and juke joints. Son and Willie attracted a growing number of fans, including Robert Johnson, who—along with Muddy Waters—became Son House's most famous disciple. In the 1930s Son married his wife, Evie, in whose Colored Methodist Episcopal Church he began preaching again. In 1941, Alan Lomax recorded him performing blues for the Library of Congress in Lake Cormorant, Mississippi, and again in 1942 in Robinsonville. About this time he moved to Rochester, New York, where he worked as a railroad porter for ten years and played little. The 1950s were transition years: Willie Brown died in 1952, and as a consequence Son nearly stopped playing, though he tried some more preaching. What he never gave up was drinking, which certainly contributed to the development of a senile tremor in his hands. In 1964, he was rediscovered by Blues researchers. Son recorded for Columbia, Blue Goose and several other record companies, toured the United States as well as Europe, and appeared on television and in documentary films. The 1970s were the years of his physical decline; from 1971 to 1975 he considerably reduced the number of his concerts, and the following year he moved to Detroit to be looked after by relatives. Later, Son House was put in a nursing home, where he died on October 19, 1988.

"A fan from Detroit visited him in a rest home a year or two before his death, bringing along a National guitar. Son could barely speak coherently, but his eyes lit up and he reached for the guitar and tried to play it before attentive relatives removed it from his hands. Would he have sung a blues or a spiritual?" *He would have preached the Blues.* This is the answer to David Evans's question closing his essay on Son House in the booklet notes to the CD *Delta Blues and Spirituals.*[2]

I intend to study the dichotomy between sacred and secular/profane in the Blues and in the life and music of Son House in the light of statements, interviews, notes and general observations pertaining to the subject, treating the topic as exhaustively as possible.[3] This accounts for the transcription of House's song "Preachin' the Blues" at the beginning of the essay, as it explicitly symbolizes the main themes in this bluesman's poetics. By making use of the critical studies at our disposal, this blues can be interpreted independently of Son House's inner conflicts.

Despite Son House's historical importance in the Blues, there is relatively little literature on him.[4] As an indication of his relevance in this field, I quote John Cowley: "During his formative years at Stovall, Muddy [Waters] obtained a wide musical experience. Above all, however, Muddy saw and learnt bottleneck from Brown's 1930s playing partner Son House." Cowley goes on, quoting what Muddy Waters himself told Don de Michael: "I had been learning guitar from this Scott Bowhandle. I thought he could play. But then I saw Son House and I realized he couldn't play nothing at all. Son House played the same place for about four weeks in a row and I was there every night. You couldn't get me out of that corner, listening to what he's doing."[5]

I will avail myself of two introductory critical theories based on an objective description. The first theory—put forward and organically explained by a linguist and not by a music critic—says, "Blues singers have in common a cultural heritage of subject matter and a regulatory system of invention that not only dictates the obvious similarities of music and structure, but also describes a particular personality, that of the bluesman who is projected in the songs. An inventory of blues formulas would reveal the existence of a very specific kind of narrator."[6] This personality type has been described as follows: "The ideal of the blues singer was to be free to move about, riding in style when times were good and hoboing when times were tough, hiring himself out to the highest bidder for his manual labor or musical services or else hustling up a living by his own wits and charm, generally living as well as he could and leaving whenever he became dissatisfied or restless."[7]

The second theory is more difficult to prove. It says that the Blues is a mixture of heterogeneous elements; all contributed to the development (and still contribute to the evolution) of this musical genre. Such coexistence already included religious components, but the profane element was predominant. Son House's historic and aesthetic importance in the Blues lies in his giving prominence to the artistic hybrid sometimes called "gospel blues."[8] Perhaps only a real bluesman/preacher like House could do so. Son House himself often referred to the B/blues as the musical genre and the state of mind directly coming from the heart, that is, from one of the places where the soul was believed to be situated. His locating in the heart the birthplace and residence of what he often called the B-L-U-E-S—that is, the personification and materialization of the "blues god"[9] ("I met The Blues this mornin', walkin' just like a man")—explains why Son House made little use (if any) of frivolously coarse and humorous language in his songs. Every possible double entendre or sexual interpretation of Son House's lyrics should be taken more literally than in any other blues singer, in that these lyrics are likely to conceal a serious, frank and unobtrusive treatment of a deeply meaningful and human (though probably ordinary and real) subject. Differently from Robert Johnson, who artistically embodied his "evil spirit" in the Devil, it was House's continuous addressing of God that eternalized his tormented soul. By making no mention of Satan in his compositions and admitting his attraction to women and the bottle matter-of-factly, Son House assumed and played the simultaneously real and allegorical role of a modern black "Everyman," because he consistently followed his principle of singing about something that might concern anybody who wanted to listen.

Despite the great influence of religion on African Americans, following the precepts of the Church was, generally speaking, of minor importance for blues people. The contrast between the religious and secular way of living (though not necessarily the philosophy of life underlying them) was the inevitable cause of the competition between church and bluesman, which took place for the winning of the same audience. The learned attitude of the preacher, who would get ready for the Sunday sermon by drawing inspiration from the Bible, was the opposite of the bluesman's, who seemed to snub that way of living probably because he felt it was of no use to him or to society. Son House was the living and active exception to that attitude. Although in many respects he conforms to the broad outlines of the "bluesman" personality type noted earlier, his artistic originality and uniqueness are inarguably also due to the fact that he had actually been a preacher *before* and not *after* he became a bluesman. This was quite uncommon among bluesmen, who usually started preaching after leading a sinful life. That is why House can be defined as an intellectual among the country bluesmen of the time, because he had in himself the mental qualities to introduce such an innovation in the Blues. Let us see what kind of qualities these were.

Precisely because he felt deeply in himself the antithetical forces of the two different worlds, Son House realized he could not do without either, and was forced to engage in an endless battle against each (their respective enemy) on both fronts, his analytic judgment being in the middle. This choice—actually quite far from the opportunism that bluesmen and preachers were often accused of, in that it was lived through a split personality—goes through the whole of House's artistic output, including that of his later years, sometimes according to typical Blues expressions ("The Jinx Blues, Part One," "The Jinx Blues, Part Two," "County Farm," etc.), sometimes according to typical religious ones ("Never Mind People Grinnin' in Your Face," "Oh, Lord, Please

Help Me on My Way," "John the Revelator"), and more rarely following both canons ("Preachin' the Blues," "Dry Spell Blues"). Through music, Son House managed to get the inner peace he could not otherwise attain in life. The "gospel blues" was for him a gradual approach to artistic invention, mental and moral exorcising and spiritual redemption.

Let us see some evidence illuminating the man Son House in relation to the dichotomy of sacred and profane, which was the spark of his artistic sensitivity. We start by examining some passages in which he himself illustrates his point of view.

In one of his few published interviews, House in 1971 falteringly answered in monosyllables Jeff Titon's question concerning the beginning of his devoutness: "I was there in that alfalfa field and I got down, pray, getting on my knees in that alfalfa. Dew was falling. And man, I prayed and I prayed and I prayed and—for wait awhile, I hollered out. Found out then; I said, 'Yes, it is something to be got, too, 'cause I got it now!'"[10] The mystical nature of Son House's devotion is clearly visible here, and this explains his inner laceration whenever he faces the Tempter.

Here is how Son House met the Blues: "I started playing guitar in 1928, but I got the idea around about 1927. I saw a guy named Willie Wilson and another one named Reuben Lacy. All before then, I just hated to see a guy with a guitar. I was so churchy! I came along a little place they call Matson [actually Mattson], a little below Clarksdale. It was on a Saturday and these guys were sitting out in front of a place and they were playing. Well, I stopped, because the people were all crowded around. This boy, Willie Wilson, had a thing on his finger like a small medicine bottle, and he was zinging it, you know. I said, 'Jesus! Wonder what's that he's playing?' I knew that guitars hadn't usually been sounding like that. So I eases up close enough to look and I see what he has on his finger. 'Sounds good!' I said. 'Jesus! I like that!' And from there, I got the idea and said, 'I believe I want to play one of them things.'"[11] In those expressions of astonishment and praise lies the beginning of Son House's existential conflict and consequently of his artistic mark. From that moment on, the attraction for the profane worked its way into Son House like a slow and sly disease, which stayed with him all his life.

Son House's mystical attitude never ceased. In the 1971 interview, he draws analogies in the composition of songs and sermons, and states the importance of the Gospel and the Bible as reference points for a Baptist preacher:

SH: I pastored a Baptist church a good while, in the Baptist church.
And then I turned a few years later on after that, then I got to be a

pastor for the C.M.E. church, which is Colored Methodist Episcopal church. Since I got this wife I got now I pastored one of them.

JT: You gave sermons.

SH: Yeah, that's was [*sic*] pastoring—pastor the people. Yeah. And
the people paid—yeah.

JT: Do you make up your sermons the way you used to make up
your songs?

SH: Mm-hm, yeah, the same way. All during the week and through
the nights or things like that I get my Bible and sit down and—
turn to such and such a chapters and verses and such and such a
books in the Bible, I'd say, "Well, I believe I'll choose this here text
for Sunday for the people and I'll start on that," I'll say maybe
around about Tuesday or Wednesday night or something like
that—come in that night, I'd set up and I'd take my Bible and I'd
study, study, read about what it's saying, what it's about, and all I
could, get it in my head, and says, "Ah, oh yeah, well I got it."
Couldn't forget it. Mm-mm.

JT: Would you write it down before you said it?

SH: No, I wouldn't even write it down. Wouldn't write it down.

JT: Do you ever use the same text more than once?

SH: No—well, but it be a long, long time between.

JT: Are you doing this now? Are you preaching now?

SH: No, I wouldn't be caught doing that.

JT: When was the last time you did it?

SH: Let's see, that's been about 15, 16 years or longer. Yeah.[12]

Son House's most significant statement, however, is probably the one he made
while introducing the song "Preachin' the Blues" during a concert at the
University of Indiana in November 1964:

I used to be a preacher. I was brought up in church and I started preaching
before I started this junk. Well, I got in a little bad company one time and
they said, "Aw, c'mon, take a little nip with us." I says, "Naw." "Aw, c'mon!" So
I took a little nip. None of the members were around, so I took the little nip.
And that one little nip called for another big nip. So there got to be a rumor
around among my members, you know. And I began to wonder, now how
can I stand up in the pulpit and preach to them, tell them how to live, and
quick as I dismiss the congregation and I see ain't nobody looking and I'm
doing the same thing. I says, that's not right. But I kept nipping around there
and it got to be a public thing. I says, well, I got to do something, 'cause I can't

hold God in one hand and the Devil in the other one. Them two guys don't get along together too well. I got to turn one of 'em loose. So I got out of the pulpit. So I said the next time I make a record, I'm gon' to name it "Preachin' Blues." I'm preaching on this side and the blues on that side. I says, "Well, I'll just put 'em together and name it 'Preachin' Blues.'"[13]

Beside the relentless struggle between the sacred and profane worlds, the poetics of the Mississippi musician explaining the genesis of the song that has made him famous and synthesizes the suffering mood of a whole life is apparent here.

While Son House concentrates on the impossible coexistence of the two conflicting existential spheres in life (though not in art), another bluesman, James "Son" Thomas, clearly expresses why we are compelled to choose one or the other solution with regard to everyday life:

Well, uh, I used to practice in a quartet some too, but after I started playing the guitar I just let the quartet go, because you can't carry blues and uh go to church and get up there and sing with them, call yourself a church member, and then you know you gonna sing the blues at night. I don't imagine it would be no harm in—to sing a church song, but I'm talking about, just like you—you gon' say you gon' be belongs to church, and then you gon' carry both of it on. So well Saturday night you go to Greenville, you gon' play at a night-club over there, Sunday morning you gon' come over here and go to the church. Now, I'd be afraid to do that 'cause something bad can happen to you.[14]

Son House's mental attitude is very similar to James "Son" Thomas's, but feeling he would never achieve his own peace of mind in life, House consciously tried to overcome this irrational "predicament" (if we want to keep the etymological root of the verb 'to preach') in a rational way by combining the two opposing activities of preaching and blues singing into a single unified expression he defined as "preachin' the blues." The hypothetical phrase "blu(e)in' the preachin'" may even be said to be one of Son House's probably unconscious alternatives, perfectly denoting this bluesman's double personality.[15] This psychological background led him to perform strange acts, such as preaching in juke joints, taking up preaching at least three different times in his life, and in his late career alternating blues and spirituals in his concerts. It is beyond doubt that the inner laceration we refer to when we are concerned with the relation between music and life in Son House was really present in his psyche. Not only that: the transposition of this torment to art stands out as one of the most original themes in the whole of Blues, despite the fact that it has not caught on in recent lyrics—where in general it has never been developed and/or modernized—thus remaining a typically country Blues theme.

Before Son House, the theme of sacred *versus* profane itself (or, if you wish, religious *versus* secular life, Spiritual *versus* Blues, God *versus* the Devil) was by no means an unusual subject in the Blues. Indeed, Son House was not the first to introduce this topic, but he was the one who went through it more intensely and deeply than anyone else, immortalizing it as a subject "worthwhile to be heard" even by a "sinful" audience, yet keeping it as sincere and genuine blues in all the accepted meanings, including psychological, of the term. Bessie Smith had already recorded a completely different song with the title of "Preachin' the Blues" in 1927 (Columbia 14195-D), which not only "lacks House's urgency, perhaps because she was a stranger to the pulpit,"[16] but fails in conveying the singer's emotive involvement in one of the black community's emerging existential quandaries. Son House was above all the man who consciously thought up the way to defeat the psychological deadlock caused by that clash, thus managing to escape the diagnosis of a real schizophrenia. The emotive tension coming from both his hypnotic and obsessive music and initiation-rite lyrics is the artistic fruit deriving from a split personality leading to the unrestrainable search for a tangible double satisfaction ("I wish I had me a heaven of my own/Then I'd give all my women a long, long happy home").[17] Here is the inner laceration, whose apparent psychological (but not artistic) impossibility of being solved is implied in the ambivalence and contradiction causing it. Son House solves his dilemma by not solving it (which explains his stylistic, aesthetic and poetic coherence in the space of almost fifty years, despite the fact that he did not make a living from music until the 1960s and played discontinuously), that is, making a destructive and constructive compromise at the same time. House realized that he had to face two enemies, the first of which tormented his mind and soul, the second his body and everyday life. He fought against the former by "preachin' the blues," that is, being actively involved in religious life as seen from a layman's perspective, and the latter by "blu(e)in' the preachin'," that is, by creating and believing in a personified (or deified) B/blues. Unlike all the other African American artists of his time and alone in his despair, Son House tried but could not or did not want to see a clear-cut difference between each of the opposing poles in the dichotomy sacred *versus* profane. His attention was drawn by the search for a more metaphysical meaning of life, but when striving to concentrate on this, all he could discern was a blurred image. Anyway, when singing his troubled sensitivity, Son House runs life-blood into the exorcising power of the Blues and at the same time overcomes his inner disease. By recording it, he brings us in on the inner torment dominating (though not killing) his person, and finally lets us know the exciting and terrifying ambiguity of the human nature when we face the transcendent. Few musicians could find such a convincing and, after all, brave solution to their problems. As we have already seen, bluesmen only used to state the impossibility of serving two masters, the Devil and God. Few people have taken a definitive (and above all definite) stand in favor of either;[18] most of them adopted a compromise attitude very different from (in fact, opposed to) Son House's, an attitude motivated by more or less different justifiable and dignified reasons, certainly not resulting from a problematic choice. Among these reasons we can find the far from remunerative—in fact alienating—condition of blindness (Blind Joe Taggart, Blind Boy Fuller), the mere purpose, often provable, of making a better living (Charley Patton), or both (Blind Lemon Jefferson, Blind Willie McTell, Blind Gary Davis). We know that House left his Baptist congregation when he was about twenty-six, and was tormented all his life by the regret and bitterness brought about by the awareness of having made a choice that would not free him from his conflict. This is the reason why taking the first tercet of "Preachin' the Blues, Part One" from its context in order to prove that a nonmystical approach to religion was the cause of his conversion does not make any sense at all. There was no conversion in Son House either to religion or to laicism, because starting from his leaving the Church he never devoted himself solely to either religion or to the pleasures of the Blues life.

"Preachin' the Blues" perfectly epitomizes Son House's poetical and musical art, painting at the same time an intimate psychological self-portrait of this man. It is likewise true, however, that other songs cryptically represent as sharp a reflection as the one visible in this prototypical 1930 recording. Some critics focused their research on House's recordings of the 1940s and later dealing with the attraction to "the opposite tugs of religious and secular callings,"[19] but this theme is present in most of House's blues from the 1930 session, including his "Dry Spell Blues." This composition can easily be interpreted either as the mere historical description of a drought's effects in 1930 or as a pure and simple invocation to God.[20] But one interpretation does not make sense without the other, and, above all, some hidden interpretations can be missed if contextual conditioning and a few complex cross-references are not taken into account. As the detailed linguistic analysis of

Table 6.1

SACRED	vs.	PROFANE
blu(e)in' the preaching ↓	vs.	preaching the Blues ↓
prayer/sermon made into a blues (blues prayer) ↓	vs.	blues having marked preaching elements ↓
"Dry Spell Blues"	vs.	"Preachin' the Blues"

this blues will prove, a song different from "Preachin' the Blues" can illuminate the issue of House's treatment of the sacred/profane dilemma and show his artistic skills in conceiving what should not be considered as a blues or a prayer only, but rather as a blues prayer.

We can try to single out a few distinctive features running through Son House's musical production, bearing in mind that time and other psychological factors may have contributed to make the dichotomy schematized in Table 6.1 more acceptable to Son House at a conscious level.

In Son House's earlier career as a bluesman, these opposing elements seem to intertwine more often and to be less distinguishable than after his rediscovery in the 1960s. Though "rapping" on the two-faced meaning of the Blues right up until he stopped performing, in his late career House took up a more mature (though not totally relaxed) attitude toward this contrast, alternating blues and spirituals in his concerts. The significant fact is that, as far as we know, he played no more versions of "Dry Spell Blues." One could maintain that his abandonment of this blues can also be considered as a sign of an achieved peace of mind. However, it is no wonder that he no longer sang it, as the Dry Spell had long been over and was therefore an irrelevant subject not only to the audience, but also to Son House himself, who in 1964 could not remember the words composed more than thirty years before.

SON HOUSE, "DRY SPELL BLUES," PARAMOUNT 12990 (1930)[21]

Part One

I   1 The dry spell blues have fallen, drug me from door to door,
       2 Dry spell blues have fallen, drug me from door to door,
       3 The dry spell blues have put everybody on the killing floor.

II   4 Now the people down south soon won't have no home,
       5 Lord, the people down south soon won't have no home,
       6 'Cause this dry spell have parched all this cotton and corn.

III 7 Hard luck's on everybody, ain't missing but a few,
     8 Hard luck's on everybody, ain't missing but a few,
     9 Now besides the shower, ain't got a help but You.

IV 10 Done got fold my arms, and I walked away,
    11 Lord, I fold my arms, Lord, I walked away,
    12 Just like I tell Y/you, somebody's got to pay.

V   13 Pork chops forty-five cents a pound, cotton is only ten,
    14 Pork chops forty-five cents a pound, cotton is only ten,
    15 I can't keep no women, Lord, Lord, nowhere I been.

VI 16 So dry, old boll weevil turned up his toes and died,
    17 So dry, old boll weevil turned up his toes and died,
    18 Now ain't nothing to do, [but] bootleg moonshine and ride.

Part Two
VII 19 It have been so dry, Y/you can make a powderhouse out of the
          world,
    20 Well, it has been so dry, Y/you can make a powderhouse out of
          the world,
    21 Then all the money men like a rattlesnake in his quirl.[22]

VIII 22 I done throwed up my hand, Lord, and solemnly swore,
     23 I done throwed up my hand, Lord, and solemnly swore,
     24 There ain't no need of me changing towns, it's a drought
          everywhere I go.

IX 25 It's a dry old spell everywhere I been,
    26 Oh, it's a dry old spell everywhere I been,
    27 I believe to my soul, this old world is bound to end.

X   28 Well, I stood in my back yard, wrung my hands and scream,
    29 I stood in my back yard, I wrung my hands and scream,
    30 And I couldn't see nothing, couldn't see nothing green.

XI 31 Oh, Lord, have mercy if You please,
    32 Oh, Lord, have mercy if You please,
    33 Let Your rain come down, and give our poor hearts ease.

XII 34 These blues, these blues is worthwhile to be heard,
    35 Oh, these blues, worthwhile to be heard,
    36 God's very likely bound to rain somewhere.

Son House's "Dry Spell Blues" is mainly a description of the weather phenomenon of a drought, which affected, among others, the southern states

starting from the spring of 1930. Giving accounts of a natural disaster was quite a frequent theme at the dawn of recorded Blues. The successful sales of Bessie Smith's "Back-Water Blues" (1927) and the popularity of Charley Patton's "High Water Everywhere, Part One and Two" (1929) paved the way for this mode of expression.[23]

Coinciding with the Great Depression that began in 1929 and following "the ravages of the boll weevil and high wartime prices,"[24] the "drought of 1930 was one of the worst in American climatological history. In contrast to previous droughts, which had been intensive but short in duration, that of 1930 gradually grew worse and lasted for almost a year." The statistics reported by Nan Elizabeth Woodruff show that twenty-three states were damaged by the drought. Owing to their fundamentally agricultural economy, the areas bearing the most dramatic consequences were those "in the plantation counties in the Arkansas and Mississippi River Deltas." The drought devastated the Midwest and northern regions of the United States from March to May; then precipitation percentages in the South started to fall in July and August.[25]

At first, the 1930 drought was overlooked by the U.S. government, but it obviously aroused a great deal of interest in the newspapers. The June 26, 1930, editorial in the *Clarksdale Daily Register* newspaper titled "Tell the World You're Cool" is a light-hearted piece still reporting that it was actually hotter north of the Mason-Dixon line. Table 6.2 dramatically illustrates the growing severity of this atmospheric phenomenon by listing headlines in the period ranging from early July to around mid-August, 1930.

Blues historians have traditionally considered Son House's "Dry Spell Blues" to have been recorded at the Paramount Studio in Grafton, Wisconsin, on May 28, 1930, at a session in which a group of other blues singers participated. In the light of the above related historical data and the fact that Son House himself told various interviewers that the session was held in July or August, it is not hazardous to assume that this session actually took place in July or August, 1930, when the drought's consequences in the Mississippi Delta were the most severe.[26]

Only two more African American original blues songs dealing with the Dry Spell of 1930 have been traced so far.[27] One is by Charley Patton, who composed "Dry Well Blues" (Paramount 13070), recorded at the same session as Son House's.[28] This tune reports the effects of the drought in Lula, Mississippi, a country town north of Clarksdale where Patton and House lived at the time of the environmental catastrophe. Although Patton's life also contained a sacred/profane dichotomy, his song was strictly a blues, not

Table 6.2

July 8	page 1	"Dry Spell for Delta without Any Surcease"
		"Hottest Day" (yesterday was 101 Fahrenheit, hottest in two years)
July 9	page 1	"Delta Sizzles Under Heat" (top headline)
		"Hottest Day in Three Years Is Official Record"
		"Blazing Wave Melts Off Old Weather Mark"
July 10	page 1	"Clarksdale Experiences Its Hottest Day Since 1925"
		"America Wilts Under Rays of Merciless Sun"
July 11	page 1	"Sizzling Wave Breaks Record in Delta Areas"
July 13	page 1	"Hot Wave Prostrates U.S." (top headline)
		"South Sizzles Under Blazing Sun; Many Dead"
July 17	page 2	"Dry Up" (editorial)
July 20	page 1	"62-Day Drought Hangs On"
July 28	page 1	"Hot Weather's Hold Is Still Firm on World"
July 29	page 1	"County Scans Skies in Hope of Heat Relief"
	page 7	"Heat Record in Delta Is Broken" (108.5 degrees in Clarksdale)
		"Catfish Raising Dust in River"
July 31	page 4	"Sunburnt South" (editorial)
August 3	page 1	"76-Day Drought in Delta Marks New Heat History"
August 4	page 1	"All Heat Records Smashed"
August 6	page 1	"Drought-Stricken Nation Demands Government Aid"
August 8	page 1	"Crop Is 500,000 Bales Short"

a prayer or preaching. A few expressions resemble the ones in Son House's song ("I sure ain't got no home" and "parched all the cotton and corn"), but they should be read according to the context, which focuses on the community and its inhabitants as well as on their love relationships. In the last tercet a typically blues erotic touch is given when Lula women are said to put "Lula men down," thus depicting a sort of sexual drought.[29]

The other blues on the drought bears the same title as Son House's and was credited on the record label as being written and recorded by "Spider" Carter (Brunswick 7181). It was recorded in Chicago a few weeks after House's session, on Saturday, September 13, 1930.[30] This beautiful, though textually acerbic, example of piano blues keeps a more general perspective, and if one excepts the recurrent references to roaming, hard luck and corn crops, it presents no original theme of its own.

Textual linguistics is becoming more and more important as a methodology in literary criticism.[31] Though it is a recent discipline, its widespread use is justified by the scientific validity of its method, the main advantage of which is to stress both the statistical-objective and the interpretative-subjective aspect of a text. The latter is obviously prevalent in my contribution, which intends to provide the Blues with a new critical method and at the same time to demonstrate that this system is valid in this particular case.[32]

"Dry Spell Blues," composed by Son House in 1930, is one of the many examples of dramatic blues, but deep down in its text lie some obscure interpretative areas that make the complex subject matter and its poetic development extremely original. Before analyzing the song's structure, it is necessary to provide precise information on the text, which is here transcribed as if it were one track. In fact, as specified in the title, "Dry Spell Blues" consists of two parts, because in the early years of this musical genre it was not customary, on account of technical limitations, to record songs much longer than three minutes. What is relevant for my analysis, however, is the stylistic uniformity of the song, and above all the consistent amalgam of structure and content. Therefore it has been copied as if it were one blues only. As a matter of fact, a separate examination of the two parts of the song would not make sense, because the global outlook on the text's structure and its real meaning would be lost.

Dwelling carefully upon the structure of this text is fundamental for an accurate analysis. It is important to prove also, in respect to content, how meaningful is the structural division of the text into two separate parts: the first thirty-three lines and the last three. The first part, consisting of eleven tercets, appears as a prayer addressed to God, whereas the second part is fully in keeping with the expressive and stylistic canons of a closing statement addressed to the listeners. In the first thirty-three lines the author addresses God directly, treating Him as a person listening to something in between a descriptive monolog and a prayer. That we are listening to a prayer can be shown by mentioning the frequent references to the Lord, which start with "You" in line 9 and are taken up again by using the direct term "Lord" or the form "Your" in lines 31, 32, and 33. "Lord" in lines 5, 11, 15, 22, and 23 is an interjection, and the pronoun "you" in lines 12 and 19/20 is probably not addressed to God; in line 12 it may refer to the audience, and in lines 19/20 it may represent the impersonal pronoun "one." Whatever the real meaning of these words, we know that Son House was a very popular musician in the Delta in that period, and so this song was very likely performed at parties, juke joints, etc. Therefore, this prayer might also have the function of a sermon for the listeners, as it deals with a problem of great topical interest to them. In the last three lines, however, Son House does not address God; in fact he speaks of Him in the third person ("God's very likely bound to rain somewhere") to men and women who, like God, should listen to this blues, which is "worthwhile to be heard" because it can better the quality of life and mankind.

The structural division of the text into two parts is evident at a first reading, since we realize that this is certainly a prayer when we read line 9. This line enables us to guess what is then made explicit in the following tercet (lines 10–12), that is, the direct reference to God ("Lord"). The first eight lines are also part of the prayer, but they may seem to be excluded from it owing to the introductory import of the monolog to God within the logical structure of the text. That these lines are part of the prayer can be proved in two ways: (1) from the point of view of meaning, so that it is their semantic homogeneity with the other stanzas of the prayer that shows their introductory import to the subject; (2) from the structural point of view, so that the juxtaposition of each one ("everybody," "all") and no one implied in lines 4 and 5 ("no") connects the first eight lines, after which "You" in line 9 comes as a release.

After proving that the first thirty-three lines are part of a real prayer while the last three are not, and after showing its uniformity, we can see what the prayer really means: human beings could not "let the rain come down" and overcome drought, but God has this power in Himself, for Himself and in itself. So He should feel "bound" to put an end to evil after the author's calling for His help by means of a prayer, which is uttered by Son House for himself, but also as a spokesman for all the human beings and animals who are suffering from the drought. Such obligation, however, is obviously moral in its nature, and comes not from praying in itself, but from the scruple of conscience that God should have when He sees the cruel actions (killings, contraband) that human beings believe themselves entitled to take in order to selfishly outlive others who suffer from natural disasters. A very assertive appeal toward God is thus made in this blues: the theme is implicit in the act of praying in the first thirty-three lines, and it is not by chance expressed right at the beginning of the song, precisely in the third line ("The dry spell blues have put everybody on the killing floor"), while the explicit prayer—compared to the implicit one in the first eight lines—is postponed and starts from "You" in line 9, and more clearly from the word "Lord" in lines 10–11. A short digression concerning the metaphor "killing floor" should be made here: this old-fashioned expression stands for a slaughterhouse and is very common in downhome Blues musicians' jargon.[33] Although one of the themes of this blues is that of abstaining from committing homicides ("killing") through the prayer as well as through a strong petition to God and its expected consequent rainfall, Son House also suggests the people who are going to be the victims of these homicides. Exactly at a distance of 9 lines (three tercets) one from the other, starting from line 3 which introduces the matter ("killing floor"), the author first tells us that if the symbolic purification does not occur, "somebody's got to pay" (line 12), then even gets to the point of indicating that the (mostly white) rich men too ("money men," line 21) are going to pay for it because, owing to the long drought, they will end up being "like a rattlesnake in his quirl."

Before starting to examine the different themes characterizing this blues, I think it convenient to carry out research on its alternately narrative and commentative structure. In order to bring the so far purely formal study to a conclusion, it is necessary to make use of a nonanalytic examination of the stanzas. This is not a contradiction with what has just been said in relation to the method of analysis that has been adopted for this blues; in fact, it strengthens it, just because such a critical excursus requires only a superficial glance at the text and few exclusively formal interpretative devices.

The introduction of the prayer, which consists of three tercets, is opened by a decidedly narrative stanza, expressed in all its shades of meaning, including the theme of killing. These first three lines perfectly illustrate the essentiality of the theme in question. The second and third stanzas are both commentative, and are closed by that "You" which makes the prayer explicit. The fourth tercet is, together with the next to last, one of the two stanzas explicitly containing the prayer. The fifth takes up the partially narrative tone again and must be read literally. The sixth and seventh enunciate the possible ways out of the actual situation and are commentative, as they do not express real but rather intentional facts, first of all by threatening to traffic in contraband and lead a life of crime (line 18), then recognizing the rich men too as dangerous victims (ready to strike and bite from their defensive position) of the human exasperation caused by the drought (line 21). The eighth stanza is narrative, except line 24 which must be interpreted separately. Following this, we find a commentative reprise in the ninth tercet, which adds little to the previous ones and stresses the tone of the second part of the prayer. The tenth stanza is narrative again and precedes the other tercet including the prayer where God is asked to let the rain come down. The last stanza, which is not part of the prayer in that it is not addressed to God, is the most commentative of all, as it is addressed to the people, who have come down to the edge of a moral abyss. This inexhaustive digression on each stanza clearly shows the structural alternation of narrative and commentative tercets, the latter being slightly but significantly prevailing. This critical dissertation on each stanza will also be useful when dealing with the thematic development of the musical composition.

Drought is, of course, the first and most apparent motif in this blues, but it is perhaps to be taken as if it were made up of two stratified planes, which may run parallel throughout the song: a literal and a metaphorical plane of drought.

The first plane refers to the physical-atmospheric phenomenon of drought—meant as an effect of a quite specific and harmful cause—and to its opposite, the rain. This theme is introduced right in the opening words of the blues/prayer ("The dry spell blues") as an objective narrative element in sharp contrast with its last line ("Let Your rain come down"), by employing the metaphorical verb antonomastically denoting rain ("have fallen"); instead, it is *the dry spell blues* that have been falling.[34] At the end of the second stanza the main subject is taken up again by describing its direct effects ("the dry spell have parched all this cotton and corn"), while the third tercet points out that the only solution to the problem is a "help" from God preventing men from being forced to commit a number of crimes. Such help is propitiated by this blues/prayer, as Son House himself seems to suggest in the last stanza.

After the pause in the stanza including the prayer, in line 13 we find a reprise of the effects of drought ("Pork chops forty-five cents a pound, cotton is only ten").[35] The sixth stanza will be analyzed separately, because it is illuminating from the point of view of meaning. The following verse presents a direct reference to the main theme ("So dry"), a reference of minor importance if seen in the general commentative tone of the stanza, and which can even be considered as a sentimental accentuation. After the other narrative pause in stanza 8, there are two tercets—the former definitely explicative, the latter mostly narrative—that add no new elements, but insist on the subject and try to generalize the phenomenon of drought to the conclusion according to which "this old world is bound to end," and that not even a blade of grass can be seen ("nothing green"). This is the preparation for the pleading that closes the prayer. In stanza 10, the effect of drought is intuitively present again in line 30 in the reiteration of negations ("And I couldn't see nothing, couldn't see nothing green").[36] These negations have the structural function of opening for the following tercet, the one containing the second supplication, and they cause in the reader/listener a strong and growing dramatic tension (inherent in the long scansion of the lines) exploding in the scream "Lord." I will deal with the metrical structure of these two lines later, though it can at this point be easily perceived how it contributes to the cadenced close of the prayer. It is not by chance that from now on there are no more references to drought, while the lexeme "rain" is used twice, first as a substantive, then as a verb; both the stanza expressing the supplication and the whole prayer concentrate on the final plea for rain ("Let Your rain come down"); now the Lord should feel morally obliged to rain cats and dogs (!) ... the way only He can ("God's very likely bound to rain somewhere"), and this downpour will spare more killings and bad actions.

The second plane of drought may metaphorically refer to Prohibition, which was in force in the United States from 1920 to 1933–34, ending at different times in different states. The theme of the extremely poor quality and the scarce quantity of alcoholic drinks in the Prohibition Era is very frequent in blues lyrics, and this was a problem dramatically felt by Son House as well, for whom drinking was a means to forget his troubles. At a superficial level, the metaphoric reference to drought meaning shortage of liquor may have been kept secret in this blues as far as line 18. The sixth tercet is fundamental in order to study in detail the meaning of the theme of drought and of the whole song, in both a literal and metaphorical sense. If we leave out the final tercet of this blues, which is no longer addressed to God, it should be noted that this stanza is exactly in the middle of the prayer. As already noticed, this central position reveals its importance, this being the only stanza in which the bluesman openly speaks of contraband liquor with reference to metaphorical and, as an alternative, to literal drought. The peculiarity here lies in presenting the two parallel themes of drought within the same tercet, but distinctly separate. Lines 16 and 17 exemplify the worrying level of drought by saying that even the boll weevil (the indestructible little insect that destroyed cotton fields) died of it; line 18 deals directly with contraband and indirectly with Prohibition. This stanza reveals, therefore, the alternative to "killing," proposing the illegal remedy of bootlegging for the privations caused by the drought.

The last point to be made on the theme of contraband concerns the reason why the author should have sharply emphasized—consciously or not—the literal rather than the metaphorical plane of drought. The reason is obvious. Drought as a natural occurrence may hit anybody, and so everybody should welcome the message inherent in this blues, which is thus "worthwhile to be heard." Metaphorical drought caused by Prohibition hits only lovers of drink, that is, a smaller group of people. Referring almost exclusively to drought as a physical-atmospheric phenomenon, Son House gives universality to his blues, and this justifies his call for attention from any human (and divine!) being, nobody excepted. If the figurative plane of drought had been pre-eminent from the purely formal standpoint of the number of lines, such a request would not have made any sense.

In light of the interpretation concerning the topic of drought in general and the sixth tercet in particular, the already analyzed theme of "killing," and consequently also that of wandering, which will soon be examined closely, acquires new importance. A key to its interpretation in this sense is present in the eighth stanza. The author does not need to solemnly swear that he is no longer going to wander in search of places not hit by the drought. In lines 22 and 23, the solemnity of gesture ("I done throwed up my hand") and action ("solemnly swore") itself is not at all justified by such a futile and liturgically insignificant oath as the one of not "changing towns." Son House is actually swearing that he (and presumably other men) is neither going to wander nor bootleg if God will be so kind as to let the rain come down. The tension of the author is, after all, typical of a person who is put in the psychological condition of having to kill other people in order to survive ("on the killing floor"). We can infer that stopping his wanderings is not the main object of the bluesman's oath from the stanzas that follow. The theme of wandering, in fact, is no longer dealt with, except provisionally in lines 25 and 26 ("everywhere I been"). The latter represent a moment of recapitulation between the much more important events expressed in the reprise of the theme of drought as the cause of crimes ("It's a dry old spell") and that of the end of the world as a direct effect of that cause ("this old world is bound to end"). In the tenth stanza, we even witness the definitive return to the theme of drought, first in the description of its psychological effects on the bluesman ("wrung my hands and scream"), then again in its direct effects on the environment ("couldn't see nothing green"). The alternation of exceeding solemnity and strong emotional tension bursts out in the final prayer (lines 31–33). The link between lines 24 and 25 is made possible by means of a peculiar stylistic device working only at a "phonic" level, but which is infallible. The reprise of "it's a drought everywhere I go" of line 24 in "It's a dry old spell everywhere I been" of the following line enables us to pick up the thread of what was being said. The logic of this connection, which is evident in the double occurrence of "everywhere" in relation to the theme of drought, is reconstructed in the song's final line by the word "somewhere" in relation to the rain. The reprise of the theme of drought starting in the ninth stanza never implies the repetition of already mentioned concepts. It is rather used to introduce new psychological and religious shades of meaning. The use of "Well" in the opening of the tenth stanza, besides departing from the solemn tone of the preceding stanza, is particularly revealing of the author's stylistic skill and technical variants. This antithetic stylistic function of "Well" is implicit in its colloquial use as the moment when one takes time to think of what should be said next. It refers to "this old world is bound to end," and increases the drama of the situation up to the physical spasm of pain in stanza eleven through the use of the iterated negations in line 30.

The two main themes of drought and "killing" are connected to what we can define as secondary themes through mutual semantic exchanges. The term secondary theme is a bit arbitrary, in that it is just the indissoluble union of all these subjects that makes this blues compact and solid. But when studying complex compositions like this, it is better to consider each topic separately and analyze it not only in relation to all the others, but also according to a wider critical line of vision. These secondary themes need to be dealt with one at a time and to be investigated thoroughly in relation to the main themes and to the prime meaning of the whole blues. Their lesser importance may be due either to the fact that they should not be considered independently—though recognized as fundamental in the song as a whole—or to the incomplete development of their topics.

An enlightening case is that of the secondary theme of wandering, which, if analyzed independently, loses a lot of its meaning. If studied in the light of the whole composition, and especially of the theme of "killing," it instead becomes extremely important for a better understanding of its cryptic implications. I start by observing the various textual references to wandering without anticipating any specific critical remarks. As far back as the beginning of the song (line 1), we can find an incontrovertible reference to forced wandering ("drug me from door to door")[37] caused by the "dry spell blues." Then in the second stanza we can find a statement, which may sound less direct than the previous one but which is just as explicit, since the people from the South, having no home, will have to leave their native territory and roam looking for a job and a home ("Now the people down south soon won't have no home"). A third reference to the theme of wandering is present in line 10, where "I walked away" is quite vague, but supports the assertion in the first line ("drug me from door to door"), taking up again its narrative tone within the prayer. Later, we can see two more allusions to the theme of wandering, which must be read jointly because they are structured in the same way from the syntactical point of view, although they have, on the whole, opposite meanings. "Nowhere I been" in line 15 refers to the impossibility of keeping a woman because of pork chops' high price and cotton's low one, while we have already made comments on the psychological function of the syntagm "everywhere I been" in line 25 when joined with the line before. A more subtle and probably unintentional hidden reprise of the theme of wandering is also present in the verb "ride" (line 18), which is tightly tied to bootlegging and infers a cause-and-effect relationship between the activity of making deliveries and that of riding around. This may unconsciously suggest an association of ideas according to which wandering in search of a place unaffected by drought ultimately leads to the criminal act of "riding" to deliver moonshine.

All these mentions of wandering can be defined as probative in that, referred to either in the past ("drug" in line 1, "walked" in line 10, "been" in lines 15 and 25) or in the future ("won't" in line 4), they express a fact that happened or will happen depending on the person wandering in search of places where drought has not yet hit. The detailed examination of lines 24 and 28, on the other hand, turns the tables: the former denotes the bluesman's surrender to the drought ("There ain't no need of me changing towns"), the latter his actual staying in one place ("I stood in my back yard"). We have already seen that an alternative to the "killing" in line 3 is pointed out here. Wandering should also represent an alternative to committing bad actions (bootlegging or murder). After the tercet suggesting action ("Now ain't nothing to do, [but] bootleg moonshine and ride")[38] and the following one not dealing with the theme of wandering, we find the stanza containing the solemn oath not to take up roaming about. We already know that swearing this oath makes no sense at all, because it actually refers to another theme. This oath does not mean that Son House really resolved not to go from town to town looking for places that had not become sterile owing to the drought. This eighth stanza—or better line 24—goes back to the theme of wandering as it is seen from a different viewpoint and expresses House's disillusion by opting in favor of a passive alternative ("There ain't no need of me changing towns"). The theme of wandering had been prevalent in the first fifteen lines, whereas the foundation of the prayer/appeal predominates after this refusal to adopt wandering as an alternative method to "killing." The most dramatic moment in this appeal can be found in the seventh stanza that follows the one concerning contraband. The assertiveness of the "petition" is here extremely evident: "It have been so dry, Y/you can make a powderhouse out of the world." Whether "you" refers to the Lord or is just an impersonal pronoun is difficult to say. Whatever the correct interpretation, this sentence means that the world is in an unstable equilibrium, which can cause an explosion, during which "all the money men" too will be "like a rattlesnake in his quirl." One more old-fashioned word can be found here: a "powderhouse" is where gunpowder is stored, and the proverbial expression "dry as a powderhouse" is an explicit reference to the danger created by the fact that powder has to be kept dry but may also ignite easily. This threat is so serious as to justify the theatrical gestures of the bluesman, who throws up his hand and solemnly swears he is not going to go away from his town.

After exhausting the subjects in the song, let us now see how the author manages to create the dramatic tension in the blues by using different tones, even though the drama is not in dialogic form as, for example, in "My Black Mama, Part One and Two" (Paramount 13042), recorded by Son House at the same session. Generally speaking, three different tones can be recognized, each in the most suitable circumstance, but all in some way concerning the theme of driving people to kill.

First, we can note a uniform way of structuring stanzas in the assertive tone of a few repeated decisively affirming or denying key words. These assertive linguistic acts enable us to find everything and nothing, everybody and nobody, everywhere and nowhere in each stanza, which introduce dramatic force into the language.

Let us see now the chronological sequence of these assertive expressions: in line 3 there is "everybody," which is very important because of its association with "everybody on the killing floor"; in the second stanza we find in line 4 the negation "no home," which continues dealing with the theme of wandering, while in line 6 "all" strengthens the catastrophic effects of drought. In the third stanza we have "everybody" linked with "hard luck" in line 7, and in line 9 "ain't got a help," which simply means "only one help." In line 12 we find "somebody," which we have seen in the middle position between lines 3 and 21 that identify the victims of "killing." Decisiveness is here expressed by means of simulated indefiniteness: "somebody" refers to the whole class of people ("all the money men"). In line 15, the assertive tone is almost exaggerated in the three extremely emphatic negations ("I can't keep no women, Lord, Lord, nowhere I been"). One more double negation ("ain't nothing") introduces in line 18 the only possible remedy to "killing," as well as the only alternative to wandering: bootlegging. In line 21, one more "all" resolutely groups together the rich men, denoting the white plantation owners, local merchants and bankers, whose unsuccessful harvest caused by the drought might make them decide to cut off credit and supplies to the poor sharecroppers, thus turning themselves into killers ready to bite ("like a rattlesnake in his quirl"). In the ninth stanza, line 27 is also extremely meaningful, because in "bound to end" there is an assertive phrase formally different from the usual ones (though expressing the same meaning), which can be compared to the final line ("bound to rain somewhere"). The correlation between the two forms of the verb makes the assertive tone of the prayer addressed to God stronger: He is "bound" to let the rain come down. Line 30 must be read parallel to line 15, because their repeated negations (four, in this case) are structured in a similar way; such negations raise the already considerable dramatic tone before the closing of the prayer ("couldn't see nothing, couldn't see nothing green"). Being the final plea directly addressed to God, the last tercet of the prayer (lines 31–33) significantly presents no assertive tone, but it is expressed differently from line 12. No room is given to either the mood of defeat, disgust and resignation exploding in the gesture "I [done got] fold my arms and I walked away," or to the one indicating defiance and resolve, resistance and determination, which is present by intuition in the sentence "I done throwed up my hand and solemnly swore." After wandering and giving vent to his feelings, Son House now stands still waiting on God, being ready for either the end of the world or God's rain.

With regard to the prayer, one can compare the structures of lines 10 and 22 whose first hemistichs are structured as in a mirror ("Lord, I [done got] fold my arms" *versus* "I done throwed up my hand, Lord"), while the structure of the second hemistich in line 10 runs parallel to the one in the second hemistich of line 22 ("and I walked away" *versus* "and solemnly swore").[39] The change in structure results from the bluesman's striving after an effect of absorption, combining solemnity of the oath and lyrical outburst.

Second, excluding the phrases "ain't got a help but You" (line 9) and the stronger "Lord, I [done got] fold my arms" (line 10), a solemn tone starts to become prevalent from line 22, and, after reaching the climax of its pleading, it tends to become pathetic in the supplication for mercy in lines 31 and 32 ("Oh, Lord, have mercy if You please"). Solemnity—seemingly at its highest in lines 22 and 23, but in fact deliberately exaggerated in order to let us understand the real object of taking such a strange oath—is caused, after all, by a strong religious yearning permeating the whole blues and coming back to the surface starting from the tenth stanza, then continuing in the following one. The uneasiness deriving from the awareness of having committed the sin of conceiving criminal intents is revealed; the solemn tone in the second part of the blues, where the theme of "killing" is abandoned, does not succeed in repressing such a strong discomfort and feeling of guilt. The rise from an assertive to a solemn tone and the sudden fall to pathos cause the growing dramatic tension in the song. This tension reflects the dichotomy between that strong religious feeling and the Blues (meant as the musical genre expressing par excellence the profane in contrast to the sacred point of view of the people). It also reflects the contrast present in this song, which resembles formally both a prayer and a blues, that is, a composition belonging to the so-called Devil's Music. It should not be forgotten that Son House was always a prey to the torments of remorse caused by the inner conflict in his capacity as bluesman and preacher, an ambiguous and ambivalent situation, artistically leading to the composition of this and other songs which are at the same time blues and preaching "worthwhile to be heard," even by God. In the term "worthwhile" (line 34) we come to the point of witnessing one of Son House's metamorphoses from bluesman to preacher.

Third, the sincere mood of the author suffering because of drought—meant both as the consequence of the weather phenomenon and, possibly, as drought in his "parched" throat—nourishes a pathetic close. The extremely original end of this blues is actually quite dramatic for an alcoholic like Son House. The few imploded words forming lines 31 and 32 serve to give prominence to the following line, where the image of liberating rainfall (and, perhaps metaphorically, whisky) may point out the best possible solution, that is, the breaking of the evil spell of drought and, by analogy, of Prohibition ("Let Your rain come down and give our poor hearts ease"). However, the hypothesis of the whisky metaphor, based on House's known severe alcoholism and on the mention of bootlegging in line 18, is very suggestive, but difficult to prove. If we keep to logical assumptions and facts, Son House's addiction to alcohol was not likely to be at such a dramatic level in 1930 as it was by the time of his "rediscovery" in 1964, and the bootlegging of liquor was an activity implying the selling and not necessarily the drinking of whisky. Moreover, if we consider that this song does not seem to have appeared in House's later repertoire, we should take the literal reference to a weather condition as being far more important than a possibly metaphorical plane of drought and confine the latter to no more than a secondary and probably unconscious relevance of meaning. This blues is about a real drought in the vein of other 1920s and 1930s blues compositions describing natural and accidental disasters.[40]

Within a whole tercet, only in line 33 (and in the word "ease" in particular) do we reach the climax of the pathetic tone. The author has now brought his supplication to God to a conclusion after putting the final accurate touch to his petition. Still using the typical language of a preacher ("worthwhile"), he can at last address human beings, convinced as he is that his appeal is going to have the desired effect ("God's very likely bound to rain somewhere").

Finally, a comprehensive study of all the themes in this blues also enables us to detect a more general overall symmetrical structure to the prayer (lines 1–33) through the principles of contrast and association, as shown in Figure 6.1.

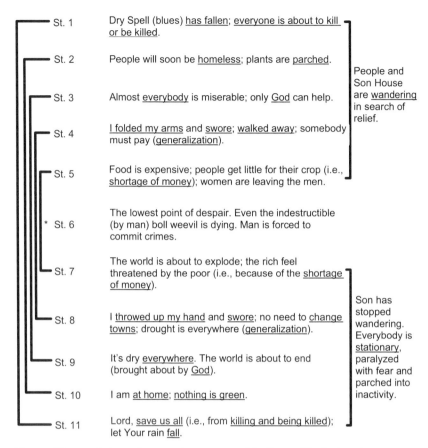

St. 1   Dry Spell (blues) has fallen; everyone is about to kill or be killed.

St. 2   People will soon be homeless; plants are parched.

St. 3   Almost everybody is miserable; only God can help.

St. 4   I folded my arms and swore; walked away; somebody must pay (generalization).

St. 5   Food is expensive; people get little for their crop (i.e., shortage of money); women are leaving the men.

* St. 6   The lowest point of despair. Even the indestructible (by man) boll weevil is dying. Man is forced to commit crimes.

St. 7   The world is about to explode; the rich feel threatened by the poor (i.e., because of the shortage of money).

St. 8   I throwed up my hand and swore; no need to change towns; drought is everywhere (generalization).

St. 9   It's dry everywhere. The world is about to end (brought about by God).

St. 10   I am at home; nothing is green.

St. 11   Lord, save us all (i.e., from killing and being killed); let Your rain fall.

People and Son House are wandering in search of relief.

Son has stopped wandering. Everybody is stationary, paralyzed with fear and parched into inactivity.

Fig. 6.1. The associative and contrastive structure of the "prayer" in the first eleven stanzas of "Dry Spell Blues."

In his study of blues lyric formulae, Michael Taft claims that "singers placed stanzas in almost any order without doing any harm to the logic of the song. [. . .] One such song is Son House's 'Dry Spell Blues' (parts 1 and 2), in which House concentrated on the themes of drought and poverty from stanza one to the next [. . .]. If one were to take all the stanzas in this song and rearrange them in some random way, the logic of the song would not be impaired,"[41] As inferable from the textual analsyis of the song above and especially from the extremely intricate symmetrical configuration of contrasts and associations and their interaction below, Taft's choice of this song is inappropriate to say the least. In order to find out why, let us focus on each linked pair of tercets, trying to examine them thoroughly in order to extract the residual interpretative areas hidden in this song.

The first and last tercet of the prayer are placed in contrast by means of an upside-down crossed mirroring (metaphorical fall of the dry spell blues→ killing *versus* salvation from killing←hoped-for rainfall), juxtaposing what has been happening and what Son House is pleading to God to make happen. The contrast is not merely thematic or structural, but also stylistic: the first verse in stanza one echoes the cadenced solitary cry of a holler, while lines 31 and 32 have the prolonged progression of a spiritual.

The two themes in stanzas two and ten (housing problem and aridity), instead, hold the same strophic position in the tercet, but are approached in a different way: in the repeated lines, by opposing the concept of forced loss of a house (lines 4 and 5) to its presumably temporary possession (lines 28 and 29), in lines 6 and 30 by associating two conditional and ineluctable facts caused by extreme dryness.

If studied apart, the third and ninth stanzas simply strike one as being assertive in an absolute way, but if seen through the magnifying lenses of mirror-like analysis, they underline the fact that a limit to people's patience has been reached. The two indefinite pronouns "everybody" and "every-where" strengthen very subtly the (literally meant) *vital* difference that exists between people's death, helplessness and suffering on the one hand, and nature's decay that causes them on the other. It is also interesting to note that these two stanzas present one more upside-down crossed mirroring similar to the one reciprocally reflected in the opening and closing of the prayer, but which now avails itself of the typically African American "call and response" pattern. Not surprisingly, especially in a (blues)man like Son House, we feel as if we are attending the performance of a religious service closely resembling a spiritual, which—deprived of the ritual linguistic and extra-linguistic utterances expressing emotional involvement—is transcribed in Table 6.3. Lines 25 and 26 provide the logical answer to a possible rhetorical question asked in lines 7 and 8, whilst the second hemistich of line 9 sounds as the abrupt and spontaneous reply to the ethical request for an explanation addressed to God in line 27.

Table 6.3

"Why is hard luck on everybody?"	lines 7 and 8
"'Cause there's the dry old spell"	lines 25 and 26
"Why is this old world bound to end?"	line 27
"'Cause ain't got a(ny) help from You"	line 9

When we link the fourth and eighth stanzas, the already noted symmetrical strophic structure of their first two lines illuminates the clash between Son House's subjective, instinctive reaction of walking away from the drought and his thoughtful, mature reflection on inaction objectively deriving from experience. Immediately afterward, such contrastive association makes room for two mirror-like generalizations, the former referring to the theme of killing (line 12), the latter to the unsuccessful remedy of wandering due to the drought (line 24).

An interaction between the fifth and seventh stanza could not have been brought to light if the reflecting construction constituting the prayer had not been discovered. Within each of these tercets, we can only find indirect implicit references to a generic shortage of money, but if we read them together as mirroring one another, they shed light on the whole blues, highlighting the fact that the reflection is always due to the persistent situation caused by the atmospheric phenomenon of drought. Just in these two most recondite stanzas we are shown that the actual shortage of money is once more only the shortage of rain in disguise. So, the overwhelming lack of rain is implicitly or explicitly present throughout the text, as if it were shaped as an invisible dry and inclement bank of clouds looming up in the sky before the cathartic liberation of human beings' (and more generally of the world's) moral and physical sins. The mirror-like matching of stanzas five and seven also allows one to make out one more correlative contraposition regarding the increasingly unbearable qualitative sphere of life under the spell of drought. When portraying the women's resolve to leave the men,[42] the former stanza alludes to a breakdown of the *domestic* order, whereas in the psychological feeling of threat pervading the "money men" the latter stanza suggests a breakdown of the *societal* order. As the longitudinal decoding of the text will soon show, the idea of juxtaposing family and societal anarchy represents a turning point and, after all, a point of no return. Moreover, while describing different (though not peripheral) serious damage caused by the drought, the conflation of these two stanzas also serves to return their two texts to the main subject, preparing for the paradoxical central stanza.

The mirror-like reflection of each tercet belonging to the prayer isolates the sixth stanza, which works as a sort of hinge around which the text of the prayer unfolds. The parenthetical mention of the boll weevil in the middle of the prayer, therefore, has a double function: (1) it is psychologically revealing, since it reminds listeners of a calamity earlier in the century that was as devastating as the present drought; (2) it is structurally meaningful, because it is the focal point on which are concentrated the fuzzy images projected in the blues by the respectively flat ("The dry spell blues have fallen") and highly-contrasted ("Let Your rain come down") pictures developed in the first and last stanza, two distant but interconnected images, which help clear up the theme of committing crimes, introducing and concluding the appeal to God.

The complex mirror-like quality of the stanzas forming the prayer is also made clearer and completed by a more visible linear reading of the whole blues through the unearthing of a second dimension, traversing the song vertically and having a double possible direction (downward or upward) as in an elevator. Both movements have a physical and moral relevance: the downward motion from the first to the sixth stanza heads down toward earthly sin and death by means of an accurate process of accumulation causing human beings' highly emblematic descent into Hell. The upward motion from the sixth to eleventh stanza lifts up toward purification and life as suddenly and "precipitately" as a long-expected shower of rain does. Choosing rainfall (that is, an exclusively downward movement) as the primary natural element tokening the ascent to purification is not contradictory, senseless or accidental, since it is Son House's (that is, mankind's) *upward* invocation to God that may get Him to rain.

As shown in Figure 6.1, the up-and-down movement covering this blues and the mirror-like reflection of the stanzas constituting the prayer not only isolate the sixth stanza, but separate the two themes of wandering and stationary waiting, placing them in sharp contrast. The latter themes are anything but new in pre-war Blues lyrics and spring from a common source. Yet, the originality lies in the way they are confronted: the deed of rambling (stanzas 1–5) leads to riding/sinning and eventually to death (stanza 6), while the notion of remaining stationary and waiting on God (stanzas 7–11) leads to salvation and rain, that is, life (stanza 12). The former theme is intrinsically secular and occurs in a number of blues compositions, such as Son House's own archetypal "Walking Blues," recorded at the same session as "Dry Spell Blues." Though also traceable in many blues, the latter theme is basically sacred in origin and very much a part of old-line Baptist and Methodist religion in often quoted biblical phrases like "watch and pray" (Matthew 26:41; Mark 13:33; Mark 14:38; Luke 21:36) and "wait till my change comes" (Job 14:14) or in the spiritual song "Keep Still, God Will Fight Your Battles." There should be no need to point out Son House's acquaintance with the Bible and his deep understanding of, serious approach to, and empathy with these two doctrines. So, the blues solution is here diluted in a gospel liquid, but retains its blues flavor.

The enumeration of disasters caused by the drought has now accumulated as a mass of clouds. On passing from one element (praying) to the other (the appeal to God), the reflected beams (the themes) of the prayer change density and are refracted in the last tercet of the blues. In the final stanza, when condensing and summarizing the content of the song, perceiving it as if after pressing a fast forward button, the petition is at first loaded in the two repeated verses ("These blues, these blues [is] worthwhile to be heard"), then triggered in the last line ("God's very likely bound to rain somewhere").

Symmetrical structures are not common in the Blues nowadays. They seem to have been statistically more recurrent in non-thematic blues—especially in folk Blues songs making extensive use of traditional phrases and lines—than in thematic ones such as this.[43] Although further rigorous and far from easy research may disprove the following hypothesis, it is very unlikely that Son House was consciously aware of this structure. So, how does the analysis of the mirror-like structure of the blues affect its meaning and scope? It certainly does not alter the former, but it contributes to broadening the latter, proving that Son House's (and in general Blues people's) ability at composing cohesive and original songs was only partly based on the tradition. Furthermore, it provides one of the most evident examples of the reason why thematic Blues lyrics should neither be considered just as the fruit of structural and compositional awareness, nor as a trivial improvisational act, but rather as a mixture of both. Such an aesthetic "duplicity" is the result of African American artists' greater confidence in, and higher awareness of, their own autonomous and innovative position in American society as spokespersons of a different culture. Independently of the exegetic method adopted, this complex blues shows Son House's musicianship and strong sensitivity to the facts of life and consequently to art.

Whether or not (or just because) Son House was aware of acting the part of an impotent pawn moved by God's hands on the scornful checkerboard of life, he stands out in the Blues sphere as one of the most brilliant stars. The essentiality of this bluesman's utterance and his stifling compression of the logically and psychologically implicit and vital assumption of a mood mix a well-blended explosive potion made up of feelings, a medicine that only a blues-suffering mind could prepare.

Notes

This chapter is dedicated to my parents.

This essay is partly based on my earlier study of Son House's "Dry Spell Blues" included in my degree thesis titled "La Lingua Inglese dei Neri d'America e i Blues: Analisi Critica di Alcuni Testi" (Black English and the Blues: A Critical Analysis of Some Lyrics), June 1985. In the present article, *Blues* with a capital "B" refers to the musical genre and to the personification or deification of the term, while *blues* with a small "b" refers to both a specific song and the psychological mood of the blues singer.

1. See Rob Hutten, "This Old House . . . ," *Blues & Rhythm* 111 (August 1996): 10–11. According to this article, the musician's year of birth is doubtfully dated back to 1886.

2. David Evans, booklet notes to *Delta Blues and Spirituals*, Capitol Blues Collection no.7, 7243 8 31830 2 9, 1995, 28.

3. Among the studies on the dichotomy under discussion, I only mention: William Ferris, "Bluesmen and Preachers," in *Blues from the Delta* (New York: Da Capo Press, 1984), 79–89; Paul Oliver, "Preaching the Blues," in *Screening the Blues* (New York: Da Capo Press, 1989), 44–89; Paul Oliver, *Songsters and Saints* (Cambridge: Cambridge University Press, 1984), esp. 140–228; Charles Keil, *Urban Blues* (Chicago: University of Chicago Press, 1966), 143–63; Albert Murray, *Stomping the Blues* (New York: McGraw-Hill, 1976), 21–42; Fabrizio Venturini, "Sacro e Profano a Confronto," in *Sulle Strade del Blues* (Milano: Gammalibri, 1984), 223–48; Julio Finn, *The Bluesman* (London: Quartet Books, 1986), 151–83; Robert Sacré, ed., *Saints and Sinners: Religion, Blues and (D)evil in African-American Music and Literature* (Liège: Société liégeoise de musicologie, 1996); Bruce Cook, *Listen to the Blues* (New York: Da Capo Press, 1995), 201–15; Jon Michael Spencer, *Blues and Evil* (Knoxville: University of Tennessee Press, 1993). The last book gives a totally different interpretation from the others, seeing no dichotomy between sacred and religious themes in the Blues but rather a "synchronous duplicity."

4. As no books on Son House have been yet published, I list here the works giving substantial space to this bluesman: Bob Groom, *The Blues Revival* (London: Studio Vista, 1970), 57–60; Bob Groom, "Down-Home Postwar Blues," in *The New Blackwell Guide to Recorded Blues,* eds. John Cowley and Paul Oliver (Oxford: Blackwell Publishers, 1996), 312–14; Paul Oliver, *The Story of the Blues* (Harmondsworth, Eng.: Penguin Books, 1972), 117–19; Alan Lomax, *The Land Where the Blues Began* (New York: Pantheon Books, 1993), 16–20; Samuel Charters, *The Blues Makers* (Part I) (New York: Da Capo Press, 1991), 57–70; Robert Palmer, *Deep Blues* (New York: The Viking Press, 1981), 79–82; Keith Briggs, Tony Burke, Alan Lomax and John Cowley, "We Called It the Walking Blues," *Blues & Rhythm* 37 (June–July 1988): 4–5; John Cowley, "Really the Walking Blues," *Juke Blues* 1 (July 1985): 8–14; Ian Grant, "Son House at 'The New Gates of Cleeve,'" *Blues Unlimited* 27 (November 1965): 8–9; Bernard Klatzko, "Finding Son House," *Blues Unlimited* 15 (September 1964): 8-9; Simon A. Napier, "Eugene Son House," *Blues Unlimited* 14 (August 1964): 6, 11;

J. Nicholas Perls, "Son House–Paramount Notes," *Blues Unlimited* 18 (January 1965): 3; J. Nicholas Perls, "Son House Interview," *78 Quarterly* 1, no. 1 (Autumn 1967): 59–61; Phil Spiro, "How We Found Son House," *Broadside of Boston* 3, no. 11 (June 24, 1964): 2, 4; Richard A. Waterman, "Finding Son House," *National Observer* (July 20, 1964): 16; Peter J. Welding, "Chicago Report," *Blues Unlimited* 30 (February 1966): 5, 7; Alan Wilson, "Son House," *Blues Unlimited Collector's Classics* 14 (October 1966): 1–16; David Evans, "Son House–Some Further Comments," *Blues Unlimited* 43 (May 1967): 8–10; William Ferris, "Gut Bucket Blues: Sacred and Profane," *Jazzforschung* 5 (1973): 68–85; Bob Groom, "An Interview with Son House," *Blues World* 18 (January 1968): 5–8; John Cowley, "Son House 1902–1988: An Historical Appreciation," *Blues & Rhythm* 41 (Christmas 1988): 8–10; Michael F. Rothman, "Son House Now: An Afternoon with the Father of Country Blues," *Talking Blues* 1 (April–June 1976): 5–6; Gérard Herzhaft, "Son House (1902–1988)," *Soul Bag* 115 (Winter 1989): 17; Sheldon Harris, *Blues Who's Who: A Biographical Dictionary of Blues Singers* (New Rochelle, N.Y.: Arlington House, 1979), 247–49; Stephen Calt and Gayle Wardlow, *King of the Delta Blues: The Life and Music of Charlie Patton* (Newton, N.J.: Rock Chapel, 1988), 208–21, 237–38; Mark Humphrey, "Prodigal Sons: Son House and Robert Wilkins," in *Saints and Sinners,* ed. Robert Sacré, 167–94; David Evans, "Ramblin'," *Blues Revue Quarterly* 8 (Spring 1993): 14; Luigi Monge, "Son House," *Il Blues* 25 (December 1988): 4–8; 26 (March 1989): 5–8; 27 (June 1989): 32–33; Bob West, "From the Vaults: Bob West Interview with Son House," *Blues & Rhythm* 207 (March 2006): 4–7.

5. Keith Briggs, Tony Burke, Alan Lomax, and John Cowley, "Really the Walking Blues," 10.

6. Dennis Jarrett, "Pragmatic Coherence in an Oral Formulaic Tradition: I Can Read Your Letters/Sure Can't Read Your Mind," in *Coherence in Spoken and Written Discourse,* ed. Deborah Tannen, Georgetown University, vol. 12, forming part of *Advances in Discourse Processes,* ed. Roy O. Freedle (Norwood, N.J.: Ablex Publishing Corporation, 1984), 155–71. The American scholar's contribution makes use of the Blues as an artistic expression closely bound to oral tradition. "Preachin' the Blues" by Son House is used to demonstrate the linguistic "coherence" and the textual integrity of fragments belonging to this tradition.

7. David Evans, "Goin' up the Country: Blues in Texas and the Deep South," in *Nothing but the Blues,* ed. Lawrence Cohn (New York: Abbeville Press, 1993), 36.

8. "Blues musicians were well aware that their singing was comparable to preaching, both in style and in the effect it could have on an audience. 'Preachin' the Blues' made the connections explicit in a manner that must have seemed scandalously outspoken to many who heard it. Much was made of Ray Charles's mixing of blues themes and gospel music in the 1950s, but House was preaching the 'gospel blues' in the late twenties." Robert Palmer, *Deep Blues,* 81. A less traditional (though questionable) meaning of the expression "gospel blues" can be found in Michael W. Harris, *The Rise of Gospel Blues: The Music of Thomas Andrew Dorsey in the Urban Church*

(New York: Oxford University Press, 1992), where the author uses this term suggesting that Dorsey's songs are a bluesy or blues-infused type of gospel song forming a separate category.

9. Jon Michael Spencer, *Blues and Evil,* esp. 71–74.

10. From the interview Jeff Titon made on May 8, 1971, at the Gopher Campus Motor Lodge in Minneapolis a few hours before House's concert at the University of Minnesota, transcribed by Titon himself and published as "Living Blues Interview: Son House," *Living Blues* 31 (March–April 1977): 14–22, esp. 15.

11. This passage is taken from Son House (interviewed by Julius Lester), "I Can Make My Own Songs," *Sing Out* 15, no. 3 (July 1965): 40.

12. Titon, "Living Blues Interview," 21–22.

13. See Julius Lester, "I Can Make My Own Songs," 46.

14. James "Son" Thomas, "Blues and Spirituals," transcribed by John Barnie in the notes to *Bothered All the Time,* Southern Culture Records SC 1703, 1983.

15. The lexeme "blu(e)in'" has been specially coined to comply with the critical method adopted in this essay. The gerundive form comes from the verb "*blue,*" which can be found in the jazz standard tune "Bluin' the Blues" and in an idiom ("I'm bluein' all the time") that Henry Thomas actually used in the song "Woodhouse Blues" (*Texas Worried Blues,* Yazoo Records 1080/1, 1989).

16. Quoted from Mark Humphrey, "Prodigal Sons: Son House and Robert Wilkins," in *Saints and Sinners: Religion, Blues and (D)evil in African-American Music and Literature,* ed. Robert Sacré, 178.

17. "Blues singers' defiant denial of the heaven and kingdom come abstractions was typically followed by a search to acquire or construct a heaven of their own—a heaven where the spirit of the blues god could reign." Jon Michael Spencer, *Blues and Evil,* 86.

18. Among those who openly sided with the Blues—also meant as a way to lead one's life—let us mention the pianist Lee Kizart, who declared: "But now I don't do that. I just serve one way. I won't cross up church stuff with my stuff, 'cause you can't do everything and be saved. I can play spirituals, but I don't like it. I won't do like a lot of folks. Disc jockeys and things, they want you to play that mix-up rhythm, but I won't do it. I figure I got enough to give account of. You know we all got a day, but I won't cross up. I'll be punished for it" (William Ferris, *Blues from the Delta,* 81–82). See also Kizart's "A Tale of Church Hypocrisy," transcribed by John Barnie in the notes to the LP *Bothered All the Time.*

19. David Evans, booklet notes to *Delta Blues and Spirituals,* 5.

20. No detailed analysis has ever been made of Son House's "Dry Spell Blues." This song has been recognized as a blues prayer by David Evans, "Early Deep South and Mississippi River Basin Blues," in *The New Blackwell Guide to Blues Records,* eds. John Cowley and Paul Oliver, 69–70; by Arnold Shaw, "The Mississippi Blues Tradition and the Origins of the Blues," in *The Voice of the Delta,* ed. Robert Sacré (Liège: Presses universitaires de Liège, 1987), 98; and as a "topical sermon" by Mark Humphrey,

"Prodigal Sons: Son House and Robert Wilkins," in *Saints and Sinners: Religion, Blues and (D)evil in African-American Music and Literature,* ed. Robert Sacré, 179.

21. The blues I am on the point of analyzing has been taken from *Son House and the Great Delta Blues Singers,* Document Records DOCD-5002, 1990. For partial or complete alternative transcriptions of both or either parts of Son House's "Dry Spell Blues," see R. R. Macleod, *Document Blues-1* (Edinburgh: PAT Publications, 1994), 27–28; Michael Taft, *Talkin' to Myself: Blues Lyrics, 1921–1942* (New York: Routledge, 2005), 247–48; Jeff Titon, *Early Downhome Blues: A Musical and Cultural Analysis* (Chapel Hill: University of North Carolina Press, 1994), 119–20; William Barlow, *Looking Up at Down: The Emergence of Blues Culture* (Philadelphia: Temple University Press, 1989), 44; Samuel Charters, *The Blues Makers* (Part I), 62; Bob Groom, Alan Grainger, and Ted Griffiths, *Blues World* 8 (May 1966): 22–23; Dave Evans and Bill Givens, sleeve notes to *The Mississippi Blues No. 2: The Delta, 1929–1932,* Origin Jazz Library OJL-11, 1965; Paul Oliver, *The Story of the Blues* (London: Barrie & Rockliff, 1969), 118–19; Paul Oliver, *Early Blues Songbook* (London: Wise Publications, 1982), 156–57; Paul Oliver, *Blues Fell This Morning* (Cambridge: Cambridge University Press, 1990), 18; Dick Spottswood, "Song Notes and Transcriptions," in *Screamin' and Hollerin' the Blues,* Revenant Album No. 212, 2001, pp. 74–75; Arnold S. Caplin, sleeve notes to *Son House—Blind Lemon Jefferson,* Biograph Records BLP-12040, 1972.

22. This dialectal term meaning "curl" or "coil" was suggested by Chris Smith in a post to the prewar blues list on July 14, 2004. For an earlier use of the word in blues lyrics see Charley Patton, "Rattlesnake Blues" (Paramount 12924), recorded in Grafton, Wisconsin, ca. October 1929.

23. See David Evans, "High Water Everywhere: Blues and Gospel Commentary on the 1927 Mississippi River Flood," in *Nobody Knows Where the Blues Come From: Lyrics and History,* ed. Robert Springer (Jackson: University Press of Mississippi, 2006), 3–75; and David Evans, "Bessie Smith's 'Back-Water Blues': The Story behind the Song," *Popular Music* 26/1 (January 2007): 97–116.

24. The best source for the study of the 1930–31 drought is Nan Elizabeth Woodruff, *As Rare as Rain: Federal Relief in the Great Southern Drought of 1930–31* (Urbana and Chicago: University of Illinois Press, 1985), esp. ix–38. All the quotations concerning the 1930 drought are drawn from this book.

25. The inexorable and merciless evolution of the 1930 Dry Spell is very evident in a table in chap. 1 of Woodruff's book, where a comparison is drawn between the actual rainfall in the critical months of 1930 (June, July, and August) and that in the corresponding period in previous years in all the states hit by the drought. I am indebted to David Evans for doing accurate research in the *Clarksdale Daily Register* newspaper and letting me appropriate the headings reported in the main text.

26. For a list of songs from this period dealing with hard times see Guido van Rijn, *Roosevelt's Blues: African-American Blues and Gospel Songs on FDR* (Jackson: University Press of Mississippi, 1997), 16–29, 216–18; see also Robert M. W. Dixon, John Godrich, and Howard Rye, *Blues & Gospel Records, 1890–1943,* 4th ed. (New York:

Oxford University Press, 1997), 404–6; Max Vreede and Guido van Rijn, "The Paramount L Master Series," *78 Quarterly* 1, no. 9 (1996): 67–87. Son House's statements on the date of the session are found in Samuel Charters, *The Blues Makers* (Part I), 188; Bob Hall and Richard Noblett, "A Handful of Keys: Louise Johnson Again!," *Blues Unlimited* 115 (September–October 1975): 21–22; and unpublished interview by David Evans and Alan Wilson, Cambridge, Massachusetts, 1964. For an overview of the entire 1930 session, see Edward Komara, "Blues in the Round," *Black Music Research Journal* 17, no. 1 (Spring 1997): 3–36.

27. Although I have as yet been unable to listen to it, another composition presumably dealing with this natural catastrophe is listed in Tony Russell, *Country Music Records: A Discography, 1921–1942* (New York: Oxford University Press, 2004), 620. It is titled "1930 Drought" (Columbia 15664-D) and was recorded in New York by white recording artist and composer Bob Miller on February 25, 1931. Bob Miller was from Memphis, but was based in New York from the mid-1920s.

28. This blues is available on the CD *Founder of the Delta Blues*, Yazoo 2010, 1995.

29. For further comments on and a transcription of Charley Patton's "Dry Well Blues," see David Evans, "Charley Patton: The Conscience of the Delta," in *The Voice of the Delta*, ed. Robert Sacré, 196–98. Other transcriptions can be found in R. R. Macleod, *Yazoo 1-20*, 2nd ed. (Edinburgh: PAT Publications, 2002), 205–6; John Fahey, *Charley Patton* (London: Studio Vista, 1970), 97–98; and Dick Spottswood, "Song Notes and Transcriptions," in *Screamin' and Hollerin' the Blues*, 77.

30. "Spider" Carter's "Dry Spell Blues" is included in *St. Louis 1927–1933*, Document Records DOCD-5181, 1993. See also Paul Oliver, *Blues Fell This Morning*, 225–26. A transcription and comment can be found in Luciano Federighi, *Blues on My Mind* (Palermo: L'Epos, 2001), 141–42.

31. Among the works making use of this method I only mention the introductory books: Robert-Alain de Beaugrande & Wolfgang Ulrich Dressler, *Introduction to Text Linguistics* (London and New York: Longman, 1981); and Harald Weinrich, *Tempus. Besprochene und erzählte Welt* (Stuttgart: Kohlhammer, 1971).

32. For further analyses of Blues lyrics where I have adopted this critical method, I refer the reader to the following works: "Il Blues del Boia di Blind Lemon Jefferson," in *Quaderni del Dipartimento di Lingue e Letterature Straniere Moderne dell'Università di Genova* (Genova: La Quercia Edizioni, 1987), 197–218; and "La Lingua Inglese dei Neri d'America e i Blues: Analisi Critica di Alcuni Testi."

33. For the meaning of the expression "killing floor," whose popularity is mainly due to Howlin' Wolf's 1964 hit with this title (Chess 1923; reissued on *The Real Folk Blues/More Real Folk Blues*, MCA Records 088112 820, 2002), see Jean Paul Levet, *Talkin' That Talk* (Levallois-Perret: Soul Bag CLARB, 1986), 194, and Keith Briggs' column "Words Words Words," *Blues & Rhythm* 192 (September 2004): 23. For an earlier use of the term see Skip James' "Hard Time Killing Floor Blues" (Paramount 13065) on *Complete Recorded Works in Chronological Order (1931)*, Document Records

DOCD-5005, 1990. For a discussion of the expression "downhome" see Jeff Todd Titon, *Early Downhome Blues: A Musical and Cultural Analysis,* xv–xviii.

34. For a similar metaphor referring to another atmospheric phenomenon, see Robert Johnson's "Hellhound on My Trail" (Vocalion 03623) on *The Complete Recordings,* CBS Columbia C2K 46222, 1990, where blues is "falling down like hail."

35. On July 18, 1930, the *Clarksdale Daily Register* published a Piggly Wiggly grocery store advertisement according to which pork chops were being sold at 25 cents a pound. As this seems to have been their actual average price during that period, Son House must have exaggerated in his song in order to show the difference in price between cotton, the chief source of cash income, and pork chops as symbolic of necessary food items.

36. For the linguistic phenomenon of multiple negation, see William Labov, *Language in the Inner City: Studies in the Black English Vernacular* (Philadelphia: University of Pennsylvania Press, 1972), 130–96.

37. The verbal form "drug" is here the dialectal past participle coming from the infinitive "to drag." Another attestation of this verbal form in the Blues can be found in James "Son" Thomas, quoted by William Ferris, *Blues from the Delta,* 86.

38. The term "moonshine" has been transcribed as a noun and therefore is not preceded by a comma, but it might also be a verb. Since bootlegging and moonshining are both illegal activities disapproved by God, the inclusion or exclusion of the comma does not make any difference for the overall meaning and structure of this blues.

39. In lines 22 and 23 "solemnly" sounds as "Solomon," which might be considered correct if Son House—in his capacity as a preacher well acquainted with the Bible—had wanted to refer to Solomon as the judge. As such a hypothesis is quite difficult to prove and the transcription "solemnly" makes more sense, the more likely interpretation has been preferred here.

40. For a comprehensive study of natural disasters, see Luigi Monge, "Topical Blues: Disasters," in *Encyclopedia of the Blues,* 2 vols., ed. Edward Komara (New York: Routledge, 2006), 995–1002.

41. Michael Taft, *The Blues Lyric Formula* (New York: Routledge, 2006), 104–5.

42. See also Charley Patton's "Dry Well Blues," recorded at the same session as "Dry Spell Blues."

43. For a similar discussion of a symmetrical structure and a study of thematic blues texts, see David Evans, *Big Road Blues: Tradition and Creativity in the Folk Blues* (New York: Da Capo Press, 1987), 68–69 and 131–44, 161–62, respectively, and David Evans, "Traditional Blues Lyrics and Myth: Some Correspondences," in *The Lyrics in African American Popular Music,* ed. Robert Springer (Bern: Peter Lang, 2001), 17–40.

7

Some Ramblings on Robert Johnson's Mind

CRITICAL ANALYSIS AND AESTHETIC VALUE IN DELTA BLUES

JAMES BENNIGHOF

The issue of aesthetic value implicitly informs most studies of the blues, as it does most studies of other musics. Fundamental decisions about which pieces are worthy of study and about the nature of their importance depend on judgments about the manner in which they are better or worse than others. Such value judgments are generally tacit, but not because they do not merit examination; indeed, we should continually examine them so as to specify assessments and criteria in the clearest possible terms.[1]

The degree to which such conclusions admit scrutiny and discussion depends on the analysis that supports them. Specific analytical observations should be made in the context of the piece as a whole, and the significance of these observations should be judged with reference to the range of possible musical choices in the relevant style. In fact these objectives have found a fairly natural home in the critical analysis of much Western concert music. Both the specificity with which musical events are notated and their abstract nature have lent themselves to this kind of assessment of their interrelationships.[2]

Less evident have been the ways that the study of aesthetic value in the blues or many other vernacular musics might incorporate such an analytical approach; this study and this approach have not commonly engaged each other in an explicit way. On the one hand, aesthetically attractive qualities of vernacular music have often been described in ways that do not readily admit discussion or debate. Observations might be either too general or too specific—the appeal of general qualities in a piece might be mentioned in a way that does not help to compare it with others, or specific features might be cited without being evaluated in the context of the whole work. Meaning-ful assessments of value are difficult in such cases. For example, such criticism would fail to show how many other works share the general qualities of the piece and how the particular piece compares with those others. Alternatively, as striking as a particular feature may be, one will still want to know whether it relates to the other features of the piece to create coherence, interest, beauty, elegance, or other aesthetic desiderata.

For its part, the analytical approach previously outlined has not easily accommodated some of the most aesthetically compelling attributes of vernacular music. In the case of Robert Johnson's "Rambling on My Mind," for example, a critical analysis should somehow address the music's often-mentioned emotional intensity and visceral appeal,[3] and it should interpret aesthetic qualities in the context of cultural, stylistic, and technical circum-stances.[4] But the variety and imprecision of these features, as compared with specifically musical events, have made it difficult to incorporate them into such an analysis.[5]

Despite these difficulties, considerable groundwork has been laid for the kind of aesthetic analysis of blues performances that I have outlined. David Evans, for example, has discussed the various aesthetic criteria that seem to have been applied to early and traditional folk blues—a sense of generally applicable "truth" (particularly as embodied in the text),[6] tradition, and fa-miliarity. He contrasts these with commercially preferred qualities of lyric originality, thematic coherence, and standardization of musical structure, and he comments on ways that folklorists have subscribed to both these approaches in various situations.[7] In *Early Downhome Blues,* Jeff Todd Titon pursues several issues relevant to aesthetic questions; in addition to discuss-ing the general milieu in which folk blues flourished and the singers' per-spectives on various aspects of performance and composition, Titon tran-scribes significant portions of forty-eight performances and uses these as a basis for developing a "song-producing system," a compositionally oriented description of customary stylistic elements.[8]

These studies notwithstanding, critics of the blues seldom examine an individual piece or performance methodically to address the nature and extent of its particular aesthetic value. Unlike scholars of Western art music, they rarely ask how *this* piece is special—how it stands out among blues pieces or uses the resources available to blues pieces to constitute a singularly striking work of art. Greil Marcus's comments on Johnson are instructive here. On the one hand, Marcus relates both personal and historical reactions to Johnson that suggest Johnson's music to be singularly striking and thus worthy of this kind of examination. At the same time, although he refers to details—"the twist of a vocal, the curl of a guitar line"—that support this evaluation, Marcus prefers to dwell on the relationship between the music's value and his own background rather than on "what-makes-the-music-great."[9]

In this chapter, then, I show how one might examine emotional and visceral attributes, along with the musical and textual aspects of a performance of "Rambling on My Mind," within a single analysis. I consider all these factors so as to address the performance on its own (various) cultural, stylistic, and technical terms, and I integrate each with the others to place it within the context of the whole. Finally, the goal of the entire study is to show the ways in which the aesthetic qualities of such a piece can be illuminated to facilitate their objective assessment and comparison with those of other works.

In this analysis, as in most studies of concert music, conclusions about aesthetic merit focus on the important relationships among elements within a piece (for example, the ways that the melody for one verse relates to that for another, the ways that each relates to a text, or the additional dimension added by the accompanimental choices for each verse). Such conclusions depend on the context in which the piece is located, however: the significance of textual material depends on its relationship to its referents, and the significance of musical syntax depends on its relationship to applicable stylistic norms and technical limitations. Although some of these issues are often taken for granted in the study of European concert music, they will need to be considered explicitly as this analysis proceeds. To do so, it is important to clarify what I am considering to be a "piece."

This study primarily addresses a single performance, Johnson's first take of "Rambling on My Mind" (recorded in San Antonio on November 23, 1936).[10] I do not assume that a given song title indicates an abstract, specifically prescribed sequence of events, as would be preserved in a notated score for performance in the case of European concert music. In situations that assume the active participation of the audience, the idea of a work can be extremely fluid. As William Ferris has observed, performances of particular songs typically flow freely together: improvised conversational transitions lead from one to the next, which is signaled by a signature opening verse but then may proceed with a variety of spontaneously selected verses and related conversations.[11]

The performance situation in a recording session was much less flexible, of course, since it was assumed that the recording would consist essentially of a continuous series of verses. Although the recording therefore does not authentically duplicate a live performance, it takes on its own value as a model for imitation and a source for material.[12] Indeed, artists who have not recorded commercially have commonly valued recordings more than they have live performances.[13] It is logical to assume that recording artists often planned their recorded performances somewhat more specifically than they might have planned a live performance. Consistent with this assumption is the "thematic" character of both takes of "Rambling on My Mind," which contrasts to the "nonthematic" (that is, thematically inconsistent at a superficial level) texts that had predominated among folk blues recordings somewhat earlier than Johnson's time.[14]

Even given the strictures of the recording situation and the thematic nature of Johnson's basic conception of "Rambling on My Mind," each performance under such a title is likely to differ significantly from all others. The two takes of "Rambling on My Mind" exemplify this in several ways. Their texts follow:

TAKE 1

1. I got ramblin', I got ramblin' on my mind.
    I've got ramblin', I got ramblin' all on my mind.
    Hate to leave my baby, but you treats me so unkind.

2. I got mean things, I got mean things all on my mind.
    Little girl, little girl, I got mean things all on my mind.
    Hate to leave you here, babe, but you treats me so unkind.

3. Runnin' down to the station, catch the first mail train I see.
    [*Spoken:* I think I hear her comin' now.]
    Runnin' down to the station, catch that old first mail train I see.
    I've got the blues 'bout Miss So-and-So, and the child got the blues
        about me.

4. And I'm leavin' this mornin', with my arm' fold' up and cryin'.
    And I'm leavin' this mornin', with my arm' fold' upped and cryin'.
    I hate to leave my baby, but she treats me so unkind.

5. I got mean things, I've got mean things on my mind.
    I got mean things, I got mean things all on my mind.
    I got to leave my baby, well, she treats me so unkind.

TAKE 2

1. I got ramblin', I've got ramblin' on my mind.
    I got ramblin', I got ramblin' all on my mind.
    Hate to leave my baby, but you treats me so unkind.

2. And now babe, I will never forgive you anymore.
   Little girl, little girl, I will never forgive you anymore.
   You know you did not want me, baby, why did you tell me so?

3. And I'm runnin' down to the station, catch that first mail train I see.
   [*Spoken:* I hear her comin' now.]
   I'm runnin' down to the station, catch that old first mail train I see.
   I've got the blues 'bout Miss So-and-So, and the child got the blues
   about me.

4. An' they's de'ilment, she got devilment on her mind.
   She got devilment, little girl, you got devilment all on your mind.
   Now I've got to leave this mornin' with my arm' a-fold' up and cryin'.

5. I believe, I believe my time ain't long.
   I believe, I believe that my time ain't long.
   But I'm leavin' this mornin', I believe I will go back home.

The text of the signature first verses is essentially the same in both takes, as is that of the third verses, but the second and fourth verses share only certain elements. Each second verse begins to address the singer's "baby" (girlfriend), and accordingly the second line of each begins with the phrase "Little girl, little girl." The fourth verse of the first take begins with the despairing line "And I'm leavin' this mornin' with my arm' fold' up and cryin'," repeated, and the same basic text forms the last line of the fourth verse of the second take. Finally, the respective fifth verses differ entirely from each other.

In general, the various instrumental licks and fills are fluidly employed—often a particular device is used in the same verse in the two takes, but at different points within that verse. Just as Johnson often follows a given signature first verse in performance with some textual variation in subsequent verses,[15] he also mixes various accompanimental devices freely with these texts instead of having devised a specifically coordinated accompaniment for each verse or possible verse of text. (Even a tremolo sound effect that represents the mail train mentioned in the third verse is employed in a different metrical position in each take.) The second take also seems a bit more frantic because its tempo fluctuates more than that of the first—the first begins at about MM = 96 and ranges up to around 105 (lasting a total of two minutes and fifty-one seconds), whereas the second starts at about MM = 100 and ranges up to about 120 (lasting two minutes and twenty seconds).

One could profitably examine the two takes as different manifestations of a single conceit to elucidate the nature of that conceit. The present study examines a single performance, however, because this is presumably the way that most listeners would experience the piece, whether hearing the original recording in person (each take was issued on the Vocalion and American Record Company labels) or on the radio or, more recently, listening to the song as one of a series of songs on an LP. (Even someone listening to the CD compilation, on which the two takes follow one another, usually tends to interpret each as a separate experience.) In focusing on a single performance, then, I aim to address the way that we can experience the unique combination of choices that constitutes this particular act of creation.

The text of this performance says that the singer is leaving his woman in despair and anger at the unkind way she treats him. Such complaints about a mistreating woman are common in Johnson's recordings. Of the twenty-nine extant titles (forty-one sides in all), twenty-three address some combination of specific complaints about a mistreating woman and general declarations of despair.[16] The thematic relationship between these specific and general laments is made clear by their common coexistence within a single song: although emphasis on each extreme varies, eighteen of the titles address both in at least one of their takes.

Since the degree to which each of these extremes is addressed in a song varies, these eighteen songs define a thematic continuum: the emphasis in some songs tilts toward the specific experiences of the persona that Johnson adopts, whereas others dwell more on the persona's more general anxieties. Furthermore the location of any song within this continuum might depend on the text selection for a given performance. For example, the second take of "Rambling on My Mind" concludes with a general lament that significantly distinguishes it from the first take, which focuses exclusively on dismay at the actions of the woman at hand. There is an ironic aspect to the way that Johnson's songs tend to link perceptions of mistreatment in love and premonitions of doom, however; although the despair may have been real (and in some cases has been interpreted as a reflection of a mystical/satanic side of Johnson), most of the information that we have about his actual love life indicates that he was generally the dominant party.[17] In this connection, too, it should be pointed out that occasionally the songs refer to distress on the part of the woman as well; the clearest examples include "When You Got a Good Friend," "Come On in My Kitchen," and, in both takes of "Rambling on My Mind," the line "and the child's got the blues 'bout me."

Two other observations may be made about this text: first, that its subject matter is drawn from Johnson's personal experience and environment, and

Table 7.1. Johnson's recorded songs, roughly categorized by tone and directness with which they relate to his realm of experience.

Light tone, metaphorical	"They're Red Hot"
Light tone, direct reference:	"Traveling Riverside Blues"
Serious tone, metaphorical	"I Believe I'll Dust My Broom," "Come On in My Kitchen," "Terraplane Blues," "Phonograph Blues," "Dead Shrimp Blues," "Little Queen of Spades," "Milkcow's Calf Blues"
Serious tone, direct reference:	"Kindhearted Woman Blues," "Sweet Home Chicago," "Rambling on My Mind," "When You Got a Good Friend," "32-20 Blues," "Walking Blues," "Last Fair Deal Gone Down," "If I Had Possession over Judgment Day," "I'm a Steady Rollin' Man," "From Four Untill Late," "Drunken Hearted Man," "Stop Breakin' Down Blues," "Honeymoon Blues," "Love in Vain"
Supernatural overtones	"Cross Road Blues," "Preaching Blues (Up Jumped the Devil)," "Stones in My Passway," "Hellhound on My Trail," "Malted Milk," "Me and the Devil Blues"

Note: Even songs that are "serious" at face value, and are listed as such here, could often have been heard by audiences as simply entertaining.

second, that it addresses this subject matter directly rather than metaphorically, as is done in a light way in some songs and more seriously in others. Table 7.1 shows the type of relationship that exists between various songs and Johnson's direct realm of experience. Rarely is a persona clearly set forth as distinct from the singer; furthermore, "Rambling on My Mind" communicates nonmetaphorically and does not have an overt light tone.

These observations invite us to interpret Johnson's poetic and musical choices in a rather straightforward way. To be sure, the song's most obvious function is to entertain, not to reveal Johnson's own life. Furthermore, there is no way of knowing whether the text is referring to a specific event in Johnson's or anyone else's life. The point here, however, is that none of the protagonist's circumstances and characteristics are foreign to Johnson's experience or, generally speaking, that of his listeners, and there is no suggestion of fantasy, irony, or self-conscious detachment from the protagonist. This attitude toward the text would also have been consistent with the rather direct communication that would normally have taken place during the performance of the song; Johnson's customary venues would not have set the performer apart from his audience to the degree usually present in concert situations.

These observations about the text provide a foundation for interpreting musical choices in this performance. This interpretation must proceed in the context of the musical premises that the piece establishes. Choices that simply conform to those premises, and thus create a generally coherent context, can then be distinguished from those that add to or deviate from this context in some way that is specifically significant for this piece.

Musical premises for the piece fall into three categories: general style characteristics, recurrent accompanimental figures, and prevalent melodic contours. The general style characteristics include the fact that the song is a blues that uses the customary open E-major guitar tuning, E-B-E–G-sharp–B-E[1] (because of this typical tuning pattern, I have transcribed the piece in E, although the sounding key is approximately concert F-sharp: F-sharp–C-sharp–F-sharp–A-sharp–C-sharp[1]–F-sharp[1], the result of a high guitar tuning or the use of a capo and possible variations in recording and dubbing speeds). It also uses a typical 12-bar harmonic structure—I-I-I-I-IV-IV-I-I-V-IV-I-V (or I at the end)—and measures normally include four beats in a shuffle rhythm that I have notated in 12/8 time.

The accompanimental figures that recur throughout "Rambling on My Mind" are abstractly illustrated in the context of a verse in Example 7.1. The harmony for each measure is often conveyed, as in mm. 1, 5, and 9, by a bass alternation of root-fifth/root-sixth.[18] In m. 11 the final dominant chord is approached by a chromatic descent from the tonic note. (Not shown in m. 4 is an optional chromatic ascent to the first subdominant.) There are three types of upper-voice material: in mm. 7–8 an inner-voice descent from A to G-sharp in the midst of the verse's central tonic harmony; a ringing E in several harmonic contexts (the chromatic turnaround in m. 11 and the subdominant harmony in mm. 5–6); and finally and most prominently, licks around a high E-major chord (which accounts for everything above the staff). These last devices are produced with a glass or metal tube (or "slide") and are made possible by tuning the open strings of the guitar to an E-major chord. This technique could be used with any harmony, by locating the slide at the appropriate fret, but in this song Johnson always uses it during a tonic harmony, at the twelfth fret.

Example 7.1 also shows the specific melodic figures that Johnson establishes as typical in the piece. Each verse of text contains two lines, the first of which is repeated (sometimes with slight variations). Each of these three lines is broken into two phrases, resulting in a total of six short melodic phrases per verse. These melodies follow similar arch-shaped contours in

Ex. 7.1. Sample stylistically normative verse.

each verse. Phrase 1a ascends from C-sharp or E to G-sharp and then descends to E; phrase 1b repeats this ascent (and usually the accompanying text) but descends to the low E. Phrases 2a and 2b trace the same process over the A harmony, lowering the G-sharp so that it is closer to G-natural. In the first three verses, phrase 3a descends from F-sharp or G-natural to E, ascends to G-natural, and descends to B over the B harmony; phrase 3b, over the A harmony, ascends from C-sharp through E to G-natural and then descends to the low E to conclude right before the turnaround. This entire melodic scheme is not only predominant throughout this performance but also typical within the blues repertory in general. For example, it constitutes one of four "tune families" that Titon identified as recurring among forty-four "downhome" blues tunes.[19]

The compositional premises established by stylistic characteristics, recurring accompanimental figures, and basic melodic outlines that Johnson has chosen form a basis for interpreting specific musical choices within this performance, which is transcribed in Example 7.2. (The measures in Example 7.2 are numbered to facilitate comparison with Example 7.1: for each measure the verse number is given first, followed by the number of the corresponding measure in Example 7.1; added measures are indicated by lowercase letters.) When Johnson simply adheres to the established norms, musical choices cannot significantly relate to specific textual elements; they can only establish a general mood. When Johnson either varies patterns or deviates from them entirely, however, the music may well carry specific significance. We can then interpret these features to determine how significant they seem to be and to form a general reading of the piece and make a specific assessment of the features within this reading.

As I examine these features in the course of formulating a general reading of the piece, it is important to remember that their significance may in some cases depend on such considerations as technical limitations, Johnson's customary techniques, and the audience and performance situation for which the song was intended. For example, one kind of variation is a flexible treatment of the bass patterns; sometimes notes are indistinct, and dotted quarter notes often occur while the slide is being used. These occurrences usually seem happenstance and result from the technical demands at the time—a thumb-bass eighth note on the offbeat might easily be blurred or omitted when attention is being given to various treble-note rhythms played with the fingers of the right hand and the slide on the left.

Another kind of variation is the alteration of the number of beats in a measure. This happens in the first, third, and fifth verses, but its significance varies, depending on several kinds of circumstances. In some cases the addition of a beat may result from a technical necessity. In m. 1.4, for example, Johnson's slide lick at the twelfth fret prevents him from using his left hand to add the sixth on the even beats of the bass accompaniment (the open fifth is played on open strings). Since measures normally end with a sixth, he

Rambling on My Mind

Transcription notes:
Notated in E major, with references to open E tuning (E B e g♯ b e1);
actual sounding key is F♯ major (tuned F♯ c♯ f♯ a♯ c♯1 f♯1).

/f = gliss on fretboard; all others use slide.

All rhythms (especially vocal) are approximate indications
of metrical locations, in some cases indicating beats that
Johnson may be feeling, more than precisely hitting.

Ex. 7.2. Transcription of "Rambling on My Mind."

Ex. 7.2. *Continued*

Ex. 7.2. *Continued*

Ex. 7.2. *Continued*

Ex. 7.2. *Continued*

extends the measure by a beat to make things come out even. The same conclusion might be drawn in the case of m. 3.1.

The metrical alteration in m. 3.4b is better read as an unmeasured, inter-jected sound effect. Those in verse 5, in mm. 5.3a and 5.4, might have several possible metrical interpretations; in any event their significance seems most naturally related to a larger-scale formal stretching toward the end of the song that I discuss later. Finally, the alteration in m. 1.1 may require the most speculation: the slide lick on the second beat would typically occur on the first beat, but it may be delayed in the interest of a leisurely beginning for the song, and this would then lead to an additional added beat so as to place a sixth on the last beat (as discussed with reference to m. 1.4).

Even if no specific significance is found in the metrical manipulations just discussed, however, it seems generally significant that metrical variation is possible. Combined with the rhythmic flexibility of the vocal line and other variations for which we find no specific significance, the metrical variation supports the sense of freedom expressed by the textual idea of "rambling"; this general mood might be represented by the fluctuating graph in Figure 7.1. It seems important to recognize such a quality, especially as it conveys the attributes that Johnson's personal and professional life has in common with the text of this song, as a context for making more specific observations. At the same time we need to remember that this rambling quality is not highly specific to this song—many of Johnson's other songs exhibit similar freedoms.

Identifying the rambling mood as a general premise does not justify locat-ing aesthetic value in every imprecision or arbitrary decision throughout the piece simply because these elements "ramble." More compelling are de-viations that seem to manipulate the established musical premises in some purposeful way. For example, as Example 7.2 shows, Johnson articulates the premise at the beginning of each verse with his slide work. In each verse the first text line states the topic; after this line is repeated, the last line comments further. The lengthy tonic harmony that accompanies the initial topic state-ment makes it easy for Johnson to comment musically with the slide on the

Fig. 7.1. Graphic representation of general "rambling" tone set by flexibility of musical choices.

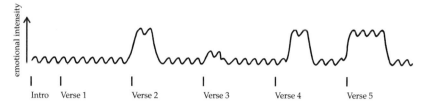

Fig. 7.2. Graphic representation of "rambling" and emotional fluctuation of text as supported by musical choices (slide licks).

high strings, since the lower strings can be played to fit the harmony without being fretted.

The singer's discussion of his actions in verse 1 is supported in mm. 1.1-4 with rather laconic licks, whereas the more emotional "mean things" of verse 2 are conveyed in mm. 2.1–2 through a more obsessive lick that dwells on the high E before its lower echo in mm. 2.3–4. The actions emphasized in the third verse receive licks more similar to those in the first verse, dwelling now on the B (in addition to the train sound effects). The fourth verse focuses at first on actions, and its first licks accordingly resemble those in verses 1 and 3, but the insertion in m. 4.2 of the emotional word *cryin'* leads to the high E and its echo in m. 4.4b. Finally, the "mean things" of verse 5 receive typically high licks again, this time reiterated at the high-E level.

Figure 7.2 shows how Johnson's slide work articulates the song. The shape imposed on the general rambling of the song is now specifically defined in terms of emotional intensity. This larger-scale motion addresses a slightly different sense of the word *rambling* here; although arbitrary meandering is supported to some extent in the text by the phrase "first mail train I see," the word seems more directly to indicate a purposeful motion, albeit one in an unknown direction. The slide work thus helps to convey the future physical motion described by the singer by emphasizing the emotional motion that takes place during the course of the song.

This emotional fluctuation is further inflected by other techniques, however, investing the latter portion of the song with increased emotional intensity. After the first three verses postulate a range of emotional levels and the fourth begins at a low level, the turning point comes in m. 4.2 at the word *cryin'*. Not only does Johnson insert "emotional" licks here, as I have mentioned, but he also inserts, in m. 4.4a, a thickened bass walk-up that seems to be headed from E to A. He then frustrates that to add two measures (4.4b and 4.4c) on the tonic chord, adds bass triplets in m. 4.4c, begins in m. 4.6

with a harsh and large vocal leap, and in m. 4.9 leaps down with his voice to a dissonant A against the B harmony.

In the last verse Johnson repeats the text of the second verse. This is not an isolated incident, for he occasionally repeats verses in other songs (although, interestingly, he does not use this text at all in the second take). The repetition here may have resulted simply from an inability to come up with the text for another verse at the right moment in the recording process or from Johnson's purposeful choice of recapitulation over the introduction of a new verse. In any event the cause of the repetition affects critical analysis only to the degree that it determines our interpretation of the piece.

For example, knowledge that a performance slip may have occurred at some point in a piece might encourage us to be satisfied with interpreting a musical event at that point as anomalous or banal. At the same time, however, even if a slip does occur, a performer might respond by making choices that "justify" the slip in some way. The result would be a performance that is different from, but not necessarily worse than, what would have happened without the slip—such situations are common, if not necessarily frequent, in improvisation-based performance (musical or otherwise). In the case of text repetition in "Rambling on My Mind," then, whether or not a slip occurred, interpretation should focus on the result—the effect of the repetition might be, for example, a simple recapitulation for the purpose of rounding off the piece or a reiteration for emphasis.

This particular repetition seems to me to express a sort of strung-out exhaustion, exhibiting both intensity or concentration and deterioration or despair at the same time. The musical characteristics of the passage support this reading. As I already mentioned, intensity is conveyed by the reiteration of the high-E lick: at first in mm. 5.1–2 its rhythm stretches out a bit from the triplets heard earlier, and it uses the affective high D-natural first presented in m. 4.3. Intensity and perhaps some deterioration are also expressed by the lack of a bass-register accompaniment at the beginning of the verse. This does not happen previously in the song at the beginning of a verse and in fact occurs only once anywhere in a verse, at the pivotal word *cryin'* in v. 4; this effect works both aurally, for it starkly exposes the whining sound of the slide work, and in a physical, structural sense for the performer, who would certainly have had the maintenance of the constant shuffle bass deeply ingrained by this point in his career, thus making its abandonment a significant interruption. The spare texture continues into mm. 5.3a–5.4, in which the high lick reappears and a total of five beats are added—this sort of indefinite extension almost literally depicts the idea of being "strung out."

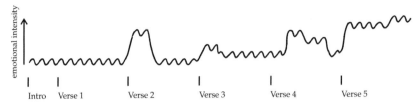

Fig. 7.3. Graphic representation of "rambling," emotional fluctuation of text, and intensification of despair as supported by musical choices (slide licks, added measures, melodic dissonance).

Finally, the melody line seems to express despair in its deterioration of pitch quality and consonance, especially since mm. 5.8–9 are even more of a departure from the typical melodic figure at this point in the verse than mm. 4.8–9 are.

We thus might interpret the whole piece as it is depicted in Figure 7.3: a general "rambling" freedom, articulated by musical choices that relate to emotional content and shaped into a gradually intensifying despair (which connects with the theme of despair seen in Johnson's other texts). Our knowledge of the close relationship between the text and Johnson's realm of experience, as well as the immediacy of his communication with his audience, supports this interpretation of the musical events as directly reinforcing and intensifying the text. These circumstances enhance the credibility of such a reading, in which Johnson's musical choices adopt the text's perspective rather than express some other outlook (the instrument might somehow convey the barriers against which the singer is striving, for example, or might even contain elements of irony) or merely establish a neutral backdrop. This account of text, vocal line, and guitar acting in concert may in turn address the common perception of powerful emotional expression in such songs.

An interpretation like this can in turn provide a basis for aesthetic discussion: once a determination of what the work is doing has been formed, one can evaluate how well it does that, how attractive various features are in the context of that endeavor, and how worthy the endeavor itself is. In this case, aesthetic value might be found in such interrelated qualities as the integrity with which music and text work together, the interesting variety of ways in which musical choices contribute to this task, the genuineness with which text and music address the song's emotional content,[20] the power of the emotional content itself, and the way that emotional intensity shapes the piece.

Of course some of these conclusions would depend on some sense of comparison with other pieces, both similar and different—one might ask, for example, how well this song does what it does compared to other Delta blues songs, or how its goals and achievement of those goals compare with those that apply to works in other styles, both vernacular and "cultured."

At this general level, the critical analysis of "Rambling on My Mind" is similar to that of Western concert music. The relationship of interpretation to evaluation seems the same in each case: an interpretation of a work in the European canon would form the basis for aesthetic discussion, and each of the evaluative questions just posed could equally apply, *mutatis mutandis*, to the European piece. Similarities might also be found on a more specific level; for example, this particular song is similar in premise to Schubert's *Winterreise,* in that the narrator is about to hit the road because of a broken relationship. The brooding, ruminative tone of Johnson's conclusion is even analogous to the final song of that cycle, "The Organ-Grinder." Of course the topical specificity of this correspondence is an isolated example, one that would not even be a possibility with a European concert piece that is not either texted or specifically programmatic.

Although general relationships between interpretation and evaluation may be shared by vernacular music and the "cultured" music that has more frequently been the object of critical analysis, and although examples of the two may happen to share specific characteristics, whether topical, structural, or otherwise, this study has shown how important analytical conclusions for a vernacular work such as "Rambling on My Mind" can proceed from premises rather different from those customarily applied to concert music. Prior to analysis came the determination that all observations would have to be based on a particular performance rather than on a published edition representing the "ideal" version of the song.

Some of the analytical decisions that followed might also occur in the study of concert music, but in most cases they would be less common than in vernacular music or would apply in a different way. For example, the interpretation of individual devices was based on their relationship to stock figures in this style, on the degree to which they seemed intentional within this performance situation, and on the technical limitations of the instrument. The first and last of these might be considered with respect to concert music, but they often are implicit rather than explicit and would in any case apply to different stock figures and different instruments; the second would rarely apply, since the analysis of concert music does not ordinarily focus on a specific performance. Melodic structures in this piece were related to repetitive contour types rather than to specific motives or Schenkerian structures, which would be more likely in the case of concert music.

I interpreted the overall theme of the song in direct relation to Johnson's realm of experience rather than assume a clearly artificial persona. This seems appropriate because of the similarity of the lyrics to Johnson's own circumstances; in fact these lyrics, the lyrics of many of his other songs, and those of contemporaneous songs by other artists seem to suggest that these performances implied less distance between performer/composer and subject of the lyrics than would commonly be assumed in a European art song. (The fact that lyrics to blues songs were commonly composed by the performer or at least were selected by him from a common repertory of ideas—unlike the common European compositional practice of using someone else's poetry—also reinforces this general analytical attitude.)

Finally, it is important to note the wide variety of issues that I explicitly considered and interrelated in forming an analytical interpretation of the piece. This breadth of inquiry seems uncommon in the study of concert music, for varying reasons. Some of the issues addressed here do not apply to that repertory, and some (such as instrumental limitations and stock figures) seem to warrant less examination because they are common to many pieces in a repertory that has been widely analyzed. Furthermore, the fact that many pieces in that repertory are examined many times may make it more often appropriate for individual writers to focus on particular facets of a piece rather than attempt such an integration (although there is still room for more integrated studies as well). The present study does not pretend to be an exhaustive account of all issues that might be considered with respect to this piece, of course. Nonetheless I intend it to show how examinations of the various terms in which this vernacular style communicates can be integrated into a critical analysis that can form an adequate basis for aesthetic discussion.

Notes

An earlier version of this essay was presented in February 1993 to the Nineteenth Annual Conference of the Sonneck Society for American Music in Asilomar, California. I am grateful to the Baylor University Research Committee for providing funds that assisted in the revision of this work. Thanks also to King of Spades Music for the use of "Ramblin' on My Mind," words & music by Robert Johnson. Copyright © (1978) 1991, King of Spades Music. All rights reserved. Used by permission.

1. Martin Williams has developed the case for this explicit consideration of aesthetic standards in American music at greater length in "On Scholarship, Standards,

and Aesthetics: In American Music We Are All on the Spot," *American Music* 4 (1986): 159–63.

2. Robert Morgan presents one account of the kinds of questions that this measurability and abstractness have tended to encourage and discourage in "Theory, Analysis, and Criticism," *Journal of Musicology* 1, no. 1 (January 1982): 15–18.

3. This is compellingly described, for example, by Greil Marcus in his chapter on Johnson in *Mystery Train*, 3d ed. (New York: Plume, 1990), 19–35, and "When You Walk in the Room," *Village Voice*, December 9, 1988, pp. 63–66; by Stephen C. LaVere and Eric Clapton in the booklet that accompanies Columbia's two-CD reissue of Johnson's work (*Robert Johnson: The Complete Recordings*, Columbia C2K 46222, 1990), pp. 18–21 and 22–23; and by Peter Guralnick in *Searching for Robert Johnson* (New York: Dutton, 1989), esp. 1–5, 37, 43, and 58–59.

4. I have discussed the need for incorporating such considerations into critical analysis, as well as other scholars' arguments toward this end, at greater length in "*Heliotrope Bouquet* and the Critical Analysis of American Music," *American Music* 10, no. 4 (Winter 1992): 391–410, and "Fluidity in Paul Simon's 'Graceland': On Text and Music in a Popular Song," *College Music Symposium* 33/34 (1993/1994): 212–36.

5. Susan McClary and Robert Walser have discussed similar problems with respect to the application of traditional musicological and theoretical approaches to popular and rock music in "Start Making Sense! Musicology Wrestles with Rock," in *On Record: Rock, Pop, and the Written Word*, ed. Simon Frith and Andrew Goodwin, 277–92 (New York: Pantheon, 1990). They claim that the implicit aesthetic of these disciplines has privileged classical music's autonomy from society, or transcendence of social interests, and they emphasize the importance of addressing its sensual dimensions in analyzing this music.

6. Throughout this essay I use forms of the word *text* to refer specifically to the lyrics of the piece rather than to the content of the piece as a whole.

7. David Evans, "Folk, Commercial, and Folkloristic Aesthetics in the Blues," *Jazzforschung* 5 (1974): 11–32.

8. Jeff Todd Titon, *Early Downhome Blues: A Musical and Cultural Analysis* (Urbana: University of Illinois Press, 1977), esp. chaps. 3 and 4, pp. 63–177.

9. Marcus, "When You Walk in the Room," 65, 64.

10. "Rambling on My Mind," take 1, was originally released as Vocalion 03519 and ARC 7-05-81, and its two takes have been compiled with the rest of Johnson's extant recordings on Columbia's CD reissue.

11. Ferris discusses and transcribes an entire evening "blues house party" in *Blues from the Delta* (New York: Anchor/Doubleday, 1978), 99–156.

12. David Evans, *Big Road Blues* (Berkeley and Los Angeles: University of California Press, 1982), 115–31; and Ferris, *Blues from the Delta*, 51–54, 61–62, and 70–71.

13. Ferris, *Blues from the Delta*, 62.

14. David Evans, "Composing Folk Blues for Live Performance and Records," *The Southern Quarterly* 26, no. 2 (Winter 1988), esp. 42–44.

15. "Rambling on My Mind" and "Come On in My Kitchen" represent the extreme in this regard among the twelve songs for which two takes are known to exist. Although no songs use exactly the same text for both takes, five ("Little Queen of Spades," "Drunken Hearted Man," "Me and the Devil Blues," "Love in Vain," and "Milkcow's Calf Blues") use essentially the same sequence of four-verse texts. The texts for the others use the following patterns, arranged roughly from least to greatest degree of variation (same letter = essentially the same text, prime symbol = significant variation of verse previously assigned a letter, x = guitar solo): "Kindhearted Woman Blues, "ABCxD, ABCDE; "Cross Road Blues," ABCDE, ABC'D; "When You Got a Good Friend," ABCDE, ABCFDE; "Phonograph Blues," ABCDA, ABCD'A'D"; "Stop Breakin' Down Blues," AA'BCA, A'A'BCD; "Come On in My Kitchen," ABCDEF, AEBCGHI; "Rambling on My Mind," ABCDB', AECFG.

16. The exceptions are "When You Got a Good Friend," "They're Red Hot," "Last Fair Deal Gone Down," "Little Queen of Spades," "Traveling Riverside Blues," and "Honeymoon Blues."

17. One account of this is found in Steve LaVere's biographical sketch in the CD reissue booklet, p. 14.

18. Although this figure is quite familiar in blues now, David Evans has pointed out in a private correspondence that it was quite rare on guitar when Johnson made these recordings, as were the particular bottleneck licks that he uses in conjunction with it.

19. Titon, *Early Downhome Blues*, 167–68. Although Titon indicates that these four families are significant, he also acknowledges that a larger or different sample would presumably yield others as well.

20. This might well relate to or expand Evans's discussion of "truth" as a common criterion by which contemporaneous listeners determined value in folk blues, as mentioned previously ("Folk, Commercial, and Folkloristic Aesthetics in the Blues," 13–15).

8

"Guess These People Wonder What I'm Singing"

QUOTATION AND REFERENCE IN
ELLA FITZGERALD'S "ST. LOUIS BLUES"

KATHARINE CARTWRIGHT

Ella Fitzgerald (1917–96), the celebrated jazz singer, was not known as a singer of the blues.[1] In fact, her blues have generally been dismissed by jazz writers on grounds they lack such attributes as "primitive guts," "raw ring," "primal" emotion, and "gruff hoarse passion."[2] As historian Albert Murray reminds us, blues singing is not "a species of direct emotional expression in the raw," but "an artful contrivance," most often one that makes us feel like dancing.[3] Nonetheless, this is no small slight. With the blues widely considered to be the foundation of jazz—along with improvisation, a *sine qua non* of the idiom—it is not surprising to find that Fitzgerald did not neglect to put her mark on the blues, artfully creating a blues persona that was virtuosic, erudite, witty, emotionally strong, and thoroughly rooted in the blues tradition. In subtle and interesting ways, she demonstrated what she knew about the blues, where she learned them, what they meant to her, and how her work grew out of and commented on that of her predecessors and contemporaries. The evidence is not so much in the timbre of her voice (though she did moan and shout on occasion), nor in the number of blues pieces in her repertoire (there were few), nor in what she said to the press (she gave interviews only rarely), but in the musical substance of her performances, particularly the narrative threads and "Signifyin(g)" gestures woven into her many musical quotations, references, and allusions in blues contexts.[4]

Fitzgerald was an inveterate user of borrowed material. "I steal everything I ever heard," she once declared unabashedly.[5] As columnist Murray Kempton put it, she "remembers everything, absorbs everything, and uses everything."[6] Pianist Tommy Flanagan, who worked with her for years, thought of her as "one of the biggest quoters of all time, she and Sonny Rollins."[7] Rollins underscored the point: "Scat singing is an art, but the way Ella uses interpolations . . . is really high art."[8] Her borrowings are remarkable for the rich diversity of her sources, the musicality with which she invoked them, the ingenuity with which she made the material her own, and her palpable enjoyment of the process. As Kempton observed, "She will not let one set pass without singing a long jump tune, all interior reference, all parody, none of it possible to appreciate altogether without having heard every jazz record since Clarence Williams."[9] While this is an exaggeration, understanding her references can indeed enhance the appreciation of her work.

References function as analytical keys of a unique sort, providing entry into aspects of an artist's musical world that might otherwise escape notice. For musicologist Lewis Porter, a jazz recording "cannot be fully discussed without reference to the influences behind it," including "borrowings from other pieces of music" and "quotation of one person by another."[10] In Porter's view, "A listener who hasn't heard the solos that are being referred to will miss a whole level of musical meaning." Kempton, a nonmusician aficionado, felt that the full force of Fitzgerald's art was ultimately created for musicians. When I asked saxophonist Phil Woods if he sometimes quoted for the band, he responded, giving a musician's perspective on references that may or may not be understood by the immediate audience. "Yes, I do," he said, "but really it's just to the world; I just kind of throw it out there and let nature do with it what it will."[11]

Through her references, Ella Fitzgerald frequently told her audiences, cognoscenti and general listeners alike, who and what she listened to, framing the allusions in specific ways. This study explores such communications, examining the substance of selected quotations, looking at her contextualizations and adaptations, examining relationships between her work and that of her sources, and looking at how multiple sources (where they occur) relate to one another. There exists a vast web of connections between Fitzgerald's work and that of her forebears and colleagues in jazz and other idioms. Below, I explore a part of this web, focusing on her blues, specifically her recordings of W. C. Handy's "St. Louis Blues," her most important blues vehicle. With its abundance of associations both within and outside her oeuvre, Handy's piece provides an exceptionally rewarding example. For no less than twenty-two years (1957–79), it served as an improvisational vehicle for her, in concert programs and in studio sessions. Five commercial recordings from concerts (1958, 1964, 1966, 1971, 1979) and two from studio dates (1957 and

1963) have been released.[12] A videotaped duet with Jo Stafford and the Benny Goodman orchestra is commercially available.[13] Another half dozen takes from live dates remain unissued.[14]

Fitzgerald acknowledged that her blues repertoire was limited, with "St. Louis Blues" serving as her main blues for many years. As she put it during a performance with Duke Ellington and his orchestra, "We had a request to do the blues; this is the only one I know."[15] After singing it and waiting for a lengthy period of applause to subside, she added ironically, "We better keep that one in." (It had been in her repertoire for nearly ten years and was to remain there for well over another decade.) It was perhaps no accident that she chose to state her feelings about it in the presence of Ellington and his audience; the prominence and longevity of the piece in her repertoire may well owe something to his example. For Ellington, even more than for Fitzgerald, "St. Louis Blues" was an essential piece. He performed, arranged, and rearranged it from the beginning of his professional life until the very end of his career, and his discography includes scores of live recordings of it. What she (as well as Ellington) chose to do with that one vehicle was extraordinarily nuanced and multifaceted. She invented and reinvented it, causing the biographer Geoffrey Fidelman to give it "the distinction of more different versions recorded by Ella than any other song."[16] Her renderings are indeed strikingly different from one another. Some feature lively scat solos full of abstract melodic quotation and paraphrase. In others, she uses text to invoke blues personae and create her own emotional contexts, drawing on the huge store of phrases that comprise traditional and popular blues idioms.

Quotation and Reference in Jazz Performance

Musical quotation is ubiquitous in jazz. Why do so many musicians—Fitzgerald, Rollins, Woods, and others—like to quote in the course of performance? There is no single universal reason, but for saxophonist Jimmy Heath the important point is that references "communicate."[17] For pianist Mike Melillo, they amount to a kind of personal history: "What's really interesting is that it's your history coming right out of you. . . . It may come out of you in a very abstract way, in all kinds of ways," as he said, but it is essentially the history of "your ears."[18]

Quotations serve not only to elucidate quoters' personal histories, but also those of the quoted phrases themselves, including their intertextuality, the "manner in which texts seem concerned to address their antecedents," as Henry Louis Gates defined it.[19] In jazz, where quoting can become a

Signifyin(g) game, the conscious (and sometimes even the unpremeditated) revisions that a musician makes in repeating a borrowed phrase contribute significantly to the story, marking the utterance in one way or another, here turning it into a gesture of respect, there imbuing it with irony. The multifarious "repetition and revision process[es]" one encounters in jazz quotation support Gates' statement that "[t]here are so many examples of Signifyin(g) in jazz that one could write a formal history of its development on this basis alone."[20]

Jazz performers and other musicians acquire (are given, borrow, trade, steal) all sorts of things from one another: a turn of phrase, an arranging idea, a tempo, an extra lyric, an emotional stance, a chord change, a few bars of an interesting solo, and so on.[21] Some ideas are picked up from recordings, others are caught in live shows. Improvisers often record tunes, arrangements, and licks that they have played in concerts and clubs, which has the effect of making it easier for other artists to study their work.

Artists whose styles are worlds apart frequently listen to one another. Reasons may be aesthetic (one wants to create a setting which pays tribute to or contrasts with another's), practical (one wants to add a particular tune to her/his repertoire and learns it by listening to a readily available recording), or simply that a hit has become inescapable. The attention often leaves its mark on the work, sometimes through conscious planning, sometimes not.

Ella Fitzgerald's work shows us that the art of interpolation is a product of how one uses, contextualizes, reconfigures, reinflects, and reinvents a given phrase. As Sonny Rollins put it, "It's one thing to put a melody of one song into another for effect, so the crowd likes it, but there's also an artistic level involved in these excursions." In his view, "Ella really brought that to a high level."[22] Part of the artistry lies in the way in which a known theme is transmuted as it is interpolated, the techniques of paraphrase and restatement. A second part of the interpolator's art involves ways in which configurations of pitches, rhythms, and words can spur musical invention, providing ready themes to be developed or broken down. These are aspects of interpolation as compositional/improvisational technique. A third part has to do with ways in which associations adhering to or meanings inherent in a reference can amplify a personal statement, adding resonance or irony, providing a kind of counterfoil or subtext to the moment at hand. These are aspects of interpolation as reference.[23]

There are multitudes of ways to use bits of borrowed material, each one lending its own character to an allusion. Some references are obvious. For instance, Ella Fitzgerald liked to quote from Koehler and Arlen's "Stormy

Weather" and interpolated its first two bars in reference-laden scat solos on "How High the Moon."[24] "Stormy Weather" is hardly an obscure melody, but what causes the reference to leap out is the way she tags it. After presenting the first two measures wordlessly, she concludes the phrase with the words "Stormy Weather," clearly reminding listeners of the tune's title.

Other gestures are much more subtle and indirect. In performances of "These Foolish Things (Remind Me of You),"[25] Fitzgerald sometimes quoted from a major hit recording of the piece made in 1936 by the Teddy Wilson Orchestra featuring Billie Holiday.[26] This was a big hit for Holiday, but Fitzgerald brought up her involvement in the recording only obliquely. She quoted not from Holiday's vocal performance, nor from the tune itself, but from a little variation Teddy Wilson played in the opening instrumental chorus; Fitzgerald paraphrased it in the parallel spot in her versions. The interpolation seems to say, "Here's a little something Teddy Wilson did on 'Foolish Things,' and—as you may remember—this was a big hit for Lady Day."

Some references poke fun. Fitzgerald's ability to mimic other musicians' styles is well known. One amusing routine in her concert repertoire, on Fields and McHugh's "I Can't Give You Anything But Love," featured two extended impersonations: Louis Armstrong and Rose Murphy (the "chi chi girl").[27] Fitzgerald liked to poke fun at songs as well as people, and was apt to turn a statement on its head by quoting it out of context. Mike Melillo remembers Charlie Parker interpolating ballad themes in up-tempo improvisations. "A sad kind of a ballad all of a sudden is a very happy quote stuck in there," he said, "and it turns out fine, but you would never think of it."[28] Like Parker, Fitzgerald was fond of including excerpts from ballads ("Stormy Weather" and others) in her up-tempo improvisations. She seemed to enjoy making light of the poetic earnestness of a slow love song by interpolating it in a boisterous, high velocity, wordless environment.

Each reference expresses a unique musical moment, a particular technique, an emotional color, a reflection on a source, a point in a performance, part of a creative flow. By looking into her references and tracking down their sources, we allow her to lead us to some of her interests and influences. The phrases and the ways in which she recalls them serve as reminders of people and circumstances that have had a bearing on her musical life, that have captured her imagination and affected her in specific ways. As she echoes some of what she has listened to, she spins it in her own way, throwing it out to us as she did to her audiences in the past, and letting us begin to chart her vast sound world with its numerous creative pathways and connections between people, events, places, times, idioms, genres.

The Stature of "St. Louis Blues"

It would be difficult to overemphasize the stature of "St. Louis Blues" in the jazz repertoire. Along with "Tiger Rag," it was one of the two most widely recorded compositions into the 1940s.[29] Written by W. C. Handy in 1914, the song had garnered a long string of popular successes by the time Ella Fitzgerald first recorded it in 1957. A chronological listing of those who scored hits with it from 1916 until the mid-1950s includes:[30]

Al Bernard,[31] vaudeville comedy singer (Emerson 9163, rec. 1919)

Marion Harris, 1920s musical theater and recording star (Columbia A2944, rec. 4/16/20)

The Original Dixieland Jazz Band, whose 1917 recording of "Livery Stable Blues" sparked an international jazz craze (Victor 18772, rec. 5/25/21)

W. C. Handy's Orchestra[32] (OKeh 4896, rec. ca. 6/4/23)

Bessie Smith, whose band included Louis Armstrong (Columbia 14064-D, rec. 1/14/25)

Louis Armstrong (OKeh 41350, rec. 12/13/29)

Rudy Vallée (Victor 22321, rec. 2/19/30)

Cab Calloway (Brunswick 4936, rec. 7/24/30; re-released in 1943)

The Mills Brothers (Brunswick 6330, rec. 4/14/32)

The Boswell Sisters (Brunswick 7467, rec. 5/28/35)

Benny Goodman Orchestra (Victor 25411, rec. 8/21/36)

Guy Lombardo,[33] the flipside of his famous "Auld Lang Syne" recording (Decca 2478, rec. 3/7/39)

Earl Hines ["Boogie Woogie on St. Louis Blues"] (Bluebird B-10674, rec. 2/13/40)

Cab Calloway (Brunswick 4936; re-release of 1930 recording)

Metronome All-Stars (Billy Eckstine with Teddy Wilson, Lester Young, and Max Roach (MGM 11573, rec. 7/9/53)

In addition to these hits, many prominent bands have included it in their repertoires, recording versions that have become familiar to jazz musicians and their audiences.[34]

Several films have adopted the title *St. Louis Blues*. The first of these, released in 1929, was one of the earliest movies to employ an entirely African American cast. Handy directed the music and co-authored the script of this sixteen-minute musical, which featured Bessie Smith in her only screen appearance. A 1939 musical entitled *St. Louis Blues* starred Dorothy Lamour,

Lloyd Nolan, and William Frawley. Maxine Sullivan, making her Hollywood debut, had a cameo role and sang the title song, while pieces by such popular songwriters as Frank Loesser, Hoagy Carmichael, Leo Robin, and Burton Lane were featured. Fitzgerald appeared briefly and sang in a 1958 film, a biography which cast singer-pianist Nat "King" Cole in the role of W. C. Handy and included performances of Handy's music by well-known musicians and entertainers, including Mahalia Jackson, Cab Calloway, Pearl Bailey, Eartha Kitt, and Barney Bigard.[35] Fitzgerald sang Handy's "Beale Street Blues" in the movie, while Bailey, Kitt, and Cole each offered versions of "St. Louis Blues."[36]

Handy is known for his role in standardizing the AAB verse and 12-bar harmonic structure of the popular blues. Despite the title, "St. Louis Blues" is not in 12-bar blues form throughout. As Handy wrote in his autobiography, "I tricked the dancers by arranging a tango introduction, breaking abruptly then into a low-down blues."[37] The tango was very popular at the time, and he expanded on the idea later in the piece, using it to underpin the third stanza, a 16-bar minor-mode section. With the exception of this verse, and two alternate texts to be sung over this part of the form, all remaining (eleven) verses use a standard 12-bar blues form and harmonic progression.

"Long, Deep, and Wide": Text Borrowing in "St. Louis Blues"

Handy described his fourteen verses as "a mosaic of characteristic Negro expressions from beginning to end."[38] He ascribed one line to "a drunken woman" he had heard singing "years ago."[39] Recordings made over the years show that musicians have tended to carry Handy's "mosaic" approach forward, treating the lyrics flexibly, adding verses from other traditional and popular blues pieces, while omitting and changing many portions of the composer's texts.

In surveying some one hundred recordings of "St. Louis Blues," I found considerable variation with regard to text usage and ordering. No performance used all fourteen of Handy's verses, nor do they all begin with his first verse. Starting with Bessie Smith in 1925, the most widely sung combination has been the first through the fourth stanzas. Nearly three-quarters of the performers used these verses together (written here with the composer's "dialect"):[40]

I hate to see de ev'nin' sun go down.
Hate to see de evenin' sun go down.
Cause my baby, he done lef dis town.

Feelin' tomorrow lak Ah feel today.
Feel tomorrow lak Ah feel today.
I'll pack my trunk, make ma get away.

St. Louis woman, wid her diamon' rings,
Pulls dat man roun' by her apron strings.
'Twant for powder, an' for store bought hair,
De man I love, would not gone nowhere.

Got de St. Louis blues jes as blue as Ah can be.
Dat man got a heart lak a rock cast in the sea.
Or else he wouldn't have gone so far from me.

Variations from one recording to the next show some of the ways in which musicians incorporated aspects of each other's performances. By quoting from two traditional blues couplets, one involving a peach metaphor, the other concerning the Mississippi River, Fitzgerald links her "St. Louis Blues" with previous versions of the tune, including those of Guy Lombardo, Ivie Anderson (with Duke Ellington's orchestra), Maxine Sullivan (with John Kirby and Claude Thornhill), and Helen Humes. Fitzgerald's stanzas recall not only other "St. Louis Blues" performances, but also older downhome/folk blues pieces and compositions of the classic/vaudeville blues era in the 1920s. In one verse ("He May Be Your Man"), she highlights the work of the vaudeville-blues women, especially Lucille Hegamin and Edith Wilson. In another ("You Ain't So Such-a-Much"), she points to the New Orleans sound and idiosyncratic lyrics of Pleasant "Cousin Joe" Joseph, a contemporary of Louis Armstrong.

References to the recordings of other artists carry meanings and associations that may be emphasized, played down, and/or changed. The approaches Fitzgerald takes toward her referents vary. She invokes myriad blues meanings as she calls upon the voices of such musicians as William Harris, Big Bill Broonzy, Mississippi John Hurt, Jim Jackson, Blind Lemon Jefferson, and Sonny Boy Williamson to resonate with those of Maxine Sullivan and Guy Lombardo in her "peach" and "Mississippi River" stanzas. With "He May Be Your Man," she chooses to maintain a posture taken in the source text. With "You Ain't So Such-A-Much" she turns the stance on its head.

PEACHES AND PEACH TREES

Among the recordings surveyed, only three versions included anything like the following verse, a stanza not written by Handy (Ex. 8.1): "If you don't like my peaches, why do you shake my tree? (stay out of my orchard, stay out

Ex. 8.1. Ella Fitzgerald, "Peach tree" stanza in "St. Louis Blues" (Verve 4062, rec. 10/29/63 [4:15-57]).

of my orchard) / If you don't like my peaches, why do you shake my tree? / Stay out of my orchard, and let my peach tree be." Fitzgerald sang the verse in both 1963 and 1964. The earliest recorded "St. Louis Blues" I found to use it is Guy Lombardo's 1939 issue, a big hit for his Royal Canadians.[41] A year later, Ivie Anderson followed suit, singing with Duke Ellington's orchestra.[42] The verse, by no means a Lombardo invention, has a particularly rich and interesting history.

Intensive exchange of texts and other musical material between musicians working within the traditional and popular blues idioms appeared in the first decades of the twentieth century with the first published blues by Handy, Perry Bradford, and others. Among folk-blues musicians, musical borrowing is a longstanding practice integral to the common aesthetic.[43] While early popular-blues composers often recalled folk-blues performances they had heard, using these recollections as raw material for new compositions, folk-blues musicians, as David Evans has pointed out, tended to "reverse" this compositional process by selecting lines and stanzas from published blues pieces to string together and combine with stock patterns and phrases, creating new songs in the traditional manner.[44] Evans observed this practice in early recordings of Handy's "The Hesitating Blues." Within a year of the composition's publication in 1915, collected versions began to incorporate traditional stanzas and lines, some presenting nothing of Handy's piece but its refrain.

It is therefore not surprising to find comparable lines about peaches and peach trees cropping up in no less than twenty different recorded blues lyrics, resembling one another to varying degrees.[45] With few significant differences, William Harris' "Hot Time Blues" contains the closest variant to those later used in "St. Louis Blues": "If you don't like my peaches, don't shake my tree / Gal, stay out of my orchard, and let my peaches be."[46] Context and content considered, Fitzgerald's use of the "peach tree" stanza in 1963 and 1964 bears the closest resemblance to Lombardo's 1939 and Anderson's 1940 "St. Louis Blues." Lombardo: "If you don't like my peaches, why do you shake my tree? (repeated) / Stay out of my orchard, and let my fruit trees be." Anderson: "If you don't like my peaches, why do you shake my tree? (repeated) / Get away from my orchard, and let my peaches be."

Did Fitzgerald get the idea to sing the couplet in "St. Louis Blues" from Anderson or Lombardo (or independently)? The evidence is in details of the presentation, including exact wording of the text. While there are marked differences between Anderson's, Lombardo's, and Fitzgerald's versions and their settings, there are significant similarities. With regard to text, the differences are small, with Fitzgerald's renderings slightly closer to Lombardo's than to Anderson's. Like Anderson, she refers to "peach" rather than "fruit" in the last line. But like Lombardo (unlike Anderson), she also mentions the tree, and says to "stay out of" rather than "get out of" her orchard. Fitzgerald emphasizes the "get out of" snippet she shares with Lombardo by repeating it as an interjection in mm. 3–4 of her versions. It is possible that Fitzgerald, remembering the Lombardo hit recording years later, and Anderson, having heard it only the year before, each decided to add the resonant "peach tree" verse to "St. Louis Blues" in response to it, independently. Both singers evidently heard the Lombardo recording (and/or live performances). It is also likely that Fitzgerald heard Anderson interpolate the peach verse in "St. Louis Blues," and may have heard interpolations of the stanza in other contexts as well, given its widespread use.

The "peach" example is particularly interesting for its multivocality, the many voices that have echoed it, and its intertextuality, the ways in which these voices seem to have spoken to one another over the years and across the genres. Fitzgerald gives it her own Signifyin(g) twist, alluding to the Lombardo and Anderson/Ellington versions, while simultaneously foregrounding the stanza's downhome-blues roots. She pulls it out of Lombardo's "sweet" dance-band setting, with its jumpy two-step (half-note) feel and impassive delivery of the text, then reinvents it, making it swinging and languorous, filling it with innuendo and subtle blues-mode inflections that affirm folk-blues practice and reflect a contemporary soul-jazz sensibility.

"MISSISSIPPI RIVER"

On Fitzgerald's first release of "St. Louis Blues" in 1957, she closed the song with a forceful full-voiced stop-time chorus that, again, is not one of Handy's: "Mississippi River, long, deep, and wide, got to meet my sweet man on the other side / Take me back to St. Louis, back to St. Louis / Got the St. Louis blues, just as blue as I can be." On all but one of her "St. Louis Blues" recordings, she ends with it, presenting it five out of six times in a stop-time rhythmic format in which the band drops out after heavy accents on the first beats of the first two measures of the tune, returning to the initial blues feel in measure five.[47] Fitzgerald's "Mississippi River" interpolation derives from a very old blues couplet, dated "back twenty years or more" in Handy's 1926 blues anthology.[48] In the Handy collection, it appears in Lucille Marie Handy's and Eddie Green's "Deep River Blues."[49] Although it has since been adopted by other performers, Maxine Sullivan is the first singer I found on record to incorporate it in "St. Louis Blues."

Maxine Sullivan (1911–87) was a stylistically "cool" singer with a distinctively restrained and understated delivery. "St. Louis Blues" was a favorite in her repertoire. Not only was it her featured number in the 1939 film by the same name, but she also released three renditions of it with the proto-cool Claude Thornhill and John Kirby orchestras.[50] Thornhill and Gladys Moser, pianist with the all-women Ina Ray Hutton Band, co-managed Sullivan's early career (ca. 1937). They strove to distinguish her sound by surrounding her voice with subdued orchestral colors and providing her with jazz arrangements of "light classical" pieces and such European folk songs as "Loch Lomond," her first big hit.[51] On all three recordings, Sullivan closed with stop-time choruses to a variant of the text: "Mississippi River, long, deep, and wide, I gotta find my sweet man on the other side / Get me back to St. Louis, get me back to St. Louis / Get me back to St. Louis, I'll lose those mean old blues."

After Sullivan, Helen Humes (1913–81) took up the "Mississippi River" couplet as a closing stanza in "St. Louis Blues," as a live broadcast shows.[52] She sang the tune at a brisk tempo (MM = ca. 200) and, like Sullivan, began the verse in stop-time, varying Sullivan's text slightly: "Mississippi River, long, deep, and wide, I got to see my daddy over on the other side / Take me back to St. Louis, take me back / Take me back to St. Louis to lose those mean old blues." Humes, who made her first recordings with such accompanists as James P. Johnson and Lonnie Johnson as a teenager in the mid-1920s, had a wide-ranging repertoire. She prided herself on flexibility, stating that she was not a blues, ballad, or jazz singer, but "just a singer."[53] She replaced Billie Holiday in the Count Basie orchestra from 1938 to 1941, during which time Jimmy Rushing was also singing with the band.[54] She had two big hits, both on the rhythm-and-blues charts: "Be-ba-ba-le-ba" and "Million Dollar Secret."[55] Humes, again following Holiday, joined producer Norman Granz's all-star "Jazz at the Philharmonic" (JATP) touring groups. Granz primarily featured instrumentalists but had, since 1946, included Holiday or Humes in his shows. Humes remained with the production for five seasons and was reported to have "stopped the show cold" on more than one occasion.[56] Ella Fitzgerald succeeded Helen Humes in JATP in 1949, becoming the third vocalist to be offered the spot.

Nellie Lutcher (b. 1915), a singer-pianist with a lively, earthy approach in the tradition of Fats Waller (and an acquaintance of Helen Humes),[57] made a popular recording of "St. Louis Blues," which featured the stop-time "Mississippi River" stanza five years prior to Fitzgerald: "Mississippi River, long, deep, and wide, I know that my man is on the other side / With that gal, yes with that wicked St. Louis woman / And I'm oh so blue, blue, blue, blue, blue."[58] In her rhythm-and-blues inflected setting, Lutcher worked it in as a penultimate verse.

Fitzgerald's "Mississippi River" stanza points to Sullivan, but she may well have known about and considered the other releases. Textually, her variant is closer to Sullivan's than to Humes' or Lutcher's, and she, following Sullivan, customarily closed with it. The evidence that, despite prominent differences in their individual styles and performance personalities, Fitzgerald and Lutcher both listened closely to Sullivan, underscores the point that musicians incorporate ideas across styles and genres.[59] Even Helen Humes, who insisted that "nobody influenced me—I didn't hear nobody," paid apparent attention to Sullivan.[60] For her part, Sullivan, whose style owes no obvious debt to Fitzgerald, reported that she was nonetheless a huge admirer, placing Fitzgerald "on a throne."[61]

"HE MAY BE YOUR MAN"

Citing Lemuel Fowler's "He May Be Your Man (But He Comes to See Me Sometimes)," Fitzgerald reminds us of earlier vocal royalty and deepens the connection between herself and Helen Humes, her contemporary. She does this in five of seven of her recordings (all but the 1964 and 1979 versions), in each case using the tune's title and opening line to create a blues chorus that is a variant of the following text: "He may be your man, but he comes up to see me sometime (repeated) / Live six flights up, and that man he sure love to climb." Fitzgerald seems to have composed the last line herself; I found no other recorded versions that use it.

The Fowler tune is not a twelve-bar blues, but a 32-bar AABA song form. It has bluesy character nonetheless, owing partly to the fact that the first eight measures follow a standard blues pattern, remaining on the I-chord for four measures, moving to the IV-chord for two bars, then back to the tonic for two measures before heading into the bridge section. The first line of text is not repeated in the original: "He may be your man, but he comes to see me sometimes / And when he's with you, he's always got me on his mind / I ain't no vampire, that is true, but I can surely take your man from you . . ."

Lucille Hegamin (1894–1970) introduced the piece, first recording it in 1921.[62] Promoted as "The Georgia Peach," "The Cameo Girl," and "The Blues Singer Supreme," Hegamin became widely known in the 1920s through her vaudeville, cabaret, and theatrical performances, as well as her recordings of blues songs and other popular material. In 1920, with the waxing of "The Jazz Me Blues" and "Everybody's Blues,"[63] she became the second classic-blues singer to be recorded. Earlier that year, Mamie Smith's release of "Crazy Blues" had sold an unprecedented number of copies, sparking an interest in women vaudeville-blues artists that would last the decade.[64] "He May Be Your Man" was Hegamin's theme song and greatest hit. She and her Blue Flame Syncopators [Syncopaters] recorded it several times.[65] It is quite likely that a young Ella Fitzgerald would either have listened to one of these records or heard Hegamin sing it on one of her thrice-weekly live radio broadcasts from The Cotton Club in Harlem in 1925.[66]

Edith Wilson (1906–81) also recorded "He May Be Your Man," first in 1922 and again five decades later.[67] Following Lucille Hegamin, she too used it as a kind of theme song, especially in the latter part of her career. Wilson, like Hegamin, was one of the top vaudeville-blues women of the 1920s. She first attracted notice through her association with Perry Bradford, who promoted her in live shows and recording sessions with Johnny Dunn's Original Jazz Hounds, initially as a replacement for Mamie Smith. During that period, Wilson recorded for Columbia and worked the TOBA (Theater Owners Booking Association) vaudeville circuit. Billed as "Queen of the Blues," a title she shared with others, she sang many of Bradford's blues compositions and played for predominantly African American audiences in theaters across the United States.[68] Upon her return to New York City, she expanded her audience, starring in Harlem cabarets and Broadway revues, and touring Europe. Her biggest hit was "Birmingham Blues," which she recorded with Johnny Dunn.[69] By the late 1940s, she had garnered some film and radio credits, but spent most of her time touring as "Aunt Jemima" to raise charitable funds on behalf of Quaker Oats.

"He May Be Your Man" became a standard of the classic-blues repertoire.[70] Notable is a 12-bar blues by Helen Humes, which she called "He May Be Your Man."[71] The opening chorus of the Humes blues, like Fitzgerald's stanza, begins with and repeats Fowler's first line, closing with something different: "He may be your man, but he comes to see me sometime (repeated) / Lord, he comes so often I'm beginning to think he's mine." The Philo session was the first, but Humes recorded it again several times three decades later.[72] Like Edith Wilson, Humes grew up in Louisville, Kentucky, and remembered Wilson's local performances, which she attended as a young girl.[73] Since "He May Be Your Man (But He Comes to See Me Sometimes)" was one of Wilson's signature tunes, Humes may have heard her sing it often.

Fitzgerald's "He May Be Your Man" verse in "St. Louis Blues" is conceptually very similar to the Humes blues that predates it. Fitzgerald is likely to have heard her do it, particularly since Humes' first "He May Be Your Man" was released as the flip-side of her greatest hit, "Be-ba-ba-le-ba."[74] Fitzgerald probably already knew "He May Be Your Man" from Lucille Hegamin's or Edith Wilson's performances, but may have taken the idea to form it into a blues chorus from Humes.[75]

Perhaps the durability of "He May Be Your Man" stems from its portrayal of a woman who is powerful and dangerous, attributes emphasized in many a blues queen's public persona. The Fowler tune is emblematic of a genre in which blues is mixed with jazz and other popular idioms: a bluesy melody with a 32-bar ABAB form, and a harmonic scheme that is blues-related but not the blues *per se.* As Fitzgerald and Humes call our attention to "He May Be Your Man," they bring up not only Hegamin and Wilson, but also the classic-blues repertoire itself, thereby connecting themselves with the great female vaudeville-blues tradition.

"YOU AIN'T SO SUCH-A-MUCH"

Shouting out a stanza from "You Ain't So Such-a-Much," Fitzgerald amplifies the "mean and evil" persona she introduces with the line from "He May Be Your Man."[76] "You Ain't So Such-a-Much," a 12-bar blues, was written by

New Orleans blues singer Pleasant "Cousin Joe" Joseph. A slightly younger contemporary of Louis Armstrong, Cousin Joe was a popular entertainer in his home city, known not only as a singer but also as a dancer, guitar (and ukulele) player, and—later—pianist. Fitzgerald worked briefly with him when he came to New York in the early 1940s.[77]

Cousin Joe began writing his own blues after he moved to Manhattan, and became known for his wit and the anti-woman postures he frequently took in his lyrics. To distinguish himself from "everybody" who sang about "how beautiful a woman was and how much they loved her and what they would do for her," as he explained, he wrote "the opposite: what I *wouldn't* do."[78] His "You Ain't So Such-a-Much," which he recorded with alto saxophonist Earl Bostic's Gotham Sextet, is one example: "I wouldn't give a blind sow an acorn, wouldn't give a crippled crab a crutch (repeated) / 'Cause I just found out, baby, that you ain't so such-a-much . . ."[79] With a "mean and evil" Signifyin(g) flip, Ella Fitzgerald adopted Cousin Joe's statement, but turned the sex roles around, substituting the image of a sparrow for that of a female pig. This is her version (with variants): "Wouldn't give a blind sparrow an acorn, wouldn't give a crippled crab a crutch (you know I'm mean and evil) (repeated) / Ain't gonna give you nothing, 'cause you think you're such a much-and-much."

Dizzy Gillespie met Cousin Joe around the same time and place as Ella Fitzgerald. Gillespie became an admirer and added "You Ain't So Such-a-Much" to his repertoire, recording it on a live date in Paris.[80] In his autobiography, stressing that "the bopper" stayed in contact with "his blues counterpart," he included Cousin Joe's name on a short list with T-Bone Walker, B. B. King, Joe Turner, and Muddy Waters.[81] Cousin Joe was (along with guitarist-singer Danny Barker) one of the two people Gillespie urged Leslie Gourse to contact as she researched Louis Armstrong's New Orleans youth.[82] Fitzgerald's renderings of "You Ain't So Such-a-Much" show no obvious debt to Gillespie, but it is quite possible that she heard him sing it as well. She and Gillespie, each in their own way, seem to share an acknowledgment of Cousin Joe as one of their "blues counterparts."

The 1958 Birthday Concert

Rather than weaving whole stanzas into one another, as Fitzgerald did in her exclusively text-based performances of "St. Louis Blues," in her scat solos she often used smaller bits of more abstract material, melodic snippets, sometimes with bits of text. Incorporating excerpts from more than a dozen sources, her 1958 "St. Louis Blues" stands apart from her other releases of the tune as an example of interpolation-based scat singing. The concert, at the Teatro Sistina in Rome, marked the occasion of her forty-first birthday.[83] The band was her working trio: Gus Johnson on drums, Max Bennett on bass, and Lou Levy at the piano.[84]

Fitzgerald began the concert with "St. Louis Blues," making it, as Stuart Nicholson writes, "a tour de force, the sort of thing a lesser singer might use to climax a set."[85] With regard to scat singing and melodic interpolation, it was indeed a tour de force. While she included scat solos on her 1957 and 1971 "St. Louis Blues" dates as well, the 1958 concert version is distinguished from these by the length of her solo and the number of quotations she uses in it. The first time she recorded the piece was on a studio session with Frank DeVol's Orchestra in 1957.[86] On this date, she took a modest two choruses and interpolated one excerpt. A year later, she extended the solo to fifteen choruses. At only one chorus in length, the 1971 solo is even shorter than the 1957 one, and does not feature quotation.[87] Table 8.1 lists interpolations in the 1957 and 1958 recordings by location within each performance and by title/composer of source material.[88] For her first two "St. Louis Blues" dates, Fitzgerald sang the piece in B-flat with arrangements that emphasized tempo

Table 8.1. Interpolations in Fitzgerald's "St. Louis Blues"

	1957
[3:10–14]	"It Might As Well Be Spring" (Rodgers/Hammerstein)
	1958
[0:38–40]	"Fever" (Davenport/Cooley)
[2:35–39]	"The Chase" (Gordon) ["High Society"—Steele]
[2:49–56]	"Later" (Bradshaw/Glover)
[3:11–13]	"Smooth Sailing" (Cobb)
[3:18–28]	"What I'm Singing" (Fitzgerald, "How High the Moon" improv., Session Disc SES 105, rec. 4/15/49)
[3:28–35]	"The Hut Sut Song" (Killion/McMichael/Owens)
[3:35–38]	"Move" (Best)
[3:39–45]	"Jumpin' with Symphony Sid" (Young)
[3:49–55]	"Swingin' Shepherd Blues" (Koffman)
[3:59–4:02]	"It Might As Well Be Spring" (Rodgers/Hammerstein)
[4:06–9]	"Mean to Me" (Turk/Ahlert)
[4:31–37]	"Chinese" idea (Fitzgerald, "Ool-Ya-Koo" improv., Jazz Live BLJ 8035, rec. 11/27/48 [1:35-8]; Parker-Gillespie, "Perdido" improv., Prestige 24024, rec. 5/15/53)
[4:40–50]	"Send for Me" (Ollie Jones)
[4:51–54]	"Only You (And You Alone)" (Ram)

and feel changes. On stage with her trio in 1958, she retained much of the feeling of the 1957 Frank DeVol big-band chart, in an informal head arrangement.

The extraordinary variety of references in Fitzgerald's 1958 scat solo (Ex. 8.2) represents a mini-typology of quotational practice in jazz. She cites her own repertoire and that of her associates and competitors, interpolating phrases from both improvisations and compositions. Some quotations point to popular hits, others emphasize particular genres, idioms, and instruments. She creates embedded references that refer to quotation of one artist by another. She inserts a meta-reference that comments on the referentiality

Ex. 8.2. Ella Fitzgerald, scat solo in "St. Louis Blues" (Verve 835-454-2, rec. 4/24-5/58).

Ex. 8.2. *Continued*

of her solo, while simultaneously bringing up similar commentaries that appear elsewhere in her work. She points to artists who—like herself—were frequent quoters, citing quotations that appear as such in the work of other performers, and those that appear elsewhere in her own work. We can trace her quotations by beginning with an allusion to New Orleans, then proceeding with references to ballads, blues, R&B, bebop, swing, and cool jazz.

Ex. 8.2. *Continued*

"THE CHASE" BEGINS IN NEW ORLEANS

Fitzgerald leads off her first scat chorus with a passage from Dexter Gordon's "The Chase" [2:35–39], a piece he performed as a tenor saxophone "duel" with Wardell Gray in a 1947 studio session (Ex. 8.2, mm. 1–4; Ex. 8.3).[89] One of the first bebop tenor players, Gordon was also one of jazz's master

Ex. 8.2. *Continued*

Ex. 8.3. Dexter Gordon, opening theme of "The Chase," mm. 1-4 (Dial 1017, rec. 6/12/47).

interpolators, the "Boss Quoter" as Phil Woods calls him.[90] Citing Gordon's work, Fitzgerald immediately calls attention to his use of quotation. She quotes the quoter quoting: embedded within the "Chase" fragment is another quotation.

The first twelve notes of Gordon's melody incorporate a clarinet obbligato from "High Society," the Porter Steele composition. Initially performed as a slow processional march, "High Society" was published as a rag in 1901, in an arrangement by Robert Recker that quickly became one of the most popular and widely recorded pieces of the early New Orleans repertoire.[91] The passage from which Gordon constructed the opening theme of "The Chase" is the first two measures of a counter line added by Recker, which marks the beginning of the trio section toward the end of the piece (Ex. 8.4). In "The Chase," the phrase is stated three times (mm. 1–6), varied slightly each time. Fitzgerald paraphrases the first two of these statements.

In Recker's orchestration, the passage is a piccolo part. Alphonse Picou, a leading New Orleans brass band and "society" clarinetist, was probably the first player to transcribe and perform it on the clarinet.[92] Because of the virtuosity it required, it became used extensively as an audition piece for brass band clarinet players. Joe "King" Oliver recorded "High Society" in 1923 with Louis Armstrong.[93] Johnny Dodds played the clarinet obbligato on this version, which was a hit for Oliver in 1924. The "High Society" passage is remarkable for linking innovative musicians who shared a fondness

Ex. 8.4. Clarinet passage (Johnny Dodds) from King Oliver's Jazz Band, "High Society Rag" (OKeh 4933, rec. 6/22/23). Originally in E-flat.

Ex. 8.5. Dexter Gordon, "High Society" interpolation in opening of tenor solo on "The Chase," mm. 1–4 of form (Dial 1017, rec. 6/12/47).

for quotation. It bridges early New Orleans and bebop repertoires, crossing boundaries of historical circumstance, instrument, and personal style. In addition to having recorded the piece itself, Armstrong liked to quote from "High Society" in his trumpet solos; for example, in a popular 1930 recording of Newman and Lombardo's "Sweethearts on Parade."[94] Fitzgerald, who was parodying Armstrong to entertain her childhood friends by 1929, is likely to have heard (and mimicked) this recording.[95] Dexter Gordon, who worked with Armstrong for a good part of 1944, may well have heard Armstrong quote the passage.[96] Charlie Parker adopted it, interpolating it in one of his most widely imitated solos on "KoKo," his composition based on the harmonic scheme of Ray Noble's "Cherokee."[97] Trumpeter Roy Eldridge is among the many other musicians who have quoted it. Creating a setting that Ella Fitzgerald would resonate with (without citing explicitly) a decade later, he worked it into two takes of an improvisation on "St. Louis Blues."[98]

By 1958, Fitzgerald is likely to have heard the "High Society" lick interpolated in a variety of settings, each musician quoting it in his own way. Armstrong employed it as a phrase ending in his final trumpet chorus on "Sweethearts on Parade." Parker, on the other hand, tended to use it to begin phrases and choruses, as musicologist Thomas Owens observed; he did this in the celebrated solo on "KoKo."[99] Gordon seems to have noticed this.[100] He not only began the melody of "The Chase" with it but cited it even more explicitly to open his tenor solo on the original recording (see Ex. 8.5).[101] Following Gordon's example, Fitzgerald kicks off her first wordless chorus in "St. Louis Blues" with it. Wherever it is inserted, the "High Society" quotation tends to be prominently displayed, worn—as it has been since the turn of the twentieth century—as a badge of virtuosity.

BALLADS

An excerpt from "It Might As Well Be Spring," which Fitzgerald interpolates in both the 1957 and 1958 solos, is one of a string of allusions to her own repertoire ("Later," "Smooth Sailing," "Swingin' Shepherd Blues"). Singers Dick Haymes, Margaret Whiting, and Billy Williams each released recordings of the ballad in 1945, all scoring in the top ten within a two-month span.[102] Fitzgerald recorded it a decade later with the André Previn Orchestra.[103] It gained a place in her live repertoire as well.[104]

"It Might As Well Be Spring" shows up most frequently in Fitzgerald's work as an interpolation. It was apparently one of her favorite quotations, inserted primarily in lively scat solos, including "Oh, Lady Be Good," "Swingin' Shepherd Blues," "I Can't Give You Anything But Love," and Duke Ellington and Sid Kuller's "Bli-Blip."[105] Perhaps her most ingenious interpolation of it appears in a ballad, however, a London performance of George and Ira Gershwin's "The Man I Love."[106] She sings the tune once through with a flexible slow pulse, then the drummer (Bobby Durham) switches to a "Latin" eighth-note feel, effecting a kind of double-time. At the end of the first A-section, she sings a melismatic double-time melodic interpolation to the words, "I'll do my best to make him, I'll do my best to make him stay."[107] Her references to "It Might As Well Be Spring" have a programmatic character. Even in a slow setting, the quotation seems to signal excitement; the "restless" feeling and "jumpy" quickening pulse suggested by the song's lyrics.

In a second ballad reference, she quotes Turk and Ahlert's "Mean to Me" [4:06–9] immediately after "It Might As Well Be Spring." A double hit in 1929, "Mean to Me" was introduced by torch singers Helen Morgan and Ruth Etting.[108] Billie Holiday, with Teddy Wilson and his Orchestra featuring Lester Young, had a top-ten hit with it almost ten years later.[109] By the mid-1950s, it had been widely recorded by singers and instrumentalists, including Lester Young, Sarah Vaughan, Illinois Jacquet, Frank Sinatra, Marlene Dietrich, the Andrews Sisters, Big Maybelle, and Louis Prima. Fitzgerald did not add it to her own discography until 1975, when she sang it on a trio session with pianist Oscar Peterson and bassist Ray Brown.[110]

BLUES

Five interpolations in Fitzgerald's 1958 "St. Louis Blues" refer to 12-bar blues forms: "Smooth Sailing," "Swingin' Shepherd Blues," "Send for Me," "Jumpin' with Symphony Sid," and "Later."

She brings us once again to her own discography with "Later" [2:49–56], a scat feature she recorded with arranger Sy Oliver's band.[111] The tune did not hold a prominent place in her subsequent recorded repertoire, but she performed it live around the time of its release, as a recording of a concert in Carnegie Hall shows.[112] She liked to quote different fragments of it in other pieces, nonetheless, including Goodman/Sampson/Webb/Razaf's "Stompin' at the Savoy" and her own "Joe Williams' Blues."[113] The "Later" quotation

draws attention to her considerable work with Oliver. A trumpeter and arranger, Oliver became known through Jimmie Lunceford's band. He was
instrumental in creating a distinctive sound for this "arranger's orchestra"
beginning in 1934, leaving in 1939 to join the Tommy Dorsey band with Frank
Sinatra.[114] Fitzgerald's tie with Oliver is strong; she recorded at least thirty-
five sides with him in the period 1949–54.[115]

The Lester Young blues, "Jumpin' with Symphony Sid," turns up in Fitzgerald's work primarily as an interpolation. She quotes it in scat solos "How
High the Moon," Ellington's "Rockin' in Rhythm," and elsewhere.[116] Although
she may have performed the piece live, it does not appear in her own discography. It was, however, a popular favorite in Young's repertoire, and by
1958, many other performers had taken it up.[117] Dizzy Gillespie arranged it
for his bebop orchestra.[118] Stan Getz, the "cool" tenor saxophonist who
acknowledged a major stylistic debt to Young, recorded it on a live date in
1951.[119] King Pleasure penned words to it, recording his "vocalese" version
in 1952.[120]

Mention of the tune also brings up the person for whom it was written:
"Symphony Sid" Torin, a disc jockey for New York City's WHOM radio in
the late forties. Torin was among the earliest to include "New York jazz"
(bebop) on his regular show, back-to-back with more popular idioms: "between and among the Basies, Louis Jordans, Wynonie Harrises, and Billie
Holidays."[121] He became known for broadcasts of informal jam sessions at
the Royal Roost, in which many bebop players took part, along with a few
of the more forward-looking big-band swing musicians, Young and Fitzgerald among them.[122] Quoting "Jumpin' with Symphony Sid," Fitzgerald highlights her involvement with this new music, bebop.

RHYTHM-AND-BLUES

As we have seen, in "St. Louis Blues" Fitzgerald demonstrates two distinct
modes of reference: a quilting of blues couplets that reflects folk-blues vocal
practice, and an interpolation of melodic fragments that reflects jazz instrumental practice. The 1958 arrangement partitions these modes, separating
them, through tempo changes, into a "vocal" presentation followed by an
"instrumental" scat solo. The melodic fragments (some texted, some not)
are primarily confined to the scat solo. A brief reference to Little Willie John's
"Fever" is an exception.

Toward the end of the first verse (m. 8), she punctuates the second statement of Handy's lyric ("I hate to see the evening sun go down") with the interjection "you give me fever" [0:38–40], a catch phrase from the Davenport/

Cooley composition. John scored an R&B hit single with "Fever" in 1956.[123] It remained on *Billboard*'s R&B charts for no less than twenty-three weeks, five of those in the top spot.[124] Fitzgerald was to interpolate excerpts from "Fever" in other contexts, including a later concert date performance of her "Joe Williams' Blues."[125]

With the "Fever" quotation, Fitzgerald foreshadows a string of five references to top 1950s R&B hits that are to appear in the scat solo. With regard to recording date, the earliest of these is Arnett Cobb's 1950 "Smooth Sailing" [3:11–13], a riff-type medium-tempo blues.[126] In 1951, Fitzgerald recorded it in a gospel-inflected setting that included organ, piano, and guitar (Bill Doggett, Hank Jones, Everett Barksdale), and featured the "easy listening" choral sounds of the Ray Charles Singers (not to be confused with the Raelettes, singers with gospel-blues singer and pianist Ray Charles).[127] It became a number three hit for her on *Billboard*'s R&B charts. Her release scored on pop charts as well, while Cobb's failed to reach the charts.[128] She kept it in her live repertoire through the end of her career, performing it as late as 1991 at the JVC Jazz Festival in New York City.[129] Her discography includes other recordings of it, *Jazz at the Philharmonic Live in Tokyo, Ella in Hamburg,* and *Newport Jazz Festival Live* among them.[130] She interpolated "Smooth Sailing" in other improvisations, such as her solo on Duke Ellington's "It Don't Mean a Thing" during a Swedish concert,[131] and on a blues jam with Joe Williams and the 1956 Metronome All-Stars ("Party Blues").[132]

Arnett Cobb, a saxophonist with a blues-based "Texas tenor" sound, gained recognition through his work with Lionel Hampton's proto-R&B jazz big band of the 1940s, a group that Quincy Jones has called "the first rock and roll band," and that Malcolm X pointed to as the favorite band among east-coast African Americans in the 1940s.[133] Cobb was not the first Texas tenor in Hampton's band with whom Fitzgerald had been auspiciously linked. In 1947, she released a recording of Benny Goodman's and Hampton's "Flying Home" in which she quoted heavily from Illinois Jacquet's trademark saxophone solo in her own scat choruses.[134] Her "Flying Home" received wide acclaim, establishing her as a vocalist with an instrumental improviser's vocabulary and giving a significant boost to her career. By quoting "Smooth Sailing," she reminds us of the successes she garnered because of her interest in Cobb, Jacquet, and the rocking sound of Hampton's band.

At slightly under four minutes into the performance, Fitzgerald quotes Moe Koffman's "Swingin' Shepherd Blues" [3:49–55] as the audience roars its recognition and approval. A flute feature for Koffman, the piece was a current hit that had been doing well on the pop charts since February.[135] As was common at the time, two other releases of it had followed on the heels of Koffman's: Johnny Pate's version with flutist Lennie Druss—which surpassed Koffman's on the R&B charts—and Hollywood songwriter David Rose's arrangement.[136] Fitzgerald had, in fact, been in the studio with arranger Paul Weston's orchestra to record it herself scarcely a month before the birthday concert.[137] Her version was not a charted hit, and the audience in Rome may not have been aware of it. But the reference stands as an example of the remarkable degree to which she had her finger on the popular pulse not only in the United States, but in Europe as well. She kept "Swingin' Shepherd Blues" in her catalogue of quotable themes at least until 1975, as a Montreux performance of "How High the Moon" shows.[138]

Fitzgerald makes two more references to R&B tunes toward the end of the 1958 scat solo, both texted allusions to vocal pieces. The first is Ollie Jones' "Send for Me," a 12-bar blues that had been a big hit for Nat Cole less than a year earlier.[139] One of the top five best-selling records for Cole during the decade from 1955 until his death in 1965 and the longest-running of his pop hits, "Send for Me" spent twenty-seven weeks on the charts, reaching a peak position of number six.

The allusion to "Send for Me" highlights her connections with Cole. Some links were recent, and pertinent to "St. Louis Blues." In 1957 and 1958, she was a periodic guest on his television show. In January of 1957, they had performed together with the Count Basie orchestra in New York City. On April 11, 1958, just two weeks before the birthday concert, they had celebrated the New York opening of the film *St. Louis Blues.* The "Send for Me" reference, like the passages from "It Might As Well Be Spring" and others, turns up elsewhere in her work. She included the two themes together in a solo on "Oh, Lady Be Good" several months before the Rome date.[140] In this instance, she identified "Send for Me" textually as she was to do in "St. Louis Blues" ("if you ever need a friend, send for me"), but created a different melody.

The final quotation of the scat solo lends a sort of referential symmetry to the performance: her first and last interpolations are texted allusions to number-one mid-1950s R&B hits. Singing "Only you can take this heart of mine," she names Rand and Ram's number one hit of 1955, "Only You (And You Alone)" [4:51–54]. Performed by the Platters, the tune topped the R&B charts for seven weeks in a row, remaining there for an astonishing thirty weeks.[141] Along with two versions of "The Ballad of Davy Crockett" (Tennessee Ernie Ford's and Fess Parker's), it placed fifth on the annual pop charts as well. The significance of its popularity—its hit factor—is under-scored by the fact that she also brings up "The Ballad of Davy Crockett" a little later on in the birthday concert. She does this mockingly, allowing her commentary to come out of the mouth of Louis Armstrong, as she parodies him while singing "I Can't Give You Anything But Love."

IMPROVISATION AND BEBOP

Not all of Fitzgerald's interpolations refer to compositions. As with the passage from "Later" and her "what I'm singing" statements (discussed below), several point to improvisations. At the top of her twelfth scat chorus [4:31–37], she quotes an idea she had used in a solo on Gillespie/Fuller's "Ool-Ya-Koo."[142] "Ool-Ya-Koo," another 12-bar blues, is one of several pieces written by Dizzy Gillespie that feature nonsemantic scat syllables as their text. In the 1948 performances of "Ool-Ya-Koo," she uses the idea as melodic material for the first four measures of the form, finishing with the words "Chinese do it, too." Her "Chinese" lick was used by Gillespie and Parker as well. In a 1953 concert, Parker played it toward the end of an improvisation on "Perdido."[143] Gillespie immediately picked it up, using it to begin his solo. The New Jazz Society of Toronto had scheduled a concert that brought together pianist Bud Powell, drummer Max Roach, and bassist Charles Mingus, along with Parker and Gillespie. The personnel had been selected by a society member poll, and the all-star quality of the date is conveyed by the title the release later received: *The Greatest Jazz Concert Ever.*

Fitzgerald's "Chinese" phrase points to her work as an "instrumental" improviser, underscoring her ties to bebop, highlighting Gillespie and Parker in particular. Gillespie put it simply: "She listens and she does all our licks."[144] Fitzgerald confirmed that "to me it's been an education with Dizzy," and that listening to him was "actually the way I feel I learned how to what you call bop."[145] He had played an engagement with her orchestra (formerly Chick Webb's) in Boston that lasted for a few weeks in 1941, and the friendship deepened when she toured with his big band five years later.[146] The two became Lindy Hop dance partners during off-hours on the 1946 tour, which led to her Carnegie Hall debut with Gillespie and Parker on September 29, 1947.

Beginning in 1949, Fitzgerald became the sole singer with Norman Granz's touring concert jam sessions (JATP). Parker and Gillespie were in the troupe in the 1950s, and jams on "Perdido" and other tunes with Fitzgerald and Parker among a host of prominent players have been preserved.[147]

SWING TO COOL

Immediately preceding the "Jumpin' with Symphony Sid" reference, Fitzgerald paraphrases a passage from Denzil Best's "Move" [3:35–38], again pointing to a landmark piece, while representing yet another genre. As "Jumpin' with Symphony Sid" connected the repertoires of swing and bebop musicians, so did "Move" bring together those of bebop and cool (and, in some instances, swing) players in the late 1940s–1950s. Best was a drummer who achieved national acclaim in the 1940s through his work with tenor saxophonists Ben Webster, Coleman Hawkins, Illinois Jacquet, and (later) pianist George Shearing. "Move," along with "Bemsha Swing" (which he co-wrote with Thelonious Monk), is one of his best-known compositions. An up-tempo bebop tune with a 32-bar AABA form, it found its way into the discographies of Miles Davis (*Birth of the Cool*),[148] Charlie Parker,[149] Stan Getz,[150] and Count Basie,[151] among others.

For her late-1950s audiences, "Move" was probably best known through pianist John Lewis' arrangement for the Miles Davis Nonet on the *Birth of the Cool* sessions. These dates, the first to document Davis's association with arranger Gil Evans, sparked a major movement in arranging and performing practice in the early to mid-1950s, quickly focusing press attention on a burgeoning "West Coast cool" school of musicians who emulated the deep timbral palette and intricacy of the charts, as well as the introspective character of the solo work. Although the Nonet recordings were made in 1949 and 1950, it was not until February of 1957 that "Move" was issued as part of the entire collection, and the dates were given the title *Birth of the Cool*. Citing "Move," Fitzgerald marks the milestone 1957 release and, once more, demonstrates her acquaintance with an important musical development.[152] She recalled the passage elsewhere as well, including live performances of Goodman/Mundy/Christian's "Airmail Special," "Smooth Sailing," and in Duke Ellington's "Cottontail."[153]

"HUT SUT": NOVELTY NONSENSE

In a wordless paraphrase of Killion/McMichael/Owens' "The Hut Sut Song (A Swedish Serenade)," Fitzgerald alludes to a genre of hugely popular "nonsense" novelty tunes. With pseudo-Swedish lyrics ("Rawlson on the rillerah and a brawla, brawla sooit"), it had produced major hits, in 1941, for Freddy Martin, Horace Heidt, and the King Sisters; and, in 1942, for The Merry Macs, a vocal group perhaps best known for "Mairzy Doats," another example of the genre.[154] By 1958, "The Hut Sut Song" had shown up in films, such as *From Here to Eternity,* and some two dozen other swing and pop artists had recorded it, including Bing Crosby (with Connee Boswell, a musician Fitzgerald acknowledged as a major early influence), The (Nat) King Cole Trio, Glen Miller & His Orchestra, and Mel Tormé.

Fitzgerald interpolated the "Hut Sut" passage in other scat excursions, including 1957 concert performances of "Airmail Special," but the tune itself does not appear in her discography.[155] Nonetheless, it represents a genre in which she had made a mark with such ditties as her own "A-Tisket, A-Tasket," a piece she quoted from time to time in other solos. Interestingly, in "St. Louis Blues" she refrains from citing her own novelty work, pointing instead to that of others, including such jazz/swing musicians as Cole, Boswell, Miller, and Tormé. Perhaps she felt that "St. Louis Blues," her major (serious) blues work, was not an appropriate context for mentioning such frivolities on her own part; though, ironically, it apparently served well enough as a setting for Signifyin(g) on the frivolities of others. Her line in a later impromptu "talking" blues is telling: "Don't want to talk about 'Mack the Knife,' don't want to talk about this *nothing*" (her emphasis).[156]

"WHAT I'M SINGING": META-REFERENCE

For the fifth chorus [3:18–28] of her solo on the Rome date, Fitzgerald improvises a verse with lyrics that comment in a unique way on the referentiality of the performance. The commentary serves as a meta-reference, framing the improvisation and its far-flung interpolations, while reminding the audience of Handy's composition: "Guess these people wonder what I'm singing / Guess they wonder what I'm swinging / Believe it or not, it's still 'St. Louis Blues.'" The statement she makes in "St. Louis Blues" harks back to one of her earlier improvisations on Hamilton and Lewis's "How High the Moon," with Hank Jones, Ray Brown, and Roy Haynes at the Royal Roost.[157]

This 1949 comment is less explicit. She points to a distance between her solo and its compositional point of departure, but refrains from naming the piece. Instead, she seems to dare the audience to recognize the references. Switching from the words and melody of "How High the Moon" to Charlie Parker's "Ornithology," his melody on the same harmonic scheme, she scats the first twelve bars. To conclude the first half of the AB form, she then inserts a 4-bar break from Lee Brown's "Oop-Pop-A-Da," a vocal feature popularized by Dizzy Gillespie's orchestra.[158] She returns to "Ornithology" at the top of the second half of the form, singing, "No, these people don't know what I'm singing" to its melody in the ensuing two measures.

As later concert dates show, the "what I'm singing" meta-reference had a life beyond 1958. In other long scat solos on "How High the Moon" she would sing: "I guess these people wonder what I'm singing / Believe it or not, it's still 'How High the Moon.'"[159] Nor was the commentary limited to "St. Louis Blues" and "How High the Moon." She used it as a text for the bridge of Billy Strayhorn's "Take The 'A' Train" during a long scat solo on a Hollywood concert date: "I guess these people wonder what we're singing / We're still swinging and singing 'The A Train' / You better hurry, hurry, hurry, and get on board."[160]

"EVERYBODY'S TOGETHER AND WE'RE ALL FOR EACH OTHER": CONCLUSIONS

The many quotations and allusions in Ella Fitzgerald's "St. Louis Blues" performances foreground her as a singer of the blues, shedding light on ways in which her improvisatory practices grew out of and continued those of traditional blues musicians, and signifying/Signifyin(g) her mastery of the idiom. The expressive range and virtuosity she displays in these performances contribute to a sense that the piece served as a proving ground for her considerable blues acumen, a place to show her critics what she knew about and could do with the blues. She infused her renderings with timbral and tonal nuances, subtle changes in rhythmic feel, and bold contrasts in mood, tempo, key, and tessitura. She growled, shouted, cried, belted, screamed, and moaned. She scatted playfully over the harmonic changes in some instances and stayed within the traditional melodic mode of the blues in others.[161] She re-inflected stanzas from the early folk-blues to contemporary rhythm-and-blues and saturated the performances with arcane as well as widely-known references to performers, arrangers, and composers of both instrumental and vocal blues. In the 1958 "St. Louis Blues" solo alone, nearly half of her quotations are from 12-bar blues forms: "Smooth Sailing," "Swingin' Shepherd Blues," "Send for Me," "Jumpin' with Symphony Sid," and "Later."

Countless blues singers have woven other musicians' lines and texts together to create their own compositions and improvisations.[162] Numerous jazz musicians, especially instrumentalists, have interpolated borrowed materials in their compositions and improvisations. Fitzgerald's blues work is extraordinary for the way she seamlessly moves between and combines the types of quotation blues singers are known for with the kinds of interpolation associated with jazz instrumentalists, emphasizing connections between these types in a unique manner. Working with texts in some instances and melodies in others, she uses the vocalist's options in ways that stretch their creative potential, while concretizing conceptual ties between distinct but related idioms and genres of African American music. As she sang to a London audience during one blues improvisation (released as "Happy Blues"), "I've paid the dues, and I've got double trouble."[163] She paid her dues at least twice, coming to terms with and contributing to the blues vocal tradition as well as the instrumental tradition of the blues in jazz.

As feminist scholars have observed, women writers, African Americans particularly, have embraced intertextuality as a means of locating themselves in stories created by men; a way of contesting narratives in which they have been rendered invisible, of providing evidence of their presence.[164] Similarly, in "St. Louis Blues," Fitzgerald mobilizes the dialogic nature of the musical utterance to activate multiple voices and multiple stories, finding her place in history in the process. In a male-dominated field such as jazz, the historical positions of women are typically hard-won. In jazz, the situation is further complicated by a culture that is more precisely described as male-instrumentalist, and one in which singing is predominantly a female-gendered role.[165]

In this context, Fitzgerald's referentiality may be seen to have a political as well as an aesthetic dimension. Through the melodic interpolations in her 1958 birthday concert, she responds to (and affirms) the utterances of great male instrumentalists (Louis Armstrong, Dizzy Gillespie, Charlie Parker, Dexter Gordon, et al.), entering their discourse, thereby assuming her place among them. On one level, these interpolations provide us with familiar phrases that help us make sense of her abstract (scat) singing and may give us a kind of comic relief ("artistic relief" as pianist James Weidman puts it).[166] At a deeper level, they remind us of how she fits into the discourse.

Fitzgerald locates herself historically through reference, providing musical evidence to support her case. She seems to ask us to evaluate this position: does she stand among the great jazz artists with whose instrumental male "voices" she engages? As we have seen, and as Jimmy Heath, Phil Woods, Sonny Rollins, and other great male instrumentalists have indicated for decades, she does. Heath, for one, places her next to Parker and Gillespie in the jazz pantheon. By contrast, she and her female vocalist peers have only recently begun to appear in historical surveys widely used as college/conservatory textbooks. For example, noninstrumentalists, Fitzgerald among them, are noticeably absent until the seventh edition of the "#1 best-selling" jazz history text, published in 2000, which nods to a handful of singers (Fitzgerald, Vaughan, Holiday, and Bessie Smith) and appends a section on acid-jazz.[167] As historian Sherrie Tucker, Signifyin(g) on the well-known

Ellington tune, reminds us, "It don't mean a thing if it ain't in the history books."[168]

Fitzgerald summed up her position "with the horns" in a television interview with pianist André Previn: "Everybody's together and we're all for each other."[169] More specifically, she once said she "should have been a tenor man."[170] Her interpolations express this strong interest in the tenor and its players. In "St. Louis Blues," she quotes pieces written and performed by tenor saxophonists, such as Dexter Gordon's "The Chase," Arnett Cobb's "Smooth Sailing," and Lester Young's "Jumpin' with Symphony Sid." She also recalls tenor features and performances which place the tenor saxophone prominently in the arrangement, including Little Willie John's recording of "Fever," her own of "Later," and Billie Holiday and Lester Young's hit rendition of "Mean to Me." She alludes to other tenor players as well, Stan Getz and Illinois Jacquet among them. Her fascination with this instrument is captured beautifully in a 1940 photograph of her orchestra (formerly Chick Webb's) in the Rutgers Institute of Jazz Studies collection (Fig. 8.1). Taken in performance at the Savoy Ballroom in New York City, it shows the young singer not in front of the ensemble, but sitting in the sax section of her band, eyes fixed on the tenor player next to her.

Fig. 8.1. Ella Fitzgerald and Her Famous Orchestra in performance at the Savoy Ballroom in Harlem, 1940 (Institute of Jazz Studies, Rutgers University). Used by permission.

Her references demonstrate an interest in trumpeters as well, particularly Dizzy Gillespie and Louis Armstrong. Along with the great singer-trumpeters, she makes mention of Miles Davis through her *The Birth of the Cool* interpolation and Roy Eldridge through the "High Society" excerpt.[171] In referring to Gillespie and Armstrong, she draws attention both to their instrumental lines and to their vocalizations.

The text interpolations are no less diverse and remarkable than the melodic quotations. She dips deeply into the blues well with the "Mississippi River" and "peach" stanzas, simultaneously connecting her "St. Louis Blues" with other jazz and popular artists' performances of the piece. Her borrowings point to ties between the referents themselves as well: Helen Humes, Nellie Lutcher, and Maxine Sullivan; Helen Humes, Edith Wilson, and Lucille Hegamin; Louis Armstrong, Dexter Gordon, and Charlie Parker; Cousin Joe and Dizzy Gillespie. She directs our attention to specific sources, Guy Lombardo's and Maxine Sullivan's versions of "St. Louis Blues" among them, amplifying certain associations these sources carry, hushing others. Especially in her recordings from the 1960s, she turns Maxine Sullivan's "Mississippi River" stanza and Guy Lombardo's "peach" reference around with a Signifyin(g) spin, pointing them back in the direction of the folk-blues. She plays up the "evil woman" persona of the classic-blues queen associated with "He May Be Your Man." With "You Ain't So Such-a-Much," by contrast, she mutes Cousin Joe's anti-woman posture, transforming it deftly into the stance of a no-nonsense woman.

The persona she creates for herself by quilting together these borrowed stanzas has its own integrity. Very much in keeping with the folk-blues tradition, she works with a common situation and musical framework, but uses it to create a distinct blues piece and blues personality. Handy's song is about a woman whose lover has taken up with someone else; she has the blues as a result. As with other blues situations, the character can be and has been fleshed out in a number of ways.[172] Fitzgerald responds to the circumstances in her own way, coloring each performance with specific emotional nuances, but emphasizing certain qualities overall. This blues woman is nobody's patsy, in love or out. She has strong appetites and a sharp tongue, flaunts an undeniable appeal, and plays a two- or three-sided game at love.

The blues aura Fitzgerald creates for herself is powerful, sexual, and emotional. In the stanza from "He May Be Your Man," she strikes back at the other woman. To paraphrase: "You may think this man is now all yours, but let me be the first to tell you that he still wants what I've got and, despite impediments, still manages to come around for it on a daily basis." In the "peach" verse, she confronts her sometime lover, telling him his free ride is over. Again, to paraphrase: "If you are not willing to commit to this relationship," she warns, "then stay away from my bed." With "You Ain't So Such-a-Much," she underlines the point, letting him know in no uncertain terms: "Ain't gonna give you *nothin'*." In the final "Mississippi River" verse, however, she lets her hair down, admitting that, even though this man is no prize, she wants him, has to have him, and won't be satisfied until she does.

Fitzgerald's blues identity contests images created in contemporary presses, which portray her as girlish and lacking in earthiness and sensuality: a singer whose "voice, image, and body" were "never the site of sexual fantasy."[173] In refuting these representations, she affirms, embraces, and merges with the voices of classic-blues queens (Lucille Hegamin, Edith Wilson, and others) and of folk-blues singers (the multitude of blues men who sang the "peach" and "Mississippi River" stanzas). In collusion with her blues counterparts, she deploys her command of the idiom to flaunt precisely those attributes her critics claim she lacks: sexual power, a growling earthiness, and a womanly perspective on adult relationships. In the process, she helps us to locate her within the greater sphere of blues history.

Through her quotations and allusions, Fitzgerald situates herself both at the headwaters of jazz and on the banks of some of its more distant tributaries. She was never content to stay in one place musically. As she once put it, "it's not where you came from, it's where you're going."[174] She was one of the very few swing era musicians to move into the bop idiom at the end of the 1940s. As Stuart Nicholson observed, "Some, like Coleman Hawkins and Don Byas, almost succeeded in adapting to bop, but only one—Ella Fitzgerald— successfully made the transition. In a music dominated by males, this was no mean achievement."[175] Her "St. Louis Blues" recordings evidence this continual artistic growth, showing us that her musical influences stem not only from what she heard as a young singer developing a personal style, but also from the many people she heard as a mature artist, still growing and changing. They show us that she listened, and was affected by what she listened to throughout her career. She demonstrates an interest in popular currents (rhythm-and-blues and hits in general) as well as in music and musicians on the margins of the contemporary jazz mainstream (bebop and cool jazz).

An evident interest in modern trends, along with a desire to satisfy her public, led her to continually incorporate contemporary sounds, both in terms of repertoire and references. Over half of the quotations in the 1958 "St. Louis Blues" are from major hit songs of various genres, blues pieces and others. (See Table 8.2 for a chronological listing of hit references with peak position, artist, and label information.)[176] The interpolation of hit material

Table 8.2. Hit references in Fitzgerald's "St. Louis Blues"

Title	Artist(s)	Label/Issue #	Genre	Magnitude/Chart(s)*	Year
[High Society Rag]	Joe "King" Oliver	OKeh 4933	rag	#15	1924
Mean to Me	Ruth Etting	Columbia 1762-D	ballad	#3	1929
	Helen Morgan	Victor 21930		#11	1929
	Billie Holiday	Brunswick 7903		#7	1937
The Hut Sut Song	Freddy Martin	Bluebird 11147	novelty	#2	1941
(A Swedish Serenade)	Horace Heidt	Columbia 36138		#3	1941
	King Sisters	Bluebird 11154		#7	1941
	Merry Macs	Decca 3810		#13	1942
It Might As Well Be Spring	Dick Haymes	Decca 18706	ballad	#5	1945
	Margaret Whiting	Capitol 214		#6	1945
	Billy Williams [Fitzgerald also recorded]	Victor 1738		#4	1945
Smooth Sailing	Ella Fitzgerald [Arnett Cobb also recorded]	Decca 27693	blues	#3 (R&B)	1951
Only You	The Platters	Mercury 70633	ballad	#1 (R&B) #5 (pop)	1955
Fever	Little Willie John	King 4935	16-bar form	#1 (R&B) #24 (pop)	1956
Send for Me	Nat Cole	Capitol 3737	blues	#1 (R&B) #6 (pop)	1957
Swingin' Shepherd Blues	Moe Koffman	Jubilee 5311	blues	#23	1958 (current)
	Johnny Pate [Fitzgerald also recorded]	Federal 12312		#17 (R&B) #43 (pop)	1958 (current)

*Hits appeared on pop charts unless otherwise specified.

reflects the desire to give her "people" what they wanted to hear, which she frequently expressed on stage. The famous Berlin performance of Weill and Brecht's "Mack the Knife" is a case in point.[177] Before beginning the piece, she explained to her audience that she had recently added it to her repertoire "since it's so popular." Forgetting some of the words, she improvised a couple of verses, reiterating her reason for including the piece. "It's a hit tune," she sang, explaining that Bobby Darin and Louis Armstrong had each "made a record," so it was her turn to "make a wreck" of "Mack the Knife."

Through her many and varied references and the emotional and musical spin she gives each one, Fitzgerald invites us, in a singular and fascinating way, to come into her mental sound library and pore over musical snapshots in her bulging "family album." As Ellington put it in the introduction to his *Portrait of Ella Fitzgerald*: "We gather the material for our musical portrait of Ella Fitzgerald by allowing our imagination to browse through her family album. We see there many people, pretty people, strong people, sturdy, solid people—people and events of great dignity and distinction, and all with a beat!"[178]

Notes

1. This paper draws on the author's Ph.D. dissertation for The City University of New York, *Quotation and Reference in Jazz Performance: Ella Fitzgerald's 'St. Louis Blues,' 1957–79* (1998). I am deeply indebted to Stephen Blum, my dissertation advisor, and to the many scholars and musicians who contributed to the research, including Phil Woods, James E. Heath, David Evans, Richard Oppenheim, Tommy Flanagan, Barry Harris, Sheila Jordan, Phil Schaap, Bill Goodwin, Mike Melillo, Cameron Brown, Bob Dorough, Flo Handy Cohn, David Liebman, James Weidman, Belden Bullock, and Steve Gilmore. Special thanks to Richard Oppenheim, Waymon Samuel, and Joe Cooper of the American Society of Composers, Authors, and Publishers, for assisting with provenance of melodic and lyric fragments; to Dan Morgenstern, Vincent Pelote, Don Luck, and Ed Berger of the Institute of Jazz Studies at Rutgers University for helping to locate recorded sources; and to the staffs of the Music Research Division and the Rodgers and Hammerstein Archives of Recorded Sound at the New York Public Library for the Performing Arts. An early draft was read at a 1996 Jazz Research Roundtable hosted by the Rutgers Institute, at which time Lewis Porter, Dan Morgenstern, and James Maher made helpful comments.

2. Rainer Nolden, *Ella Fitzgerald: Ihr Leben, ihre Musik, ihre Schallplatten* (Gauting-Buchendorf: Oreos, 1986), 183; Sid Colin, *Ella: The Life and Times of Ella Fitzgerald* (London: Elm Tree Books, 1987[1986]), 60; John A. Tynan, "Ella Fitzgerald: Stairway to the Stars (Decca 74446), These Are the Blues (Verve 4062)," *Down Beat* 31/13 (1964): 28; Stuart Nicholson, *Ella Fitzgerald: A Biography of the First Lady of Jazz*

(New York: Charles Scribner's Sons, 1993 [discography by Phil Schaap]), 201; Will Friedwald, *Jazz Singing: America's Great Voices from Bessie Smith to Bebop and Beyond* (New York: Collier Books, 1992 [1990]), 145.

3. Albert Murray, *Stomping the Blues* (New York: McGraw-Hill, 1976), 87.

4. Henry Louis Gates Jr., *The Signifying Monkey: A Theory of African-American Literary Criticism* (New York and Oxford: Oxford University Press, 1988). Gates designates "Signifyin(g)" as a particularized spelling of "signifying" that captures African American intertextuality. I adopt his spelling in discussing varieties of "repetition, with a signal difference" that one encounters in jazz quotation (51).

5. Will Friedwald, *Jazz Singing,* 142.

6. Geoffrey Mark Fidelman, *First Lady of Song: Ella Fitzgerald for the Record* (New York: Citadel Press, 1994), 103. Friedwald (*Jazz Singing,* 142) reports that Fitzgerald herself made this comment to Kempton.

7. Conversation with the author, 6/20/97.

8. Nicholson, *Ella Fitzgerald,* 92.

9. Fidelman, *First Lady of Song,* 103.

10. Lewis Porter, "Some Problems in Jazz Research," *The Black Perspective in Music* 8, no. 2 (1988): 203–4.

11. Conversation with the author, 3/19/97.

12. The Fitzgerald "St. Louis Blues" studio sessions are Verve 10128, rec. 7/24/57; and Verve 4062, rec. 10/29/63. The live dates are Verve 835-454-2, rec. 4/24-5/58; Verve 4065, rec. 7/28/64; Status DSTS1013, rec. 9/23/66; Pablo 2308 234, rec. 7/21/71; and Pablo Today 2312 110-2, rec. 7/12/79.

13. Video Yesteryear 763, rec. 7/27/66. On television, she appeared in a couple of other performances of "St. Louis Blues" with singers, including a duet medley with Dinah Shore during a 1960 spot on NBC's *The Dinah Shore Chevy Show,* and a November 1978 trio with Pearl Bailey and Sarah Vaughan in a *Salute to Pearl Bailey* (Fidelman, *First Lady of Song,* 130, 243).

14. Phil Schaap, "Discography," in Nicholson, *Ella Fitzgerald,* 259-324. Unissued recordings were made on the following concert dates: 4/25/58, 8/10/58, "possibly" 4/5/61, 5/14/61, 7/29/64, and an unknown date in 1967 (Schaap, "Discography").

15. Status DSTS1013, rec. 9/23/66.

16. Fidelman, *First Lady of Song,* 246.

17. Conversation with the author, 5/23/97.

18. Ibid.

19. Gates, *The Signifying Monkey,* 51.

20. Ibid., 63.

21. As J. Peter Burkholder ("'Quotation' and Emulation: Charles Ives's Uses of His Models," *Musical Quarterly* 71, no. 1 [1985]: 1–26) has argued, musical borrowing has been central to musical practice in the U.S. and elsewhere for centuries. Regarding African American musical tradition, Gates (*The Signifying Monkey,* 63–64) goes so far as to say that improvisation, a *sine qua non* of jazz, rests ultimately on "nothing

more" than "repetition and revision," the creative restatement of materials and ideas, given a new twist in the retelling.

22. Nicholson, *Ella Fitzgerald*, 92.

23. For an exploration of quotation in various idioms, see David Metzer, *Quotation and Cultural Meaning in Twentieth-Century Music* (Cambridge: Cambridge University Press, 2003).

24. Examples include Verve 4041, rec. 2/13/60 [4:12-5]; and Pablo Live 2308-242, rec. ca. 1/66 [4:16-8].

25. Verve 8264, rec. 10/9/57 [1:04–7]; Verve 835 454-2, rec. 4/25/58 [1:48–51].

26. Brunswick 7699, rec. 6/30/36. The Wilson passage is mm. 14-15 [0:43–45].

27. Tax CD 3703-2, rec. 4/29/57; Verve 835-454-2, rec. 4/24-5/58. Singing bassist Slam Stewart is another musician Fitzgerald frequently parodied.

28. Conversation with the author, 5/23/97.

29. Richard Crawford, *Jazz Standards on Record, 1900–1942: A Core Repertory* (Chicago: Center for Black Music Research, Columbia College Chicago, 1992), 10.

30. Joel Whitburn, *Joel Whitburn's Pop Memories (1890–1954)* (Menomonee Falls, Wisc.: Record Research, 1986).

31. Al Bernard made three other recordings of "St. Louis Blues" (Brunswick 2062, rec. 11/20; Brunswick 3547, rec. 4/5/27; OKeh 40962, rec. 11/14/27).

32. Handy recorded "St. Louis Blues" on two other occasions (Paramount 20098, rec. 1/22; and Varsity 8163, rec. 12/26/39).

33. Lombardo had recorded an earlier version of "St. Louis Blues" (Columbia 50256-D, rec. 10/1/30).

34. This very long list includes a half dozen other versions by Louis Armstrong (Victor 24320, rec. 4/26/33; Brunswick A-9683, rec. 10/34; Jazz Society AA550, rec. 2/8/47; Columbia 5-2012, rec. 7/12/54; Decca DL8169, rec. 1/2/55; Columbia CL1077, rec. 7/14/56), along with recordings by Bing Crosby with the Duke Ellington Orchestra (Brunswick 20105, rec. 2/11/32), numerous other Ellington recordings (including Jazz Guild 1006, rec. 9/7/40; Palm 30-11, rec. 11/7/40; Sunbeam 214, rec. 9/6/41; Victor 20-2327, rec. 9/13/46; London HMP5036, rec. 6/9/47; Columbia CL1198, rec. 4/2–3/58; Foxy 9003/9004, rec. 7/4/59), Ethel Waters (Brunswick 6521, rec. 12/23/32, among other issues), Ray Noble's orchestra (Victor 25082, rec. 6/10/35), Stephane Grappelli [Stephane Grappelly] and Django Reinhardt (Decca 23032, rec. 9/30/35), Count Basie and his Orchestra featuring Jimmy Rushing (Jazz Archives JA16, rec. 2/8/37, among other issues), Mildred Bailey (Vocalion 4801, rec. 9/29/38), Billie Holiday (OKeh 6064, rec. 10/15/40), Maxine Sullivan (Victor 25895, rec. 6/29/38; Columbia 36341, rec. 5/1/40; Decca 4154, rec. 6/17/41; Victor 27926, rec. 2/11/42), Dizzy Gillespie (Victor LJM 10009, rec. 4/14/49), Billy Eckstine (MGM 11573, rec. 7/9/53), and Nellie Lutcher (OKeh 7030, rec. 8/25/53), among many others. Walter Bruyninckx, *60 Years of Recorded Jazz* (Mechelen, Belgium: Bruyninckx, 1980?); Walter Bruyninckx, *Jazz: The Vocalists, 1917–1986; Singers and Crooners* (Mechelen, Belgium: Bruyninckx, 1988?); Walter Bruyninckx, *70 Years of Recorded Jazz* (Mechelen, Belgium: Bruyninckx,

1991–?); Brian Rust, *Jazz Records, 1897–1942,* 4th ed. (New Rochelle: Arlington House, 1978).

35. Other musicians and entertainers appearing in the film were Teddy Buckner, Red Callender, Lee Young, George Washington, Ruby Dee, Juano Hernandez, and Billy Preston. Nelson Riddle was conductor and arranger.

36. The Nat Cole Trio and Nelson Riddle Orchestra also recorded "St. Louis Blues" for Capitol records (Capitol W993, rec. 1/29-31/58).

37. W. C. Handy, *Father of the Blues: An Autobiography* (New York: Collier Books, 1970 [1941]), 122.

38. W. C. Handy, ed., *Blues: An Anthology* (New York: Albert and Charles Boni, 1926), 31-2.

39. "My man's got a heart like a rock cast in the sea." Ibid., 25.

40. Ibid.

41. On The Royal Canadians' 1939 issue of "St. Louis Blues" (Decca 2478), the vocal performance is credited to "the ensemble." James T. Maher, co-founder of the Institute of Jazz Studies at Rutgers University, reported that Lombardo's band was hugely popular among the African American community in New York City, setting the all-time attendance record at the Savoy Ballroom. After World War II, Maher reports (conversation with the author, 12/11/96), Russell Sanjek was looking for good pressings of Louis Armstrong recordings and other jazz releases to reissue on his Hot Record Society label. Sanjek rang doorbells in Harlem, inquiring about residents' jazz collections. He turned up so many of Lombardo's releases, and so few of Armstrong's, that he gave up this method after about a week.

42. Palm 30-11, rec. 11/7/40. Ellington first recorded "St. Louis Blues" with Bing Crosby, who did not use the "peach" stanza, in 1932 (Brunswick 20105, rec. 2/11/32). From 1940 to 1973, the piece was an Ellington staple, evidenced by no less than forty-three recordings, the majority made live and unissued (W. E. Timmer, *Ellingtonia: The Recorded Music of Duke Ellington and His Sidemen,* 3d ed. [Metuchen, NJ, and London: Institute of Jazz Studies and Scarecrow Press, 1988]). After Crosby, Ivie Anderson—in 1940—was the first singer to appear on Ellington's "St. Louis Blues" dates.

43. David Evans, *Big Road Blues: Tradition and Creativity in the Folk Blues* (New York: Da Capo Press, 1987 [1982]).

44. Ibid., 61.

45. These include Garrett and Wand's "Dallas Blues" (Handy, *Blues: An Anthology*), Frank Stokes' "Half Cup of Tea" and "Mr. Crump Don't Like It" (Paramount 12531, rec. 8/27; Paramount 12552, rec. 9/27), Walter 'Buddy Boy' Hawkins' "Number Three Blues" (Paramount 12475, rec. ca. 4/27), Jim Jackson's "Kansas City Blues" (Vocalion 1144, rec. 10/10/27), William Harris' "Hot Time Blues" (Gennett 6707, rec. 10/10/28), Blind Lemon Jefferson's "Peach Orchard Mama" (Paramount 12801, rec. 8/29), Joe Linthecome's "Pretty Mama Blues" (Gennett 7131, rec. 11/20/29), Bumble Bee Slim's [Amos Easton's] "Squalling Panther Blues" and "Lemon Squeezing Blues"

(Bluebird B-5517, B-6649, rec. 3/23/34; Vocalion 03005, rec. 7/11/35), Art McKay's "She Squeezed My Lemon" (Decca 7364, rec. 4/30/37), and Sonny Boy Williamson's "Until My Love Comes Down" and "Black Panther Blues" (Bluebird B-7576, rec. 3/13/38; Bluebird 34-0701, rec. 12/11/41). Other "peach" variants are found in Trixie Smith's "Sorrowful Blues" (Paramount 12208, rec. 5/24), Memphis Jug Band's "Peaches in the Springtime" (Victor 21657, rec. 2/13/28), Edward Thompson's "Showers of Rain Blues" (Paramount 13018, rec. ca. 10/23/29), and Joe Williams' "Peach Orchard Mama" (Bluebird B-7770, rec. 6/17/38; Bluebird B-8774, rec. 3/27/41) and "Little Leg Woman" (Bluebird B-5900, rec. 2/25/35).

46. Gennett 6707, rec. 10/10/28.

47. Fitzgerald's 1963 studio recording of "St. Louis Blues" (Verve 4062) is the only date not to include the "Mississippi River" couplet. The 1964 concert version (Verve 4065), which re-creates many features of the 1963 arrangement, includes it, but not in a stop-time format.

48. Handy, *Blues: An Anthology*, 3.

49. Ibid., 106. Michael Taft lists several blues musicians recording in the early 1930s who used close variants of the text in their compositions, including Ruby Glaze's "Lonesome Day Blues" (Victor 23353, rec. 2/22/32), Big Bill Broonzy's "Mississippi River Blues" (Banner 32670, rec. 3/23/34), and Hosea Woods' "Wolf River Blues" (Victor 23272, rec. 11/24/30). Two other variants of the couplet ("deep and wide"/"side to side") appear in Joe McCoy's "That Will Be Alright" (Columbia 14439-D, rec. 6/18/29) and Mississippi John Hurt's "Got the Blues Can't Be Satisfied" (Okeh 8724, rec. 12/18/29). Michael Taft, *Blues Lyric Poetry: A Concordance*, 3 vols. (New York and London: Garland Publishing, 1984).

50. Victor 25895, rec. 6/29/38 [Thornhill]; Columbia 36341, rec. 5/1/40 [Kirby]; Decca 4154, rec. 6/17/41 [Kirby]. The stanza shows up in recordings of "St. Louis Blues" by Kansas City blues "shouter" Big Joe Turner, but not until very late in his career (Atlantic 1234 [K.C. 108], rec. 3/7/56, does not include it, while Telefunken 28572, rec. 5/23/81, and Southland SLP-13, rec. 5/18/83, do).

51. Dempsey Travis, *An Autobiography of Black Jazz* (Chicago: Urban Research Institute, 1983), 454.

52. Swing House SWH8, rec. ca. 7/45.

53. Whitney Balliett, *American Singers: 27 Portraits in Song* (New York and Oxford: Oxford University Press, 1988), 53.

54. Rushing sang "St. Louis Blues" with the Basie band but did not include the "Mississippi River" couplet on recorded versions (Jazz Archives JA16, rec. 2/8/37; Swing House SWH41, rec. 7/5/43). On the 1937 recording, a live broadcast, the band plays a truncated arrangement that segues into Basie's closing theme; it is impossible to say how the piece would have ended, but the verse is also absent from the 1943 recording, a complete performance of the tune.

55. "Be-ba-ba-le-ba" (Philo/Aladdin 106, rec. 1945) and "Million Dollar Secret" (Modern 20-779, rec. 8/50).

56. Nicholson, *Ella Fitzgerald,* 102.

57. Linda Dahl, *Stormy Weather: The Music and Lives of a Century of Jazzwomen* (New York: Limelight Editions, 1992 [1984]), 233.

58. OKeh 7030, rec. 8/25/53.

59. As noted above, Lutcher and Humes were acquaintances (at least in the latter part of their careers). If their friendship predated 1953, it would strengthen the possibility that Lutcher got the "Mississippi River" idea from Humes. However, her version shares more (melodic and textual) features with Sullivan's than Humes', and—like Sullivan—she took the piece in the key of C (not B-flat).

60. Dahl, *Stormy Weather,* 225.

61. Sally Placksin, *American Women in Jazz: 1900 to the Present* (New York: Wide View, 1982), 122.

62. Arto 9129, rec. 1/21.

63. Arto 9045, rec. ca. 11/20.

64. OKeh 4169, rec. 8/10/20.

65. Hegamin's "He May Be Your Man" recordings include Arto 9129 (rec. ca. 1/21); Puritan 1108 and Paramount 20108 (rec. 2/26/22); and Cameo 287 (rec. ca. 1/23). Bruyninckx, *60 Years of Recorded Jazz,* indicates that different takes of the tune from the 2/26/22 session were released on two contemporary labels; matrix 997-1 was for Puritan and 997-2, -4 were for Paramount. As was common practice at the time, her first sides for Arto were copied for eight labels (Derrick Stewart-Baxter, *Ma Rainey and the Classic Blues Singers* [New York: Stein and Day, 1970], 16–17, 19). A version of "Arkansas Blues" (Arto 9053, rec. ca. 2/21) appears on between nine and eleven issues. Daphne Duval Harrison, *Black Pearls: Blues Queens of the 1920s* (New Brunswick and London: Rutgers University Press, 1988), 230; Robert M. W. Dixon, John Godrich, and Howard Rye, *Blues & Gospel Records 1890–1943,* 4th ed. (Oxford: Clarendon, 1997), 373.

66. Hegamin credited herself with popularizing "St. Louis Blues" in Chicago (ca. 1914–18) by using it as one of her "feature" numbers (Stewart-Baxter, *Ma Rainey,* 19). She did not record it, however, until quite late in her career (Bluesville BVLP1052, rec. 8/16/61). Because Fitzgerald was so young when Hegamin's career was blossoming, it is only remotely possible that she would have been aware of Hegamin's live versions of "St. Louis Blues"; if so, it could have influenced her to associate "He May Be Your Man" with "St. Louis Blues" as a tribute to Hegamin's repertoire.

67. Columbia A3653, rec. 6/9/22, and Delmark DS637, rec. 4/16/75.

68. Harrison, *Black Pearls,* 177.

69. Columbia A3558, rec. 1/22/22.

70. New Orleans–based Creole ballad and blues singer Lizzie Miles is one of the better-known contemporary singers to feature "He May Be Your Man" in her shows (Stewart-Baxter, *Ma Rainey,* 25). Pearl Bailey recorded it as well (Coral 61487, rec. 11/53; Coral 57162, rec. 2/1/54).

71. Philo/Aladdin 105, rec. 8/45.

72. Classic Jazz CJ120, rec. 8/73; Jazzology J55, rec. 9/74; Columbia PC33488, rec. 2/18/75. Another blues by Humes, entitled "He May Be Yours" (Discovery 520, rec. 5/9/50), offers a text that is a loose variant of "He May Be Your Man."

73. Dahl, *Stormy Weather*, 230.

74. Philo/Aladdin 106, rec. 1945.

75. Joe Williams seems to have gotten the idea from Humes as well. He borrowed more than one verse from her "He May Be Your Man" to create his own blues, which he called "Who She Do" (Fantasy F9441, rec. 8/7/73).

76. Fitzgerald interpolates "You Ain't So Such-a-Much" in the 1957, 1958, and 1966 "St. Louis Blues" performances, three of the five that include "He May Be Your Man."

77. Pleasant "Cousin Joe" Joseph and Harriet J. Ottenheimer, *Cousin Joe: Blues from New Orleans* (Chicago and London: University of Chicago Press, 1987), 110, 115.

78. Ibid., 120.

79. Gotham 501, rec. ca. 3/46.

80. Vogue V5136, rec. 4/11/52.

81. Dizzy Gillespie with Al Fraser, *To BE, or not . . . to BOP* (New York: Da Capo Press, 1979), 294.

82. Leslie Gourse, *Louis' Children: American Jazz Singers* (New York: William Morrow, 1984), 13.

83. Verve 835-454-2, rec. 4/24–5/58. The compact disc jacket erroneously lists it as her 40th birthday concert.

84. On a few of the tracks—not including "St. Louis Blues"—she was joined by Oscar Peterson, Herb Ellis, and Ray Brown.

85. Nicholson, *Ella Fitzgerald*, 182.

86. Verve 10128, rec. 7/24/57.

87. Pablo 2308 234, rec. 7/21/71.

88. This is not an exhaustive list, and excludes more ambiguous allusions (for example, James/Lawrence/Pestalozza's "Ciribiribin" [2:42–44]).

89. Dial 1017, rec. 6/12/47.

90. Conversation with the author, 3/19/97.

91. Crawford, *Jazz Standards on Record*, 28–29.

92. Nat Shapiro and Nat Hentoff, *Hear Me Talkin' to 'Ya: The Story of Jazz as Told by the Men Who Made It* (New York: Dover Publications, 1966 [1955]), 23–24; William J. Schafer, "Breaking Into 'High Society': Musical Metamorphosis in Early Jazz," *Journal of Jazz Studies* 2, no. 2 (1975): 53–60. Gunther Schuller (*Early Jazz: Its Roots and Musical Development* [New York and Oxford: Oxford University Press, 1968], 183, 195) credits another New Orleans clarinetist, George Bacquet, with having transcribed the passage for clarinet.

93. OKeh 4933, rec. 6/22/23.

94. Columbia 2688-D, rec. 12/23/30.

95. Annette Miller in Nicholson, *Ella Fitzgerald*, 9.

96. Gordon recorded over forty sides with Armstrong from May to October 1944.

97. Savoy M9-12079, rec. 11/26/45. Parker's interpolation of "High Society" in "KoKo" is transcribed in Thomas Owens, "Charlie Parker: Techniques of Improvisation" (Ph.D. dissertation, University of California, Los Angeles, 1974), vol. 2, 219 [chorus 2a, mm. 1–2]. See also Owens' *Bebop: The Music and Its Players* (New York and Oxford: Oxford University Press, 1995), x.

98. Keynote 607, rec. 1/24/44.

99. Owens, "Charlie Parker," vol. 1, 25.

100. With Sir Charles Thompson and His All-Stars, Gordon and Parker recorded four cuts together (Spotlite [E] SPJ 150, rec. 9/4/45), two months prior to the waxing of Parker's landmark "KoKo" solo.

101. Like Dexter Gordon, Jay Peters—a tenor saxophonist with the Lionel Hampton band—reinforced the "High Society" reference in the opening measures of his solo on a live recording of "The Chase" (Columbia CL711, rec. 7/22/54). Eldridge seems to have combined Armstrong's and Parker's approaches in his "St. Louis Blues." Like Parker, Gordon, and Fitzgerald, he quoted it to begin both phrase and chorus, but—like Armstrong—he brought it in toward the end of his improvisation.

102. Decca 18706, Capitol 214, and Victor 1738, respectively.

103. Decca DL8155, rec. 4/1/55.

104. Verve 4052, rec. 5/19/61.

105. "Oh, Lady Be Good" (Verve 8264, rec. 10/9/57 [1:19–21]), "Swingin' Shepherd Blues" (Verve 10130, rec. 3/19/58 [1:41–43]), "I Can't Give You Anything But Love" (Pablo 2310-829, rec. 1/8/74 [4:02–5]), and Duke Ellington and Sid Kuller's "Bli-Blip" (Verve 4010-4, rec. 6/27/57 [0:18–22]).

106. Pablo 2310-711, rec. 4/11/74 (mm. 7–8 of the new feel [ca. 2:16–21]).

107. On a recording several months earlier (Pablo 2310-829, rec. 1/8/74) Fitzgerald used a similar arrangement of "The Man I Love" (initial rubato section followed by Latin-feel voice/drum interlude and full ensemble sections), but did not interpolate "It Might As Well Be Spring."

108. Morgan (Victor 21930, rec. 3/6/29) and Etting (Columbia 1762-D, rec. 3/11/29).

109. Brunswick 7903, rec. 5/11/37.

110. Pablo 2310 759-2, rec. 5/19/75.

111. Decca 29198, rec. 6/4/54.

112. Verve 815147-1, rec. 9/17/54. Prior to recording "Later," she "worked it up" on live dates with JATP (Nicholson, *Ella Fitzgerald,* 145). Tenor saxophonist Sam Taylor was featured in these performances.

113. "Stompin' at the Savoy" (Verve 6026, rec. 9/29/57 [5:12–16]) and "Joe Williams' Blues" (Verve 837 758-2, rec. 2/11/61 [3:21–26]).

114. Gunther Schuller, *The Swing Era: The Development of Jazz, 1930–1945* (New York, Oxford: Oxford University Press, 1989), 206.

115. Billie Holiday also recorded a number of sides with Oliver's orchestra during that same period. Decca scheduled sessions for both singers during the month of September 1949. Holiday's September 30 date featured two duets with Armstrong (Decca 24785).

116. "How High the Moon" (Pablo 2310-751-2, rec. 7/17/75 [2:38–40]) and "Rockin' in Rhythm" (Pablo 2310-829, rec. 1/8/74 [3:49–50]).

117. Aladdin 163, rec. 2/18/47. In an interview with Phil Schaap, pianist Sadik Hakim [Argonne Thornton] said that he had improvised the "Jumpin' with Symphony Sid" melody during the 1947 recording session (Aladdin 163) but that the song was released with credit to Lester Young instead. Lewis Porter, *Lester Young* (Boston: Twayne, 1985), 110, n.2.

118. Victor LJM 1009, rec. 4/14/49.

119. *Live at Storyville*, Roost LP 411, rec. 10/28/51.

120. Prestige 821, rec. 12/12/52.

121. Ira Gitler, *Swing to Bop: An Oral History of the Transition in Jazz in the 1940s* (New York: Oxford University Press, 1985), 6.

122. Fitzgerald's *Royal Roost Sessions* documents a jam at the club on "How High the Moon" in which she and Young participated (Cool n' Blue C&B CD 122, rec. 11/27/48).

123. King 4935, rec. 1956. In November of 1957, "Fever" was recorded by the Ray Peterson–Shorty Rogers Orchestra, featuring the Jack Halloran Singers. This version was not a charted success but may have been known to Fitzgerald, as Rogers was a prominent figure in the influential "West Coast cool school." Peggy Lee sang "Fever" as well, recording it for Capitol records in 1958 (F-3998 and EAP 1-1052). It became a big hit for Lee that year and has since remained associated with her. However, Lee did not record the tune until June of 1958 (it hit the charts in August), several months after Fitzgerald's 1958 "Fever" reference in "St. Louis Blues."

124. The term "rhythm-and-blues" (R&B) was coined by *Billboard* in 1949 to replace "race records" as a category charting sales in predominantly African American communities. The rubric initially took in a variety of genres; R&B charts in the early to mid-fifties were indicative of a range of contemporary African American popular tastes.

125. Verve 837 758-2, rec. 2/11/61 [2:30–50].

126. Columbia 39040, rec. 12/4/50.

127. Decca 27693, rec. 6/26/51. Composer-arranger Ray Charles (b. 9/13/18) led this date. Also in the ensemble were Arnold Fishkin on bass and Jimmy Crawford on drums.

128. Other artists who recorded "Smooth Sailing" include trumpeter Cootie Williams (Mercury 8073, rec. 1947) and Count Basie and his Orchestra with Lester Young (Unique Jazz 004, rec. 1/8/53).

129. Nicholson, *Ella Fitzgerald*, 135.

130. *Jazz at the Philharmonic Live in Tokyo* (Pablo 22620-104, rec. 11/4-9/53), *Ella in Hamburg* (Verve MGV 4069, rec. 3/26/65), and *Newport Jazz Festival Live* (CBS 68279, rec. 7/5/73).

131. Tax CD 3703-2, rec. 4/29/57 [1:03–6].

132. Clef MGC 743, rec. 6/25/56 [2:01–3].

133. Malcolm X and Alex Haley, *The Autobiography of Malcolm X* (New York: Ballentine Books, 1993 [1964]), 113. Quincy Jones is cited in Lewis Porter and Michael Ullman, *Jazz from Its Origins to the Present* (Englewood Cliffs, N.J.: Prentice Hall, 1993), 356.

134. Decca 23956, rec. 10/4/45. "Flying Home" had been in her live repertoire since 1943 (Nicholson, *Ella Fitzgerald,* 83).

135. Jubilee 5311, rec. 1957.

136. Druss (Federal 12312, rec. 1958) and Rose (MGM 12608, rec. 1958).

137. Verve 10130, rec. 3/19/58.

138. Pablo 2310-751-2, rec. 7/17/75 [6:02–6].

139. Capitol 3737, rec. 6/17/57.

140. Verve 8264, rec. 10/9/57 [3:13–17].

141. Mercury 70633, rec. 1955.

142. Jazz Live BLJ 8035, rec. 12/4/48 [1:17–20]; and a variant rec. 11/27/48 [1:35–38].

143. Prestige 24024, rec. 5/15/53. Parker also used the "Chinese" idea in a live performance of his "Cool Blues" (Stash CD-10, rec. 1/18/54 [1:00–4]).

144. Gillespie, *To BE, or not,* 350.

145. Ibid., 273.

146. Although they had met in 1945, she became romantically involved with Ray Brown, who was later to become her husband, on tour with Gillespie's band in 1946.

147. For example, Verve 837 141–42, rec. 9/18/49. Parker and Gillespie's use of the "Chinese" idea in the 1953 concert brings up the common practice of quoting from a preceding soloist's improvisation. In this context, quotation has a quality of immediate "addressivity"; one performer "speaks" directly to another (Mikhail M. Bakhtin, "The Problem of Speech Genres," in *Speech Genres and Other Late Essays* [Austin: University of Texas Press, 1986], 60–102). While Fitzgerald responds across a greater expanse of time—nearly a decade—her allusion nonetheless highlights this dialogic aspect. She and her band engage in this sort of communication—picking up and returning ideas from one another—elsewhere during the 1958 birthday concert ("Stompin' at the Savoy" [2:15, 3:47, 6:06], "Just Squeeze Me" [0:30, 0:51, 2:33, 2:44]).

148. Capitol LP T-762, rec. 1/21/49.

149. Charlie Parker Records CPR 701A, rec. 6/30/50.

150. Roost LP420, rec. 10/28/51; Session Disc 108, rec. 8/9/52; Alto AL704, rec. 8/16/52. Getz recorded "Jumpin' With Symphony Sid" and "Move" on the same date (10/28/51). The fact that Fitzgerald, like Getz, put the two tunes together—he, as

complete performances; she, as interpolations—may be coincidence, or she may have been listening to him. Several months earlier, she and Getz had been featured together on an album arranged by Frank DeVol entitled *Like Someone in Love* (Verve 6000/4004, rec. 10/15,28/57).

151. Giants of Jazz LP1002, rec. 1/17/51; Verve 89177, rec. 1/11/56.

152. "Move" does not appear in Fitzgerald's discography.

153. "Airmail Special" (Verve 8231, rec. 8/15/56 [0:55–56]), "Smooth Sailing" (Verve MGV 4069, rec. 3/26/65 [1:18–19]), and "Cottontail" (Verve V6-4070, rec. 10/18–20/65 [1:38–39]).

154. See Table 8.2.

155. Verve 8231, rec. 8/15/56 [2:46–2:52]. Gene E. Davis, *Ella Fitzgerald: Forever Ella* (New York: A&E Television Networks AAE-17767), 2000 [video of 1957 concert in Brussels].

156. Ella Fitzgerald, "Happy Blues" (Pablo 2310-711-2, rec. 4/11/74) [2:11–2:15].

157. Session Disc SES 105, rec. 4/15/49 [2:35–37].

158. Victor 20-2480, rec. 8/22/47.

159. Verve 4041, rec. 2/13/60 [4:44–50]; Pablo 98.819-2, rec. ca. 1/66 [4:48–54].

160. Verve 4052, rec. 5/21/61 [ca. 5:37–45].

161. Fitzgerald's 1963 "St. Louis Blues" is an excellent example of her use of traditional blues mode.

162. In traditional blues practice, borrowing is well documented. David Evans (*Big Road Blues*, 60) describes ways in which blues musicians "string various traditional stanzas together." Jeff Todd Titon (*Early Downhome Blues: A Musical & Cultural Analysis*, 2d ed. [Chapel Hill: University of North Carolina Press, 1994 {1977}], 38–39) writes of "fitting together stanzas" by reworking traditional material and "alternating" it with "borrowed" verses and new lyrics.

163. Pablo 2310-711-2, rec. 4/11/74.

164. Mary O'Connor, "Subject, Voice, and Women in Some Contemporary Black American Women's Writing," in *Feminism, Bakhtin, and the Dialogic*, ed. Dale Bauer and Susan Jaret McKinstry (Albany: State University of New York Press, 1991), 115. See also Elaine Showalter, "Piecing and Writing," *The Poetics of Gender* (New York: Columbia University Press, 1986), 223–47.

165. See Sherrie Tucker, *Swing Shift: 'All-Girl' Bands of the 1940s* (Durham and London: Duke University Press, 2000); Burton Peretti, *The Creation of Jazz: Music, Race, and Culture in Urban America* (Urbana and Chicago: University of Illinois Press, 1992); Dahl, *Stormy Weather*.

166. Conversation with the author, 5/23/97.

167. Mark C. Gridley, *Jazz History: Styles and Analysis*, 7th ed. (Upper Saddle River, N.J.: Prentice Hall, 2000). Earlier editions cite "space limitations" as justification for a categorical omission of singers (Ibid., 6th ed. [1997], xi).

168. Tucker, *Swing Shift*, 1–29.

169. Video reproduced in Charlotte Zwerin, *Ella Fitzgerald: Something to Live For* (New York: Educational Broadcasting Corp., 1999).

170. Carter Harman in Fidelman, *First Lady of Song,* 70.

171. Her connections with Eldridge are deeper than those with Davis; she both toured and recorded with Eldridge under Norman Granz's auspices. Eldridge was known among musicians and fans as "Little Jazz," and she recorded his self-titled instrumental composition, "Little Jazz," on two occasions: once with Marty Paich's group and arrangement (take 1—Verve [J] J28J-25118; take 2—Verve 6019/4021, both rec. 11/23/58), and again with Ray Brown in 1989 (Pablo PACD 2310-938-2, rec. 3/15,16,20,22/89).

172. For feminist perspectives on this process and its implications, see Hazel Carby, "'It Just Be's Dat Way Sometime': The Sexual Politics of Women's Blues," *Unequal Sisters: A Multi-Cultural Reader in U.S. Women's History,* ed. Ellen Carol DuBois and Vicki L. Ruiz (New York: Routledge, 1990), 238–49; and Angela Y. Davis, *Blues Legacies and Black Feminism: Gertrude "Ma" Rainey, Bessie Smith, and Billie Holiday* (New York: Pantheon Books, 1998).

173. Francis Davis, "One Scats, the Other Doesn't," *The New York Times Book Review* (9/25/94), 14.

174. Nicholson, *Ella Fitzgerald,* 243.

175. Ibid., 97.

176. Whitburn, *Joel Whitburn's Pop Memories,* 1986; Joel Whitburn, *Joel Whitburn's Top Pop Singles: 1955–1986* (Menomonee Falls, Wisc.: Record Research), 1987; Joel Whitburn, *Joel Whitburn's Top R & B Singles: 1942–88* (Menomonee Falls, Wisc.: Record Research), 1988; Joel Whitburn, *Joel Whitburn's Pop Hits: 1940–1954* (Menomonee Falls, Wisc.: Record Research), 1994.

177. Verve 314 519 564-2, rec. 2/13/60 [1:41–2:07, 2:36–3:02].

178. Verve 4010-4, rec. 6/24-7/57. E. K. (Duke) Ellington, *Music Is My Mistress* (New York: Da Capo Press, 1973), 236.

9

Beyond the Mushroom Cloud

A DECADE OF DISILLUSION IN
BLACK BLUES AND GOSPEL SONG

BOB GROOM

The commercial issuing of African American blues and gospel recordings effectively began in 1920 (a very few religious recordings were made before that date).[1] Although the gospel songs mostly stressed the devotional element in their lyrics, and many were in fact traditional spirituals, there was an increasing trend toward reflecting social issues. Some of the powerful and popular singing preachers (notably Rev. J. M. Gates and Reverend A. W. Nix) commented on all sorts of issues, from women's hairstyles and the length of their skirts to the risks of flying in airplanes. Similarly, although the majority of blues song lyrics revolved around the male/female relationship (albeit more candidly than the popular songs of the day), many examined other themes such as alcoholism, hunger, loneliness, and wanderlust. The Depression generated many hard-time blues and there was an increasing awareness of politics in song lyrics. Particularly interesting were the recordings devoted to praising President Franklin Delano Roosevelt, whose revolutionary politics rescued the United States from economic disaster.

America's involvement in World War I triggered a number of blues and gospel recordings about the conflict or that made some reference to it; most were made in the 1920s, several years after the war had ended. But even as late as the 1960s artists like Joe Calicott, from Mississippi, and South Carolina songster Pink Anderson could still recall (and record) songs about the Kaiser and the fighting in France. Many more recordings in both genres were made about World War II, and this considerable body of song lyrics has received a certain amount of critical attention in print. In general, after some initial ambivalence about the prewar military draft, these songs supported the war effort enthusiastically, viewing Hitler, Mussolini, and Tojo as arch villains. Some, however, expressed discomfort over domestic rationing and fears that women would be unfaithful to their men in service.[2]

Less well known are related songs of the interwar years, such as Sister Cally Fancy's prophetic two-part 1930 recording of "Death Is Riding Through the Land" (Vocalion 1663), and those that reflect on the events of the decade following World War II, which provide the topic for this article.[3] In order to set the scene for examination of that time through contemporary recordings, we need first to refer to the later stages of the war.

In April 1945, the storming of Berlin by Allied forces prompted Hitler's suicide and the surrender of the German armies. The war in Europe was over; in Asia, Japan fought on alone, though its overseas empire was crumbling. By the summer, Japan was fiercely defending the homeland, and it seemed that many more lives must be lost before it was defeated. Memphis blues singer Willie Borum, singing retrospectively in 1961, expressed the fears of soldiers who had survived in Europe only to face transfer to the Pacific theater of war, when he stated in his "Overseas Blues" (Bluesville BVLP 1034) that he did not want to go because "I had so much trouble with them Germans, don't send me over in Tokyo." In July 1945, America tested an atomic bomb at Los Alamos, New Mexico, and the Allies called on Japan to surrender or face complete destruction. Japan was now on its knees but still had two million men under arms. It rejected the ultimatum, confident that it could not be successfully invaded, its warlords unaware of the immense destructive power of nuclear fission.

President Harry Truman (who had succeeded FDR on the latter's death on April 12) and British Prime Minister Winston Churchill considered the huge Allied casualties that would have been inevitable and made the fateful decision: on August 6 an atomic bomb was dropped on the city of Hiroshima. But Japan still procrastinated, its fanatical military leaders convincing Emperor Hirohito that they must fight on to the finish. Three days later, a second bomb destroyed the city of Nagasaki. The devastation was immense, the loss of life horrific. Seventy thousand died at Hiroshima, forty thousand at Nagasaki. Thousands more were injured and many died later from the effects of radiation. Japan finally surrendered on August 14. The surrender terms were signed on September 2, 1945, and soon many American troops were on their way home, expecting homes and jobs fit for heroes, just as troops had after World War I. And just like their predecessors, many of them—particularly the black soldiers—were doomed to disappointment. In a January 1946 recording, "I Got My Discharge Papers" (Savoy LP 2223),

Joe Turner stated that during the war he was fighting and didn't give a damn as long as he was "fightin' for the woman I love and my dear old Uncle Sam." The euphoria of victory was soon to pass, however, and the mood of the day became increasingly bitter as wartime production quickly ran down. In October 1945, Louis Jordan had recorded an optimistic "Reconversion Blues" (Decca 18762), highlighting what the soldiers would do when they returned home. The following year, Ivory Joe Hunter recorded a different and much gloomier "Reconversion Blues" (Pacific 601) about the shutting down of the defense plants that during wartime had brought urban blacks a brief taste of prosperity. "The war is over; now, baby, what are you going to do? [x2] I used to give you twenty but now one or two will have to do." John Lee Hooker expressed similar sentiments in a November, 1948, recording, "The War Is Over" (Specialty LP 2127): "Well, the war is over and I'm broke and I ain't got a dime [x2]; Well, all my money's gone, and my friends don't know me no more." In 1946, Roosevelt Sykes had described in "Sunny Road" (RCA Victor 20-1906) the retreat to the South as war plants closed down: "Well, the war is over, I'm goin' back down that sunny road [x2]; Well, I ain't getting nothing in Chicago but my room and board."

Louis Jordan's upbeat recording of Johnny Mercer's "G.I. Jive" (Decca 8659) had been a No.1 R&B hit and a considerable pop hit in the summer of 1944, but his November 24, 1947, "Roamin' Blues" (Decca 24571) mentioned standing in line for work with other ex-GIs; by then the bubble of optimism had well and truly burst. A week later he was bemoaning the high cost of living in a heartfelt "Inflation Blues" (Decca 24381):

> Now listen, Mr. President, all you congressmen too;
> You got me all frustrated, and I don't know what to do.
>
> I'm trying to make a dollar, can't even save a cent;
> It takes all my money just to eat and pay my rent.

He goes on to plead with the president to cut the price of sugar so that he can make his coffee sweet.

A few days before Jordan entered the studio to comment on inflation, a bitter Jimmy Witherspoon had recorded his own observations on the economy in "Money's Getting Cheaper (Times Gettin' Tougher Than Tough)" (Supreme 1501):

> Money's gettin' cheaper, prices gettin' steeper.
> Found myself a woman but I just couldn't keep her.
> Times gettin' tougher than tough; things gettin' rougher than rough.
> I make a lot of money, but I just keep spendin' the stuff.

Witherspoon goes on to sing about the rising cost of pork chops, which had served as the barometer of the cost of living for black singers as far back as the 1920s.[4] The money he lays down in front of the butcher won't any longer buy a pound. He concludes that the only people doing well are the funeral directors and that while he can't afford to live, he'll have to try as dying is too expensive.

"Cootie" Williams had sung enthusiastically "Gotta Do Some War Work" (Hit 8090) in January 1944, but even the good pay produced its problems. In "Defense Blues" (Disc 5085) recorded in June 1946, Leadbelly pointed up the heightened expectations of spending power, which had caused a rift between him and his woman:

> Just because she was working, making so much dough, (x2)
> That woman got to the place she did not love me no more.
>
> Every payday would come, her check was as big as mine; (x2)
> That woman thought that defense was gonna last all the time.

Shifty Henry in his "Hypin' Women Blues" (Enterprise 105), recorded ca. late 1945, expressed his distrust of the women angling to get their hands on his money now that the war is over: "Yes, women are so mysterious, they will hype you for your gold."

In October 1943, Louis Jordan had recorded a "Ration Blues" (Decca 8654), which caught the mood of both blacks and whites (Uncle Sam rationing food was unfortunate but patriotically accepted) and became a crossover pop hit (from the R&B charts) in January 1944. His "You Can't Get That No More" (originally recorded as V-Disc 237B in November 1943) was similarly upbeat; the unpopular OPA (Office of Price Administration) has rationed food, the fittest men have gone off to war, so the girls have to settle for the ones left behind, and Uncle Sam demands that you work or fight. Jordan also highlights the then unusual situation that some women received a bigger check than the men. When Bobbie Robinson in 1946 ("Meat Situation Blues," Aladdin 170) and Rubberlegs Williams in 1945 ("Pointless Mama Blues," Savoy 564, in which he begs for ration "points" to buy meat) recorded their pleas a couple of years later, the situation seemed much less acceptable. The United States had sent millions of dollars of aid to a Europe exhausted by the war. In particular, bankrupt Britain had benefited from both "Lend-Lease" and then in 1947 the Marshall Plan to alleviate its acute shortages of food, fuel, and other resources. But now inflation was beginning to bite back home and inevitably hitting the poorest strata of society first, as Ivory Joe Hunter recounted in 1947 in "High Cost Low Pay Blues" (Pacific 630): "When

I go down to the store and try to buy at pre-war price, the man behind the counter look at me and say 'No dice.'" The song is full of striking images with Hunter complaining that his bank account is "flatter than an undertaker's chest" and asking, as many Americans were, "Who cut down that doggone money tree?" Who indeed? Victory was bought at high cost for black labor. Having briefly enjoyed better times, many workers were soon reduced to the austerity that prevailed in bankrupt Britain. For returning GIs the lack of jobs was a bitter pill to swallow. The sacrifice was, of course, unequal. Black labor tended to be laid off first, and for professional white families there was barely a hiccup. After the unity and common cause of the war years, American society was polarizing again.

Many blues artists relocated from the South to Chicago in the 1940s and, accompanied by bands using heavily amplified instruments, started to produce a harder edged blues that combined the deep feeling of rural blues with the harsher sounds of the urban ghetto. In the early 1950s their darker toned music began to replace the jumping, swinging sound of artists like Louis Jordan and Wynonie Harris on the R&B charts. As the major record labels turned their backs on what had been known as "race music" (black blues and gospel), a host of small, independent labels sprang up to take advantage of the "new" market for what had become known as "rhythm and blues." The economic situation worsened and, by 1949, the American economy was in recession, albeit one considerably less deep than Britain's. Records like John Lee Hooker's 1950 "House Rent Boogie" (Staff 710, "I didn't have the rent and out the door I went") were very much in keeping with the mood of the time. The 1940s had seen a steady decline in the percentage of black workers in agriculture as opposed to industry and commerce. There was a blip in 1950 as the recession encouraged some to return to field work, a move rationalized in lines like "going back south where the weather suits my clothes" in several blues.

Back in March 1945, Johnny McNeil, with Charles Brown and Johnny Moore's Three Blazers, had sung the "End o' War Blues" (Exclusive 205), suggesting that if U.S. citizens bought sufficient war bonds and stamps Germany and Japan would soon be defeated and "We'll soon be marching home" to the waiting loved ones. In October of that year, Cousin Joe had fantasized about his "Post-War Future" (Philo 118). Understandably, he comments that after fighting in the East and fighting in the West he's "goin' back home to take my proper rest." His dream is to marry his little woman, build a little cottage and raise a family (specifically "two little boys" and "a little girl") so that "we can live our happy lives in this free and peaceful world." The romantic idyll of the soldier overseas was, however, soon to be shattered. There had already been serious race riots in several cities, with some whites resenting the influx of blacks into war plants and attempts to integrate them into local housing communities. Many returning black soldiers encountered hostility. Air Force veterans in Los Angeles were bombed out of their homes. Isaac Woodward was blinded by a policeman in South Carolina while on his way home from military service, and in Georgia Maceo Snipes, another black veteran, was shot and killed at the polls. Several race riots also took place in 1946, all too reminiscent of the horrific violence of the summer of 1919, following the end of World War I.

It's not surprising that these returning soldiers experienced the same disorientation and disillusionment that followed after World War I. Walter Davis encapsulated their feelings in 1947 in his heartfelt "Things Ain't Like They Used to Be" (RCA Victor 20-2335):

> I spent two years in the European country, way out across the deep blue
> sea. (x2)
> And since I been 'round here, don't seem like home to me.

> If I would enlist back in the army, wonder could I go back across the
> European sea. (x2)
> I don't like it here no more; things ain't like they used to be.

Records like "Re-enlisted Blues" (Trilon 1058) by Turner Willis (1946) and Lawyer Houston's 1950 "Lawton Oklahoma Blues" (Atlantic LP 7226) indicate that many black servicemen became so disillusioned that they rejected civilian life. Even back in uniform Houston had his troubles:

> When I reenlisted in the army, they sent me down to Fort Sill. (x2)
> Well, I know that the women in Lawton will get a good soldier killed.

> Well I started drinking at the House of Joy, then went to Willie's Grill. (x2)
> I made a date with a beer-drinking woman and got clipped out of two
> twenty-dollar bills.

Woman trouble as a result of absence due to military service was a common thread in many wartime blues. Even the most faithful wife or girlfriend found it difficult to reassure her soldier boy that she was still true when an infrequent letter was the only means of communication. Others succumbed to the temptations of the flesh and, to judge by such boasting blues as Brownie McGhee's 1941 "Million Lonesome Women" (OKeh 06329) and Bukka White's "Army Blues" (Takoma LP 1001), recorded retrospectively in 1963, there were plenty of slavering wolves, who, declared unfit for military service, were obviously well enough equipped for extra curricular duties! McGhee declared that when the young men have gone to the camps, "Gonna be many a young wife left back here cold in hand," and sought to "reassure" them that in the meantime "I'll be tryin' to carry your business on." In his 1940 "When You Are Gone" (OKeh 05756) Blind Boy Fuller put it even more bluntly: "When Uncle Sam call you, be about one, two and three. [x2] Yeah, there's no use a-worryin', leave all these women back here with me."

In complete contrast to his romantic "Post-War Future Blues," Cousin Joe's 1946 "Desperate G.I. Blues" (Savoy 5526) evokes the outrage of the cuckolded soldier. While he was overseas, his woman was "living a life of ease," and "While I was in a foxhole in no-man's-land, Lord she would give my money to some Jody man." The cold fury of one verse is quite chilling in its intensity: "I'm goin' to kill that woman and I don't tell no lie; I'm goin' to kill her and dare her spirit to rise." Equally violent is the retribution posited in the 1946 "World War 2 Blues" (Queen 4162) by the Al (Stomp) Russell Trio:

I've just got back from World War Number Two, (x2)
But it seems to me I still got some shootin' to do.

My baby, she's been runnin' 'round.
My baby, my baby, she's been runnin' 'round.
I'm goin' to take my German Luger and blow their playhouse down.

I've slept in foxholes, bombs land in my bed.
I've slept in foxholes, bombs fallin' over my head.
Now I come back home and find a bum layin' in my bed.
[*Spoken:*] Get out of there.

I could forgive her, I could if I would,
Said I could forgive her, I could if I would,
But I'm not gonna do that, 'cause she's no darned good, no darned good.

In his October 24, 1945, recording of "Get Ready To Meet Your Man" (Columbia 36948) James "Beale Street" Clark is the "other man" (or "Jody man") who needs to get out of the way before his girl friend's husband returns from the war:

Now, babe, I been worried ever since Victory Day.
Everytime I pick up the paper, your man is coming thisaway.

Now your man been to the army; I know that's awful tough.
I don't know how many men he done killed, but I think he done killed
    enough.

The Yalta Conference in February 1945, at which President Roosevelt, U.K. Prime Minister Winston Churchill, and Russian dictator Josef Stalin agreed on the carving up of Eastern Europe after the anticipated defeat of Nazi Germany, sowed the seeds for the dissolution of the uneasy wartime alliance of the three major powers, who then followed their own agendas. In Stalin's case this meant replacing the German Empire with a Russian one and promoting the Soviet Union's impure version of Communism worldwide. Socialism does not seem to have appealed to the mass of black workers, and most blues singers followed the "patriotic" line of viewing it with grave suspicion and viewing Communism, espoused by some academics and entertainers, with abhorrence. The 1948–49 Berlin Blockade, in which Russia and East Germany tried for ten months to starve out non-Communist West Berlin, was recognized in 1949 by Lightnin' Hopkins, a Texas blues singer always alert to the news, as a threat to world peace. In "European Blues" (Gold Star 665) he alluded to the very real danger of war in Europe "on sea, land, and in the air," warning his girl friend that "your man may have to go over there."

The crisis passed, but the Cold War deepened. The USSR and its European satellite countries, along with Red China, were seen as increasingly belligerent by America and its Western European allies, several of whom had joined it in forming the North Atlantic Treaty Organization (NATO). Anti-Communist fever gripped the United States and Senator Joseph McCarthy became increasingly powerful and influential. His witch hunts ruined many lives and careers. Prominent black singer Paul Robeson suffered along with Hollywood stars, writers, and folk singers. Folk-blues singer Josh White was summoned and intimidated by the House Committee on Un-American Activities, which began to resemble the Spanish Inquisition in its insatiable search for victims. White's reputation would not be restored until the folk boom of the 1960s. During World War II, he had recorded blues praising Russia's resistance to the Germans on the Eastern Front and condemning racial discrimination in the armed forces and defense factories.

On June 24–25, 1950, the Communist forces of North Korea invaded South Korea. Historical evidence now indicates that the Russian dictator, Josef Stalin, knew of Kim Il Sung's plan and condoned it. It is even possible that Stalin actively encouraged the invasion, on the assumption that North Korean forces would overwhelm the South before America could become actively involved. He certainly provided covert Soviet military assistance, even though he was aware that escalation could lead to World War III. Lightnin' Hopkins, tuned in, as ever, to world events, sang in his contemporary 1950 "War News Blues" (Kent LP 9008): "You may turn your radio on soon in the morning, sad news every day [x2]; Yes, you know I got a warning, trouble is on its way."

Vocal group The Four Barons, in their 1950 recording of "Got to Go Back Again" (Regent 1026), voiced the discomfiture of soldiers recently returned from tours of duty overseas, only to be shipped out again to fight half-a-world away in East Asia. "Well, I just got home and I got to go back again; Uncle Sam don't know what kind of fix he caught me in." They concluded that "Uncle Sam don't ask no questions." He just expects the soldier to do his duty. A January 1951 recording by Johnny O'Neal, "War Bound Blues" (King 4441), updated a 1940 recording by the Five Breezes entitled "My Buddy Blues" (Bluebird B8614), stating, "If you're eighteen, buddy, I advise you not to hide [x2]; Because Uncle Sam is calling you now, and I declare you've got to ride." In the 1950 "Back to Korea Blues" (Sunny 101), Sunnyland Slim similarly commented on being wrenched away from home affairs to go back in uniform: "I was layin' in my bed, turn on my radio [x2]; All I could hear was the news about the war." He continued, "I got to go back in the army, but I hate to leave my baby behind." Bob Kent in 1952 endorsed the feeling of double trouble in "Korea, Korea" (Parlophone 1303). He'd "got a letter this morning saying I got to go," which would result in him being "right where I started from." Presumably, he meant fighting in Asia again.

In an amusing blues recorded in 1950, Rufus Thomas sang about the "Double Trouble" (Star Talent unissued) that caused him (or, rather, his persona in the song) to enlist in the army rather than choose between two attractive ladies vying for his affection:

> Yes, I've got double trouble, and I'm blue as I can be; (x2)
> I've got eyes for two women, and they got eyes for me.
>
> Well, one's a high yaller, the other's a teasin' brown; (x2)
> I had to volunteer for the army so I could leave town.
>
> Well, six weeks in this man's army, well it ain't no fun,
> I took my basic training, they had me on the run,
> Every day I went on maneuvers, with a five hundred pound pack,
> I hope both of them are married when I get back.

In 1965, a dozen years after the effective end of the war, J. B. Lenoir in "Korea Blues" (Spivey LP 1009) still recalled with bitterness:

> Went to the army, I stayed two long years,
> Fought twelve months in the heart of Korea.
> Sent my money to my wife and child;
> She didn't even write me a single line.

When he got back home, his woman didn't want him any more.

Recording in 1951, Dr. Ross evokes in "Little Soldier Boy" (Arhoolie LP 1065) the feeling of the draftee transplanted from small town America into an alien environment to face a fanatical enemy equally as willing as the Japanese in World War II to sacrifice great numbers of fighters in order to overwhelm the opposition:

Now I gets up early in the morning, my face all full of frowns;
Sometimes I get to thinkin' about that little girl of mine.
Baby, please, now baby, please pray for me, (x2)
Because I am a little soldier boy; I will need your prayer to get me free.
[*Spoken:*] Pray for me, little girl; I'm sittin' over here in Korea.

At first there was optimism that the war would soon be over. After the initial reverses suffered by United States forces, more than 15,000 casualties in the month of July 1950 alone, the arrival from late August onward of United Nations forces, and in particular contingents of Commonwealth troops from Great Britain, Australia, Canada, and New Zealand, began to turn the tide of the invasion. Through September the North Korean army was driven back to, and in October beyond the 38th Parallel, which divided the two Koreas. In November U.N. forces were not far short of the Yalu River, which divided North Korea from Manchuria, a province of China, when the nature of the war changed completely. First, Communist China announced that it was entering the war on behalf of North Korea, having through the autumn assembled an army of nearly a million troops in Manchuria, half of which were frontline fighters who now poured across the border to join the North Korean army. The United States Army, which had already started to ship troops out, swung from the jubilation of victory to near panic as division after division was swept away by the Red Tide. There was full retreat all along the United Nations front, and only the indomitable Turkish battalions were able to put up sufficiently fierce resistance to slow down the Chinese hordes. The second setback to the Allies was the arrival of appallingly cold weather from Siberia, with night temperatures falling as low as minus 45 degrees Fahrenheit with awful wind chill; conditions rapidly became close to intolerable. Everything liquid froze, including antifreeze, and even boiling water poured into vehicle radiators.

There was now a need for reinforcements. General Douglas MacArthur's "Home for Christmas" prediction had come to nothing and the morale of the United States Army, and increasingly the country generally, was at low ebb as the Chinese counterstrike began to seem unstoppable. In his 1951 recording of "The Lazy J" (Sittin' In With 648), L. C. Williams voiced the fear of all young men eligible for conscription: "If I should happen to go to the army, who gonna take care of my wife and child? [x2]. Well, you know, if I happen to get out in the battlefield, she'll never know the death I died."

Clifford Blivens even anticipated the war spreading across the Pacific, such was the fear of Communism at this time, but verse 2 of his 1951 "Korea Blues" (Swing Time 236) still dismissed the conflict as a "squabble":

> Yes, I've been called to the army, going over to Korea; (x2)
> So I can stop these Communists before they come over here.
>
> Well, I gotta go, baby, goin' far, far away; (x2)
> So I can stop this squabblin'; then I'll come home to stay.

Air power became increasingly important in the attempt to stem the Communists, but as J. B. Lenoir indicated in his 1951 "Korea Blues" (Chess 1449) there was the danger of being shot down and either summarily executed or "brainwashed" in a prisoner of war camp:

> Lord I got my questionnaire; Uncle Sam gonna send me away from here. (x2)
> He said, "J. B., you know that I need you; Lord, I need you in South Korea."
>
> Sweetheart, please don't you worry; I just begin to fly in the air. (x2)
> Now if the Chinese shoot me down, Lord, I'll be in Korea somewhere.

Arthur "Big Boy" Crudup, who in 1942 had recorded the intensely patriotic "Give Me a 32-20" (Bluebird B9019, "Now if I go down with a red, white and blue flag in my hand; then you can bet your life poor Crudup's sent a many man"), had by 1951 become much more ambivalent about military service. In the up-tempo "I'm Gonna Dig Myself a Hole" (RCA Victor 22-0141), he is reluctant to go to war, preferring to "go underground" with his baby:

> I'm gonna dig myself a hole, move my baby down in the ground; (x2)
> You know, when I come out, there won't be no wars around.
>
> Well, they take me to the riverfront, cross the deep blue sea;
> My baby begin to wonder what in the world become of me.

In his 1952 "Mr. So and So" (RCA Victor 20-4572), Crudup expresses the serviceman's apprehension about being supplanted while he is away overseas:

> Yes, I don't mind leavin', Lord, and I ain't scared to go; (x2)
> Darlin', only thing worries my mind, you and Mr. So-And-So.

Yes, I'm leaving in the morning, I'm goin' way out 'cross the sea; (x2)
Darlin', while I'm gone, will you sometime remember me?

For Willie Mae "Big Mama" Thornton, however, it was once bitten, twice shy. She explains in her 1951 "No Jody for Me" (Peacock 1587) that if her man goes to war again she's going to use her head, as after the last war a no good Jody fooled her and spent all her money, disappearing when the war was over.

When my man came back home again, he really took me by surprise;
He gave me a good beating and blackened both of my eyes.
That Jody said he loved me, well, I know it's just a lie,
'Cause if Uncle Sam can't use him, why oh why should I try.

As the grim reality dawned that the Chinese ignored enormous casualties and kept on coming so that it was impossible to kill them fast enough, it became clear that the Allies would inevitably suffer heavy losses also and many families would lose loved ones. In 1952, Gatemouth Brown sang in "Sad Hour" (Peacock 1576):

This is a sad, sad hour; you know my story's true; (x2)
Better get on your knees and pray, 'cause that's the only thing to do.
I want to tell all you wives just what you must do. (x2)
If you don't believe my story, you will feel the sad hour too.

It was becoming clear that the whole character of the Korean War was changing and that it was going to be equally as vicious and bloody as the struggle to defeat the Japanese only six years earlier. In his September 1950 "Korea Blues" (Imperial 5099), Fats Domino commented on the need for reinforcements to show that the Chinese Communists couldn't defeat Uncle Sam either:

Uncle Sam ain't no woman, but he sure can take your man. (x2)
He's taking 'em day and night to go to Korea and fight.

The people over there have messed up; they have made it very rough. (x2)
We'll have to go there and show 'em what it mean to be real tough.

As winter deepened, so did the depression of the military and the politicians, as what had seemed to be a short-term policing action became a desperate struggle for the survival of South Korea as an independent, non-Communist nation. Only big business was happy, as the demand for munitions began to stimulate America's flagging economy. Lightnin' Hopkins perfectly captured the somber mood with his 1952 "Sad News From Korea" (Mercury 8274).

[*Spoken:*] Sad news . . .

Whoa, I got sad news this morning; people havin' trouble over in Korea.
Whoa, I got sad news this morning; people havin' trouble way over in
    Korea.
Well, some of their friends is missing,
[*Spoken:*] They don't know whether they's over yonder,
They don't know whether they's over there.

Well, poor mother cryin', wonderin' where my poor son could be.
[*Spoken:*] Don't worry, mama.
Whoa, poor mother runnin' cryin', "Ooh Lord, where could my poor
    child be.
Whoa, I just want you to answer my prayer, please sir, God, send my poor
    child back to me." [*Spoken:*] . . . just can't help it.

You know it's sad, ain't it sad, when the rain come fallin' down,
Ain't it sad, ain't it sad, when the rain come fallin' down,
Well, when you got a lot of playmates in this world somewhere; they can't
    be found.

Increasing numbers of soldiers were indeed "Missing In Action," helping
the Republic of Korea, as L. B. Lawson recounted in January 1952 in a song
of that name, which he recorded in the Sun studio in Memphis, Tennessee
(Sun CD29). Setting the scene with "Well, they said I was missing in action,
they thought that I was dead," he goes on to describe how he was made
captive:

Whoa, yes I know the Lord is on my side,
Yes my mother, she's back on earth, says she worried about her child,

Now said "Son, don't worry about the night being long.
I know you're way over here in Korea; you know you a long old way from
    home."
They say I was missing in action; by the help of the Lord they're wrong.
Yes, I know mother's goin' to jump and shout, just when I get home.

Yes now, you know the day they captured me and I fell down on my knees,
I said I want everybody just to hear me, "Lord, I want to pray one time if
    you please.
Lord, have mercy; will you please make a way.
Yes, you know I'm missing in action; Lord I was helping the R.O.K."

Rosco Gordon's curious "A Letter from a Trench in Korea" (Chess 1489)
was of topical interest when issued in 1951. It positively drips with sentimen-

tality, but no doubt draftees identified with its message to the wife or girl friend back home to wait patiently (and faithfully) for the soldier's return: "Darlin', here I lie in my foxhole; I have tears in my eyes. But I'm sure you're true, no matter what they say or do."

On Sherman Johnson's "Lost in Korea" (Trumpet 190), recorded in 1952, the noises of bombs, shells, and firing provide a constant, atmospheric background throughout the recording, while the lyrics evoke the desperation felt by the troops in that terrible winter of 1950–51.

> Baby, please write me a letter, because I'm lost and all alone. (x2)
> Well, I have no one to love me, and I'm a million miles away from home.
>
> World War Two was bad, but this is the worst I've ever seen. (x2)
> Every time I think it's over, I wake up and it's just a dream.

And still the men were summoned to war, as Lloyd Price recounted in his March 1952 "Mailman Blues" (Specialty 428):

> Oh mailman, mailman, tell me what you got for me. (x2)
> He said "A long letter, brother, it'll lead you across the sea."
>
> Now all day long it's one, two, three and four. (x2)
> Well, I'm so unhappy, I can't see my baby no more.

The name Korea literally means "land of high mountains and sparkling streams" and, while the troops had some doubts about how pristine the latter were, there was no arguing with the accuracy of the former; the 525-mile-long peninsula of Korea is covered with hills and high mountains. Many of the hills were named or numbered as they became fiercely contested strong points. Duke Upshaw, singing with Red Callender's Sextet in 1953, in "Soldier's Blues" (Bayou 002) described the (literally) "bloody hills" that gave him the "blues in Korea," while J. B. Lenoir referred to a particular location in his 1954 recording "I'm in Korea" (Parrot 802):

> Yes, I am in Korea, north-east side of Kim-Foy. (x2)
> Lord I don't have no idea, I never will see you no more.
>
> I'm on a hill called Ten Sixty-Two, machine guns firing all over my head. (x2)
> Darling, I was thinking about my kids and you; if I die, what you goin' do?

He concludes by reminding his woman of his warning not to let any other man lay his head in Lenoir's bed. (In his 1951 "Korea Blues," Chess 1449, Lenoir had sung, "I just stand here wonderin' who you gonna let lay down in my bed.")

Homesick James Williamson was one of the many blues singers anxious to profit from the discomfiture of the draftee. In his January 1953 "Wartime" (Pea Vine LP 706), he sang:

> Everytime I pick up a newspaper, I can read something about the war, (x2)
> Well, then you know all the Chinaman do is eat rice and start to take some good man's life.
>
> Well some of you go to the army, boys, ain't no need [for] you to weep and moan. (x2)
> Well, she always got a smile on my face; well, I can lay down in your house anytime.

In his 1951 "Questionnaire Blues" (Gotham 509), John Lee Hooker expressed confidence that his woman would be faithful while he's away, singing:

> I done got my questionnaire, and it leads me in the war. (x2)
> I got to go to the army and try to win the war.
>
> But I believe in you, baby; I'm goin' far, far away.
> I believe in you, baby; I be goin' far, far away.
> I ain't goin' say goodbye, baby, 'cause your daddy will be back someday.
>
> She said, "Don't worry, daddy; everything goin' be alright.
> Don't worry about me. I be happy until you go and come again."

On April 3, 1951, American forces recrossed the 38th Parallel. General Ridgway's plan was to press on into North Korea through the center of the country, but on the night of April 22–23 the Chinese launched a counteroffensive across the Imjin River that threatened to overwhelm the Allied forces with sheer weight of numbers. There were many deeds of heroism over the following week. By April 30, U.N. forces had retreated to positions north of Seoul and regrouped.

A momentous event occurred during this period. On April 11, President Truman relieved General Douglas MacArthur of all his commands, including Supreme Commander of U.N. forces (General Ridgway replaced him in this post). MacArthur had refused to accept the political decision not to carry the war to Red China and had instigated a press campaign to influence American and world opinion to demand retaliation against the Chinese mainland. President Truman, Prime Minister Winston Churchill, and other heads of state involved feared that escalation would lead to another world war. General Douglas MacArthur returned to the United States a national hero, reciting the famous line "Old soldiers never die; they just fade away."

But when the dust had settled, the dangers of his proposed policy were generally understood and his popularity quickly declined. These events inspired the chorus of "Fade Away Baby" (Mercury 8240), recorded in May 1951 by Ray Snead, in which he is trying to get rid of his woman: "Do The MacArthur, baby; I don't want you to die, just fade away."

Many of MacArthur's supporters had favored "nuking" the enemy out of existence, failing to understand the consequences if Russia retaliated on behalf of China. The lethal power of the nuclear weapon was not readily apparent from recordings like "Atom and Evil," a humorous parody recorded by the Golden Gate Quartet on June 5, 1946 (Columbia 37236), and the Spirit of Memphis Quartet's "The Atomic Telephone" (King 4521), recorded August 14, 1951. It was hard to imagine the devastation of Hiroshima and Nagasaki happening in America, and the government promoted among the population the naïve belief that fall-out shelters would protect most people from harm. The development of the hydrogen bomb offered an even speedier path to annihilation, but even this weapon could become a macho image. Certainly singer Bob Ferguson used it to stress his power as a performer when he adopted his nom-de-disque "H-Bomb" Ferguson in 1951.

The New Year of 1952 dawned with peace talks hopelessly deadlocked and the American and Chinese delegates unable to agree on anything positive, the suspicion being that the Communists were simply buying time to build up their military strength. In the meantime, hostilities continued unabated, albeit the war was becoming geographically static and relatively uneventful. But soldiers were still dying, and in New York on January 20 Joe Turner recorded the classic "Sweet Sixteen" (Atlantic 960), later revived by B. B. King and Chuck Berry: "Well, my brother's in Korea, and my sister down in New Orleans; Well, my mother's up in heaven, Lord, what's gonna happen to me?"

The Five Blind Boys of Alabama considered the worries of mothers in "All I Have Is Gone" (Gospel 138):

> Some mothers have sons in the army, in the navy, Lord, and the Marines,
> They are fightin', Lord, over in Korea; some of their faces never more will
>   be seen.
> If Uncle Sam call your son to the service, tell him to go ahead.
> He may not have water, he may not have a piece of bread.
> Mother, pray to the Lord above, watch over [the] child you love.

The bitter winter ended and summer came again, with its sultry heat and drenching rain. No wonder draftee Bobby "Blue" Bland sang, "The sun rose this morning; that awful day has dawned" ("Army Blues," Duke 115). Uncle

Sam had got him and he would have no more fun until "my army life is through." (When recording, Bland was on furlough, a year into his three-year military service.) May saw General Mark Clark take over as Supreme Commander, succeeding General Ridgeway. Peace talks dragged on at Panmunjom but broke down completely in October.

In December 1952, General Eisenhower, who had just won a landslide victory in the U.S. presidential election, flew to Korea to try to speed up a settlement. In the event he had to renew the threat to extend the war into China, with the use of atomic weapons. (The political climate had obviously changed considerably since Truman dismissed MacArthur for making the same threat!) In "Drive Soldiers Drive" (Excello 2016, recorded in 1953), Little Maxie expressed considerable faith in the new president's ability to end the war and also took pride in the integration of the army, which had actually been ordered by President Truman:

> President Ike is a mighty man;
> He called for the whites and the brown and tan.
> "Come on, boys, and follow me;
> We're goin' to end this war in old Korea."
> Drive soldiers drive, drive on. (x3)
> Drive on, drive on, drive on.
>
> Don't worry about your wife and be no slacker.
> Uncle Sam is your financial backer.
> All you got to do is follow through.
> We'll take care of you and your families too.
>
> Well, everybody knows that Ike's the one;
> He knows and I know there's work to be done;
> We can win this war, but make it fast.
> And Uncle Sam won't have to ration that gas.
>
> Well, I know you boys have got a lot of ambition;
> You can tear up things with that new ammunition.
> We're in this war, but we're not alone;
> Let's finish this war, then we'll all go home.

"Hup, Hup, Hup, Ho" is chanted over the instrumental choruses, giving the atmosphere of the parade ground, concluding, "Look out, soldiers!"

As late as March 30, 1953, Bob White, vocalist and organist with the Emitt Slay Trio, recorded a humorous trouble-at-home piece with the group, "Male Call" (sic, Savoy 1101), in which he reads a letter from a buddy back in the States to an illiterate fellow soldier. This recounts the soldier's wife's infidelity, her wrecking the car, all his pay sent home being used for booze, etc., etc., concluding, "But do me one big favor. Give all of those Communists heck, huh?" The narrator realizes that he has read out the wrong letter just as the soldier reaches for his gun and shoots himself.

In his December 24, 1952, "Back Home" (Federal 12128), Jimmy Witherspoon, in a serious vein, refers to the same scenario:

> Have you ever been to Korea? Know what I'm talkin' about. (x2)
> Well, you come back home and your woman wants to put you out.
>
> Well the war's over in Korea, fightin' to save the land.
> You women over here, well, you fightin' over each other's man.

He concludes that if the women don't put things right, the "wrong man" will come back and put everybody out of the house. Eddie "Guitar Slim" Jones echoed the fears of the absent husband in his "Feelin' Sad" (J-B 603), recorded in 1952. Ray Charles was so impressed with the emotional impact of the song that he recorded it (Atlantic 1008) the following year: "I was in Korea in '51, I had no love and that was no home; I was sending you all my money, baby, and all the time you was doing me wrong."

When a cease-fire was finally signed in July 1953, America had suffered more casualties in Korea than in World War I. Diplomatic wrangling continued, and the repatriation of prisoners did not begin until January 1954. The armed truce between South Korea and North Korea has remained precarious right up to the present day, with numerous flare-ups of hostilities over the years. A permanent peace treaty has never been signed, and the two sides are still technically at war. The demilitarized zone along the 38th Parallel that forms the border is guarded by two million troops on both sides, and from time to time the North accuses the South of armistice violations and threatens "retaliation."

In "The War Is Over" (Decca 48842), recorded July 29, 1953, Lightnin' Hopkins celebrated the armistice in characteristic fashion, assuming the persona of a returning GI who finds his woman has spent all his money in his absence but is determined to have a good time anyway:

> Yeah, you know the war is over, man; I've got a chance to go back home. (x2)
> You know, if that woman done spent all my money, I'm gonna whup her
>   for doing me wrong.
>
> Man, the war is over; baby, now ain't you glad? (x2)
> You know you can get back to that old used to be, have the same good
>   times you used to have.

Perhaps the most fitting celebration of the cease-fire was gospel singer Sister Rosetta Tharpe's joyful "There's Peace In Korea" (Decca 48302), recorded two days earlier:

> I'm so glad at last, there's peace in Korea,
> Yes, I'm so glad at last, there's peace in Korea,
> Don't you know, I'm so glad at last, there's peace in Korea,
> Because President Eisenhower has done just what he said.
>
> We're hoping there will be no more misery and no more sadness,
> No, no, no, no, no more dyin' there'll be in the land;
>
> Hope we'll have happiness, and joy and peace of mind.
> Because we know God has made this world and made it for the good and
>   kind.
>
> I'm saying to all you mothers, now don't you weep and moan.
> I know that you are glad because your sons are coming home.
> Now you wives, sisters and brothers, you can wipe your teary eyes;
> Because, sure as I am singing, the sun has begun to shine.

There was an assumption among American politicians that America and its allies had proved their might, and such conflicts could be avoided in the future, but little more than a decade later American forces became embroiled in the conflict in Vietnam, the unhappy outcome of which began to make the United States question the role of "World Policeman," which it had unwittingly assumed in the aftermath of World War II. Not until the Persian Gulf War of 1991 would American military confidence and prestige be fully restored. Even then there would never again be the certainty of successful outcome that the American public had assumed in the 1940s, when James McCain could sing, "Well, I said, we just got to win this war now, people, because this country have never failed" ("Good Mr. Roosevelt," Chicago 103, recorded in 1945).

While there had been advances in integration in the armed forces, change "back home" was disappointingly slow. The Echoes of Zion gospel group, who, in a September 1950 recording, urged listeners to "Please Pray for South Korea" (Sittin' In With 2018), also about this time made a very telling comment about racial double standards in "Keep Still (God Will Fight Your Battles)" (Gerald 105). Having referred to the black soldiers who in two world wars "died that democracy might have a chance," they state that in Korea "our boys were fightin' to keep the Reds on the run" while "down in Florida our homes being bombed." A veiled threat was contained in the penultimate verse:

> Our boys were fightin' in far off Korea,
> For American democracy they loved so dear.
> Their blood has flowed in foreign lands,
> They're comin' home to take a stand.

Such determination would be needed, as the arrival of Dwight D. Eisenhower in the White House meant a slowdown in the progress of civil rights legislation to correct racial discrimination. Blacks suffered disproportionately in the economic recession of 1953–55 with high and increasing unemployment. The separatist Black Muslim movement attracted many converts after the Korean War. Blacks had finally achieved integration in the armed services, but the battle was still to be won in civilian life. New hope would come with the inauguration of President John F. Kennedy in 1961, but in the meantime there had been a deepening mood of despair and disillusion.

In his 1954 "True Blues" (Ace LP 206), James Wayne had recounted his bad luck, including an alleged false imprisonment that led him despairingly to state, "I believe I'll join the army, let the North Koreans take aim at me, 'cause I would rather be dead than to be living in misery." Wayne accepted the status quo, even pleading guilty (presumably under duress) "because they asked me to," but J. B. Lenoir was made of sterner stuff. In the controversial "Eisenhower Blues" (Parrot 802), recorded October 6, 1954, he directly challenged the economic oppression experienced by blacks: "Takin' all my money to pay the tax; I'm only giving you people the natural facts." But his chorus, "Oh, oh, oh, I got them Eisenhower blues; thinkin' 'bout me and you; what on earth are we gonna do?" led to the record being blacklisted and withdrawn soon after its release. Lenoir recorded a slightly changed version of the song, now titled "Tax Paying Blues," and it was released under the same issue number. Equally hard-hitting was a related recording made for Chess a few months later but which was only issued as recently as 1976. "Everybody Wants to Know (Laid Off Blues)" again invokes the president in its chorus: "Oh, oh, oh, I got them laid off blues; thinkin' 'bout me and you; what the president gonna do?"

In 1944 Franklin D. Roosevelt had gained an unprecedented fourth term as president, riding on a tide of national pride as the United States saw itself winning the war for the Allies. A survey of servicemen in August of that year had shown that blacks were much more positive than whites about the impact of military service on their lives and, even more telling, were much more optimistic than whites about improving their lives after the war. Failure to progress significantly, either socially or economically, over the next ten years, plus involvement in another bloody war far away in Asia, turned that optimism to pessimism. The scene was set for the long Equal Rights struggle that began with the 1955 bus boycott in Montgomery, Alabama.

A decade of disillusion had produced a long series of relevant recordings, some indulging in caustic comment, some humorous, others more simply reportage. Those about the Korean War, however, were increasingly ambivalent and several unequivocally antiwar, anticipating the stand of boxer Muhammad Ali on the Vietnam War issue. More than a decade would have to pass before James Brown could speak without apology for the majority of black Americans, declaring in 1968, "Say It Loud—I'm Black and I'm Proud" (King K6187). Black servicemen had been proud to serve in two world wars, but it took a long time for Uncle Sam to show that he was proud of them. Arthur "Big Boy" Crudup's 1942 plea ("Give Me a 32-20," Bluebird B9019) rings down through the years: "Mmm, 'Hero' is all I crave; Now when I'm dead and gone, write 'Hero' on my grave."

Notes

I would like to offer special thanks to, among others, Ray Astbury, Dave Clarke, John Cowley, Kip Lornell, and David Evans for help in providing information and recorded examples.

1. Discographical details of the examples discussed here can be found in Mike Leadbitter and Neil Slaven, *Blues Records 1943–1970, A Selective Discography, Vol. 1, A to K* (London: Record Information Services, 1987); Mike Leadbitter, Leslie Fancourt, and Paul Pelletier, *Blues Records, 1943–1970, "The Bible of the Blues," Vol. 2, L to Z* (London: Record Information Services, 1944); and Cedric J. Hayes and Robert Laughton, *Gospel Records, 1943–1969: A Black Music Discography*, 2 vols. (London: Record Information Services, 1992). There are a number of other relevant blues and gospel recordings, particularly about the Korean conflict, not quoted here. Some, like "Uproar about MacArthur" by the Five Voices (Five Voices 3500) and "Korea (Fighting in the Foreign Land)" by the Gospel Pilgrims (Atlantic 928), were not available for assessment. The war also sparked recordings in other musical genres, an example being "The Battle in Korea," a country and western record by L. W. and Harold and the Carolina Neighbors on the Blue Ridge label.

2. Important studies of blues records dealing with social issues and problems, the Depression, President Franklin D. Roosevelt's administration, and World War II are Paul Oliver, *Blues Fell This Morning: Meaning in the Blues*, rev. ed. (Cambridge: Cambridge University Press, 1990; first published in 1960); Guido van Rijn, *Roosevelt's Blues: African-American Blues and Gospel Songs on FDR* (Jackson: University Press of Mississippi, 1997); and Bob Groom, "Tiger in the Night," *Blues & Rhythm* 66 (January 1992), 12–15, and unpublished manuscript *Blues for Uncle Sam*. Subsequent

to my writing of this article, an important study of postwar recordings has been published, Guido van Rijn, *The Truman and Eisenhower Blues: African-American Blues and Gospel Songs, 1945–1960* (London: Continuum, 2004), with accompanying CD (Agram ABCD 2018), including twenty-six selections from the recordings quoted in the book.

3. Historical sources for this era include Tim Carew, *The Korean War* (London: Pan Books, 1970); Neil A. Wynn, *The Afro-American and the Second World War* (London: Paul Elek, 1976); and John Modell, Marc Goulden, and Sigurdur Magnusson, "World War II in the Lives of Black Americans: Some Findings and an Interpretation," *Journal of American History* 76, no. 3 (December 1989): 838–48.

4. An example is "Dry Spell Blues" (Paramount 12990), recorded in 1930, in which Mississippi blues singer Son House sang about a prolonged drought that reversed normal values: "Pork chops forty-five cents a pound; cotton is only ten."

Houston Creoles and Zydeco

THE EMERGENCE OF AN AFRICAN AMERICAN
URBAN POPULAR STYLE

JOHN MINTON

"Play 'Jole Blon'!"

It's Saturday afternoon at Pe-Te's Cajun Bar-B-Que House, a tavern and dance hall in the South Houston suburb of Pasadena. Under the aegis of Cajun entrepreneur, music promoter, and disc jockey Les "Pe-Te" Johnson, L. C. Donatto and the Slippers (Fig. 10.1), one of the Bayou City's premier zydeco bands, are holding their weekly matinee for a mixed crowd of Creoles and Cajuns. This particular request comes from a young lady among the latter.

"All right!" L. C. responds, pumping his accordion. "Somebody wanted 'Jole Blon.'"

> Of course, I don't know what she talking about; I'm not a Frenchman [shouts and laughter]. I'm glad I'm not a Frenchman. And I know Pe-Te, Pe-Te ain't no Frenchman. He talk that stuff on the radio every Tuesdays and Saturday morning, but Pe-Te is not no Frenchman. And I *know* I'm not no Frenchman. But now I'm going to tell you, anytime that you want to ask somebody if they're a Frenchman, and they tell you a lie, I'm going to tell you how to find out if they're a Frenchman. Anybody you ask, "Is you a Frenchman?" they tell you, "No," I'm going to tell you a secret. Don't step on all their foot. Step on that little toe, and they going to holler "*Ayy-yee-yai!*" Now that's a Frenchman.

And with that L. C. launches into "Jole Blon," punctuating the traditional paean to an idealized "pretty blonde" with an unmistakable index of musical performance on the French Gulf Coast, *une crie de danse*, that is, a high-pitched yell sounding something like "*Ayy-yee-yai!*"[1]

Fig. 10.1 L. C. Donatto and the Slippers Zoddico Band at the Texas Folklife Festival, San Antonio, August, 1986. Left to Right: L. C. Donatto Jr., Lonzo Woods, and L. C. Donatto Sr. (Photo by Lynn Gosnell.)

I begin with L. C.'s tongue-in-cheek exegesis of the telling relation between French ethnicity and musical style as an especially apt indication of that identification on the contemporary Gulf Coast, particularly in urban areas such as Houston, where other components of Creole culture (most conspicuously the French language itself) are rapidly fading. In fact, this symbolic function largely accounts for the present popularity in Houston of zydeco, customarily defined as a combination of Cajun accordion and African American urban blues originating among the French-speaking blacks—the "Creoles of color"—of rural South Louisiana.[2]

There are, however, other reasons for beginning a history of Houston zydeco with L. C.'s facetious prescription for detecting Frenchmen. That is, even in establishing the obvious tie between Creole ethnicity and ethnic tradition, L. C. simultaneously implicates the problematic qualities of both these phenomena, especially today in America's fourth largest city, where to be black *and* French *and* a traditional musician is altogether more than a little anomalous—and thus all too easily overlooked or undervalued by a dominant culture in many ways inimical to such marginalized groups. Then again, from an insider's perspective, the seemingly unequivocal connection between Creole music and ethnic identity can just as easily obscure the idiosyncratic, even contradictory qualities that individual tradition bearers attribute to such subjective constructs, qualities indicative of endemic conflicts and contradictions within the Creole community itself.

In this last respect as in many others, L. C.'s example is typical. Consider, for instance, how such performers challenge the conventional definition of zydeco as a hybrid of Cajun accordion music and rhythm and blues played by French-speaking blacks on the rural Gulf Coast. Notwithstanding zydeco's obvious affinities to Cajun music and blues, notwithstanding the near universal acceptance by outsiders of its status as an offshoot of these traditions, I have found virtually no consensus whatsoever among Creoles themselves concerning the precise relation between such categories as "zydeco," "Cajun," or "blues"—provided, that is, that the individual in question distinguishes among them at all. Anderson Moss, like L. C. a longtime exponent of Houston zydeco, seems entirely comfortable with an orthodox definition, evincing little interest in hard-and-fast typologies. When I asked, "How would you define zydeco, . . . like, a combination of Cajun music and blues?" he simply replied, "Yeah. It's a mix, uh—Creole? You know what I'm talking about? It's Creole music. That's all it is." Queried more specifically on the relation of Cajun to zydeco, he rejoined, "The same thing!" About the relation of zydeco to blues, he said: "Well, you can play blues with it. You can play blues. You can play slow pieces. Blues. Play slow stuff, you know. Play the blues, I can play blues on that thing [his accordion]. Play all that!"

The late Lonnie Mitchell, another of Houston's zydeco stalwarts, was only a bit more particular. Asked to define zydeco, he simply responded, "Well, it's different from other music, you know. I don't know—it's some way or another people just love that type of music, really love that type of music, and it's come up like that." When pressed on the Cajun connection, he conceded, "Well, it's related, yeah, Cajun music, sure is. Just, uh, blacks play a little different." And he had this to say about the relation of zydeco music to blues:

> It's related to blues, but a little different than the blues. You know, mostly
> blues is played with a guitar, and, uh, course you can play blues on accordion
> if you know how . . . , 'cause I know I can play blues, whole lot of pieces of
> blues, and you know all the guys that play accordion, some of 'em can't and
> some of 'em can. Yeah, you can play a blues and play zydeco, and you play it
> in a different tone, you know, but you can still play blues on the zydeco music.
> Course, they call it—when you play a blues—they call it a "slow drag," you

know, for blues with accordion. Yeah, I play a whole lot of blues myself, but most people want that regular zydeco. [JM: Like a fast two-step?] Fast two-step, yeah. That's a fast two-step, um-hm.

As do most Creoles, Mitchell here employs *zydeco* both as a generic term and as the description of a particular tune type and the dance figure it accompanies, specifically a fast, syncopated two-step. This partly explains why he and Moss differentiate zydeco and blues—that is, "slow drags," or "blues with accordion"—on the basis of tempo. That explanation is not entirely satisfactory, however, since both Mitchell and Moss (and Creoles generally) include many tune types other than zydecos in the generic class of zydeco, including many played at much slower tempos (for example, waltzes), while fast blues—which are, in their view, neither zydecos nor zydeco—are equally common.

L. C. draws finer distinctions than does either Mitchell or Moss, even introducing additional categories—while claiming fluency in all of them. "You see that's a difference," he insisted. "Like, a whole lot of people, they hear the Cajun music, see, 'cause they have a whole lot of blacks play them little bitty button accordions just like the Cajuns do, and they call that zydeco, but it's not—it's not zydeco; it's French music. What I play, I can play French *and* zydeco *and* blues *and* rock and roll. Now that's zydeco!" Asked to elaborate, he explained, "It's a whole lot different between French and zydeco. . . . See, they [French musicians] playing that one-row button accordion, see, but zydeco, we playing them three-row button accordions. . . . Well, we most can play anything on it, but those one-row button accordion, you can't play anything you want like you can a [three-row] button accordion or a piano accordion."

So although contemporary Creole music is clearly related to, and in some instances virtually indistinguishable from, Cajun tradition, this aspect of black French music is just as clearly distinct from zydeco—at least in the view of many Creoles, who refer to this strain as "French La La" or simply "French music," reserving *zydeco* for the bluesy, percussion-driven, highly amplified urban style developing after World War II. The distinction is related in part to the characteristics of different accordions. "Cajun" or "French" music—distinguished as, respectively, white and black subtypes of a single idiom—constitutes an older style reflecting the adaptation of nineteenth-century rural traditions to the diatonic one-row button accordion. Zydeco, by contrast, is usually played on two- or three-row models or, especially today, on the chromatic piano accordions Creoles adopted in the late 1940s and

1950s, instruments better suited to the blues and pop tunes they increasingly assimilated in Texas cities. Incidentally, L. C., who is somewhat unusual in playing one-, two-, and three-row button accordions as well as the piano model, prefers to perform "Jole Blon" on the single row instrument, since in his view this piece properly falls within the Cajun-French domain (not surprisingly his rendition closely follows the now "standard" arrangement recorded in Houston in 1949 by Cajun fiddler Harry Choates).[3] That opinion is further reflected in his atypical use of the high, tense singing and *crie de danse* ("*Ayy-yee-yai!*") characteristic of Cajun-French music, a marked contrast to the open-throated African American singing style more usual to zydeco.[4]

In short, although zydeco clearly constitutes a fundamental expression of French identity on the contemporary Gulf Coast, it is only one of many musical styles fulfilling that function—hardly surprising, since French identity is no more uniform or univocal than French music is. On the one hand, the seemingly clear-cut distinction between Cajuns (white) and Creoles (black) is tempered by a close-felt affinity between these two groups. Accordingly, Creoles may appreciate Cajun music—or Cajuns, its Creole equivalents—as an expression of their own "Frenchness," at the same time regarding such productions as something apart from their own culture. And such ambiguities figure within as well as between groups, as individual Creoles distinguish among, or variably identify with, different musical subtypes within their own cultural repertories, most significantly because of those idioms' relative affinity to Cajun-French or African American traditions.

Not coincidentally, *Creole* is no easier to define than is *zydeco*, even within the Gulf Coast area, where the term is applied to a bewildering range of human populations or cultural phenomena, some of them mutually exclusive. In this essay *Creole* denotes a complex of cultural, linguistic, and genetic variables characterizing persons from southern Louisiana and southeast Texas whose ancestry lies in the successive interactions, beginning in the 1700s, of various African, European (most notably French), and Native American populations. It is this African ancestry that primarily distinguishes the persons described here as "Creoles" from other Gulf Coast Francophones (many of whom are also identified as "Creoles"), just as their French heritage distinguishes them from their black neighbors. In other words, the latter characteristic places Creoles within the broad category "French," while the former differentiates them from other "Frenchmen," a factor underscored by other traditional epithets: *créoles de couleur, mulâtre, nèg, noir*, and so forth. Although justifiably deemed "a gross misnomer," "nonsense," or a "racial impossibility,"[5] the term "black Cajun" is still occasionally employed by both scholars and Creoles.[6] Other terms—for example, "African-French"—seem peculiar to academicians.

Once again, L. C. Donatto illustrates the difficulty of applying even such a qualified definition without further allowances. Although L. C. unequivocally regards himself, and is regarded by others, as "Creole"—that is, as both "French" and "black"—he simultaneously allows that he is actually neither. His parents were bilingual, but they taught their children only English. "I was born in Louisiana and I can't talk French," he marveled. "My mother and father didn't teach me French, but the few words that I did learn, I learned it by listening at the records." Moreover, by his account he possesses neither African nor French ancestry; rather, he reckons himself to be of mixed Irish, Italian, and Native American descent. "You see my mother there, she's white. And my dad's full-blooded Mohawk," he explained (we were examining a photograph). "But see, where we come from in Louisiana, they raised us up as black, so I just stayed like that. But I don't have a drop in me."

It is significant that, his ancestry aside, L. C. insists that he was "raised as black" and so "just stayed like that," which is to say that on the Gulf Coast, as elsewhere, "blackness" is more a subjective cultural than an objective biological category, potentially encompassing more than one group (for example, French Creoles and "American" blacks). Much as this African American identity separates Creoles from their Acadian neighbors, their identification with other styles of black music has increasingly distinguished Creole from Cajun performances. Indeed many Creoles prefer other African American genres—R&B, jazz, and soul or, more recently, funk, disco, and rap—to any and all varieties of "French" music, including zydeco, which indisputably assumed its current form through an increasing affinity to such black popular styles.

Given such factors, there is a certain validity—not to mention a considerable utility—in describing zydeco as a combination of Cajun-French music and blues. Recall, though, that Creoles distinguish these as *three* (in some cases *four*) different genres. It accordingly seems somewhat misleading simply to characterize zydeco as a combination of Cajun or French music and blues. Even Anderson Moss, who evinces little interest in rigid typologies, seems to regard the blues as something apart from zydeco proper ("Well, you can play blues *with* it [zydeco]"), a view with which Mitchell concurs ("You can play a blues *and* play zydeco, and you play it in a *different* tone"). L. C. Donatto is characteristically adamant, even if he identifies personally with both blues and zydeco.

Like many Creoles, L. C. has a longstanding love of downhome blues—epitomized by the records of Houston's greatest bluesman, Sam "Lightnin'" Hopkins (1912–82)—which he very much regards as an expression of his own ethnic identity. "Aw, no, we heard *blues* [in Louisiana]," he assured me when asked. "We had Lightnin' Hopkins music all over. Yeah, now that's the blues I heard—Lightnin' Hopkins, Muddy Waters, Howlin' Wolf, Blind Boy Fuller. . . . Them old blues, way back yonder, man, in '45 and '50—now that was blues!" In fact, after coming to Houston, L. C. got to know Hopkins personally. "Yeah, was my brother-in-law and myself, we used to play with Lightnin'," he remembered. "We was real good friends and played for a long time together." When I asked, "Would you just do blues or would he try to do zydeco?" he was categorical: "Just blues. Just playing with him. I'd be hitting the rubboard or sometimes take my accordion, and I'm the onliest, I'm the onliest black could take, I'm the *onliest* black man could take a piano accordion and play the same thing with Lightnin' playing on the guitar! Well, I'm the onliest black man could play Lightnin's music on the *guitar* and sound just like him." Indeed, L. C. still has a guitar Hopkins gave him, which he plays in his friend's style. And he indisputably ranks among the best I have ever heard at playing blues on accordion. (Then again, Hopkins was himself more attuned to Creole music than L. C.'s comments suggest; after all, he was apparently the first person to document the term *zydeco*.)

Yet as the foregoing commentary also suggests, L. C. still holds to the ideal that zydeco and blues—*and* French music *and* rock and roll—are and should remain separate. When I asked whether the blues or rock had affected his music, he responded, "Naw, especially when we playing it, you know. . . . See, you have to mix it up. See, you might like zydeco; the next person, they love zydeco too, but they want you to mix, play a little rock and roll once in a while, then blues. Yeah, that's how we do it, . . . just mix it." "Mix it," then, apparently does not mean "mix it together." To the contrary, L. C. is critical of such synthetic trends in zydeco, innovations invariably credited to the performer who more than any other thereby created the style, Clifton Chenier. "Now, you see, the real zydeco band was accordion and a rubboard, accordion and a rubboard, and one of those little angle irons [a triangle]," he explained. "Now that's the real zydeco. But now some of the latest, like Clifton Chenier, my cousin, that's my first cousin, well, he started to come up with guitars and saxophones and stuff that really don't go in no zydeco band."

Nor is L. C. alone in these sentiments. Curiously, *combat* may be a more appropriate term than *combination* to describe the perpetually uneasy relationship between French music and blues. Especially today, a cluster of interrelated if seemingly irreconcilable factors—the remarkable popularity of zydeco, coupled with the marked decline in a black audience for blues, almost perversely counterbalanced by many Creoles' preference for Chenier's style of bluesy accordion backed by a heavily amplified R&B band—have forced some French musicians to play blues and some blues musicians to play French, sometimes to the satisfaction of no one.

These aesthetic conflicts are merely one dimension of a wider dilemma within Creole culture, arising, like this expanded range of musical options, from Creoles' greater contact with and participation in "American" culture, most conspicuous in urban Texas, where French Louisiana's relatively fluid ethnic taxonomy is replaced by a two-caste system in which individuals are either black or white. In such settings, then, Creoles find themselves increasingly identified with "American" blacks (to cite only one especially revealing cultural index, marriages between Creoles and non-Creole blacks, relatively rare only a couple of generations ago, are now commonplace), yet few are willing or able entirely to discard the French identity that historically has tied them more closely to their white neighbors, the Cajuns, from whom they're now distanced by their redefined "blackness."[7] The stylistic conflicts embodied in zydeco are thus very much an expression of the problematics of Creole ethnicity in an urban environment.

This brings me to a final, fundamental contradiction in zydeco. That is, while Creoles and critics alike conventionally associate this genre with rural Louisiana, zydeco is—if only circumstantially—as much and perhaps more an urban Texas tradition. Granted, the style's formative influences are easily traced within the folk traditions of South Louisiana. In actuality, however, zydeco constitutes a postwar popular music that first made its mark in Texas cities such as Port Arthur, Beaumont, Galveston, and Houston (Fig. 10.2). It was in Texas cities that aspiring professionals such as Clifton Chenier first combined Creole accordion music with black R&B to create the music they then called "zydeco," a term appearing in Houston only in the late 1940s. It was in Texas cities that these performers first tapped the commercial venues capable of sustaining full-time musicians, including the electronic media so essential to zydeco's development and diffusion. And it was in Texas cities too that these performers initially established the logistical bases from which to tour as the new style's popularity spread.

Ironically, the belief that zydeco first emerged in rural Louisiana is both a cause and effect of the genre's success, since zydeco—like many urban ethnic traditions—represents both a response to and a reaction against the socioeconomic, demographic, and cultural stresses under which it evolved.

Fig. 10.2. The French Gulf Coast. (Drawing by James E. Whitcraft.)

In this respect, zydeco resembles a number of contemporary popular styles—for example, country and western or bluegrass—that deliberately emphasize their distant sources in folk traditions, providing adherents with a symbolic link to an idealized rural past. This probably explains why the word *zydeco* itself is now often applied generically to all Creole music, incongruously attached to forms bearing little resemblance to the accordion-based R&B originally described as "zydeco," or anachronistically applied to traditions antedating that style's appearance by decades or more.

Ironically, too, this urge to invent a romanticized rural past for newly coined urban traditions most plausibly explains the relative neglect of Houston's central role in zydeco, since that cosmopolitan setting is hardly consistent with the genre's stereotypical association with the Gulf Coast's French Creole hinterlands. Not that this circumstance has been completely overlooked.[8] It does fly in the face of received wisdom, though, which definitely casts Texas as peripheral to, rather than central within, the zydeco genre. However, while Texas zydeco may be a cluster of contradictions, it is not, conventional wisdom to the contrary, a contradiction in terms; in fact, at the beginning Texas zydeco *was* zydeco—period.

Given these considerations, a more complete history of Texas zydeco than presently exists is significant not only in and of itself; rather, such an account addresses a major imbalance in our view of this genre as a whole. This essay, then, is intended to counter the conventional notion that "zydeco music is a unique blend of African-American and African-French traditions indigenous to southwest Louisiana"; that "born out of close interaction between the Cajun (white) and Creole (black) populations of Louisiana, zydeco music developed into a distinctive genre when it received a healthy dose of rhythm and blues influence from the urban areas of east Texas"; that "its initial spread can be linked to Creole out-migration from Louisiana"; and that its "subsequent diffusion can be attributed to the commercial recording and distribution of the music and the national and international concert tours of zydeco musicians."[9] Given the empirical evidence, it is more accurate to state that zydeco represents a unique *confrontation* between African American and African-French traditions indigenous to southeast Texas (in some cases played by musicians who are technically neither African American nor French); that, born of the displacement of Louisiana Creoles, zydeco emerged as a distinctive genre through an ambiguous and ambivalent relationship with rhythm and blues within urban Texas; and that its initial spread back to the Creole hearth area of South Louisiana, as well as its subsequent diffusion, is attributable in part to Creole return migration and in part to recording and touring by musicians operating from East Texas—and especially Houston—or even southern California.

Although the urban popular style now known as zydeco first appeared in southeast Texas after World War II, its roots undeniably reach to Louisiana's colonial era. The most significant forebears of the present-day Creoles were the French-speaking slaves and *gens de couleur libres* ("free persons of color") of eighteenth- and early-nineteenth-century Louisiana and the French West Indies, usually, in the case of these free *créoles,* the manumitted offspring of French or Spanish planters and their black chattel. Much of this free-black population eventually settled the bayous, marshlands, and prairies to the west of New Orleans, subsisting as small farmers, fishermen, ranchers, and trappers or, in some instances, as slave-owning planters themselves. Besides continuing to associate with Francophone slaves and their descendants, or with the heirs of the colonial French and Spanish of pre-1803 Louisiana, these *créoles de couleur* intermingled in subsequent generations with later European emigrés, prominent among them Germans, Italians, and Irish; with Scotch-Irish *Américains* and Anglophone slaves (the *Noir'méricains*) arriving from the Deep and upper South after the Louisiana Purchase; and with the remnants of the region's indigenous peoples. However, the Creoles' most numerous and influential neighbors were the Acadians and their descendants, the Cajuns, the French colonists expelled from "Acadia" (now Nova Scotia) by the British during the French and Indian War.[10]

Predictably a kindred complexity characterized the early musical traditions of Louisiana's rural "Creoles of color." Many were simply adaptations of European genres: ballads and love lyrics, game songs, lullabies, and Africanized versions of Celtic fiddle tunes imported both from Brittany via Acadia and from Britain and Ireland via the American South. Other forms more directly reflected the Creoles' African American heritage, paralleling other New World black traditions: worksongs and hollers, topical satires, and the dance songs known as "*juré* singing." Deriving its name from the traditional expletive "*Jurez* (testify), my Lord," the last is a localized form of the African American "ring shout," consisting of a counterclockwise procession accompanied by antiphonal singing and the shuffling, stamping, and clapping of the dancers, occasionally supplemented by simple percussion such as the ubiquitous metal-on-jawbone scraper or its descendant, the washboard. Percussive traditions themselves were also important, as Louisiana blacks were generally free from the prohibition on drumming imposed throughout much of the South.[11]

Although many Creole genres perpetuated African or European traditions, these were substantially modified in South Louisiana, and local developments were also significant. The most important innovation was the adoption of the diatonic button accordion sometime after its invention in Austria in the 1820s. Conventional wisdom holds that this instrument was introduced by German immigrants during the 1880s, but other data reveal that it was already current among Creoles (and possibly Cajuns) before 1850, merely one instance of the accordion's popularity among antebellum blacks.[12] In any event, by the early twentieth century the accordion had come to dominate both Creole and Cajun traditions, replacing the fiddle as lead instrument in most rural dance bands.

Born in Opelousas, Louisiana, in 1932, Alcide "L. C." Donatto Sr. is today regarded by many Creoles and Cajuns alike as the finest accordionist in Houston, Harris County, or even Texas as a whole. Asked about zydeco's origins, he replied,

> I couldn't tell you, 'cause if I'd tell you, I'd be lying, 'cause I was too small when that started. I wasn't even born. It would take some of them old, old

fellows to tell you. . . . Some of them I don't think could tell you really how it started, but I know some of it. You work in the field all day, pick cotton all day and plow, then when you get home, get out of the field, get home and take your bath, all the neighbors want to have a party and have fun, take your bath and put—they ain't had no electricity, had some lamps—put the lamps all around the wall and some benches, and play, especially on the weekends. Start that Friday night, then they didn't quit till that Sunday night, about twelve o'clock Sunday night. Gumbo, popcorn, aw, hell, we had a good time!

L. C.'s descriptions of the performances themselves evoke the Africanized pole in the prewar stylistic spectrum, typified by a syncopated accordion technique subordinating melodic development to rhythmic complexity, complemented by the washboard accompaniment unique to black tradition. ("The real [that is, original] zydeco band was accordion and a rubboard," he asserted. "Now that's the real zydeco!") Other Creoles played in a style indistinguishable from that of their Cajun neighbors—what L. C. calls "French"—a strain epitomized by legendary Creole accordionist Amédé Ardoin, who recorded extensively in the 1920s and 1930s, often with Cajun fiddler Dennis McGee. In fact, although contemporary zydeco musicians often cite Ardoin as an inspiration, his lasting influence has really been in Cajun-French tradition. (L. C., who knew Ardoin only from records, insisted "Some of the people today call him zydeco, but it's French—whole lot different from zydeco.")

The precise role of the blues in early Creole music is difficult to ascertain. Although the blues shares many of the traits distinguishing black French tradition from its Cajun analogues, this may simply reflect their common African American provenance. Residing between East Texas and the Mississippi Delta, two of America's premier blues regions, Creoles must have been exposed to the genre from an early date, either through records or itinerant performers, and scattered accounts support that assumption. Indeed, blues records in particular apparently had considerable impact on Creole musicians; however, the performers they most often name—Muddy Waters, Lightnin' Hopkins, John Lee Hooker, and so forth—began recording after World War II and represent national as well as regional trends. Even before the war but especially after, Louisiana produced many fine bluesmen, but most came from outside the Creole region, either from along the Mississippi to the east or around Shreveport to the north. In the 1920s and 1930s Creole musicians sometimes included the term *blues* in song titles (such is the case, for example, with many of Ardoin's recordings), but that tag is an unreliable indicator at best, and these items bear little definitive resemblance to "American blues."[13] In sum the blues does not appear to have greatly influenced Creole music before World War II. And the early evidence for that relationship comes not from the rural Creole heartland but from outlying enclaves in Texas cities.

The twentieth-century migrations of Creoles are consistent with demographic trends in the South as a whole. Beginning between the two world wars, but especially during and after World War II, rural Creoles inundated industrial centers such as Lake Charles, Port Arthur, Galveston, Beaumont, and Houston. In Houston they initially settled around 1919 in the area of the old Fifth Ward now known as "Frenchtown," the core of that city's Creole community.[14] At the time of its formal incorporation in 1922, Frenchtown consisted of approximately five hundred residents inhabiting a dozen or so city blocks. As Creole migration increased, especially after the great Mississippi River flood of 1927, the district expanded accordingly, eventually including three times its original area (roughly the tract bounded by Liberty Road, Collingsworth Avenue, Russell Street, and the East-Tex Freeway), although later arrivals also moved into other black neighborhoods just beyond Frenchtown's formal boundaries.

The recollections of Anderson Moss typify the experiences of these first migrants. Born in Louisiana on February 11, 1917, just southwest of Lafayette, near Mauriceville, Moss arrived with his family at the peak of the first major wave of Creole migration. "We moved here in 1927," he recalled six decades later, sitting in the living room of his home on Houston's northeast side. "Why? Well, I'm going to tell you; the crop in Louisiana went down to nothing. And so I had two—my older brothers was living here in Houston, they had good jobs. And so my mother came over here and my baby brother, and she seen how things was going over here; she come back home and told my daddy, says, 'It's the best thing to move to Houston.' Says, 'There's plenty of work; they's begging for men to work.'"

Labor was indeed in demand in Houston's expanding economy. The Southern Pacific Railroad in particular provided employment for many Creoles. Others worked on Houston's waterfront, still others as skilled craftsmen—carpenters, mechanics, brick masons, paper hangers, plumbers, and so forth—or in the industrial or service sectors (Moss, for example, was first employed digging sewers). Women worked as homemakers or as domestics.

Distinguished by their language and culture from the balance of Houston's African American population, Creoles have to the present remained something of a community apart. Admittedly the Creole language has suffered in this predominantly Anglophone setting. At present conversational French is increasingly rare, the use of patois primarily limited to highly formalized expressions such as singing and songs. Even then texts are often simply memorized rote from older singers or from recordings, while "French music" in English has long been commonplace.

The family, on the other hand, was and still is of inestimable importance, easing the transition between rural Louisiana and urban Texas while preserving ties between these milieus. Even today Houston Creoles routinely rely or expound on subtle degrees of filiation antedating by decades these prewar migrations, and persons born and raised in Texas, sometimes as second- or third-generation Texans, still refer to Louisiana as "back home." The Catholic religion has likewise endured. Our Mother of Mercy, the city's first Creole parish, was founded in 1928, its building and adjoining convent school completed just outside Frenchtown the following year. Today there are a dozen such congregations around Houston, constituting the focal social institution outside the kin group for most Creoles, although family and church are for many persons practically inseparable. Not surprisingly, then, other formal organizations are usually closely aligned with, or even modeled after, these familial and religious units—for instance, the Creole Knights fraternal order (est. 1936) or the men's and women's auxiliaries of the various churches. Family-owned businesses also originally doubled as social centers.

Thus in the prewar period especially, Houston's Creole community retained much of the air of rural Louisiana. Many elderly persons remember hunting or fishing in areas that only a half-century later rank among the planet's most urbanized. Early Frenchtown residents also routinely kept large gardens and even chickens and pigs—practices that still have not died out entirely—so that agrarian customs like the *boucherie* (communal hog killing) have survived in Houston much longer than one might expect.

While many rural traditions were transplanted to Texas, some, such as Mardi Gras, never took hold. (Although both Moss and Donatto recalled pre-Lenten festivities from Louisiana, they agreed that these never transpired in Houston.) Music, by contrast, flourished in Frenchtown, a circumstance frequently remarked, if but vaguely, by outsiders. The WPA's Depression-era *Houston: A History and Guide* almost certainly overstates the case when, after noting that "this part of the [city's] Negro population [that is, Frenchtown's Creole enclave] has a characteristic passion for music and dancing, and performs elaborate rituals through both mediums," it goes on to claim that "nearly every person in the Frenchtown community can play a musical instrument."[15] Nonetheless, older Creoles still vividly recall

Frenchtown's prewar "house parties with zydeco music played on accordions and rub boards for rhythm," where residents "danced the lala, the two step, and other popular steps."[16]

Again, Anderson Moss exemplifies these migratory traditions. "I was raised in a place they call Mauriceville, Louisiana," he explained.

> And I was about nine years old. They—long time ago, they used to give them zydecos, see? It was close by where I lived at. They had a big hall; they would give a zydeco every two weeks. And I was go down there, and I was too little to go inside, 'cause my mother and daddy was there. I would stay on the outside, me and my sister and little brother. You see, they was dancing, and we looking. And they had a fellow named Johnson would play. He had a washboard, accordion; the one beat the washboard, and one played accordion. They didn't had nothing electric them days, they play just—and they had some little iron [a triangle], they call 'em "*tit fer*" [literally, "little iron"].
> . . . And there'd be three or four hundred people in that hall, man. And the people would be enjoying theirself. That's way back. And the guy was playing was named Johnson. And he weared a shoe, 15 1/2—big foot man, big man. But he pulled that thing. That'll go until about two o'clock at night, start about eight to two. That's for every two weeks. Now they had another man they would call Bidon. *Bidon.* He had a head about that long. But brother, you talk about lay that stuff down, he laid it down. He *played* that accordion. Well, I know'd a whole lots of 'em would come down there and played in that hall.
> That's how I become to play accordion, now you see. In 1927 we moved here in Houston. I went downtown and bought me an accordion. And I learned myself. Then I started playing. I learned; it didn't take me long. 'Cause I come from down there, you know. I knew how it'd go. . . . My mother and daddy—both of them was living—they used to laugh at me. But my daddy was a harp player, had a great big harp. I guess I took after him. And that's the way—*zydeco!* I come from the zydeco country—I knew a *whole lot* of musicians.

These musicians included not only Johnson and Bidon, renowned accordionists from the Lafayette area, but also many other major figures of the prewar tradition, foremost among them Amédé Ardoin. "Amédé had a long head," Moss recollected. "But that man, he was good!" He also remembered Claude Faulk and the Reynolds brothers, Jesse and Joseph.[17] "And they had Chilook and Cha Bec," he continued. "They lived in Galveston, but they were raised up in my home." Other accordionists who came west to Texas included Joe Jesse and Jack George. "They lived there all across that San Jacinto River. They all dead." However, when I first asked Moss, "Who would've been playing around in Houston back in the twenties, when you started?" he without hesitation named the individual whom elderly Creoles invariably credit with establishing French music in Houston: "The fellow they call Willie Green. . . . Willie Green! One while we was the onliest two here in Houston playing. He played most in the Sixth Ward, back up in there. Well, I played in the First Ward, and Third Ward, Fifth Ward. I had this end covered!"

During this formative period, music making was featured primarily on the same occasions as it was "back home": house dances, birthday and anniversary celebrations, picnics or barbecues, and the like. "I used to play, uh, I started when I first started, you remember—?" Moss began, trailing off before suddenly catching himself. "Oh no, you wasn't born! When the 'St. Louis Blues' come out and, uh, 'Stormy Weather'? 'Keep raining all the time'? Then they came out with 'Black gal, what makes you doggone head so nappy?' Them times.[18] They used to give house dances. You pay a dime, a quarter to come in. That's last all night, brother. It ain't like it is now. All night. And plenty of foods to eat. Plenty to drink. And plenty pretty women [laughs]. Yes sir!"

Despite the early importance of such domestic functions—house parties and other "casuals" still occasionally feature live music, but this is hardly the norm—these gatherings were already losing ground by the 1940s, when more and more Creoles began frequenting establishments such as Houston's famed El Dorado Ballroom, where they could dance to the trendier sounds of big bands or urban "jump" blues. Ironically, it was then that French music experienced a rebirth, coinciding with the second wave of Creole migration, when Willie Green moved his music from private homes into public taverns.

Among the Creoles then pouring into Houston was fourteen-year-old L. C. Donatto, who as a member of Green's circle would help to inaugurate the next phase in Houston zydeco. Like Moss, L. C. was from an early age acquainted with the major exponents of the rural Creole tradition. His own family was not especially musical, however. "My mother played a French accordion like the Cajuns play," he acknowledged. "Yeah, one of them one-row button, and she could play a harmonica, too. But other than that I'm the only one, you know, left in the family playing now, and nary one of 'em play, no one but my mother." Fortunately, the Donattos numbered among their neighbors the now-legendary Reynolds brothers, Jesse and Joseph, who early on sensed L. C.'s potential. "One day my daddy was coming from work," he recalled. "And we was sitting on the porch, and he [Reynolds] was teaching [me]. He told Joseph Reynolds, he said, 'You just losing time.' And he told my daddy, he said, 'No, he'll be better than me and all my brothers.'

Because all the family of them could play. And sure enough that's what happened."

"That's where I started, but I end up finishing here," L. C. concluded. In fact his apprenticeship was interrupted when Joseph Reynolds moved to the tiny Texas community of China, just over the Louisiana border near Beaumont. "And when he moved the first time that he moved to China, well, I stayed maybe about a year or two years later with his brother Jesse," L. C. continued. "And his brother could play. But the one was teaching me was the best. So that's where I got it, from Joseph Reynolds. That's how I started. But when I come here, I was fourteen—I been here ever since."

Despite his relative youth, L. C. was soon performing with established players like Willie Green. His musical prowess aside, little else is known about Green. What seems certain is that he was born in Louisiana, that he came to Houston during the 1920s, and that he died there of heart trouble in the mid-1960s. Moss recalled that Green was already an established local performer by the early 1930s, although the most influential phase of his career began on Christmas Eve 1949, when he became the first Houston Creole to perform French music in a public venue. L. C., seventeen at the time, provided this recollection:

> One Christmas Eve we was riding, just riding around in a car, and we happened to be riding around in the Sixth Ward. And we just sitting in the car, driving and playing that thing and drinking and having fun, and there's some tall black fellow, just sitting on his porch, had his wife fussing at him. He's banging on a guitar but he couldn't play it. And he hollered at us to stop. Well, so we backed up, and he told us pull in the drive. We pulled into the driveway, say, "Y'all come on the porch and play." One Christmas Eve. And we started playing that—it was Willie Green and I, and, uh, got a rubboard man—we started playing, but you know something? That yard was full, full of people, done tramped all the lady's flowers in the ground. She raised sand but she didn't say nothing to us 'cause she enjoyed, and when we look around, they had—uh, Miss Irene—well, she dead now, but she had a café, a nice place, and she heard that, and she come on 'round there, her and her husband, and seen all them people, said, "Well, why don't y'all come to the café?" And we started from that day. Started from that, and Count Basie or Benny Goodman couldn't draw no bigger crowd than that. And that, you know that, it looked funny to them 'cause they never seen that before. And we the first one played, that's right, zydeco in Houston.[19]

So began Willie Green's long tenure at Irene's Café, where he performed until his death. Because of his success, moreover, French music was soon featured at other establishments with Creole clienteles. Already, like Green, a performer of some local renown, Moss remembered first meeting Donatto around this time, when the few established players suddenly had more work than they could handle.

> See L. C. start about the time with me, almost the time with me, see. Lot of time, I would walk way from Third Ward to Fifth Ward, to save that dime [for bus fare]. I'd go way down on Liberty Road, I was living way in Third Ward, now. I walk across and tell him [L. C.], I say, "I got enough to play, now; you want to play some sets tonight?" He would tell me, "Okay, Moss," say, "I'll be there." Well, all his children was small, see. Say, "Okay. I can depend on you?" I say, "Yeah, 'cause," I says, "I got too much." . . . Man, sometime I would play every night! And then I would work, you understand? Course, I got used to it, you know, playing, you know, after I found out the dope on it. But it wasn't no strain.

Among the era's other top-ranked accordionists was Alfonse Lonnie Mitchell, who, like Donatto and Moss, was a fixture in Houston's Creole community for over four decades. Mitchell was born around 1925, between Beaumont and Houston at Liberty, where his parents had moved from Louisiana. Like L. C., he was the only musically inclined member of his immediate family. "I'm the only one out of ten [children] that wanted to play music," he laughed. "The rest of them didn't want to fool with it. But I just love music ever since I heard, you know, zydeco music." His first inspiration was a prominent prewar accordionist often recalled by elderly Creoles. "It was a guy here in Houston, name of Joe Jesse," Mitchell averred. "He was playing—my uncle live in Raywood, a little town, and he would get that guy to play every other Saturday. And so he would—it's my older brother and him was good friends—and he would come over there and spend the night with my brother. And he showed me how to play the accordion, and I just started from there coming up. I was about twelve, I guess, something like that when he first started coming to my mother's. And so my mother bought me one, and I just took up from there."

For a few years, Mitchell performed intermittently around his hometown, quitting altogether when he got married around 1940. After the war he moved to Houston and went to work in an auto body shop in nearby Alvin. It was then that a chance encounter with Willie Green prompted Lonnie Mitchell again to take up the accordion. "I could play good enough for dancing when I was eighteen," he continued, "and just start from there. And early '50 I moved here to Houston. And so I hadn't heard nothing about zydeco music for about a year after I moved here, and then I heard about a guy named Willie Green was playing out in Sixth Ward, so that's when I went over there, played some, and a guy heard me, and so they said that, well, 'If you get your music, I'll hire you to play.'"

The "guy" who approached Lonnie Mitchell that night was Charley Johnson, a local nightclub owner who had previously declined to book French musicians. (His flagship operation—Johnson's Lounge—featured an orchestra and floorshow at the time.) The booming business at Irene's had apparently changed his mind, however, and he was just then in the market for a black French accordionist. Lonnie Mitchell thus began a four-decade stand in Frenchtown. By the mid-1960s Johnson's, often featuring Mitchell six nights a week, was Houston's premier Creole nightspot. And while most of the Gulf Coast's zydeco greats have played the club over the years, Mitchell was by all accounts—his own and others'—the man people came to see. "Most everybody wanted to hear me play, what come out there," he confessed. "Honest true. I remember the time, if I would take off, that, you know, Old Man Johnson had it, I take off, wife and I go somewhere, and I'll get back, oh, around ten or eleven, you know, there'd be people standing around on the outside, 'cause they don't want to hear nobody else but me." In fact, after Johnson passed away in the mid-1960s, Mitchell took over "running the place, the dances, and playing my own dances too." Mitchell's, as the club was then called, lasted for five years, when the lease reverted to Johnson's granddaughter, Doris McLendon. She changed the name to the Continental Lounge but wisely kept Lonnie Mitchell, who played there almost up to his death in September 1995.

Other early Frenchtown accordionists included Albert Chevalier. Born in Lafayette, Louisiana, in 1909, Chevalier moved in 1943 to Port Arthur and then in 1952 to Houston. In fact he was one of the musicians originally rejected by Charley Johnson. Chevalier later told Chris Strachwitz that "people made fun of him and his music when he auditioned at Johnson's" and that Lonnie Mitchell was eventually hired "because, according to Mr. Chevalier, he would play for less." Never really breaking into clubs, Chevalier played primarily at house dances until his death in Houston in the mid-1960s.[20]

Born at Opelousas in 1919, Vincent Frank was another important accordionist arriving in Houston just after World War II. Recorded by folklorist Mack McCormick in 1959, he also cut a few sides for the local Ivory label during the 1960s. He was reportedly still living in Houston in the mid-1980s, but I was never able to contact him, and he has since passed away.[21] Also from Opelousas was Herbert "Good Rockin'" Sam, who, as his nickname implies, was an early exponent of the bluesy urban accordion style. Born in 1924, he spent many years in Houston before returning to Louisiana, where he now manages a popular group comprising his sons, the Sam Brothers Five.[22] In fact, as Houston's Creole population and musical venues expanded apace, more and more musicians came from Louisiana specifically to exploit the city's possibilities. Anderson Moss also remembered Marcel Dugas: "Live up in there in the Lake Charles—play good. He come here and play some time. . . . He been playing ever since I been playing!"[23] Similarly, Claude Faulk, who although much admired in South Louisiana never recorded and played mainly around Lafayette, occasionally performed in Port Arthur and Houston.[24] But without question the most important figure emerging from Texas during this period was Clifton Chenier, who almost single-handedly pioneered and popularized the urban accordion music now known as "zydeco." In fact, Chenier, who is often justifiably credited with having "invented" the genre, seems also to have named it.

Admittedly, the term *zydeco,* much like the music it describes, is rooted in rural Creole traditions. In Creole folk etymology, *zydeco* is said to be cognate with the French *les haricots,* or "beans." In other words, *zydeco* and its many variants (for example, *zodico, zotico, zadeco, zordico, zarico*—there is no standard spelling, although *zydeco* is today the most common) are simply phonetic representations of "*les haricots,*" or more specifically, of the liaison between the plural article's final consonant and the noun ("*'s'haricots*"), with the tongue-flapped French *r* assuming the character of an English *d.*[25]

The term's musical associations are customarily traced to a floating lyric— "*les haricots sont pas salés*"—literally, "the snap beans aren't salted," a metaphor for hard times. As one of Nick Spitzer's informants explained, "In the old days somebody would meet you and he'd say, 'Tu vas faire z'haricots?' and that would mean are you gonna get your beans in this year or really 'How are you doin'?' So you might say back to him, 'Ouais, Je vas faire z'haricots, mais z'haricots sont pas salé.' That would mean that you were gonna have beans, but no meat. You'd have no meat not even salt-meat, to flavor the beans. You was barely gettin' by."[26] Even today in urban areas, one may still encounter this conversational usage. So from the vantage of Houston's late-1980s "oil bust," Anderson Moss volunteered,

> What you call this pressure is a high-class depressure. That other one in 1927, '28, '29 into the thirties, there was plenty of work, now. You want to work, you have the work, but the salary, you know what I'm talking about? But if you had five or six children, you could feed them for twenty-five cents a day,

you understand? Meat what you pay a dollar sixty for it or a dollar fifty a pound, in them days you pay ten cents a pound. Said the neck, cost you six cents a pound. Pork bones, things like that, three cents a pound. You understand? But go down there in them stores and try to get that. Ain't nothing but a zydeco [that is, beans but no meat], that's all it is [laughs]! Yeah. You'll have to pay, man.

Its more literal applications aside, this figure functions in folk songs as a metaphor for romantic difficulties signified through the familiar "food-as-sex" (or lack thereof) analogy. The earliest of these musical examples were recorded by Alan Lomax in South Louisiana in 1934. In one, a traditional love lyric performed as a *juré*, the group's leader, Jimmy Peters, enumerates various misfortunes—in one verse, for instance, he laments "Toi, comment tu veux je te vas voir, / Mais quand mon chapeau rouge est fini? / Toi, comment tu veux je te vas voir, / Mais quand mon suit est tout déchiré?" ("You, how can you want me to see you / When my red hat is worn? / You, how can you want me to see you / When my suit is all torn?")—underscored by the refrain "O mam, mais donnez-moi les haricots. / Mais ô chérie, les haricots sont pas salés" ("Oh momma, give me some beans. / But oh dear, the beans aren't salted").[27] In another of Lomax's recordings—"*Dégo*"—the singer, Wilbur Charles, complains that his wife is lying ill in a ditch with some Italian fruit vendors, the result of having eaten their rotten bananas; his own situation is summed up by the insistent refrain: no meat, no nothing, only beans in the pot and the beans aren't salted (obviously the "food-as-sex" metaphor works on a number of levels in this one).[28] After World War II this refrain often appears in another traditional love lyric, "*Hip et Taïaut*," or occasionally by itself in otherwise instrumental performances.[29]

Barry Ancelet seems close to the mark when he writes that "'Zarico' in Louisiana French, like 'blues' in American English, describes hard times and the music that expresses them and eases the pain."[30] (Or, as Texas bluesman Lightnin' Hopkins would sing, "Let's go zydeco 'cause times gettin' hard down here.") Intriguingly Ancelet also suggests that, folk etymology to the contrary, this cognomen may derive from the coincidental phonological resemblance of the French word for green beans and various West African phrases associated with dancing.[31] Whatever its West African contacts—Ancelet's data are inconclusive—zydeco is, in current Creole usage, indeed analogous to the English word *dance*: as a noun it can refer to a social occasion involving music and dancing, to the music played at such an occasion, or to a particular dance step or the accompanying tune. In other cases it acts as a verb— "to zydeco" is to engage in any or all of the foregoing—or more particularly as an imperative, commanding the listener to dance or just to party in general ("Zydeco, baby! Et toi!").[32] Of these various senses, the first is apparently the oldest, putatively employed in South Louisiana before World War II. Curiously, however, conclusive documentation appears only in the postwar period. And the earliest indisputable evidence comes not from Louisiana but from Houston.

The first writer to remark the term *zydeco* was apparently Marie Lee Phelps, who in 1955 contributed the article "Visit to Frenchtown" to the *Houston Post*. Describing the pastimes of Houston's Creoles, she wrote that "on Saturday night, somebody holds a 'zottico' in his home. Out come the accordion, banjo and rub bo'd. The latter is an oldtime washing board. The musician plays it with a thimble on his finger. Off they whirl in a folk dance similar to the square dance."[33] Actually, the term had surfaced nearly a decade before, not in print media, but on commercial recordings by black Houstonians. And the earliest mention comes not from a Creole but from Houston's top bluesman, Lightnin' Hopkins. In 1949 Hopkins re-created a Frenchtown soirée for Gold Star Records. Issued as "Zolo Go," the piece features Lightnin' on electric organ instead of his usual guitar, imitating an accordionist at a "zolo go" ("zydeco") dance. (Indeed this release may thus also constitute the first use of this term in print, that is, as given on its label; Fig. 10.3.) As the recording begins, Hopkins exclaims, "Gonna zydeco a little while for you, folks. You know young and old likes that. Wake up directly."

> Wake up, old maid: don't you sleep too long,
> Wake up, old maid: don't you sleep too long,
> You know, we got a zydeco dance: it's just going on.
>
> [instrumental chorus]
>
> Yes, here come a-Johnnie: with her head rag on her head [*Spoken:* Hold it, lord!],
> Yes, here come a-Johnnie: with her head rag on her head,
> Yes, she's got to zydeco 'cause she woke up out of her bed.
>
> [instrumental chorus] [*Spoken:*] Whoo-ee!
>
> Well, two old maids: they're laying in the bed,
> Yes, two old maids, boys: they're laying in the bed,
> Well, one turned over and this is what they said.
>
> Let's go zydeco 'cause times getting hard down here,
> Let's go zydeco 'cause times getting hard down here,
> I'm going back tomorrow: see who feels my care.[34]

Although the song's basic structure (three-line stanzas accompanied by a twelve-bar I-IV-I-V-IV-I chord progression) obviously reflects Hopkins's background as a bluesman, the piece also echoes contemporaneous trends in Creole music. Around the same time, in fact, the term *zydeco* first appeared on a recording by a Creole, although Clarence Garlow was hardly more a traditional French musician than was Lightnin' Hopkins. Born in 1911, just east of Lake Charles in Welsh, Louisiana, Garlow learned a little fiddle as a boy from his father, who played "stomps and hoedowns" with his two brothers. Garlow did not tackle music in earnest, however, until moving to Beaumont during the 1940s. Inspired by the records of T-Bone Walker, he bought an electric guitar, joined the musicians' union, and formed his own R&B band. Soon afterward a gig in Houston led to a session with the local Macy's label. The result was an unexpected hit, "Bon Ton Roula," a number in "kinda broken dialect," as he described it, "born right in the studio when we was trying to find something to record."[35] Notwithstanding its folksy persona—"You see me there, well, I ain't no fool," the singer begins, "I'm one smart Frenchman never been to school"—"Bon Ton Roula" is anything but rural French music. Over a jump blues guitar riff backed by piano, saxophone, and drums, Garlow evokes a series of backcountry tableaux, culminating in the final verse:

> At the church bazaar or the baseball game,
> At the French La-La, it's all the same,
> If you want to have fun, now, you got to go,
> Way out in the country to the zydeco.
> Well, let the bon ton rouler.[36]

Garlow subsequently recycled the "Bon Ton Roula" formula for Los Angeles's Aladdin and Modern labels, but he never matched the original's success. "Crawfishin'"/"Route 90" (1954) came close.[37] More tantalizing is "Jumping at the Zadacoe," recorded for Aladdin in July 1953 but unissued until 1996. Aside from its title, though, this track likewise bears little resemblance to rural French music, not too surprising given the presence of Maxwell Davis's Orchestra, then also backing such artists as B. B. King and Percy Mayfield.[38] In fact, except for a few such "novelty" items, most of Garlow's recordings were in the mold of his idol, T-Bone Walker. He never enjoyed much success in this vein, however, and when his West Coast prospects played out in the mid-1950s, he returned home to Beaumont, recording a few more sides for small independent labels and even taking up the accordion to court the French market. (Although that move was not especially

Fig. 10.3. The original label for Lightnin' Hopkins's "Zolo Go." (Courtesy Chris Strachwitz/ Arhoolie Productions.)

successful either, he was something of a trendsetter in this as well.) Eventually, however, Garlow gave up music to work as a disc jockey, television repairman, and restaurateur.

By then (the mid-1950s) *zydeco* was applied to Creole music as well as to the occasions at which it was played, although both were increasingly removed from their rural antecedents. The first person to use the term in this sense was another Louisiana-born but Texas-based R&B aspirant whose frustration in that field eventually forced him back to French music, an accordionist who occasionally played at Clarence Garlow's "Bon Ton Drive-In" in Beaumont: Clifton Chenier. And, once again, the first conclusive evidence for this semantic shift comes from a commercial recording, Chenier's "Zodico

Stomp," cut in Los Angeles in 1955.[39] Nearly three decades later Chenier explained how he came to call his music "zydeco." "When I made a hit with 'Ay Tete Fee' [another of his first recordings] and stuff and called it 'zydeco' everybody started saying 'zydeco,'" he told Anne Savoy. "See, the old people used to say 'Let's go to the zydeco,' meaning the dance. And I kept that in mind, and when I started playing music I called my music 'zydeco.'"[40] Although researchers have generally dismissed or disregarded this account, apparently preferring to believe that *zydeco* is the traditional name for this music, Creoles—and especially musicians—invariably back Clifton's claim.

Take, for example, Ashton Savoy, whose comments are typical. Born near Opelousas in 1928, Savoy has played both zydeco and R&B—he is currently the guitarist in Donatto's band—although he definitely prefers the latter. His father was an accomplished Creole fiddler, however, and Savoy also numbers several accordion players among his immediate family. "Back a long time ago ... they didn't call it 'zydeco,'" he insisted. "Clifton and them started that 'zydeco' stuff. They used to call that 'French la la.' . . . 'Well, we going around to listen at the French la la tonight,' you know. You know, then Clifton's the one that came up with that 'zydeco'—'Allons danser le zydeco.'" Savoy also confirms that this terminological shift coincided with stylistic changes after World War II. "They call it the 'French la la,'" he reiterated. "But when they started putting them horns and saxophones and all that stuff in there [guitar, drums, and so forth], well, then they started playing the blues, they started mixing that stuff up then, you know. Well, that's when they started calling it 'zydeco' then." He underscored the point with a cogent analogy to white country music: "Stuff like that, that violin, well, then they call that 'French music,' you know what I'm talking about? [Just like] they couldn't call it [prewar white country music] 'bluegrass' or 'country and western' [terms appearing only after the war], they couldn't call it—and they call that 'hillbilly.' . . . Couldn't call it 'bluegrass.' It was 'hillbilly.'"[41]

Creoles and non-Creoles alike have often done just that with *zydeco*, however, anachronistically applying this term to any and all varieties of Creole music, including prewar styles that may have been played at dances called "zydecos"—even here, conclusive evidence is lacking—but that were never in themselves known by that name. Obviously the confusion stems in part from an awareness of the historical and stylistic continuities between prewar traditions and postwar developments—evinced, for example, in the traditional line about unsalted snap beans. Nick Spitzer neatly illustrates the problem when, noting that "the merging of styles resulting in a music actually called 'zydeco' in the Cajun/black Creole areas of southwest Louisiana cannot be exactly pinpointed as to date," he allows that general opinion places its origins in the postwar period, "when black American music style fused with the Cajun French style of rural black Creoles." "However," he writes, "my oldest informants have consistently told me that fast syncopated music like zydeco existed in the 19th century. As the late accordionist Eraste Carrière, born in 1900, said: 'My old pop, he was playin' Zydeco back before I was born.' . . . However, he noted in another interview that even though the more creolized fast two-steps existed during his earliest comprehension of music, 'C'est pas nommé zarico' (It wasn't named zydeco then)."[42]

We can categorically state that, musically as well as nominally, this nineteenth-century tradition was not zydeco either, even if certain stylistic traits foreshadowed the postwar, urban dance music to which that term was first applied. In fact, the merging of styles into a music called "zydeco" *outside* the Cajun/black Creole areas of southwest Louisiana can be pinpointed with reasonable certainty in both time and space: the best evidence indicates that all this occurred in southeast Texas after 1940. At least there is considerable support for that claim—and none to the contrary.

The foregoing data suggest a further cause for all the confusion, as the earliest documented instances of the term *zydeco*—whether applied to dances or dance music—share yet another factor: that is, they all represent an urban and mass-mediated perspective on a vanishing agrarian milieu and its folk traditions. "If you want to have fun, now, you got to go," Clarence Garlow advised from a Houston recording studio, "way out in the country to the zydeco." "See, the old people used to say 'Let's go to the zydeco,'" explained Clifton Chenier, recalling the days of his own first recordings. "And I kept that in mind, and when I started playing music I called my music 'zydeco.'" In this sense too, Savoy's analogy between *zydeco* and *bluegrass* or *country and western* is wonderfully apt, for these terms are all creations of urban or recently urbanized professionals, terms idealizing obsolete, even extinct agrarian or pastoral cultures from the vantage of persons somewhat removed from such lifestyles.

Indisputably, then, as both a musical and linguistic idiom, zydeco is distantly tied to a culture approximating the ideal "folk society," a self-sufficient, nonindustrial, geographically isolated collective of kith and kin, cooperatively producing only what they consumed, consuming only what they produced, communicating exclusively through oral/aural conduits.[43] In reality, though, as both a musical genre and a generic term, zydeco was coined by urban wage earners, more specifically by professional musicians—hardly a fixture in settings where people routinely subsist on unsalted snap beans—

whose technological and musical sophistication, reliance on electronic media, geographic and socioeconomic mobility, and more general relations to urban industrial or even international consumer economies are all more consistent with mass popular music than they are with local folk tradition. And as both a musical and a linguistic entity, zydeco first appeared not in rural Louisiana—the "back home" of the zydeco ethos—but in urban Texas.

Creole accordionist Clifton Chenier personifies these contradictions, and Chenier's role in zydeco invites comparison to other postwar performers identified with such stylistic innovations—Bill Monroe and bluegrass, Muddy Waters and Chicago blues, Elvis Presley and rock and roll—typically through the adaptation of folk or regional idioms to the conventions of urban popular music, and especially to electronic media.[44] At the pinnacle of his later success, Chenier himself defined zydeco as "rock [his term for R&B] and French mixed together, you know, like French music and rock with a beat to it," providing this résumé for interviewer Ben Sandmel:

> I'm born and raised in Opelousas, I left Opelousas way back there in 1946, and went on to Texas. And I learned how to play the accordion in 1947 and '48. From there, I played all around Texas and everywhere, you know, and in 1955 I started recording for Specialty Recording Company, first one was "Eh, tite Fille," "Boppin' the Rock," and the next one, recorded on down the line, and I started jumping from company to company. . . . And after that well, I started nationwide, traveling you know from Texas, to California, Chicago, New York, all them places, up to now.[45]

Clifton Chenier was born in 1925 near Opelousas, where his family farmed on shares. His father played the accordion—the single-row button variety—as did many of his family's acquaintances, among them such influential performers as Claude Faulk and the Reynoldses. "I used to love to hear them play, yeah," Clifton told Anne Savoy. "They played zydeco but they played different. Old-timey, you know. See, they had just rubboards and triangle iron, and they didn't have no drums or nothing."[46] Although Chenier eventually took up the accordion himself, his first instrument was a piano model. Moreover he began playing only after he and his older brother, Cleveland, moved to Port Arthur in the mid-1940s.[47] There he quickly mastered the accordion and began performing publicly, working by day at local refineries and gigging nights and weekends at taverns and house dances, often backed only by Cleveland on rubboard. Despite that "old-timey" lineup, Clifton even then aspired to a more cosmopolitan idiom: when later asked to name his early influences, he typically began with such recording artists as Lightnin'

Hopkins, Muddy Waters, or B. B. King. The first song he remembered learning to play on the accordion was Joe Liggins's R&B hit "The Honeydripper."[48]

Indeed, Cleveland—and the rubboard—were absent when Chenier made his own first recordings. Instead, his 1954 inaugural session featured drummer Robert Pete and Clifton's uncle, bluesman Morris "Big" Chenier, on electric guitar. Held at a Lake Charles radio station, the date was produced by Los Angeles promoter J. R. Fulbright, who issued two tracks—"Louisiana Stomp" and "Cliston [*sic*] Blues"—on his Elko label, leasing the others to Imperial. The results did not sell especially well, but with their bluesy accordion and vocals in English over a straight R&B backing, they established the pattern Chenier would faultlessly follow for at least the next decade.[49]

These early sides also attracted the attention of California's Specialty label, which in 1955 brought Chenier to Los Angeles for the first of several sessions. Again, except for Clifton's accordion, the results were straight R&B, which is not surprising since he was accompanied by the band he was then using in Texas (electric guitar and bass, piano, and drums, sometimes with a saxophone or two). Ironically, the one track he sang in Creole—"Ay-Tete Fee" (that is, "*Eh, 'tite fille*," or "Hey, little girl")—became a minor hit.[50] The resulting exposure kept him on the road for the next several years, working either with his own group out of Port Arthur or on R&B package tours. Specialty dropped him in 1956, however, and his subsequent sides for Argo and Checker (both subsidiaries of Chicago-based blues giant Chess) or for Crowley, Louisiana, producer Jay Miller's Zynn label never came close to matching the success of "Ay-Tete Fee." By 1958 Chenier was back in Texas, living in Houston and playing local clubs or sporadically touring. Although he was still something of a celebrity on the Gulf Coast, he was out of the national limelight for the time being—possibly for good.

Nonetheless, his stature among Houston's Creoles was boosted by another development reflecting their growing acceptance of his urban accordion style: the appearance of zydeco dances in Catholic halls, which was the work of Clarence Gallien Sr. Born in Opelousas in 1913, Gallien had some experience as a music promoter before coming to Houston in 1952 and so in the mid-1960s organized a zydeco dance as a fundraiser for his parish, St. Francis Assisi. The event proved immensely successful, and soon other parishes were holding French dances, usually with Gallien's assistance. In fact, by the late 1980s over a dozen area churches were regularly hosting zydecos, which today constitute the largest regular social functions in Houston's Creole community, sometimes drawing a thousand or more persons.[51] Until his death in January 1989 Gallien was involved in most of these dates, booking the bands, handling security or other arrangements, or acting as an emcee. Presently providing work for scores of Gulf Coast musicians, these church dances have largely eclipsed Houston's zydeco clubs. Early on, however, they were dominated by Clifton Chenier, so much so that I have often heard Gallien referred to as "the man who gave Clifton his start." But while the church zydecos may have sustained Clifton through some lean years, the real turning point occurred in 1964, when an encounter with California record producer Chris Strachwitz revived his recording career.

Fittingly, that meeting was arranged by one of Clifton's early inspirations, by this time also his cousin by marriage, the omnipresent Lightnin' Hopkins. Remembering his introduction to Chenier, Strachwitz has written,

> I met him through Lightnin' Hopkins, who told me one night in Houston that we ought to go out and hear his cousin (on his wife's side) in French Town. I had heard the name before and was familiar with Clifton's records on Specialty and Checker, but at that time I was rather more interested in pure country blues and recall going along, but with little enthusiasm, since I remembered the records as being more in the rhythm and blues vein. However, when we got to the little beer joint, what I heard quickly brought on a rush! Here was this man with an accordion singing his head off in French, accompanied only by a drummer, while a few couples shuffled across the small dance floor. I had never heard the blues done like this before. Mixed with that addictive Cajun sound![52]

Over the next few years the recordings Chenier made for Strachwitz's Arhoolie Records would establish him as an international celebrity.[53] However, his fame as the world's foremost black French musician came largely at the expense of his own musical preferences, since even though Chenier deferred to the demand for French music, he always preferred to perform straight R&B. After Chenier's death in 1987, Strachwitz summed up the dilemma. "Over the years Clifton Chenier became the undisputed king of Zydeco as well as my best selling artist on Arhoolie Records," he acknowledged. "Every recording session however would be a compromise between what Clifton wanted to record which was mainly rock and roll [that is, urban blues] and what I wanted which was the 'French numbers.'"[54] Or, as Clifton's son, C. J. (now a well-known accordionist himself), put it: "He [his father] played zydeco, but he just had that blues all in his soul. He was the Zydeco Man, but also he was the Blues Man too, 'cause he hummed the blues all the time, just sitting around."[55]

Even if by his own account the world's most renowned black French musician did not particularly relish that role, Clifton Chenier's grudging concessions to "French stuff" have proven still more discomfiting for those Texas Creoles who have persevered in the once-vital albeit now moribund urban blues scene. Consider Freddie "Big Roger" Collins. Born in Ville Platte, Louisiana, in 1935, Collins is as frank about his aversion to accordion music as he is unswerving in his devotion to blues, habitually representing himself as "the only Frenchman that don't like zydeco." "Now when I was young, down in Louisiana," he explained, "only time I would hear zydeco, somebody would have like a house party or something. They'd play it, but you never see it in a club. They always nearly have blues, and so I got away from zydeco and went into blues, and I been in 'em ever since, and I go to zydeco dances and I admire *all* musicians; I don't damn *no* musician. But to me liking zydeco, I don't like zydeco."

Further inspired by the big-city blues he heard on neighbors' windup phonographs or his grandmother's battery-powered radio (T-Bone Walker, Muddy Waters, Lightnin' Hopkins, and John Lee Hooker all ranked especially high in his estimation), Collins eventually took up the drums and the life of the itinerant bluesman. His first steady gig was with "a little band in Ville Platte we used to call Johnny Jones and the Cotton Pickers." This was an exception during his early career, however, since he usually worked simply as a "pickup" whenever and wherever opportunities arose. He even occasionally traveled over to Texas to perform with Clifton Chenier. "I played drum with Clifton long time, just he and I. We used to travel, man, we'd sleep side of the road, wake up and go on some more." But before long, he confesses, "I got to where I—I just—I just didn't *like* zydeco. Now Clifton Chenier's the only player that kind of satisfied me with zydeco, 'cause he more play it with blues, you know, and he make his accordion so clear, but just to me liking zydeco, I don't like it."

Actually, Collins seemed hard pressed to distinguish zydeco from the blues. "Well zydeco, it is the blues," he allowed. "But it just in a different angle than what we're doing. See, I'm doing straight, I say, American blues, and this [zydeco] is, uh, Creole blues, it's—most people call it 'French.' . . . Mostly everything that you catch that Buckwheat, Clifton Chenier, everybody doing, it's blues, but you just doing it in French." After 1960, anyway, his aversion to French blues was no longer a matter of much concern. That year he moved to Oakland, joining a pool of transplanted southwesterners (Jimmy McCracklin, Pee Wee Crayton, Lowell Fulson, Sonny Rhodes, and L. C. Robinson, among others) plying northern California's blues clubs. Eventually a spot opening for Bobby Bland brought him back to Houston, where he's remained, despite the diminishing returns on his efforts. "Well, this year [1986] and last year been my baddest years I have in Houston, 'cause everything have just dropped—dead, like the *world*," he lamented. "But when I came here all the best musicians, blues musicians about had gone. Albert Collins, and all them, they'd moved on—Johnny Copeland—there just wasn't much." Ticking off the names of the few others ("Rockin' Douglas, . . . Clarence Green, . . . Buddy Ace, . . . Jerry Lightfoot, . . . Andy William") still scuffling for jobs, he glumly pronounced, "We just about the only stone blues musicians working around here now."

Clearly, it has been tough going for Collins since he returned to the Gulf Coast. Although he has managed to cut a fine album[56] and a couple of singles, most of his work has been in local clubs—that is, when he can find a club whose clientele appreciates or even just tolerates his music. "I don't care who play it, I enjoy the blues," he mused. "Shoot me to death, but somebody else have to like it. A lot of places I go, people laugh at me. But it doesn't bother me, 'cause I might leave this club and go over there, they have a barroom full of people who love it." Finding that crowd is no easy task, though. "A lot of places I go, they got a bunch of youngsters, and you know, youngsters don't like no blues, only the young whites," he explained. "I gets a young black crowd, they wants disco." Then again, "If you go in a white club and play the blues, they're gonna run you out of there. You have to play something, Hank Williams or somebody like that, old country-western."

As a result Collins has turned to performing largely within the Creole community, where he can still sing the blues, but only by accommodating the demand for zydeco. "I enjoy all of the zydeco musicians," he reiterated. "But for me to *like* zydeco, I don't like zydeco. . . . But I go along with 'em. I got a lot of guys that we do zydeco and blues together, you know, just whatever it takes to make a show." His stand at Frenchey's Golden 19th Hole during the summer of 1986 typifies his recent experiences (tellingly the club itself, located in an especially depressed section of the Sixth Ward, stayed open only a couple of months). Friday nights would find the bar half full of middle-aged or older blacks, most of them Creoles, whose tastes were nonetheless fairly eclectic. Although there was plenty of zydeco on the jukebox, the most popular selection that summer seemed to be Bobby Bland's "Members Only." Aiming to please, Roger would trade sets with his band, a group of younger musicians with pop aspirations, and accordionist Ron Broussard. The band usually opened the evening, interspersing original disco with familiar pop items (for example, "Purple Rain," by Prince, or Wilson Pickett's "Don't Let the Green Grass Fool You"). Afterward Roger and Broussard would each do a couple of sets, with Roger relying heavily on well-known standards (for example, Bobby Bland's "Turn on Your Love Light," Lowell Fulson's "That's All Right," or John Lee Hooker's "Boogie Chillen"), occasionally slipping in a few of his own compositions ("Houston Blues," "I Got to Start Making Love to You") when the crowd's mood permitted. Broussard, at one time Lonnie Mitchell's guitarist (Mitchell was himself performing at Frenchey's on Sundays), complemented Big Roger with the "soul zydeco" sound favored by younger Creoles. The band's reception was usually cool, with Broussard and Collins both faring well, although the accordion usually had the edge. On one occasion, after introducing Broussard and two other local accordionists in attendance, one of whom (Dan Rubin) eventually played a set on audience demand, Roger told the crowd in good-humored disgust, "I'm the only Frenchman in the house that don't like zydeco."

Although some Creole performers continue to struggle in the declining black R&B market, others have left professional music entirely. Such is the case with Ivory Lee Semiens.[57] Born near Washington, Louisiana, in 1931, Semiens came from a family of French musicians. ("I had some uncles that, you know, they played guitars and accordions and the violin," he recounted. "They played that kind.") Like Collins, however, he too preferred the blues that he heard on records and radio and, after experimenting with saxophone and bass, settled on drums, casually gigging "with different other guys" before moving to Houston around 1950. "Well, I came over for work and then I began to get interested in it [music] again; I began to start playing," Ivory recalled. "I knew Johnny Clyde Copeland, Joe Hughes, just a whole lot of different local [blues] musicians in Houston." Thereby inspired to pursue music professionally, he formed his own band and as "King Ivory Lee" began touring the Gulf Coast, eventually even founding his own record company. His first effort, Alameda, folded in the late 1950s after only a couple of singles by Semiens himself. Shortly thereafter, though, he launched Ivory Records, producing a string of releases by other Houston blues notables (Lightnin' Hopkins, D. C. Bender, Earl Gilliam, and others) as well as his own, promoting them as a local disc jockey or at his television repair shop. His greatest success was with East Texan Harding "Hop" Wilson (1927–75), the guitarist in Ivory's own band. One of a "school" of Texas and Louisiana bluesmen playing steel instead of standard guitars, Wilson arrived in Houston from Crockett, Texas, around the same time as Semiens. The two soon joined forces and in 1958 cut a few sides together for the Lake Charles–based Goldband label. They would later re-record most of these items for Ivory's own fledgling line, where Wilson enjoyed his greatest success. ("I didn't have any trouble selling Hop's discs," Ivory assured me. "It didn't take a whole lot of pushing.")

In fact, Wilson proved to be the label's bestseller, although he could not sustain the company by himself. Never caring much for zydeco, Semiens nonetheless felt compelled to plumb its potential by occasionally recording such hometown favorites as Lonnie Mitchell and Vincent Frank. Those concessions aside, the collapse of the local blues market in the late 1960s, closely followed by Hop Wilson's death, marked the end of King Ivory Lee's career. Inactive for over a decade when I visited him in 1988, he seemed especially chagrined that zydeco has prospered in direct proportion to R&B's decline and that many Creoles who formerly played or patronized blues have returned to French music. He is also acutely aware of the renewed interest in blues among young white consumers (much of the Ivory catalog has been recently reissued on LP and CD in the United States and abroad). "I believe blues is coming back," he told me. "And it's a big market for blues, but for some reason, they don't push it on the air. In other words, they not giving the public what they really wants." At that time he even spoke of resuming his career and resurrecting his label, but given his long inactivity and the changes in musical tastes and media markets, his ultimate success even then seemed uncertain, and not long after our first meeting, he again dropped out of sight.

Although some Creole bluesmen have struggled on in the field, with others leaving the business entirely, more and more are acquiescing to the upsurge of zydeco, grudgingly casting their lot with accordion music. Such is the case with L. C. Donatto's present guitarist, Ashton Savoy. Born near Opelousas in 1928, Savoy grew up hearing both "them old downhome blues" and "what they used to call that 'French La La.'" His own preferences were unequivocal, however: "That's my real thing, blues, you know. That's the only thing I was playing when I first started, the blues." He received his first music lessons from his father, who played both guitar and violin, but he was also inspired by an Opelousas street musician he knew only as "Crippled Bob." ("Oh Lord, he was a *blues!*" he remembered with relish. "He could play like them old stuff, like old Blind Lemon, back then, you know? All that stuff!") Records served as Savoy's primary resource, however. (Curiously, whereas L. C. grew up speaking only English but learned French from records, Savoy grew up speaking just French but now sings only in English, another capability that he acquired from phonograph discs.) By the time Savoy moved to Lake Charles in the early 1950s, he was thus solidly versed in the postwar R&B idiom.

Savoy remained in Lake Charles through most of the decade, fronting bar bands, doing some session work for local labels, and even recording a few sides on his own or with Houston-born singer-pianist Katie Webster.[58] Eventually, though, he too headed for Houston, prospering for a time in its thriving blues scene. Even in those years, however, he sometimes resorted to zydeco. "Aw, that zydeco, well, you know, I started—I played with Clifton for a while, when Clifton was in Port Arthur, before he got famous," he conceded. "I used to go play with him. He used to come pick me up and go play with him in East Texas, we play around Port Arthur, Beaumont, Lake Charles." During the same period he often backed Marcel Dugas at clubs in Texas and Louisiana, and when Houston's blues scene finally atrophied in the mid-1970s, he signed on as Lonnie Mitchell's regular guitarist.

In the early 1980s, Mitchell was temporarily sidelined by illness, and Savoy teamed up with L. C. Donatto, with whom he has played ever since. Although he still sometimes grouses about being stuck in an accordion band, the arrangement has actually proved beneficial to both. Besides coanchoring one of the bluesiest zydeco groups in Houston today, Savoy invariably plays a set or two of straight R&B during the course of an evening. He even recently bought himself a button accordion, expressing his intention to master the instrument (this has itself become something of a tradition among Creole guitarists; recall Clarence Garlow's example). At present, however, Savoy is still playing only guitar, nor has he ever seemed at all dismayed by his own repeated predictions of zydeco's imminent demise.

Many Creole bluesmen may thus be ambivalent about the potential benefits of playing zydeco, but Creole accordionists are similarly tentative concerning the profits they have reaped from rhythm and blues. Anderson Moss is characteristically positive about the changes he has witnessed. "It's getting better and better," he affirmed. "Oh yeah! You take . . . all the Catholic halls. They raise a whole lot of money, man. . . . Shoot, man, it be four, five hundred, six, seven hundred people, that you can't come in." In recent years he has followed the lead of Clifton Chenier, working with bands including guitar, bass, and drums, as well as the traditional rubboard, even trying his hand at recording. This last experiment ended in frustration, though. "I made a record and I didn't get nothing out of it!" Moss exclaimed in disgust. "They beat me out of it. Right here in town here. I made four—four records! And so there's lots of people have asked me to make some, now. And with what happened to me the first time, I said, 'Well, forget about records.'"[59] His experiences with the new "high-powered" accompaniment have not been entirely happy either, for younger musicians especially are "hard to keep"— "pulled a lot of ways," as he put it, by the present profusion of musical options. "There's a lot of people think, uh, say like a guitar man, it's a disgrace to play with a zydeco band," he confided. "They're hard to keep. Then there's some of 'em, you know, you get a-hold on to, and some of 'em ain't going to—people now, I don't know what it is, they're just pulled a lot of ways, you know? They play with you a while and they're gone!"[60]

The late Lonnie Mitchell also spoke approvingly of recent developments, for example, the expanded ensemble popularized by Chenier. "It sound better, you know, a guitar and drums, to me," he told me. "I don't know if I could play now with just a washboard. It'd have to be a mighty good one." Nonetheless he took a dim view of accompanists who drown out the accordion. "See, I been in music many years," he confided. "They [audiences] want to expect the accordion. They want to hear it more than they do the other guys, and that's right—the leader, he's the leader." As proof, Mitchell recalled an elderly admirer who for years had driven from Galveston to Houston every Friday, Saturday, and Sunday to hear him play but who stopped coming around altogether when he added guitar and drums. "Yeah, he's still in Galveston," Mitchell acknowledged ruefully. "He been promising me he would come where I play at but he say he just don't like too much guitar music. Just one of the old guys that doing, you know, he come up, . . . want it to be just washboard and accordion; he thinks that best way to have zydeco music." And Mitchell's experiences with recording were of a kind with Moss's. "I cut one record, but it didn't go very—course it was a little small place," he acknowledged, referring to his 1961 single for Ivory,[61] then launching into a bitter indictment of another local producer: "They used to have a guy named, black guy named ———. But that guy was crooked as a bad old snake. He'd tell you, you know, that record didn't go nowhere, and then you was singing way off—he's disgusting, aw, man, he's disgusting so bad!"

Curiously, Donatto, who of these three has enjoyed the most recent success, is also most critical of recent trends. Retiring briefly after Willie Green's death, L. C. returned to find the music transformed by its growing resemblance to urban blues, rock, and soul. And although he excels in the new style, aided in no small part by Ashton Savoy, he is not entirely pleased with these changes, which in his opinion are often simply a cover for inept accordionists. "These days, anybody, you can get up there with an accordion and you got guitar, saxophone. Well, people say 'Aw, well, he's really good,'" he scoffed. "But you put 'em by theirself, just with a rubboard and accordion, like I played mostly all my life, just me and a rubboard, then you'll know who can really play accordion."

Nevertheless, L. C. and the Slippers Zoddico Band remain atop Houston's growing field of zydeco players. Besides playing weekly gigs at Frenchtown's

Silver Slipper Lounge and Pe-Te's in South Houston, or at church dances and other area taverns, L. C. and the Slippers have played clubs and festivals all over the Gulf Coast and the United States, in 1991 completing a second European tour. At Savoy's instigation L. C. has recently even added a sax to the group—this despite his objections to "saxophones and stuff that really don't go in no zydeco band"—and, rather unusually, a second rubboard player. And although L. C. has never had a hit record as such, he has cut three singles since the early 1970s, more recently branching into audiocassettes and even videotapes.[62]

On the whole, however, the Lone Star State's zydeco players have watched as Louisiana Creoles have reaped most of the benefits of the recent zydeco boom. For decades known only to Creoles or vernacular music enthusiasts, zydeco is currently enjoying the celebrity occasionally accorded ethnic traditions, bringing fame to a few of its Creole practitioners, influencing world popular music, and even entering the vocabulary of mass consumer culture, as evinced in the ersatz zydeco themes of recent television commercials.

Despite its status as an urban, mass-mediated, popular style, however—and truly a Texas-born style at that—zydeco is now ensconced in popular consciousness as *the* folk music of Louisiana's rural black Creoles, often at the expense of their own indigenous traditions and certainly at the expense of Texas Creole musicians. These circumstances partly reflect the prevalence in South Louisiana of the conditions that, forty years ago, fomented zydeco in southeast Texas, for example, the urban-industrial economic base at one time more characteristic of Texas cities, enabling many more Creoles to remain at home and prompting many more to return. In later years Clifton Chenier himself finally returned to Louisiana to live. (As he told Ben Sandmel at the time, "I stay in Louisiana and Texas, but I'm more in Louisiana than I am in Texas. . . . Texas, man, is crowded; Houston is getting crowded.")[63] Already he was locally revered as a "cultural spokesperson," since, despite his efforts to escape French music, he had *defined* that tradition for a new generation. And paradoxically, Chenier's nontraditional approach largely explains this acceptance, since, as South Louisiana itself has come increasingly to resemble urban Texas, most Louisiana Creoles are no more disposed to rural folk traditions than are average Americans.[64]

Somewhat surprisingly, then, these nontraditional qualities are precisely what render zydeco such a salient symbol of contemporary Creole ethnicity, one that subsumes most other markers of black French identity. (So, for example, besides encompassing music and dance, zydeco as a cultural complex also includes foodways, libations, and ritualized sociability among family and friends, often under the auspices of the Catholic church.) Or, from another perspective one can state that zydeco's relation to Louisiana Creole folk culture is purely symbolic. Often cited by Creoles as a pillar of the "real French" sound, the late Louisiana accordionist John Delafose clearly if perhaps unintentionally enunciated this focal paradox. "Zydeco is really not Creole French anymore," he once stated, echoing a common complaint. "One of the problems right now with zydeco players, they can't speak French. Your young generation, they can't talk French. So how are you going to play zydeco if you can't speak French. You can say a few words but mostly the songs are English. And most of your music nowadays is blues and rock. . . . I'm the one more do the Frenchy-style zydeco than anyone else right now." But Delafose himself admitted, "I do all kinda . . . music, you know . . . rock zydeco . . . French . . . country and western. . . . The blues, whatever. . . . Feel the audience and give them what they want." And he also insisted "Clifton Chenier, that's my top man. The only man I respected in the music"—this despite the fact that Chenier is personally responsible for the very qualities Delafose laments in zydeco, which has always been as much blues and rock as Creole French.[65]

In Louisiana, of course, such real or perceived threats to "traditional" French culture have spurred a nativistic revival, abetted by folklorists and cultural activists, state and local organizations, the tourist industry, and especially the appeal of such "invented" (and, in this case, largely imported) traditions as zydeco—itself now a threat to older French music.[66] In the Bayou City, by contrast, such official validation—and the visibility it bestows on officially sanctioned versions of "Frenchness"—is lacking, so much so that Houston Creoles seem almost compelled to deny their own city's central role in zydeco, submitting instead to the cultural-programing blitz from "back home." Consider, for instance, the preference that many Texas Creoles now express for Louisiana zydeco bands, which are on that score regarded as more "authentic" than local performers[67]—or that in still another reversal, Houston's zydeco players are today more likely to record for Louisiana labels than for local concerns.[68]

Accordingly it is at once perverse and appropriate that today's dominant black "French" musicians are frustrated rockers in the mold of Chenier. Take, for example, Sidney "Count Rockin' Sidney" Simien. Born in 1938 in St. Landry Parish, the son of an accordionist, Simien instead took up the guitar and by the late 1950s had established himself as a regional R&B recording artist. By the 1970s, however, his career was at a standstill. Impressed by Chenier's success with French rock and roll, he began experimenting with that style and in 1985 scored big with "Don't Mess with My Toot Toot," recorded in a home studio with only a drum machine and Sidney on vocals, accordion, bass, and guitar. The track was a runaway hit, the closest thing to a "zydeco crossover" to date (on the Gulf Coast it was programmed by both pop and country and western stations), unexpectedly establishing Count Rockin' Sidney as a major figure in "French" music.[69]

Still better known is Stanley "Buckwheat" Dural, no more a traditional French musician than is Simien, which is to say very much a traditional zydeco musician, at least in the tradition of Clifton Chenier. Born in Lafayette in 1947, Dural began his career touring as a keyboardist with R&B artists Clarence "Gatemouth" Brown, Little Richard, and Barbara Lynn. By the early 1970s he was back in Lafayette, playing "rock 'n' roll disco" and eventually joining Chenier's band on keyboards. Dural took up the accordion only in 1978 but, leaving Chenier the following year, soon achieved international stardom as "Buckwheat Zydeco." (Indicative of that stature, his recent work features collaborations with English blues-rock superstar Eric Clapton, with whom he has also toured; country singers Dwight Yoakam and Willie Nelson; and David Hidalgo, of the Chicano rock group Los Lobos.) At present the best-known zydeco artist outside the Creole community, he is also among the most popular on the Gulf Coast, a major draw at Houston's French dances, which he dominates much as Chenier did two decades ago.[70]

To be sure, Dural has his detractors; in fact many Creoles employ "Buckwheat music" as a pejorative, signifying everything that zydeco is not, or at least should not be—sentiments themselves constituting something of a Creole "tradition." After all, from the time he began playing "rock and French mixed together" nearly a half century ago, Clifton Chenier was similarly censured, dogged by complaints that since "Clif got hooked up with that city sound, he don't play zydeco no more. He thinks he's the king of rock 'n' roll."[71] In sum, zydeco's efficacy as a symbol of postwar Creole ethnicity appears always to have derived from this ongoing conflict between French vernacular and urban popular styles—which perhaps is why many Creoles find it easier to state what zydeco is not than to explain what it is. This returns me to the problem with which I began: how, after all, does one discover a Frenchman in this postmodern milieu? What, after all, distinguishes those of Louisiana's rural black Creoles who do not speak Creole, may not be black, and often reside in urban Texas? The most obvious answer is zydeco, a Creolized hybrid of Cajun accordion and black urban blues that, in reality, is neither Cajun, blues, nor necessarily even Creole.[72] Today, in fact, more and more Creoles follow the lead of Big Roger Collins, asserting their Frenchness by *not liking* zydeco. Of course, many of these same Frenchmen insist that, appearances notwithstanding, Buckwheat Zydeco and his acolytes are themselves also doing just that. (Take Roger Collins, who, while deferential to most zydeco players, flatly states that he "don't like *no* Buckwheat music.")

Having had the first word, L. C. Donatto deserves the last. Discussing the difficulties of preserving zydeco's integrity despite the mounting temptation to "mix it" with other styles, L. C., who himself professes to "play French *and* zydeco *and* blues *and* rock and roll," offered this parable: "See, like Buckwheat and them, well, I know one night at the Catholic hall, the priest went and told him, the priest told him, father told him, said, 'If we want rock and roll, we'll hire a rock and roll band, but we want zydeco.' And the father asked him, say, 'You know this man?' Say, 'Yeah, that's L. C. Donatto.' And father told him, said, 'Now that's a man that play zydeco, that's a zydeco man.'"

Which is one, but only one of many ways of saying, "Now that's a Frenchman."[73]

Notes

Most of the fieldwork for this study was sponsored by the University of Texas Institute of Texan Cultures at San Antonio, whose support I gratefully acknowledge. I wish also to thank David Evans, Pat Jasper and Texas Folklife Resources, Jim McNutt, Linda Frame Minton, Betsy Peterson, Gary Smith, Chris Strachwitz, and Steve Stuempfle for their advice or assistance at various stages during its completion. Finally—but especially—I am most deeply indebted to the many great musicians and gracious music lovers in Houston's Creole community, all of whom have proven invariably and unfailingly unselfish with their time and talent: *et toi!*

1. From a recorded performance by L. C. Donatto and the Slippers Zoddico Band at Pe-Te's Cajun Bar-B-Que House, Pasadena, Texas, July 12, 1986. Unless indicated otherwise, all direct quotations are taken, with occasional emendations (the elimination of false starts, pauses, and so forth), from the following taped interviews, all in the archives of the Institute of Texan Cultures: Alcide "L. C." Donatto, Houston, March 25, 1986, JM86-1-1:1; Anderson Moss, Houston, July 11, 1986, JM86-2-1:1; Freddie "Big Roger" Collins, Houston, July 13, 1986, JM86-5-1:1; Lonnie Mitchell, Houston, July 14, 1986, JM86-8-1:1; Ashton Savoy, Houston, July 26, 1986, JM86-11-1:2 and JM86-11-2:2; Ivory Lee Semiens, Houston, July 10, 1988, JM88-1-1:1.

In addition to recording the Slippers' July 12 performance at Pe-Te's, I have been able to tape a few of the other zydecos I have attended in Houston: L. C. Donatto and the Slippers Zoddico Band, Pe-Te's Cajun Bar-B-Que House, Pasadena, July 12 and 19, 1986, JM86-4-1:2, JM 86-4-2:2, JM86-10-1:2, and JM86-10-2:2; Jabo and the J.B.'s, Continental Lounge, Houston, July 13, 1986, JM86-6-1:1; "Big Roger" Collins with Ron Broussard and the Soul Kings Blues Band, Frenchey's Golden 19th Hole, Houston, July 18, 1986, JM86-9-1:3, JM86-9-2:3, and JM86-9-3:3; Lonnie Mitchell and the Zydeco Rockers, Continental Lounge, Houston, July 31, 1987, JM87-1-1:3, JM87-1-2:3, and JM87-1-3:3; L. C. Donatto and the Slippers Zoddico Band, the Silver Slipper, Houston, August 2, 1987, JM87-2-1:2 and JM87-2-2:2.

2. See, for example, the most thorough and penetrating account of zydeco with which I am acquainted: Nick Spitzer, "Zydeco and Mardi Gras: Creole Identity and Performance Genres in Rural French Louisiana" (Ph.D. diss., University of Texas, Austin, 1986). "Zydeco is the traditional dance music of black Creoles in rural Louisiana. . . . Musically zydeco is a mixture of Cajun dance songs (tunes, texts, rhythms), Afro-American blues (tunes, texts, tonality) and Afro-Caribbean rhythms" (Spitzer, "Zydeco," 300). Purely for the sake of the present argument, I have omitted from my own "definition" one element included by Spitzer and others, that is, those features of zydeco reflecting the close historical and cultural ties between Louisiana and the French West Indies. If Gulf Coast Creoles disagree widely on the relationship of zydeco to Cajun music or blues, they appear in tacit agreement on one point: I have never, in either my personal experience or extensive reading, encountered any intimation that the tradition bearers themselves explicitly recognize Caribbean influences in zydeco.

Other basic works on zydeco and its antecedents include: Barry Jean Ancelet and Elemore Morgan Jr., *The Makers of Cajun Music: Musiciens cadiens et créoles* (Austin: University of Texas Press, 1984); Barry Jean Ancelet, "Zydeco/Zarico: Beans, Blues and Beyond," *Black Music Research Journal* 8 (1988): 33–49; John Broven, *South to Louisiana: The Music of the Cajun Bayous* (Gretna, La.: Pelican, 1983); John Minton, "Zydeco on CD," *Journal of American Folklore* 111 (1998): 417–34; Robert Sacré, *Musiques Cajun, Créole et Zydeco* (Paris: Presses Universitaires de France, 1995); Ann Allen Savoy, *Cajun Music: A Reflection of a People,* vol. 1 (Eunice, La.: Bluebird, 1984), 300–402; Nick Spitzer, liner notes and booklet for *La La: Louisiana Black French Music,* Maison de Soul Records LP 1004, 1977; idem, booklet for *Zodico: Louisiana Créole Music,* Rounder Records LP 6009, 1979; Chris Strachwitz, booklet for *Zydeco: The Early Years (1961–1962),* Arhoolie CD 307, 1989; and idem, "Zydeco Music—that is, French Blues," in *The American Folk Music Occasional,* ed. Chris Strachwitz and Pete Welding (New York: Oak, 1970), 22–24.

Although most of these studies acknowledge Houston's zydeco scene, many treat its role as peripheral, and others ignore it altogether. Works on zydeco in Houston specifically are fewer, briefer, and of varying quality but nonetheless useful in addressing this lapse. See Robert Damora, "Houston Zydeco: From Churches to Clubs," *Living Blues* 116 (July–August 1994): 44–47; Mike Leadbitter, ed., *Nothing but the Blues: An Illustrated Documentary* (London: Hanover, 1971), 170; Joseph F. Lomax, "Zydeco—Must Live On!" in *What's Going On (in Modern Texas Folklore),* ed. Francis Edward Abernethy, Publications of the Texas Folklore Society 40 (Austin: Encino, 1976), 204–23; Mack McCormick, booklet for *A Treasury of Field Recordings,* vol. 1, 77 Records LP 77-LA-12-2, 1959, pp. 9–10; Susan Orlean, "Socializing: Houston, Texas," *Saturday Night* (New York: Knopf, 1990), 176–97; Joe Nick Patoski, "The Big

Squeezy," *Texas Monthly* 16 (August 1988): 98–103, 126–27; and Roger Wood, "Southeast Texas: Hot House of Zydeco," *The Journal of Texas Music History* 1, no. 2 (2001): 23–44. Some of my own research has appeared in "Creole Community and 'Mass' Communication: Houston Zydeco as a Mediated Tradition," *Journal of Folklore Research* 32 (1995): 1–19.

Ancelet and Morgan, Broven, and Savoy also provide excellent introductions to Louisiana's Cajun traditions, although accounts of Cajun music in East Texas are similarly rare. See, however, Carl Lindahl, "*Grand Texas:* Accordion Music and Lifestyle on the Cajun *Frontière,*" *The French American Review* 62, no. 2 (Winter 1991): 26–36.

3. Harry Choates and His Fiddle, "Jole Blond (Pretty Blond)," Gold Star 1314, 1946; reissued on *J'ai été au bal (I Went to the Dance): The Cajun and Zydeco Music of Louisiana,* vol. 1, Arhoolie CD 331, 1990.

4. Compare Spitzer, "Zydeco and Mardi Gras," 357.

5. Lomax, "Zydeco—Must Live On!" 210–11.

6. See, for example, John S. Ambler, "French," in *The Ethnic Groups of Houston,* ed. Fred R. von der Mehden, 195–204, Rice University Studies, new ser., no. 3 (Houston: Rice University Press, 1984), 203; Broven, *South to Louisiana,* 101, 105, 113; and Harry Oster, *Living Country Blues* (Detroit: Folklore Associates, 1969), 9, 415–18.

7. For closer considerations of these complex issues, see James H. Dormon, "Louisiana's 'Creoles of Color': Ethnicity, Marginality, and Identity," *Social Science Quarterly* 73 (1992): 615–26; and Spitzer, "Zydeco and Mardi Gras," 343–45, 522–51.

8. Revealingly, British writers generally acknowledge the centrality of East Texas to zydeco, while the case for a Louisiana provenance is espoused primarily by folklorists or cultural activists from that state. For the former perspective, see Broven, *South to Louisiana,* 101–2; Bruce Bastin, booklet for *Zydeco Blues,* Flyright FLY CD 36, 1989; and Paul Oliver, *The Story of the Blues* (Radnor, Pa.: Chilton, 1982 [1969]), 161–62.

9. Robert Kuhlken and Rocky Sexton, "The Geography of Zydeco Music," *Journal of Cultural Geography* 12 (1991): 27–28. I quote from Kuhlken and Sexton's recent survey as in that capacity representative of current opinion.

10. Basic histories of Louisiana's *créoles de couleur* include Virginia R. Domínguez, *White by Definition: Social Classification in Creole Louisiana* (New Brunswick, N.J.: Rutgers University Press, 1986); Dormon, "Louisiana's 'Creoles of Color'"; Thomas Fiehrer, "Saint-Domingue/Haiti: Louisiana's Caribbean Connection," *Louisiana History* 30 (1989): 419–37; Gwendolyn Midlo Hall, *Africans in Colonial Louisiana: The Development of Afro-Creole Culture in the Eighteenth Century* (Baton Rouge: Louisiana State University Press, 1992); Nicholas Spitzer, "Cajuns and Creoles: The French Gulf Coast," *Southern Exposure* 5 (1977): 140–55; and idem, "Zydeco and Mardi Gras," esp. 1–224.

11. On nineteenth-century Creole music, see Harold Courlander, *Negro Folk Music, U.S.A.* (New York: Dover, 1992 [1963]), 162–74; Hall, *Africans in Colonial Louisiana,* 196–200; and Spitzer, "Zydeco and Mardi Gras," esp. 304–23. On *juré* singing and

"Easter Rock," the parallel English-language tradition of Louisiana's black Baptists, see Ancelet, "Zydeco/Zarico," 43–45; Courlander, *Negro Folk Music,* 194–200; Hiram Gregory, "Africa in the Delta," *Louisiana Studies* 1 (1962): 16–23; Harry Oster, "Easter Rock Revisited: A Study in Acculturation," *Louisiana Folklore Miscellany* 3 (1958): 21–43; Lea Seale and Marianna Seale, "Easter Rock: A Louisiana Negro Ceremony," *Journal of American Folklore* 55 (1942): 212–18; Spitzer, "Zydeco and Mardi Gras," 195–97, 330–35; and Doris White, "*Jouré* My Lord," *Louisiana Folklore Miscellany* 4 (1976–80): 143–45.

12. This claim is based primarily on my own unpublished research with testimonies from elderly Creoles in the WPA ex-slave narratives. The recollections of Virginia Newman, a free Creole of color born in 1827 near Franklin, Louisiana, are typical. Describing dances during her youth in the region between St. Mary and Evangeline Parishes, she reported "W'en dat ol' corjian (accordion) start' t' play, iffen I ain' eben got my hair comb yit it don' neber git comb. I d' fus' one t' git t' dat dance 'n' d' las' one t' leabe.... Dey hab fiddle music 'n' 'corjian" (in George P. Rawick, ed., *The American Slave: A Composite Autobiography,* supplement, ser. 2, vol. 7, *Texas Narratives, Part 6* [Westport, Conn.: Greenwood, 1979], 2905).

13. An almost casual inclusion of the term *blues* in song titles was at this time something of a fad in American music generally, although the motivations of black French musicians seem more complex and revealing. At the least this trend appears to confirm that Creoles were indeed listening to blues before World War II, perhaps beginning to absorb the idiom or anyway to register those traits it shared with their own traditions, for example, "hot" rhythms, lyric structure/emotional content, the use of "blue notes," and so forth. Nevertheless the connection remains at this stage tenuous.

14. Established in the late nineteenth century, Houston's former political wards are of little practical importance today, although the predominantly black neighborhoods of the inner city, mainly the old Third, Fourth, Fifth, and Sixth Wards, are still referred to by these designations. In addition to coming from my own field research, data on Frenchtown are from David Kaplan, "Houston's Creole Quarter," *Houston Post,* March 19, 1989, F:1, 4; Marie Lee Phelps, "Visit to Frenchtown," *Houston Post,* May 22, 1955, 5:2; Patricia Smith Prather, "A Unique Houston Neighborhood Called Frenchtown," *Houston Chronicle,* September 15, 1986, 5:1, 4; James M. SoRelle, "The Darker Side of 'Heaven': The Black Community in Houston, Texas, 1917–1945" (Ph.D. diss., Kent State University, 1980), 222–23; Richard West, "Only the Strong Survive," *Texas Monthly* 7 (February 1979): 176; and the Federal Writers' Program, Work Projects Administration, State of Texas, *Houston: A History and Guide* (Houston: Anson Jones, 1942), 173.

15. Federal Writers' Program, *Houston,* 173.

16. Prather, "A Unique Houston Neighborhood," 4.

17. On Bidon, Claude Faulk, and the Reynoldses, see Broven, *South to Louisiana,* 110; and Savoy, *Cajun Music,* 316–18, 371. Most of the works on Cajun and Creole

music cited herein consider Ardoin and his influence. His thirty-two extant record-ings have been reissued on Amédé Ardoin, *"I'm Never Comin' Back,"* Arhoolie/Folk Lyric CD 7007, 1995, and *Cajun Dance Party: Fais Do-Do,* Columbia/Legacy CD CK 46784, 1994.

18. Moss was, of course, referring to popular prewar recordings. Of particular interest is "Black Gal What Makes Your Head So Hard?" Bluebird B5459, 1934, by Joe Pullum, a resident of Houston's Fourth Ward, which proved so popular that Pullum recorded several sequels. The song also eventually became a standard among zydeco musicians. Cf. Clifton Chenier, "Black Gal," 1966; reissued on *Bon Ton Roulet! And More,* Arhoolie CD 345, 1990.

19. In July 1961 Chris Strachwitz recorded Green and his group, probably includ-ing Donatto, at Irene's Café. Four selections appear on *Zydeco: The Early Years.* In his introduction to one—"Green's Zydeco"—Green corroborates L. C.'s account, telling the audience, "We been playing over here off and on for twelve year. The zydeco got started what we get that name with that push and pull, rub and scrub. Right over here at Miss Irene, it was a Christmas morning—you better hurry up and knew it."

20. Information on Chevalier is from Strachwitz's notes to *Zydeco: The Early Years,* which includes one song by this artist.

21. McCormick recorded Frank with Dudley Alexander's Washboard Band, rep-resented by one track on *A Treasury of Field Recordings* (McCormick's complete field tapes are part of the Texas Music Collection, Barker Texas History Center, University of Texas, Austin, reel F190—Cajun French Songs). The other group members were Alexander (born 1914 in New Iberia), who alternates with Frank on accordion and washboard, and fiddler Alex Robert Jr. (born 1916 at Opelousas). One of Frank's Ivory sides—"Vincent's Blues," Ivory 1-128, 1968—appears on *Texas Zydeco Greats,* Home Cooking COL-CD-5286, 1993.

22. Sam was also recorded in Houston by Chris Strachwitz in the early 1960s; his signature song, "They Call Me Good Rocking," appears on *Zydeco: The Early Years.*

23. A native of Church Point, Louisiana, Dugas had reputedly played dances around the region since the 1930s; he was also often reported in southeast Texas during the postwar period. Between the late 1950s and mid-1970s he recorded for the Ivory, Goldband, and Blues Unlimited labels; some of the last sides appear on *Zydeco Blues.*

24. Savoy, *Cajun Music,* 316–18.

25. The spelling *zydeco* is usually credited to Mack McCormick, who in 1959 used it to represent the term as then current among Houston Creoles (*A Treasury of Field Recordings,* 9–10; but see Spitzer, "Zydeco and Mardi Gras," 407–8, n. 12). Although McCormick is often cited as the first outsider to document this word in print, that distinction probably belongs to Marie Phelps—or arguably even to Texas bluesman Lightnin' Hopkins and Bill Quinn, the owner and operator of Houston's Gold Star Records.

26. Spitzer, "Zydeco and Mardi Gras," 327.

27. Jimmy Peters and the *juré* singers, "*J'ai fait tout le tour du pays*" ("*Les haricots sont pas salés*"), recorded by Alan Lomax, Jennings, Louisiana, 1934, issued on *J'ai été au bal (I Went to the Dance): The Cajun and Zydeco Music of Louisiana,* vol. 2, Arhoolie CD 332, 1990; transcribed in Ancelet, "Zydeco/Zarico," 45–46; and Spitzer, "Zydeco and Mardi Gras," 333–35.

28. Wilbur Charles, "*Dégo,*" recorded by Alan Lomax, New Iberia, Louisiana, 1934; transcribed in Ancelet, "Zydeco/Zarico," 39–40; and Spitzer, "Zydeco and Mardi Gras," 331–32.

29. The best-known example of the former is Clifton Chenier's "Zydeco Sont Pas Salé," 1965, reissued on *60 Minutes with the King of Zydeco,* Arhoolie CD 301, 1986. See also Ancelet, "Zydeco/Zarico," 38–39; Spitzer, "Zydeco and Mardi Gras," 327–29. Examples of the latter appear on *Zydeco: The Early Years.*

30. Ancelet, "Zydeco/Zarico," 41.

31. For example, the Yula *a záre,* Diwala *na sá,* Ashante *ma sa/mére sa,* and so forth, all translated as "I dance." Although these linguistic data are hardly compelling, Ancelet's hypothesis is not inconsistent with the general process of creolization, and he uncovers one tantalizing parallel from the Creole islands of the Indian Ocean, populated in the 1700s by French planters and their West African slaves: there the accordion-based style known as "*séga*" is reportedly sometimes also called "*séga zarico,*" ostensibly after a dance song not dissimilar in form to a *juré* in which a "pretty girl" is likened to "*cari zarico*" ("hot bean soup"). See Ancelet, "Zydeco/Zarico," 35–36; and Spitzer, "Zydeco and Mardi Gras," 332.

32. Actually this polysemic quality is commonplace in African American musical idioms, for example, *boogie, breakdown, rag/ragtime, jubilee, stomp, bop, rock,* and so forth.

33. Phelps, "Visit to Frenchtown." The mention of the banjo is quite unusual for the urban context, although the ex-slave narratives reveal that this instrument was frequently teamed with the accordion among both American blacks and Creoles during the nineteenth century (see n. 12). Or perhaps Phelps observed the four-string tenor banjo commonly employed for rhythmic chords in New Orleans jazz.

34. Lightnin' Hopkins, "Zolo Go," Gold Star 666, 1949; reissued on *Lightning Hopkins: The Gold Star Recordings, 1948–50, Volume 1,* Arhoolie CD 330, 1990. Words and music by Sam Hopkins, copyright Arhoolie Productions/Tradition Music, administered by Bug Music; used by permission. Hopkins's spoken introduction was omitted from the original 78-rpm release; Chris Strachwitz discovered it on the acetate when he first reissued this selection on *Zydeco,* Arhoolie LP F1009, 1967. (Two decades later, incidentally, another Houston bluesman, Weldon "Juke Boy" Bonner, re-created a zydeco dance in his "Jumpin' at the Zydeco," in this case imitating the accordion on harmonica, accompanied by his own guitar; the track appears on "*I'm Going Back to the Country Where They Don't Burn the Buildings Down,*" Arhoolie LP F1036, 1968.)

35. Broven, *South to Louisiana,* 106. On Garlow, see also Leadbitter, *Nothing but the Blues,* 177–78.

36. Clarence Garlow, "Bon Ton Roula," Macy's 5002, 1949; reissued on *Zydeco: The Early Years.*

37. Clarence "Bon Ton" Garlow, "Crawfishin'"/"Route 90," Flair 1021, 1954; reissued on *Texas Rhythm and Blues,* Ace LP CH 29, n.d.

38. Clarence Garlow, "Jumping at the Zadacoe," Aladdin (Los Angeles), July 24, 1953; issued on *Louisiana Swamp Blues,* Capitol CD CDP 7243 8 52046 2 3, 1996.

39. Clifton Chenier, "Zodico Stomp," Specialty LP 2139, 1955; reissued on Clifton Chenier, *Zodico Blues & Boogie,* Specialty Records CD SPCD-7039-2, 1993.

40. Savoy, *Cajun Music,* 373.

41. For corroborations of Savoy's testimony from Cajun accordionist Marc Savoy; "old-time Creole" musicians Freeman Fontenot, "Bois Sec" Ardoin, and Canray Fontenot; and zydeco accordionist Alton "Rockin' Dopsie" Rubin, see Savoy, *Cajun Music,* 313, 330–31, 361, respectively. Savoy's analogy with white country music is well taken indeed, especially for *bluegrass,* whose etymology reveals a similar range of ambiguity or even latent antagonism. Moreover, although as a musical genre bluegrass is similarly rooted in, and popularly identified with, rural Appalachian traditions, it too really emerged in an urban milieu (for example, Nashville, Washington, D.C., Detroit), propelled by the same forces as was zydeco (the growth of professionalism, the increasing role of electronic media, accentuated cross-influences with other styles, and so forth). See Neil V. Rosenberg, *Bluegrass: A History* (Urbana: University of Illinois Press, 1985), esp. 95–131.

42. Spitzer, "Zydeco and Mardi Gras," 323–24.

43. The classic formulation of this "ideal type" is Robert Redfield, "The Folk Society," *American Journal of Sociology* 52 (1947): 293–308.

44. Compare the comments of Samuel Charters, "Workin' on the Building: Roots and Influences," in *Nothing but the Blues: The Music and the Musicians,* ed. Lawrence Cohn (New York: Abbeville, 1993), 20. Biographies of Chenier include Ancelet and Morgan, *The Makers of Cajun Music,* 88–91; Broven, *South to Louisiana,* 109–13; Greg Drust, booklet for *Zydeco Dynamite: The Clifton Chenier Anthology,* Rhino Records CDs R2 71194, 1993; Savoy, *Cajun Music,* 370–402; and Strachwitz, *Zydeco: The Early Years.*

45. Quoted in Savoy, *Cajun Music,* 379, 375.

46. Ibid., 371.

47. Although it is sometimes reported that Chenier began playing the accordion as a boy in Opelousas (see, for example, Broven, *South to Louisiana,* 110), Chenier himself consistently maintained that he took up the instrument only after moving to Texas. See Savoy, *Cajun Music,* 370, 375.

48. Savoy, *Cajun Music,* 371, 378–79; and Chris Strachwitz, booklet for Clifton Chenier, *Louisiana Blues and Zydeco,* Arhoolie CD 329, 1990. The record in question is Joe Liggins and His Honeydrippers, "The Honeydripper, Pts. 1 and 2," Exclusive 207, 1945.

49. Cliston Chanier [*sic*], "Louisiana Stomp"/"Cliston [*sic*] Blues," Elko 920, 1954; reissued on *Zydeco: The Early Years* and, with four other selections from Chenier's

first session, on *Louisiana Swamp Blues*. On Morris Chenier, see Leadbitter, *Nothing but the Blues,* 159. Coincidentally, another 1954 recording from Lake Charles—Boozoo Chavis's "Paper in My Shoe," Folk Star 1197, 1954; reissued on *Louisiana Swamp Blues*—also combines Creole accordion with an R&B accompaniment and in fact proved to be much more successful than Chenier's own debut, selling over 100,000 copies; it is thus sometimes cited as the first zydeco "hit." In reality, though, Chavis's disc seems merely to confirm how distant French music and urban blues were at the time in South Louisiana. As producer Eddie Shuler explained, "Boozoo played a German button accordion . . . and had no band of his own. I decided to record him and went out and found [Lake Charles guitarist] Classie Ballou, who then had the best R&B band in the area. I didn't know it, but Ballou's band had never heard of zydeco music, let alone played it, and after eight hours in the studio no mentionable results were forthcoming. Ballou's boys just couldn't dig Boozoo's music, and Boozoo didn't know that they weren't with him!" Having written off the date as a failure, Shuler released the record as an afterthought, with entirely unexpected results. Nonetheless Chavis soon became disenchanted with the music business and quit performing for nearly three decades, resuming only in 1984, after Clifton Chenier had demonstrated the commercial potential of French R&B (Broven, *South to Louisiana,* 108-9). See also Leadbitter, *Nothing but the Blues,* 161–62; and Edward R. Silverman, "Boozoo Chavis: Beyond the Crawfish Circuit," *Living Blues* 98 (July–August 1991): 16–19.

50. Clifton Chenier, "Ay-Tete Fee," Specialty 552, 1955; reissued on *Zodico Blues & Boogie.*

51. In 1986 the following Houston parishes were hosting zydecos: St. Peter Claver, St. Philip Neri, St. Gregory the Great, St. Peter the Apostle, Our Lady Star of the Sea, St. Anne De Beaupré, St. Francis Assisi, St. Francis Xavier, and Our Mother of Mercy. Two churches just outside the city—St. Mark the Evangelist in Missouri City and St. Martin the Poor in Crosby—were also holding Saturday night dances, and Houston's St. Monica sometimes sponsored a Sunday matinée. (Data from conversation with Clarence Gallien and Pearl Gallien, Houston, March 27, 1986. See also Damora, "Houston Zydeco"; Orlean, "Socializing: Houston Texas"; and Patoski, "The Big Squeezy.")

52. Chris Strachwitz, "Recording Louisiana Folk Music for Arhoolie Records," in *Louisiana Folklife: A Guide to the State,* ed. Nicholas R. Spitzer (Baton Rouge: Louisiana Folklife Program/Division of the Arts, 1985), 243. Admittedly, Strachwitz's description might suggest that Chenier had reverted to "French music" by the time the two met ("Here was this man with an accordion singing his head off in French, . . . that addictive Cajun sound!"). It is notable, however, that Chenier was using a drummer instead of the more traditional rubboard and that Strachwitz also describes the music as "blues." Moreover it does not appear that this performance was entirely representative of Clifton's approach at the time. In fact, much to Strachwitz's surprise, Chenier arrived for the session they scheduled for the next day with a five-piece band. As Strachwitz remembers, "Clifton insisted that he sounded much better

with piano, guitar, bass and other instruments added and that he sing in English. He was obviously hoping to make another hit in the style of *Eh Tite Fille*" (Strachwitz, booklet for Clifton Chenier, *Out West*, Arhoolie CD 350, 1991; see also Drust, *Zydeco Dynamite*). As it turned out, the guitar and bass amplifiers malfunctioned, so this first session took place with just accordion, piano, and drums. Nonetheless, Chenier's own inclinations seem obvious, and much of what he recorded for Strachwitz over the years, at least when he was given free rein, was wholly "in the rhythm and blues vein" of his Specialty and Checker singles.

53. For Chenier's discography, including recent CD and cassette reissues, see Savoy, *Cajun Music*, 382–91; and Chris Strachwitz, booklet for Clifton Chenier, *Clifton Sings the Blues*, Arhoolie CD 351, 1992. Although most of his later sessions took place in California or Louisiana, it is revealing that of the 171 tracks Chenier produced during his formative phase (1954–70), 107 were recorded in Texas (94 in Houston and 13 in Pasadena), 43 in California, and only 17 in Louisiana, with two each from Chicago and London.

54. Strachwitz, *Zydeco: The Early Years*. See also Broven, *South to Louisiana*, 113; and Drust, *Zydeco Dynamite*.

55. Drust, *Zydeco Dynamite*.

56. Big Roger Collins, *Houston Blues*, Lunar no. 2 Recordings LP L2S-20012, n.d.

57. On Ivory, his label, and his bandmate Hop Wilson, see also Broven, *South to Louisiana*, 157; William Orten Carlton, "Hop Wilson," *Living Blues* 26 (March–April 1976): 8–9; Brian Cope, "Living Blues—Houston," *Blues World* 37 (December 1970): 11–12; Leadbitter, *Nothing but the Blues*, 169–70, 193–95; Mike Leadbitter and Neil Slaven, *Blues Records 1943–1970, Vol. 1, A to K* (London: Record Information Services, 1987), 151, 422–23, 460, 607, 767–68; Mike Leadbitter, Leslie Fancourt, and Paul Pelletier, *Blues Records 1943–1970, "The Bible of the Blues," Vol. 2, L to Z* (London: Record Information Services, 1994), 250, 280, 774–75; Joseph F. Lomax, "Hop Wilson," *Living Blues* 26 (March–April 1976): 8; Minton, "Creole Community and 'Mass' Communication," 6–9; and Ray Topping, liner notes for *Hop Wilson and His Buddies: Steel Guitar Flash!* Ace LP CHD 240, 1988. Most of the Ivory titles by Wilson and King Ivory Lee have been reissued either on this last album or on *Houston Ghetto Blues*, Bullseye Blues CD BB 9538, 1993. Two of Ivory's zydeco sides appear on *Texas Zydeco Greats* (see nn. 21 and 61), and one track from Lightnin' Hopkins—"War Is Starting Again," Ivory 91272, 1962—is included on *Mojo Hand: The Lightnin' Hopkins Anthology*, Rhino Records CDs R2 71226, 1993. Semiens's and Wilson's Lake Charles recordings have also been reissued on *Hop Wilson: Blues with Friends (at Goldband)*, Goldband LP G-7781, 1981.

58. One of Savoy's own sides—"Tell Me Baby," Storyville LP 177, 1959—appears on *Hop Wilson: Blues with Friends*, while a duet with Webster—Katie Webster & Ashton Conroy [*sic*], "Baby, Baby," Kry 100, 1958—has been reissued on *Katie Webster: The Legendary Jay Miller Sessions, Volume 48*, Flyright LP 613, 1988. An alternate take, "No Bread, No Meat," appears on Katie Webster, *Whooee, Sweet Daddy: The*

Legendary Jay Miller Sessions, Volume 9, Flyright LP 530, 1977. See also Broven, *South to Louisiana,* 146–49; Leadbitter, *Nothing but the Blues,* 158, 163; and Leadbitter, Fancourt, and Pelletier, *Blues Records,* 458–59, 692.

59. Moss could not recall the name of the label for which he recorded, and I have been unable to trace these items.

60. When I met Moss in 1986, he had temporarily quit performing out of respect for an older brother who had recently died (such hiatuses are a common custom among Creole musicians), but he has since resumed.

61. Lonnie Mitchel [*sic*], "Watusi Beat"/"Louisiana Slo-Drag," Ivory 136/137, 1961. The latter appears on *Texas Zydeco Greats.*

62. L. C.'s first single was "My Baby Left Me"/"Lafayette," Maison de Soul 1001, ca. 1970. He has since independently produced two 45s ("Don't Tell Me about Your Worries"/"The Pop Special," Special Edition Records ACA 6991/6992, 1985; and "You're In Trouble"/"Good Morning, Virgie Mae," Special Edition Records ACA 7019/7020, 1986); an audiocassette, *L. C. Donatto & Slippers Recorded Live at Pe-te's Bar-B-Que House—Houston, TX: Various ZADECO Selections* (ca. 1989); and, most recently, a series of videotapes also intended for eventual distribution. See Minton, "Creole Community and 'Mass' Communication," 11–12.

63. Quoted in Savoy, *Cajun Music,* 376.

64. Such circumstances are common in contemporary "folk" music. Once again Ashton Savoy's analogy between zydeco and bluegrass or country-western is characteristically astute. Similarly, as David Evans has observed (personal communication), the present status of zydeco in South Louisiana is also reminiscent of what now often passes for "Delta blues," in many cases simply a reflex of the Chicago blues pioneered by Muddy Waters or the soul blues of such artists as B. B. King. The leaders of these urban styles were often born in the Delta, and there are even early manifestations of these later trends in larger Delta towns such as Clarksdale and Greenville, Mississippi, or Helena, Arkansas. Generally speaking, however, these styles first emerged in urban areas outside the Delta (for example, Memphis, Chicago, and Los Angeles), although as that region has itself become more urbanized and less regionalized, local musicians have increasingly assimilated these big-city idioms.

65. Sunny Slim Baker, "From the Heart of a Sharecropper: John Delafose," *Living Blues* 98 (July–August 1991): 28.

66. Cf. Dormon, "Louisiana's 'Creoles of Color'"; Spitzer, "Cajuns and Creoles," 150–55; and idem, "Zydeco and Mardi Gras," 522–51.

67. Between 1986 and 1992, the period covered by my own field research, I constantly encountered this opinion among audience members at Catholic halls, clubs, and festivals. For their part, Houston's zydeco players often complain of this bias, just as quickly dismissing it. (As Anderson Moss told me, "It's all the same thing [that is, zydeco in Louisiana or Texas]; don't let the people fool you!")

68. Such artists include Willie Davis, who has recorded for Crowley-based Blues Unlimited (*Little Willie Davis and His Zydeco Hitchhikers,* Blues Unlimited cassette

5028, 1985), and Donald "Jabo" Glenn and Wilfred Chevis (also the host of "Zydeco Dawn" on Houston's Pacifica station, KPFT), who, like Donatto (see n. 62), have releases on Ville Platte's Maison de Soul label (Jabo, *Texas Prince of Zydeco*, Maison de Soul LP 1032, 1990; Wilfred Chevis and His Texas Zydeco Band, *Foot Stompin' Zydeco*, Maison de Soul LP 1013, 1984, and *"Let's Go to P.T.'s,"* Maison de Soul cassette 1040, 1992).

69. Rockin' Sidney, "Don't Mess with My Toot Toot," *My Toot Toot*, Maison de Soul CD 1009, 1985. See also Broven, *South to Louisiana*, 227; Leadbitter, *Nothing but the Blues*, 163–64; Leadbitter, Fancourt, and Pelletier, *Blues Records*, 428–30; and Spitzer, "Zydeco and Mardi Gras," 353–54, 537.

70. On Buckwheat, see Broven, *South to Louisiana*, 115; and Spitzer, "Zydeco and Mardi Gras," 365–66, 537. His collaborations with Clapton, Yoakam, Hidalgo, and Nelson appear on *Taking It Home*, Island CD 422-842 603-2, 1988; *Where There's Smoke There's Fire*, Island CD 422–842 925-2, 1990; and *Five Card Stud*, Island CD 314-524 018-2, 1994.

71. Spitzer, "Zydeco and Mardi Gras," 351.

72. Indeed, much as whites have borrowed blues idioms, zydeco-based forms are now often played by non-Creoles. One example from Houston—the case of Pierre and the Zydeco Dots—is especially striking. The group is led by accordionist Pierre Blanchard, who is French but neither Creole nor Cajun. Born in Nice, Blanchard came to Houston at age fourteen, first taking up blues harmonica and later accordion. See Paula Felder, booklet for *Texas Zydeco Greats*, which features three cuts by the Dots.

73. Except for a couple updated references, this article appears just as it was originally published a decade ago. In that time, there have been many changes in Houston zydeco. Lonnie Mitchell passed away in late 1995, L. C. Donatto in 2002. Other key actors have come and gone. Then, too, there have been important developments in the scholarship, most notably the publication in 2006 of Roger Wood's *Texas Zydeco* (Austin: University of Texas Press). Roger's book incorporates many of the ideas first presented in this piece, a fact he graciously acknowledges.

Contributors

GERHARD KUBIK is a professor at the Institute for Psychology at the University of Klagenfurt and the Institute of Musicology at the University of Vienna. Since 1959 he has conducted fieldwork in sixteen countries of sub-Saharan Africa and in Brazil and the United States. His more than three hundred publications include books, articles, and recordings of African music and oral traditions and related material from the New World. His work has resulted in many fellowships, awards, and guest lectures. In 1999 he published the book *Africa and the Blues*.

DOUG SEROFF AND LYNN ABBOTT are independent researcher-writer-historians. Seroff lives near Nashville, Tennessee; Abbott, in New Orleans. Their individual and collaborative articles have appeared in *American Music, JEMF Quarterly, 78 Quarterly,* and elsewhere. They have also coauthored two books: *Out of Sight: The Rise of African American Popular Music, 1889–1895* (2003) and *Ragged but Right: Black Traveling Shows, "Coon Songs," and the Dark Pathway to Blues and Jazz* (2007).

ELLIOTT S. HURWITT was educated at the Royal Conservatory of Music in The Hague (Netherlands), and at Hunter College and the Graduate Center of the City University of New York. His doctoral dissertation, "W. C. Handy as Music Publisher: Career and Reputation" (CUNY, 2000), won the Barry Brook Dissertation Award. Professor Hurwitt has written nearly fifty entries for recent reference works, including the *International Dictionary of Black Composers, American National Biography, Encyclopedia of the Harlem Renaissance,*

Encyclopedia of New York State, the *Routledge Encyclopedia of the Blues,* and *African American National Biography.* He has taught at Vassar College, Columbia University, Hunter College, Brooklyn College, and Fordham University.

ANDREW M. COHEN divides his time between organizing and participating in folk musical events in and around Memphis, Tennessee, where he lives, and playing a variety of gigs far from home. He has studied with and served as "lead boy" for a number of blind musicians, including Jim Brewer, Dan Smith, Daniel K. Womack, and (briefly) Reverend Gary Davis. He has recently recorded for the Riverlark and Wepecket labels and written occasional pieces for such magazines as *Sing Out!* and *Old Time Herald.*

DAVID EVANS is First Tennessee Professor of Music at The University of Memphis. He has been involved in blues research since the 1960s and is the author of *Tommy Johnson* (1971), a biography of a traditional blues singer, *Big Road Blues: Tradition and Creativity in the Folk Blues* (1982), and *The NPR Curious Listener's Guide to Blues* (2005), as well as many scholarly articles, book chapters, encyclopedia entries, and record album notes on blues and related types of music. He is the producer of many albums of field and studio recordings of blues. In 2003 he received a Grammy™ Award for Best Album Notes for his essay in *Screamin' and Hollerin' the Blues: The Worlds of Charley Patton.* He has performed blues in twenty countries and recorded three CDs as well as accompaniments to other artists.

LUIGI MONGE is a freelance teacher and translator in Genoa, Italy. He is a member of SIdMA (Italian Society of African American Musicology) and a blues and gospel lecturer in Italy and abroad. In Italian, he writes for the magazine *Il Blues* and for *World Music Magazine.* In English, he has published articles in *Black Music Research Journal, Journal of Texas Music History, Popular Music,* and in the books *The Lyrics in African American Popular Music* and *Nobody Knows Where the Blues Come From,* both edited by Robert Springer. He has contributed entries to *The Encyclopedia of the Blues* and the *Encyclopedia of American Gospel Music,* both published by Routledge.

JAMES BENNIGHOF is a professor of music theory and vice provost at Baylor University. His scholarly work, much of which focuses on the critical analysis of twentieth-century American vernacular music, has appeared in his book *The Words and Music of Paul Simon* (2007) and in the *Journal of Music Theory,* the *Journal of Music Theory Pedagogy, American Music, College Music*

Symposium, and the *International Dictionary of Black Composers.* Several of his choral works, mostly for treble choir, have been published by Oxford University Press and Heritage Music Press.

KATHARINE (KATCHIE) CARTWRIGHT is an assistant professor of music at Northwest Vista College in San Antonio, Texas. She has received Fulbright grants for residencies in Greece and Lebanon and has performed and conducted workshops in South Asia, West Africa, South America, the Caribbean, and Europe. Her recent recordings as a singer and flutist include *A Mumbai of the Mind: Ferlinghetti Improvisations, La Flaute de la Musique: Songs of John Cage,* and Mark Holen's *Zambomba: Noches Flamencas.* She serves as chair of the International Association for Jazz Education's Sisters in Jazz mentoring program, on the board of the International Women in Jazz, and is an active member of the International Association of Schools of Jazz.

BOB GROOM is an independent blues researcher based in Knutsford, England. He was the founder and editor of *Blues World* magazine (1965–74) and is the author of *The Blues Revival* (1971). In recent years, he has contributed articles to *Blues & Rhythm* and *Juke Blues* magazines and album notes for reissues of early blues recordings on Document Records. His article "Tiger Man: Elvis and the Blues" is included in *Aspects of Elvis,* edited by Alan Clayson and Spencer Leigh (1994).

JOHN MINTON is a professor of folklore at Indiana University–Purdue University Fort Wayne. In addition to his many articles on American folk music and song, he is the author of *"Big 'Fraid and Little 'Fraid": An Afro-American Folktale* (Folklore Fellows' Communications No. 253, 1993); with David Evans, of *The Coon in the Box: A Global Folktale in African-American Tradition* (Folklore Fellows' Communications No. 277, 2001); and of *78 Blues: Folksongs and Phonographs in the American South* (forthcoming).

Index

Abbott, Lynn, 4

accordion: aversion to, 379, 383; banjo, 371, 393n 33 (371); blues, 352–53, 356–57; Ron Broussard, 380–81; Cajun, 351–54, 360, 365, 387; C. J. Chenier, 378; Clifton Chenier, 356–57, 376–77; chromatic button accordion, 353–54, 356, 376; Creole, 357, 360, 367–68, 371, 373–74, 381; John Delafose, 386; diatonic button accordion, 353–54, 360, 365, 376; Ashton Savoy, 383; "Count Rockin' Sidney" Simien, 386–87; zydeco, 353, 356–57, 361, 364, 376, 379. *See also* zydeco

Ace, Buddy, 380

Ace, Johnny, 207

Acey, Johnny, 207

Africa and the Blues, 28 fig. 1.4

African-American newspapers, 49–50: *Baltimore Afro-American*, 124, 126; *Chicago Defender*, 69–70; *Indianapolis Freeman*, 5, 60–72, 78–80, 83, 85, 87–91; *Kansas City American Citizen*, 50; *Leavenworth Herald*, 50–51; *Topeka Weekly Call*, 50

African ethnic groups: Azande, 19; Baule, 16; Chamba, 24; Cokwe, 16; Fang', 16, 36; Fulbe, 24, 26; Hausa, 21, 24, 26; Kutin, 24; Lucazi, 16; Lwena/Luvale, 16; Makua, 43; Manding', 24; Mangwilo, 36; Mbwela/ Nkhangala, 16; Tikar, 26; various ethnic groups of Moçambique, 36; Wagogo, 42;

Zanganyi, 24. *See also* African instruments; African music

African instruments: *algeita*, 21; *bangwe*, 11; *gogé* (or *gojé*), 21, 46n. 29 (21); *likembe*, 19; mouth bow, 35; *mvet*, 16; *sese*, 36; *takare*, 36; *tong'*, 24; xylophone, 36. *See also* African ethnic groups; African music

African music: blues, 3–4, 21; Islam, 24; harmonic series, 28–31, 36, 42–43; neutral thirds, 16; melisma, 21; pentatonism, 4, 24, 26–27; retention/reinterpretation in blues, 24–27, 30–31; scalar patterns, 25 fig. 1.3, 27–29; tonal systems, 15–16; tunings, 13. *See also* African ethnic groups; African instruments; blue notes; blues

"African Princess," 73

A. G. Allen's Minstrels, 89

Ahlert, Fred, 303

"Ain't Dat a Shame," 58

"Ain't Gonna Give It Away," 192

"Airmail Special," 308–09

"Alabama Blues." *See* "I'm Alabama Bound"

Aladdin label, 372

Alameda label, 381

Alderson, Mozelle, 189

Alexander, Alger "Texas", 44

Alexander, Dudley, 392n 21 (368)

Alger, Horatio, 143n 52 (117)

Ali, Muhammad, 348

"All I Have Is Gone," 343

Allen, India, 80

AFRICAN AMERICAN MUSIC IN GLOBAL PERSPECTIVE

The University of Illinois Press
is a founding member of the
Association of American University Presses.

Composed in 10.5/13 Adobe Minion
with Meta display
by BookComp, Inc.
for the University of Illinois Press
Manufactured by Thomson-Shore, Inc.

University of Illinois Press
1325 South Oak Street
Champaign, IL 61820-6903
www.press.uillinois.edu